Advance Praise

"Pinsky offers a gripping tour de force of crime journalism as he documents the fatal disintegration of a vulnerable young man under the spell of a malignant hustler." — DR. KATHERINE RAMSLAND, author of *How to Catch a Killer*

"A captivating tale of madness, manipulation, and murder. I simply couldn't stop turning the pages." — DIANE FANNING, crime writer and television commentator

"Detailed and deeply compelling, *Drifting Into Darkness* radiates with a veteran investigative reporter's drive to 'shake the tree' on his cross-country quest to uncover the criminal and cultural complexities of a family's dysfunction." — JOE SHARKEY, author of *Above Suspicion*

"A lavishly detailed story of murder, madness, and treachery in Alabama and parts beyond. Mark Pinsky's prose is as sweetly beckoning as a Southern breeze." — MICHAEL CUNEO, *New York Times*-acclaimed author of *Almost Midnight* and *American Exorcism*

"Descend and drift into madness in journalist Mark I. Pinsky's second work of true crime. To report on the Springford case, Pinsky personally had to comprehend his subject's sociopathy, immersing himself in a story of parricide. To lay down with sociopaths is to risk getting fleas, but that is the only way to get the story. Then came the sociopath I wasn't expecting . . . " — ARTHUR JAY HARRIS, investigative true-crime author of *The Unsolved Murder of Adam Walsh* and *Speed Kills*

"A fascinating work of true crime, superbly written. Anyone who cracks this book open will not want to put it down. Be prepared to miss work and social events!" — PHIL CHALMERS, criminal profiler, host of the *Where the Bodies Are Buried* podcast

DRIFTING INTO DARKNESS

Drifting Into Darkness

Murder, Madness, Suicide, and a Death 'Under Suspicious Circumstances'

MARK I. PINSKY

NewSouth Books

Montgomery

NewSouth Books
105 S. Court Street
Montgomery, AL 36104

LIBRARY OF CONGRESS CATALOGING-IN-PUBLICATION DATA
Names: Pinsky, Mark I., 1947– , author. Title: Drifting into darkness : murder, madness, suicide, and a death "under suspicious circumstances" / Mark Pinsky. Description: Montgomery : NewSouth Books, [2021] | Includes index. | Summary: "Two grisly murders-a brutal double parricide-a suicide, and a fourth death under suspicious circumstances. Drifting Into Darkness is a tangled tale of family dysfunction, fatal attraction, and greed, a saga that wends its way from the elegant Southern mansions of Montgomery, Alabama, to the New Age salons of Boulder, Colorado, to rural, windswept Wyoming. On Thanksgiving weekend in 2004, philanthropists Charlotte and Brent Springford Sr.—a wealthy, socially prominent Montgomery couple—were brutally beaten to death with an ax handle, echoing the infamous case of Lizzie Borden. Suspicion quickly fell on the Springfords' gifted but troubled son Brent Jr., who would be tried and sentenced to life without parole. But a mystery remained: Who was the mysterious, elusive woman who claimed to be a Native American shaman that investigators believed manipulated Brent into this murder? Journalists solving murders is a time-tested trope in movies, mysteries, and on television. But cops and cop reporters know that rarely happens in real life. Except when it does. Veteran crime reporter Mark I. Pinsky, who covered the sensational cases of serial killer Ted Bundy and Green Beret Dr. Jeffrey MacDonald, broke the cardinal rule of journalism by involving himself in the story. Pinsky's extensive research prompted investigators to invite him to join their dogged pursuit of justice. His access to unique and heart-breaking behind-the-scenes material enables him to take readers with him into the troubled, tortured minds of the case's main players" — Provided by publisher. Identifiers: LCCN 2021045569 (print) | LCCN 2021045570 (ebook) | ISBN 9781588384577 (paperback) | ISBN 9781588384584 (ebook) Subjects: LCSH: Springford, Brent, Jr., 1976-2013. | Parricide—Alabama—Case studies. Classification: LCC HV6542 .P56 2021 (print) | LCC HV6542 (ebook) | DDC 364.152/3085409761—dc23 LC record available at https://lccn.loc.gov/2021045569 LC ebook record available at https://lccn.loc.gov/2021045570

Design by Randall Williams

Printed in Canada by Friesens

The Black Belt, defined by its dark, rich soil, stretches across central Alabama. It was the heart of the cotton belt. It was and is a place of great beauty, of extreme wealth and grinding poverty, of pain and joy. Here we take our stand, listening to the past, looking to the future.

In memory of Dr. Norman M. Wall

Contents

DRIFTING INTO DARKNESS

Justice, justice, you shall pursue.
DEUTERONOMY 16:20

Prologue

The Weston County courthouse, in Newcastle, Wyoming, is a majestic, three-story, sandstone and brick building. Four tall pillars support the front portico and a copper-plated, octagonal dome. It was built in 1911, two decades after Weston was carved out of neighboring counties in the northeastern corner of the state, not far from Mount Rushmore in neighboring South Dakota.

Riding up in a small elevator, built years later along the outside of the structure, I sense that there must not be much crime in the county of seventy-two hundred residents. After all, there is only one working courtroom in the building, on the top floor. It is a paneled, windowless chamber with padded wooden pews, where a large-faced, old-fashioned Papillon clock on the right wall keeps the time. And it is here that an arcane proceeding known as a coroner's inquest is underway.

For the first time in forty years of covering murder cases around the country, I hear myself called to the witness stand. I take the oath and face the jurors. I am a long way from my home in the Central Florida suburbs, and from the tragic chain of events that brought me to this place. Why am I here, in the middle of a tangled tale of family dysfunction, fatal attraction, and greed, a saga that wends its way from the elegant Southern mansions of Montgomery, Alabama, to the New Age salons of Boulder, Colorado, to this rural, windswept county seat? More to the point, how can I tell the people staring at me so intently what—or who—connects four violent and unnatural deaths? Well, I say, it's a long story.

Part One: The Springfords

Garden District

Brutal, bloody murder is an unlikely intruder in the sedate Garden District of Montgomery, Alabama. Long autumn weekends in the neighborhood—home of the governor's mansion and many of the city's wealthiest citizens—tend to be quiet, punctuated by group dog walks and preservation-association picnics. But not Thanksgiving of 2004. Just after 8 a.m. on Friday, November 26, subcontractor Michael Shelton and two tile specialists working with him on a home-remodeling project pulled up to 1944 South Hull Street. On that sunny day, the elegantly restored 1920s house looked like what it was: the comfortable home of an affluent family. In the front yard, which sloped to the street, the leaves had turned red and gold on the young maples. From a fan-shaped, brick entrance to the sidewalk, a curved stone pathway led to the front door. Four windows ran along the front of the two-story, white-brick house, two on each side of the portico. The side and rear of the property were surrounded by an eight-foot brick wall and a section of wooden fencing. A black wrought-iron gate provided a side entrance to the yard.

There was no hint of the carnage within.

Montgomery is a city of contrasts and contradictions, a riverside city once the capital of slavery and segregation, now an open-air civil rights museum. Nowhere is that mix more evident than in the 325-acre Garden District, the neighborhood of choice for the city's business leaders throughout the twentieth century, listed since 1984 on the National Register of Historic Places. Today, what remains of the old elite mingles with post-civil rights-era immigrants from outside the South. About twenty-five hundred of these affluent empty-nesters, upwardly mobile gentrifiers, and urban pioneers have settled in the leafy district, all within walking distance of downtown and the monumental, white stone buildings of state government. Not all structures are restored mansions on large lots, like the house the construction crew approached at 1944 South Hull. Others range in value and include modest apartment complexes and smaller, contemporary homes on the edge of decay. "Today's Garden District," a local real estate website brags, is "ethnically varied, socially diverse, and still every bit as genteel as any small town in the old South." The site quotes one longtime resident who described it as a neighborhood "where civility never went away." Yet no urban area is immune from crime, and occasional sidewalk stickups are not unknown in the neighborhood.

What the workmen were about to discover was of another magnitude.

Parking on a side street so they wouldn't block the pebbled driveway on the right of the house, they walked up to the garage. The previous Wednesday the men had been laying kitchen tile to match the new yellow cabinets. Now, the holiday over, they were back to finish the job. Shelton had the keys to the house and the alarm codes. He knew the dwelling and the occupants well, having worked on various projects for them in the previous eight years. Using one of his keys to get into the detached, four-car garage, he noticed that the alarm reset was not on. He used the remote control to lift the garage door so he and the other two men could retrieve their tools from the garage's fourth bay. While using a bathroom in the garage, Shelton and the others noticed that the family's Jaguar was gone and the garage office was in disarray, with drawers pulled out, doors open, and papers scattered. This seemed odd to the men, since they knew that the owner, Brent Springford Sr., who owned the Pepsi bottling plant in Luverne, about an hour outside of Montgomery, always kept a clean work area. The three men headed along a vine-covered breezeway to the glass door in the rear of the house. They walked up the two shallow brick steps to the kitchen entrance, which was flanked with large pots of dwarf camellias. But the door was locked from the inside with what they knew was a floor-level deadbolt.

Shelton called Jerry Armstrong Jr., who managed the Luverne bottling plant and was close to the family. Armstrong also owned the construction company that was overseeing the remodeling. He advised Shelton to do as they had in the past when they found the door bolted: remove a glass door panel so they could reach in and release the deadbolt. Once inside, the three men carefully laid the panel on the kitchen counter and shouted for the residents or the housekeeper, without response. Then they called the cell phones of Brent Springford and his wife Charlotte, whose numbers Armstrong had given them. Again, there was no answer.

The kitchen, with its floor still half stripped, looked barren and forlorn, just as they had left it last week. Shelton and the others inspected the rest of the downstairs and found more evidence of disturbance. A small office area, including a built-in closet under the rear stairs where a fax machine was kept, was a mess. In the book-lined library and the high-ceilinged Florida room, things were thrown everywhere. Eight white shopping bags of kitchen supplies from Linens 'n Things lay on the floor. Shelton's first thought was that there had been a burglary. He and another of the men cautiously made their way up the narrow back staircase to see if there was more evidence of a break-in, again calling out for the Springfords.

At the top of the landing, the men stopped cold. The carpeted floor was splotchy and much darker red, with a large pool of what Shelton was sure was drying blood. They backed down the stairs, filled with foreboding.

Shelton called Armstrong back, saying there was something wrong, that there was blood on the landing. Armstrong told him to leave the house immediately while he called Lois Truss, Charlotte Springford's half-sister, to ask if she knew where the Springfords were, and, if so, to try to reach them. Rather than telling the contractor to call the police, or contacting them himself, Armstrong drove over to the house. When he got there and saw the blood on the landing, he knew something dire had occurred. He suspected a break-in while the Springfords were away, and that an intruder might have injured himself. So he dialed 911 and asked the operator to send the police. While Armstrong and the three workmen waited, they circled the residence to see if they could locate a possible point of entry to the house. They did—a broken window on the second floor at the rear of the house.

When the uniformed officers arrived, Armstrong followed one of them up the stairs. "It was a lot of blood—lots of blood," Armstrong told the Alabama News Network. "And it was in a couple of different areas. It was pretty obvious that something really, really bad had happened." Swerving

9

tracks of blood on the cream carpet indicated that a body had been dragged along the narrow foyer outside the TV room. Armstrong and the officer followed the blood trail into a nearby bedroom and then to the closet, where Brent Springford's slashed and battered body lay. Armstrong's first thought was that Brent had surprised a robber. As a trained EMT, Armstrong had seen damaged bodies before, but this time he was looking down at a man who was not only his longtime employer, but someone he considered a second father. Armstrong thought to himself, *this is not happening*. Shaken, he went back downstairs, while the officer went to another, larger bedroom, where he found Charlotte Springford's body. "It was the worst day of my life," Armstrong told a reporter in July 2014, almost a decade after the murders. "No doubt."

On those rare occasions when Garden District residents are crime victims, they expect the police and the power structure to respond, promptly and efficiently. And they did. A radio call went out noting a "Double Code Five"—two bodies found, and it didn't appear to be a murder-suicide. Detectives and death scene investigators arrived within five minutes. They sealed the grounds with yellow tape and uniformed officers set up a cordon around the lot. A patrol car pulled up and blocked the one-way street out front. Police officers, photographers, and death-scene investigators, most dressed in regulation khakis and blue departmental golf shirts, swarmed the yard. Police officials notified Montgomery Mayor Bobby Bright, who made it a practice to go to every reported homicide scene; the politician rushed to the Garden District, not knowing who the victims were.

Upstairs, investigators wearing latex gloves and sterile booties clustered around the bodies of Winston Brent Springford Sr., sixty-two, and his wife, Charlotte Turner Springford, sixty. It was a grisly sight, even for veteran officers, one of whom said it was the worst he had ever seen. There seemed to be blood, bloodstains, and spatter everywhere, along with skull fragments, bits of brain tissue, teeth, broken nails, and hair. Brent Springford—who went by his middle name—was found, face-up and ankles crossed, in the closet of the bedroom their adult daughter Robin occupied until she left for college and then work years before. He was clothed all in brown—slacks, a patterned, long-sleeved shirt, and shoes. His shirt cuffs were turned up a few times, and near his open, bandaged right hand were a bloody mattock* handle and an equally bloody serrated six-inch kitchen knife. His pants pockets were turned out, but he still had a gold watch on his wrist. Brent, investigators believed, had been hit from behind, bludgeoned to death with a blunt instrument in a sudden, furious attack, and then stabbed so violently in the neck that he was nearly decapitated.

Charlotte Springford's body lay face-up in a dressing-area closet near a small walkway between the master bedroom and an adjoining gallery. Shoeless, she had been dressed in a beige vest outfit, with a teal top, a wide leather belt, brown and green paisley-pattern slacks, and a blue jacket. Next to her shoulder was a gold watch bracelet, the smashed quartz face stopped at 6:28. The bloodstains and spatter on the walls, the floor, and an area rug indicated that there had been a struggle, that she had been attacked between the bed and a wall, and that she had crawled or been dragged to where her body was found, not far from a telephone. Scattered on the carpet were a pen, makeup, one sock, a lone, high-heeled black boot, and an open Louis Vuitton handbag. Drawers from her nightstand were pulled out, and a lamp lay on the floor. There were deep dents in the wall above her body, indicating the killer's fury. She, too, had been bludgeoned and stabbed, her left arm fractured several times in a classic defensive injury familiar to investigators. Her throat was also cut, but not as severely as her husband's. Mayor Bright inspected the scene, still unaware who the victims were. *My God*, he thought, *what happened? How could someone do this to another human being? Someone must have hated them so much!* Years later, the scene was still etched in his memory: "I'm *still* seeing it." Forensic investigators first put the time of death sometime during the early morning, which they later moved back to the previous evening.

Before noon investigators concluded that Brent was killed first, hit from behind in an explosive assault in the foyer landing, and that Charlotte was then attacked in the master bedroom. A search of the house's exterior by investigators found a short, sickle-shaped saw with an orange handle, used for pruning shrubbery. It was just outside what they took to be the killer's

---

* A garden/farm tool similar to a pickax but with a wide blade for digging on one end.

point of entry, a window in Robin's old second-floor bedroom. Both the pane and part of the frame were broken from the outside, leaving glass shards on the desk beneath the window. The smashed window was partially concealed from the outside with a pillow and by two audio speakers holding the blinds in place. From the ground, a trellis and a pillar had provided climbing access to the bedroom. There were scuff marks on the pillar, and on the ground near the base a trail of boot prints led to a line of bamboo in the backyard. On the tiled back patio, some potted plants had been disturbed and more muddy, waffle-soled footprints had been left in the spilled potting soil. Inside downstairs, two land-line phones were off their cradles.

Police would find more than twenty thousand dollars in cash in various safes around the house, as well as a large amount of foreign currency. There were numerous pistols and rifles in Brent's gun safe in the basement, and a handgun in one of the master bedroom's night stands. Parked in the garage were two of the couple's vehicles, a gray Chevy Caprice station wagon and a white Chevrolet Silverado pickup. Brent's 1998 black Jaguar XJR, registered to his Pepsi bottling company, was missing. Investigators separated members of the remodeling crew and Jerry Armstrong, took their phones, and began questioning them individually on the lawn. They asked Armstrong if Brent Sr. had any enemies. Later, they asked Armstrong if he knew where the couple's son, Brent Jr., was, and he told them Greeley, Colorado. Armstrong called the bottling plant office in Luverne to get the Jaguar's license tag number. But police wouldn't let Armstrong call his wife from the scene, and by the time he finally got home, sixteen voicemail messages from *Montgomery Advertiser* reporters were waiting.

Brent Sr. and Charlotte were not church-goers, but in the wake of the murders their daughter, Robin, who was living with her new husband in a Birmingham suburb, reached out to the mother of one of her good friends. Robin asked about the possibility of holding a memorial service. The murdered couple was deeply woven in the social fabric of Montgomery, both in business and philanthropy. As a result, the civic trauma of their deaths was so great that friends thought there was a need for some sort of community gathering to share their grief. Robin's friend's mother, a longtime member of St. John's Episcopal Church downtown, contacted the rector, the Reverend Robert Wisnewski Jr., asking if a memorial service could be held there. Wisnewski, as shaken as everyone else in Montgomery by the slayings, readily agreed. He met with Springford family members to plan the service, guiding them toward a simple Episcopal ceremony, with no sermons, homilies, or eulogies—no speakers at all—and no choir or musicians.

That approach also saved the minister from the sermon so many clergy dread—trying to make theological sense out of a pointless tragedy. For Wisnewski, much of the time between the murders and the service was a blur, infused by shock and incredulity. That Wednesday morning the historic, vaulted sanctuary, which seats five hundred, was overflowing. Robin asked members of the news media to respect the family's privacy by remaining outside the sanctuary, which they did. The family also requested that in lieu of flowers donations be made to the Charlotte Stephanie Springford Memorial Scholarship Fund at the University of Alabama School of Communications, Charlotte's alma mater. Members of the congregation, with Robin, her husband, and her aunt, Lois Truss, in the front row, recited the Apostles' Creed and the Lord's Prayer, and sang "A Mighty Fortress Is Our God," "Amazing Grace," and "O God, Our Help in Ages Past." The hymns did little to lift the mood. To Armstrong, Robin appeared numb. "It was the bleakest funeral I have ever attended," recalled a woman who was another good friend of the Springfords and, a decade later, did not want to be named. "At most occasions like that, there are bright spots, recalling high points in a life or humorous anecdotes from the life of the deceased, but not that morning. Mostly, it was disbelief and devastation." Her husband added, "There was no way to grieve normally when you lose close friends that way." After the service, some close friends gathered for lunch at the home of retired Circuit Court Judge Sally Greenhaw, Charlotte's close friend. In keeping with the Springfords' dual civic loyalties, they were buried on Saturday, December 4, in Luverne, at the small Emmaus Cemetery outside of town.

2

Family

Charlotte Turner met Brent Springford in 1963 in Panama City, Florida, where he was taking flight training at Tyndall Air Force Base, and she was teaching school after graduating from the University of Alabama. They married in 1969. After being discharged from the Air Force, Brent took a job with the Corning Glass Works in Corning, New York. Their first child, daughter Charlotte Stephanie Springford, was born in Corning on December 8, 1971, sharing her mother's first name but called by her middle name, Stephanie. In May 1972, Charlotte and Brent planned a trip to Mexico, their first excursion since their daughter's birth. They left the baby with Charlotte's father George Turner and stepmother Dee in Luverne. On May 29 a sudden, devastating fire broke out at 1:30 a.m. in the den at the rear of the Turners' ranch-style brick house. The baby was sleeping in her grandparents' bedroom. All three died of smoke inhalation. Charlotte's half-sister, Lois, then twenty-two, had graduated from college that day, but she was awake reading when the fire broke out. She panicked, but had enough presence of mind to break a window and struggle through the aluminum frame. In the process she severed an artery on the back of her leg. A passerby saved her life by applying a tourniquet, but the leg had to be amputated. Baby Stephanie, Dee, and George were buried in Luverne two days later, after Charlotte and Brent rushed back from Mexico. The arrangements were handled by Turner Funeral Home, founded by Charlotte's father's family. Charlotte, understandably devastated by the tragedy, was hospitalized for depression. She took a year to slowly emerge, still anxious and fragile.

With his father-in-law's death in the house fire, Brent moved back to Alabama to assume control of the Pepsi bottling company that George had run. In the years following the Luverne house fire, Charlotte had a tubal pregnancy, which made the birth of her next two children all the more precious. Their son, Winston Brent Jr.—called Brent, like his father—was born in 1976. Although nonreligious herself, Charlotte nonetheless asked her old debate coach and mentor at the University of Alabama, Annabel Hagood, to be Brent Jr.'s godmother. The couple's daughter, Robin, was born two years later. Friends thought the parents indulged their children, possibly a result of the earlier tragedy, and young Brent was thought to be particularly spoiled. "He had everything," one contemporary observed, and his parents rarely, if ever, said no to things he wanted, or wanted to do.

The parents were considered, for Alabama, unconventional—worldly as well as liberal, with Charlotte working outside the home from time to time. The couple was also well-traveled. In addition to Europe and the Caribbean, they visited China, Nepal, and Morocco, in all more than sixty countries over three decades. Charlotte and Brent Sr. were inquisitive, sensitive, and philanthropic, reading up on all aspects of their destinations before leaving, and always hiring guides so they could meet some of the local residents. When possible, they presented spur-of-the-moment gifts that could make a great difference in people's lives. In one country, they bought a man a refrigerator so he could start a food bank. They developed a sophisticated understanding of social changes in areas where they traveled, often sharing their travel experiences and slides with friends, formally and informally— sometimes late into the night at their showcase home. The Springfords wanted their children to have every possible cultural advantage, and they encouraged them to seek stimulating experiences, to explore the world with them. From the time the children were in kindergarten the family spent parts of each summer at the Mesoamerican University in Oaxaca, Mexico, in part so that Robin and Brent Jr. could learn Spanish from native speakers.

The family did not attend church regularly, although the children went to services some Sundays with the family's African American housekeeper. In the Deep South in the 1980s it was difficult for many to separate white, evangelical religion from its ultra-conservative political dimension—and racism. Charlotte noticed that this was the case with her son. She wanted to impart skepticism and critical thinking to Brent Jr., without his succumbing to a different kind of intolerance. She was, she recalled in a letter, "trying to make him understand that 'Christian bashing' was simply not acceptable, certain insufferable right-wingers notwithstanding. Christianity, at its core, is a beautiful religion—as all major religions are."

Charlotte participated in local interfaith activities, and read widely, telling one friend how much she enjoyed Roger Kamenetz's *The Jew in the Lotus*, which got her interested in Jewish mysticism. She was also attracted to the paranormal, a predilection her agnostic husband did not share. However, she shared this interest with her children, teaching them about the presence of spirits and psychic events. Using Tarot cards and a Ouija board, she talked to the children about her supernatural sensations. She also read palms to entertain friends. More than once she told her husband she had a premonition he should not go to work that day, and to placate her he stayed home. At the age of three, Brent Jr. told his mother that he had lived an earlier life in the Old West, giving a detailed account of his life as a ranch hand and gunfighter who was fatally wounded at eighteen in a shoot-out, and whose father had been murdered. He talked about this past life with his mother for about six months. When Brent was in tenth grade, Charlotte reminded her son of the episode. He told schoolmates about it. "I soon came to believe that I was here for *a great purpose*," he wrote years later. "But I didn't know what that purpose was. . . . I had delusions of grandeur to say the least." In high school, Robin wrote a school research paper on reincarnation.

Brent Sr. grew the business he inherited and the family prospered. By the time of his murder, as much as $250,000 a month was passing through the couple's joint personal checking account at Regions Bank. Usually, the balance ranged from $7,000 to $60,000, averaging $30,000. The Springfords lived well, and as the years passed, it showed. Charlotte fretted about high cholesterol and battled to remain slender, ultimately resorting to a personal trainer who came to her house; cosmetic surgery; and residential diet programs. Brent put on weight as his hairline receded. He drank, at home most nights, but was also known to hit Montgomery bars with his friends. "He had a confidence bordering on arrogance," a family friend said. "He embraced risk." Brent earned a black belt in karate and was licensed to carry a concealed weapon. He drove a Jaguar, often at excessive speeds. However, Charlotte set limits on Brent's lifestyle, as she remained traumatized for years after the house fire that had killed their baby daughter and her parents. While the children were still young, Brent Sr. wanted a motorcycle, but his wife threatened to divorce him if he got one. She insisted he keep his impressive pistol collection in a safe. He bought a small plane, a Piper Dakota, which he piloted himself and kept in a private hangar on the far side of Montgomery's regional airport. Charlotte secretly went to her husband's flying instructor to take lessons so she could land the plane in the event that something happened to Brent while he was at the controls.

Although Brent Sr. had a temper, and the couple argued from time to time, their children considered the marriage stable. When they dined with friends, one recalled, "Charlotte was the bigger personality in the room," which her husband did not find threatening. As he grew older Brent Sr. devoted time to more sedate hobbies like genealogy and studying gemstones. Close friends noticed a strong devotion and a mutual solicitousness in the couple's relationship, and they continued their globe-trotting.

The family was social, for years hosting a black-tie Christmas gathering at their home, a sit-down dinner party for more than a hundred guests, including their children and their friends. They also opened their home to benefits for various charities. Robin was a source of considerable pride for her parents, graduating from Vanderbilt University in 2001. Later she became engaged to Gregory Lee Crouch, a local schoolmate. Their wedding in Seaside, Florida, in October 2004 was one of the social events of the season. So, when Brent Sr. and Charlotte and Robin and Greg sat down for Thanksgiving dinner on November 25, 2004, at the Birmingham home of Charlotte's sister, Lois Truss, and Lois's physician husband Christopher, there was much to give thanks for. The Trusses' older daughter Anna was also a newlywed, so the conversation naturally centered on the two young couples. But just as Brent and Charlotte were about to leave for Montgomery, the mood turned bittersweet. Brent Jr., the Springfords' estranged son and Robin's older brother, known as "Little Brent," was absent from the table, as he had been from Robin's wedding a month before. "The subject of Little Brent was the elephant in the room," Lois recalled. The Springfords were concerned that their son, living across the country in Colorado, was having mental problems, and they were troubled by his—and their—relationship with his Native American caregiver, Caroline Scoutt.

: *3*

Fortunate Son

As a child, Brent Jr. was indulged with all manner of toys and gadgets, as well as personal field trips with his mother. He remained close with Charlotte through adolescence, confiding in her about things like school and girls. By contrast, Brent Sr.'s love of his son seemed more conditional. Some friends observed that in personality the boy was more like his mother than his father. Still, when he was still in kindergarten Brent Sr. would take the boy with him to shoot targets. In the years that followed, Brent Jr.'s personality evolved into a sometimes volatile, seemingly contradictory mix of entitlement, idealism, rebellion, insecurity, and a competitive drive to excel at all costs. After church day care, his parents enrolled him at the Montgomery Academy, a private K-12 day school, considered one of the most academically rigorous in the state, and the school of choice for the city's wealthy. It was founded in 1959 as an all-white, "segregation academy" in response to the civil rights movement and impending public school integration. By the time Brent Jr. entered, the Academy was nominally desegregated, although less than 10 percent of the student body was nonwhite. Given her liberal political beliefs, Charlotte must have had mixed feelings about sending her son to the school.

As an adolescent, Brent felt close to his parents and looked forward to a bright, if conventional future. When he was twelve, he did a school project on family history, called "Brent's Beginnings," drawing on his parents' recollections. Brent's feelings for his mother, he wrote, were strong: "My mom is a very kind, sweet, gentle, loving person. . . . She gives me a lot of attention and loves me a lot. . . . I try to make good impressions on her and make her proud of me." As for Brent Sr., Brent Jr. wrote, "I think my dad is the greatest dad in the world. He loves me a lot and I love him. We

do a lot of things together. We build models, we go on camping trips"—
something his mother and sister had no taste for—"and we ski together. . . .
Both of us are stubborn as a bull and love to laugh. Dad is very smart and
knows what's good for me. I love my dad." In the same paper, Brent said
he wanted to go to Princeton, Harvard, or Yale, and return home to take
over his father's business.

In addition to the family skiing trips to Montana, during middle school
Brent Jr. started playing golf and learned to dance. In his early years, he
often relied on his mother to initiate his social interactions. For a party
at his house, where he first asked a girl to dance, his parents had rented a
jukebox. In eighth or ninth grade, Brent confided to his mother that he was
depressed, but he rejected her suggestion that he see a psychiatrist. In tenth
grade, he took up debate, perhaps to emulate his mother, who had been a
college debater. That same year, at fifteen, he began drinking, sometimes
heavily. His parents knew about it and didn't like it, yet they were aware
of the fierce peer pressure from his school friends, so they looked the other
way. When he briefly made bad grades, he was grounded and seemed embarrassed. Brent Jr. and Robin were under strict curfews, which they observed
for the most part, and could go out only on weekend nights. So they and
their friends drank at the Springford home. There was considerable drinking at teen parties for the next few years, and he later recalled sometimes
being drunk for days. In high school, he grew into a handsome young man,
with dark hair and pale blue eyes, chiseled features, and a rosy complexion.

In high school, he was on the track, baseball, and tennis teams, rode
the bench on the basketball team, and was a member of the Fellowship of
Christian Athletes. "I was popular and smart," he wrote years later, "the
strongest and fastest guy in the class, and my parents were the wealthiest."
He acknowledged that he had been "given every opportunity and advantage
in life." Sometimes, he admitted, he was arrogant and felt superior, because
so many things came easily to him. "My ego was huge, and it would be
many years before I understood what humility meant." A good student, he
earned A's and B's in his classes, including six Advanced Placement and four
honors courses, ultimately graduating with a 3.6 GPA, and was a favorite of
many of his teachers, known for his writing ability. One teacher in particular

recommended Hermann Hesse's *Siddhartha*, the 1922 novel popular in the 1960s, which ignited Brent's lifelong fascination with Buddhism. On the other hand, he also read the conservative icon Ayn Rand. He spent part of three summers during high school, and another after his first year at college, at the Instituto Allende in San Miguel de Allende, Mexico, sometimes with his parents, in "total impact" language study. In his senior year he tried to bulk up his five-foot-ten frame by lifting weights. Instead, he developed a hernia, which required an operation to repair.

By all accounts, Brent was sociable and liked by his classmates, lighting up any room he entered. He wore a suit to most social events and liked being the center of attention. Yet he also made a point of including classmates who were on the fringes of his circle, even when it annoyed others. Friends say he had a strong personality and was a gracious host, especially at gatherings at his home, when he often cooked. He liked to host parties, sometimes in formal dress, where he joined others in drinking and, eventually, smoking marijuana. Weed largely eclipsed drinking by his senior year, supplemented by LSD and psychedelic mushrooms when they were available. In the "pot den," as they called his bedroom, friends crowded onto his studio bed. As his father had in college, Brent Jr. took up the electric guitar, playing stand-in with three local bands. Sometimes, though, smoking marijuana—he could stay high for six hours—made him paranoid and caused his thoughts to race. The Springfords tended to be permissive with their children, as long as things did not get out of hand. Charlotte had smoked marijuana when she was younger, but stopped because it made her paranoid as well. But Brent Sr. passed along his own marijuana paraphernalia from his youth. When Brent Jr. was sixteen, Brent Sr. bought him a red sports car, an IROC-Z Camaro, which did nothing to diminish his social status. Like his father, Brent liked to drive fast, well over a hundred miles an hour on the interstate.

Brent Sr. once walked in on his son having sex in his bedroom with a sixteen-year-old tenth-grade schoolmate, but the father quietly backed away. Brent Jr. had several other sexual and romantic relationships in high school, but only one developed into something significantly deeper. It was with

Andrea Jameson,* the beautiful daughter of his parents' good friends, who lived nearby. The two met in kindergarten at the Montgomery Academy. For most of the years that followed, Andrea and Brent were just friends, although they grew increasingly close as the years went by. In the tenth grade, he would sit with her on bus rides to debate tournaments, instead of with his buddies. "He had the confidence to sit with me," she recalled, more than a decade later. Andrea did not smoke or drink, and, throughout her high school years, remained a virgin. She won a statewide beauty pageant, and Brent spoiled her, treating her as precious to him. As graduation neared, the relationship turned romantic; their first kiss was on the way to the Senior Cruise. On Senior Prom night, Brent hosted an after-party at his house, with Andrea acting as hostess, at his request.

Friends saw Brent and Andrea as an ideal couple. "I was the only woman in his life," she recalled later. "I know he loved me. We were the very closest of friends for years. We were alike and comfortable together, we talked about everything. He knows everything about me." In December 1996, when Brent was twenty, they slept together for the first time, and again in March 1997, in both cases in his bedroom when his parents were out of town. Both sets of parents were aware of the situation, but did not appear concerned, perhaps hoping it would blossom into permanence. Charlotte and Brent Sr. loved Andrea, always complimented her, and told their son that he was lucky to have such a wonderful, beautiful girlfriend. The four parents socialized together with the young couple, along with Robin and her boyfriend, Greg Crouch. Brent Sr., who referred to Andrea as their "probable daughter-in-law," supported her ambitions to become a singer. Even later after Brent Jr. seemed to have lost romantic interest in her, Andrea was welcomed at the Springfords' Garden District home, where she spent many hours with Charlotte.

Psychologically, Brent Jr. seemed reasonably well adjusted in high school. He was never violent, always sensitive, polite, and helpful, although he had poor short-term memory. There was one troubling sign: he was obsessive about his bedroom, sometimes staying up all night, organizing and

---

*   Not her real name.

reorganizing, rearranging posters, creating a theme, and trying to make it perfect. There were some incongruities, as with most teenagers. While he liked to quote Rudyard Kipling's poem, "If," especially the phrase, "to walk with kings but never lose the common touch," he insisted on using expensive cosmetics to maintain his appearance. And from time to time he dismissed his parents as "tourist snobs," though they were anything but typical in their traveling habits. Brent Jr. traveled a good deal himself, with his parents, with others, and by himself. He collected ornate knives from his travels, but when he later thought they had bad karma, he sealed them all in a box and stored them on a high shelf. Andrea worried that he never talked about his plans for the future, or a career, except for vague talk about "the arts."

Dow Harris was another of Brent's friends since they were in kindergarten. Harris, whose life in many ways would parallel Brent's, observed later that something in his friend's early life seemed to undermine him, in particular his parents' permissiveness. Harris would later write:

> Charlotte and Brent Sr. never ever disciplined him. He never once in his life showed any sign of respect for any authority whatsoever. At the same time, he never once in his life took personal responsibility for his actions. He got everything he wanted and he could always afford to fuck up. I can't tell you how many times I watched him, growing up, and thought that he had broken one boundary too many and that he just didn't know how lucky he was that he could get away with, and that one day it was going to come to haunt him. Somehow I think he thought that that allowance was his birthright. [At the same time,] I saw so many beautiful things about him, his passion, his strength, his determination; but he never developed a self-regulating mechanism that could limit his appetites and focus his mind on legitimate goals. Because he did not understand how to be truly independent, most of his ideas were completely off the chart of reality. This made him very impressionable and susceptible to people who seemed to know what they were talking about and, if they curried to his notion of a romantic rebellion, they had him.

: 4

Wild Child

It would be difficult to imagine an upbringing more different from Brent Springford Jr.'s than that of Caroline Scoutt, the woman whose life would be inextricably linked to his. She was born Carol Eileen Gonzales on July 31, 1951, in Rancho Cucamonga, a suburb of Los Angeles, and was listed on her birth certificate as Caucasian. Her father, Robert J. Gonzales, left the family when Carol was a toddler, and she was raised by her stay-at-home mom, Celia C. Quiroz in Alhambra, another Los Angeles suburb. Carol had three younger siblings, twin brothers and a sister, all of whom used their mother's last name. The family spoke Spanish at home and attended All Souls Catholic Church. As she grew up, Carol encountered one stumbling block after another, attending three different primary schools. In fourth grade, her teacher reported that she was hyperactive but "a likeable, conscientious girl." She was referred to the school's guidance and special education staff, who reported that despite an impaired self-image she demonstrated a willingness to improve. Because of her "below grade level work" and her difficulty following directions, the school considered holding her back, but did not. Her grades through middle school were C's and D's, possibly because of absences due to illness—anemia and frequent upper-respiratory infections.

In the late 1960s Carol attended Alhambra High School, and then Mark Keppel High School, in the same town. At Mark Keppel, she was thrown into a difficult environment. The school's official website reports that the counterculture then engulfing the nation, with its attendant drug use and anti-authority attitudes, surfaced on the campus. The school's website history reported other challenges: "As some whites began moving out of Keppel's attendance area, Mexican-Americans were moving out of East Los Angeles and into the area. As the stability of long-time residents weakened, racial tensions began to emerge."

Keppel's students also found life daunting in the classroom. During the 1950s, the San Bernardino Freeway was built along one edge of the campus, separated by only a chain-link fence. The website said, "By the '60s, students had to either endure the deafening din of freeway noise or close the windows and swelter in non-air-conditioned classrooms. By the end of the 1960s the face of Mark Keppel High School had completely changed. School apathy, the counterculture, and anti-war and ethnic activism dominated the atmosphere of the time and accurately mirrored the growing cynicism of society."

Carol continued to earn C's and D's, although school records indicate that she and her mother disagreed over her academic track. Her mother favored secretarial studies, while Carol wanted college preparatory, with an interest in social work or psychiatry. Mother and daughter compromised, with Carol taking academic courses as well as typing and business correspondence. Still, her grades never improved, which must have been frustrating to the teen, believing she could succeed academically under the right circumstances; she earned A's and B's at summer school between tenth and eleventh grades. A happy-looking Carol Gonzales is pictured as a junior in the 1970 Mark Keppel High School yearbook, and again with a women's athletics support group called the Red Suits. Tragedy intervened in her home life when one of her brothers was killed in a car crash that may have been a suicide. Her grades dropped precipitously and after eleventh grade she became pregnant and dropped out to marry her high school boyfriend, whom she lived with until their son was about ten, when she abandoned her family.

At this point, the background of the woman who came to be known as Caroline Scoutt becomes difficult to pin down. Years later she boasted of a colorful life—serving as a personal mystic to Hollywood stars like Boris Karloff (who died in 1969, when she was in her teens), and traveling as a groupie with heavy-metal rock groups like Great White (who she said played at one of her birthday parties) and Black Sabbath. At various times Scoutt has claimed Native American heritage, variously Apache, Comanche, Oglala, and Lakota Sioux. Over the years, she began giving different birth years, ranging from the 1950s to the 1960s, and used different first and last names, spelling each differently. Her names on documents vary, from Hispanic to Anglo to Native American, and she has several Social Security numbers. After a lengthy separation, Caroline and her husband divorced in 1983. At the time she left him, she was pregnant with her second son, who was subsequently adopted by her second husband, with whom she had another son. The first-born son contacted Caroline in 1991, just after her younger daughter was born, and he visited her twice. Caroline's third husband, the father of her fourth child, was a long-haul trucker who came and went in his family's life, and whose relationship with Caroline ended when he came home one Thanksgiving and found her with another man.

The names on birth certificates of Scoutt's four children list different last names and spellings. Alhambra school records documenting her early home life notwithstanding, Scoutt claimed she was raised by her great-grandmother, the last of the Apache medicine women, who trained her as a spiritual successor. After her grandmother's death at 108, Scoutt has said that she lived for many years in unhappy foster homes in Wyoming, and for a time slept under a park bench. This was the story Caroline shared with her children. "She told me that she was adopted, that she never knew her parents," Scoutt's younger daughter, Star Fosheim, recalled. "By the age of eighteen she was on the street living behind bushes and under park benches. She said that she remembered something about an older grandmother, but she always changed the story." In any case, this exotic tale would prove to be demonstrably false.

Late in the 1980s, Scoutt found her way from California to Newcastle, in northeastern Wyoming near the South Dakota border, working as a low-paid health aide. By the early 1990s, she was caring for a man named Larry Price, the town's engineer, who became ill with cancer. Sometimes she would bring her children with her to his office, and shortly after the family moved into Price's basement. When Price was diagnosed with cancer, his wife left him. Price legally adopted Caroline in 1995, when she was in her forties. The event was so odd that it made the local paper, the *News Letter Journal*. But at some point Price became involved romantically with another woman, and one of Caroline's daughters believes that he cut her mother out of his will. Still, in the years to come Scoutt would sometimes use the name "Carol Price."

Scoutt became active in a local group in Newcastle called FOCUS, which tried to educate the community on domestic abuse. Scoutt claimed that she, too, was a victim, and convinced the editor of the paper to profile her—anonymously. This, her younger daughter insisted, was not true. In the course of Scoutt's work with FOCUS, she attempted to cultivate close ties to local law officers. One she couldn't cultivate was Andrew Macke, the Newcastle police chief. Rather than calling 911 or the police department with her frequent complaints about her neighbors—squabbles that would become a lifelong habit—she would send her son up the street to knock on Macke's door. But he was not taken in. "She was tight with the then-sheriff and was gaining the confidence of local enforcement," said Macke, who would play a significant role in Scoutt's life decades later. "I didn't care for her," he said, for reasons he couldn't put his finger on.

Whatever the facts of her upbringing and early adulthood, Scoutt fully embraced Native American culture, transforming herself into a convincing teacher and spiritual leader. People in several western states—Colorado, Wyoming, the Dakotas—paid her to share with them some of the truths that she had learned from her life experiences and her informal studies. By the late 1990s, Scoutt was living in a trailer on her land outside Newcastle and making month-long trips to Boulder, Colorado, giving counseling, breathing, and "rebirthing" sessions. During that time, Scoutt left her elementary school-aged daughter in the care of the girl's older brother and sister, and created a new identity in Boulder.

Searching

By the summer of 1994, when he was eighteen, Brent Jr. had seen much of the world. His friend Dow Harris believed that, as a result, he came to resent the provincialism of Alabama and the South. Though he was eager to escape the region for college, his good-but-not-great combined SAT score of 1220 meant he had to lower his sights from attending one of the top-tier Ivy League schools. He applied to Dartmouth and Cornell and was naturally disappointed when he was rejected, despite his heartfelt application essay in which he credited his parents for their generosity in providing him opportunities for personal growth. He was accepted at Vanderbilt, a highly regarded university in Nashville, but he seemed to have felt it was a fallback choice.

After a six-week Lions Club youth trip to Europe that summer, Brent went off to college—with an ample supply of alcohol, including a case of Old Forester bourbon, provided by his father. He pledged Alpha Tau Omega and liked to party, mixing pot, acid, and mushrooms with large amounts of alcohol. Incongruously, he settled on religion as his major and over time grew more interested in spiritual matters. One of his early courses was a seminar called "Concepts of God," in which he read C. S. Lewis's *Miracles*. The class accelerated his introspection and spiritual awareness and deepened his inner focus as he read books like *The Dharma: The Teachings of the Buddha*. That course's professor remembered him as a charming and popular exception to the upper-class frat boys who often filled his classes. Brent told his ATO pledge trainer that the course was a transformative experience, the first of many. "Partying became less meaningful, but I was still doing it," Brent recalled years later. Strangely, the more he studied Buddhism, the more distant he felt from his mother.

Yet while he saw his parents as materialistic, he saw no contradiction in taking money from them.

Brent continued to respond to the altruistic impulse his parents nurtured in him, and his own growing contemplation. Freshman year, he joined eleven other Vanderbilt students in a social-service program called "Alternative Spring Break," in which they traveled to Honduras to help build a cobblestone and concrete roadway in a rural village. In the early summer of 1995, he went on another Vanderbilt trip, this one with his Latin American literature class to the Dominican Republic and Peru, where he climbed the Incan ruins of Machu Picchu. There, he later told a friend, he ingested powerful hallucinogenic plants (possibly ayahuasca), "traveled to the inner regions of my mind," and "experienced my own immortality." After that mountaintop experience, he told friends, he gave up LSD and mushrooms, although not marijuana and alcohol. He read *The Tao Te Ching* that summer and met an antiques dealer in Peru who read his aura and introduced him to the writings of a spiritual teacher named Osha. When he returned from the trip, he spent the rest of that summer (and those that followed) in more mundane pursuits, working at the family's Pepsi plant in Luverne.

For most of his first two years at Vanderbilt, his grades were good, even as his spiritual reading was making him more reclusive. As freshman year progressed, he began spending more time at the international student center than at the ATO house. In the fall of his sophomore year, 1995, he moved into McTyiere International House, living on the Spanish hall and working as the hall's program director. Otherwise, he spent the semester in virtual isolation, reading increasingly esoteric books. He was fully consumed with a quest for personal enlightenment, to become like the Buddha, he told friends, and he began seeing parallels and messages from his own life experiences in what he was reading. In a sense, Brent had embarked on what would be his version of Joseph Campbell's classic myth, the hero's great search.

At Thanksgiving break of his sophomore year, when he came home for the holidays, he began reading and rereading two books he later said further transformed his life: *The Celestine Prophecy* by James Redfield, a spacey New Age work, and his well-worn copy of *Siddhartha*. Home again for Christmas vacation, Brent hosted a sleepover at his family's weekend vacation home on

Lake Martin, in Elmore County, about forty miles north of Montgomery. He and Andrea Jameson spent the night in sleeping bags on the dock and talked about being soul mates. He told her that the *Celestine Prophecy* had convinced him that what he had taken for coincidences in his life were in fact examples of synchronicity, messages from "the Spirit."

At Vanderbilt as he had been in prep school, Brent was a favorite of his teachers, including a Spanish professor who was also the dean of students. Brent was one of two student leaders of the 1996 Alternative Spring Break, which worked on projects in Monterrey, Mexico. Yet he was unhappy and increasingly restive. So the dean was sympathetic and supportive when at the end of his sophomore year in the spring of 1996 Brent, then twenty, announced that he wanted to take time off. His grades were good, A's and B's, with a 3.7 grade point average. Confusion and burnout, the dean told his parents, were not uncommon for young people who attended high-powered prep schools and competitive colleges. "I'm absolutely losing it," Brent confided to Andrea. He wrote her in an email that he could no longer attend a conservative college in a conservative part of the country.

Brent's parents agreed to his plan, at least in part, although they worried that he might drop out for good. As a compromise, the Springfords agreed to support him in taking a year off to study Eastern philosophy and mysticism, hoping that he might satisfy his spiritual quest and return to Vanderbilt. He would also have to work periodically at the Pepsi plant in Luverne to support any travel and outside study. So in June 1996, Brent hit the road in his Chevy Blazer, driving around the country for ten weeks. He crisscrossed the U.S., Canada, and Mexico, camping out and staying at nine different Hindu ashrams and Buddhist monasteries.

One year of seeking stretched into four. Brent alternated between extended periods of reading, meditation, and contemplation at his family's lake house, drives around the country, staying at various retreats, camping at national parks, and one long stay in Mexico. Throughout, he read widely and deeply, but also unevenly. The spectrum tended to be undifferentiated—serious classics, together with light-headed New Age fare. He kept reading and, while he drove, listening to books on tape, some Russian and Arab history, but mostly books on Eastern religion and philosophy.

By the end of the summer of 1996, Andrea felt "the last remnants of normalcy" in Brent were starting to slip away. Earlier, seeing him in Montgomery and at Vanderbilt, she became convinced that his spiritual quest was fueled by incipient mental illness, a growing obsession that was inseparable from escaping the "mess in his head." His early obsession with decorating his bedroom got worse. "He'd get in that room," Andrea recalled, "changing, cleaning everything. There was a constant search for organization." His gregarious personality atrophied, and the young man who was once the life of the party was now only comfortable in small groups. "We lost the wonderful social person who loved being surrounded by friends, and loved to entertain people." She also noticed that his sex drive waned, along with his enjoyment of women. "He was a very sexual person—not in a weird way, just in a very masculine way," she recalled. "But that completely disappeared as he came to view sex as an earthly weakness. He lost all sense of enjoying and participating in the world around him." She felt he wanted to present himself as enlightened, yet he said he felt self-loathing, feeling that he was failing in his goal of "being something other than what you are."

In September 1996 Brent went to work as an account auditor at the Pepsi plant, which turned out not to be a good fit. He had worked at the plant for part of every summer since ninth grade, rotating from department to department, enjoying it, although he was uncomfortable being thought of as "the boss's son." He told the Springfords' longtime housekeeper, Maggie Johnson, who had become a confidant, that he liked working at the plant but wanted to be treated like anyone else. "He wanted to be humble," she recalled. The money he earned seemed unimportant; he sometimes just left it on his desk. Now, though, his growing fixations hampered his productivity. He told friends he developed the position of account auditor, evaluating the performance of sales teams. Yet after writing a computer program designed to grade and chart store displays, he would obsessively rotate the two-liter bottles on shelves, take them all out, and then return them for no apparent reason. He told Andrea that working at the plant was a valuable experience but also convinced him that a career at Pepsi wasn't for him.

Throughout this time, Brent kept reading, diving into the works of the philosopher Jiddu Krishnamurti, and also novels like W. Somerset Maugham's

The Razor's Edge, a tale of a young man's spiritual quest, which he listened to on tape while making occasional drink deliveries. On October 22, 1996, the day before his work at the Pepsi plant was to end, he wrote a letter to Andrea. He said he had finally gotten around to reading a book she had sent him the year before, *Soul Mates: Honoring the Mysteries of Love and Relationship*, by Thomas Moore, a contemporary therapist. He also talked about the European philosophers Soren Kierkegaard and Georg Wilhelm Friedrich Hegel. The next day, in another letter—possibly unmailed—he addressed her as "Dearest Andrea," and shared his relief that it was his last day as a Pepsi delivery man.

Suddenly, it seemed, Brent had decided he wanted to renounce the world and become a monk, an announcement his father greeted with distaste. He began spending more time reading at the Lake Martin house, where his mother would recall him being "happy and utterly absorbed." In late October, Andrea came home from Columbia University to celebrate her twenty-first birthday. Brent told her he was reading, fasting, and praying, although his friends thought he was mostly smoking weed. She suspected he was pulling away from her, which he confirmed, telling her face-to-face that he no longer had romantic feelings for her. She was devastated. "I really missed him," she recalled. "It was a long, drawn-out progression, but I was losing him to the Search." But the relationship wasn't completely over, as she feared.

In November 1996 Brent moved to the lake house full-time, where he lived as what he described as a "hermit monk." He studied Tibetan Buddhism, with a cache of books and a regime of meditation, including an abridged version of *Isis Unveiled: Secrets of the Ancient Wisdom Tradition*, by Madame Helena Blavatsky, founder of the esoteric occult belief called Theosophy. Charlotte, concerned, wanted to support her son, so she also moved to the lake house and began working her way through the same ambitious book list her son had compiled. He was reading voraciously: Carl Jung, Thomas Merton, Nikos Kazantzakis, Sri Ramakrishna, Swami Vivekananda, Lao Tzu, and more Hermann Hesse. Also *The Tao Te Ching* (again) and *Walden*—with the sci-fi classics *Dune* and *Dune Messiah* by Frank Herbert mixed in. He discovered a book by the Tibetan Buddhist Sogyal Rinpoche, *The Tibetan*

Book of Living and Dying. Once again, Brent was keeping a journal, recording some of his adventures on the road.

For his twenty-first birthday, on March 24, 1997, Brent's present from his parents was another road trip. So he headed west almost immediately, and stayed on the road until May, listening to Eric Fromm's *The Art of Loving* on tape, as well as the *Bhagavad Gita* in Spanish. Later that month, on the way back home from California, Brent stopped at Monument Valley, Arizona, which he found "mystical." He retained tentative connections to Vanderbilt. Although he was already planning his next road trip, at his parents' insistence he returned to Vanderbilt for "May-mester," a one-month course on "Religion and Politics in America." He got an A in the course, yet the experience clarified for him that he wasn't ready to return to traditional academic study. Nonetheless, he thought he might need to return to Nashville for the fall semester to bump up his GPA in order to transfer to another school, perhaps Williams College in Massachusetts. "I could not return to what I felt to be [the] stifling atmosphere at Vanderbilt," he later wrote.

Soon, Brent was again restless to continue his search for enlightenment, although his father was starting to balk at the cost of his odyssey. So he made another agreement with his parents for them to support him for a summer trip to Mexico. The previous year, their Christmas gift to him that year had been round-trip airfare to Mexico. Instead, he turned in the tickets for money and took the bus to Mexico, to "follow my bliss," where a three-month sojourn turned into six months. He ended up in San Cristobal de las Casas, in the state of Chiapas near the Guatemalan border. There, he spent the first month at a house owned by an old friend of Charlotte's from the University of Alabama debate team, reading more about Eastern religions and philosophy, mostly in Spanish translation. But the Christmas money only went so far, and in the months and years to come, Brent would have to put in more time at the bottling plant to finance his extensive travels.

Brent's parents were relieved when he told them that, since he was already in Mexico, he wanted to enroll in classes at the Mesoamerican University in Oaxaca, where the family had studied in previous summers. The lone American among six hundred students, he took two classes, "History of Western Philosophy" and "Theories of Personalities," both in Spanish. Brent did not find the classes academically demanding, although speaking and thinking in another language was. One of his professors asked him to give lectures on philosophy, Taoism, Hinduism, and Buddhism, and he used a Spanish translation of Huston Smith's *The World's Religions* to prepare. He was also asked to lead a discussion on meditation. In the process, he found that his longtime fear of public speaking had largely disappeared. He studied Spanish five hours a day, exercised, and meditated. On his own, he also studied more worldly subjects like Latin American history and politics, particularly the Zapatista uprising, which had taken place in neighboring Chiapas State in 1994.

Brent had moved to a shared room in a seven-person boarding house, owned by his yoga teacher, near the town market. He earned rent money teaching English to five local waiters. After six weeks at the boarding house, he found the tumult too distracting. So for the last ten weeks of his stay he moved to what was in effect a hermit's cabin in an Indian community atop Huitapec, a nine-thousand-foot peak. He pedaled to and from classes on a mountain bike. The political lesson of that living experience, he wrote, was that "excessive materialism can interfere with personal growth, but there is little time for growth when people live on a subsistence level."

Throughout his stay in Mexico, Brent kept a diary, partially in Spanish, still trying to puzzle out his path ahead. In one English entry, he asked himself:

> Do you really want to waste your life in a monastery? Why don't you do something constructive for the world? Brothers and sisters, the purpose of life is to know God. I will go to a good university because I feel that is my duty. Then I will become a monk and dedicate my existence to realizing God. Once he tells me what it is I'm supposed to do in my life, then I will do it. If that means plunging into a life of incessant work and action then that is what I will do. If it means teaching, then I will do that. If it means I will do nothing but worshipping God for the rest of my life, then I will do that. There is no such thing as a wasted life.

But when his parents visited him in Mexico, they were shocked to see that their son's once-muscular 190-pound body was emaciated. He had become a vegan, but he was existing for the most part on organic muffins. When he ate vegetables, they were sprouted beans and, once, a raw leafy vegetable the size of a football, which made him very ill. "Equally disturbing," Charlotte wrote later, "was the intensely superior and condescending way he treated us about the way we ate. We were just ignorant fools who knew nothing about spirituality." There was more to Brent's psychological change. He told his parents he wanted to become a Buddha in his lifetime, even though his behavior appeared to his parents to be un-Buddha-like. His mother wrote, "What was frightening was the way he would tenaciously hold on to completely bizarre ideas in the face of overwhelming evidence," from nutrition to his spiritual superiority.

If his religious and dietary ranting were not enough to frighten his parents and drive off his friends, Charlotte noticed that Brent was drinking more and smoking more pot. From personal experience, she recognized the mania and sense of superiority, as well as the substance abuse, for what they might be: an early sign of her family's troubled psychological history, which she had intentionally not shared with her son. This sad litany included bipolar disorder, schizophrenia, alcoholism, and suicide stretching back three generations. In particular, Charlotte's mother had been hospitalized numerous times for mental illness and alcoholism, which placed a great strain on the mother-daughter relationship. Charlotte knew enough about Eastern philosophy (and alcoholism) to recognize that her son seemed more concerned with power than enlightenment. Even after this disastrous visit, Brent did not relent. He wrote his mother a long, rambling email lecture on nutrition and spirituality, attacking her for not accepting the theories of healer Paul Pitchford, later the author of *Healing With Whole Foods: Asian Traditions and Modern Nutrition*. "My purpose is enlightenment, not for my own pleasure but so that I may be a guiding light for the rest of humanity," Brent wrote.

Brent was back in Montgomery for his parents' formal Christmas Eve party in December 1997, where it became clear he was going off the rails. He appeared with a shaved head and in a monk's robe, mortifying his mother. Charlotte warned arrived guests not to say anything, because Brent Jr. "was finding himself." A friend recalled that Charlotte seemed alarmed by Brent Jr.'s appearance and behavior. Brent Sr. was clearly disappointed in his son, and Brent Jr.'s friends made fun of his growing eccentricities. Charlotte privately suspected that it was drug use rather than a search for enlightenment that had led to her son's decision to leave Vanderbilt.

Charlotte, with Brent Sr.'s support, was still pushing their son to return to college. While in Mexico, Brent Jr. met some American students and graduates of Oberlin College in Ohio, and based on their accounts of the liberal school and its curriculum he decided he might want to apply there, rather than to Williams College. Instead, in May 1997, after his last, month-long course at Vanderbilt, Brent had told his parents he wanted to apply to Naropa University, a Buddhist institution in Boulder, Colorado, which he had read about online. His parents said no, but they were now amenable to his applying to Oberlin. One of his Vanderbilt professors later said he mourned the loss of such a good, engaged student.

Again, Brent retreated to the family's Lake Martin house for two months of reading and meditation. His book list included more of his typical spiritual and metaphysical fare. On January 23, 1998, he wrote "A Dialogue With Myself." It began: "Hello myself. Where have you been? I have been looking for you but couldn't find you. I searched in books, spices, sexual thoughts, facts, where else? Lots of places, but no luck." After all his traveling, study, and self-examination, he confessed, "I still haven't come close to knowing myself during the last year and a half."

Although the Oberlin College deadline to apply for the fall 1998 semester had passed, Brent Sr. apparently pulled some strings and in March Brent Jr. sent his application. At last he had a concrete goal, to be admitted to the school. In his admissions essay, he finessed his complex and evolving religious background. "Rather than reducing my perspective to a single belief system, my parents fostered the exploration of many traditions and helped me to develop an open mind." Yet he was eerily prescient when writing about his social consciousness: "It is easier to feel compassion for those who are obviously suffering than for those who, on the surface, appear to have everything but who may actually be suffering underneath." On the subject of his own recent growth, through reading and travel, Brent wrote, "I have undergone a shift from material desires and concerns to spiritual ones." He mentioned his lectures on both Eastern and Western traditions, in Spanish, in Mexico, and his patronage of the co-op vegetarian dining hall there. After a campus interview at the Ohio school, the wandering seeker was admitted for the fall 1998 term.

In the spring and summer of 1998, Brent was back on the road to en-lightenment. He stayed at five Buddhist and Hindu retreats in Manhattan, Massachusetts, and West Virginia—all paid for by his parents. The Buddhist monasteries were in a variety of traditions: Burmese, Tibetan, Sri Lankan. For a time, his reading took him on a more syncretic spiritual path, this time through the writings of Krishnamurti, an early adherent of Theosophy who developed his own philosophy. Brent began to describe himself as "Buddhist Hindu," in the Vedantin tradition. Charlotte supported what she called her son's "great religious quest," yet acknowledged that "it did concern his non-religious father." Brent Jr. went backpacking and camping in Yosemite and Sequoia national parks and visited still more monasteries and retreats. With his friend Mike Carver, he hiked the Appalachian Trail in Maine. Then for three weeks, he stayed with Andrea Jameson in New York City. She recalled that he was severely depressed for the entire visit, spending most of the time lying on her couch, barely functional. In her journal, she wrote that Charlotte had told her that—like Andrea—she had a sense she was losing her son, either to mental illness or his search for enlightenment. Despite what Brent had told Andrea earlier about ending their romantic relationship, they slept together sporadically through the fall of 1998. Jameson felt that while Brent approached lovemaking enthusiastically, he seemed also to be struggling against his sexuality, feeling it was too worldly, a weakness. At the same time, he could revert to being a demanding and spoiled son, with a dogged sense of entitlement. Yet something of the old, thoughtful Brent still survived. That winter, when Andrea herself fell into a severe depression, Brent returned for a visit to offer comfort and support.

Charlotte's primary hope was that her son ultimately would finish college, so she and Brent Sr. were optimistic as they helped him pack for Oberlin, as planned, in September. They found him a nice apartment and felt they could begin a scheduled trip to Indonesia. However, during their second night in Indonesia, they received a 2 a.m. phone call from Brent, who said that after spending a week "fixing his room," three days of classes, and a "tumultuous internal debate," he had decided to withdraw. Brent told Oberlin officials that he would become a monk at a Buddhist monastery in Redwood Valley, California. The chairman of Oberlin's religion department suggested that he spend a month at the monastery, but then enroll at Naropa University for the spring semester. At Naropa, he could blend the study of Buddhism with meditation.

So yet again, Brent was back on the road. He begged his mother to join him in California for a retreat, she recalled, "so I could find out how wonderful it was. I went, and I did have a good experience. I never met such loving men. They knew that I was frantic, and each one spent time with me explaining what had led to their decision to be a monk. I can tell you that anybody raised in the American culture is not happy when her son is contemplating becoming a Buddhist monk, but I will say that these men were a centered, peaceful and loving group." Charlotte spent a month at the monastery and concluded that it wasn't a cult, but the visit wasn't entirely successful. "She wanted to help him make a connection between the search for enlightenment and the real world, but Brent didn't want it to be that way," Andrea Jameson remembered.

By this time, both parents felt emotionally battered and exhausted, and on the Oberlin chairman's advice, they agreed to let Brent apply to Naropa after the monastery stay. Naropa accepted him for the spring term of 1999, and he planned to major in religious studies with an emphasis on Buddhism. In Boulder, he wrote, he wanted to study for a BA and an MA, with a focus on spirituality and environmentalism. Though he missed the October deadline to send his fees, Naropa held his place. As they had so many times before, his parents supported this move, and Brent came back to Montgomery for a pleasant visit, as did Andrea Jameson. "He was still interested in being a monk," Charlotte wrote, "and we had decided that we could accept that if it made him happy. We were glad to have him back in school."

: 6

Boulder

Boulder, Colorado, remains one of the centers of America's organic, touchy-feely universe, as well as an outdoor health and fitness haven. So it was no surprise that Brent gravitated to the city and loved it. He later explained that Boulder "is kind of a Mecca for Eastern religious traditions." One of its landmark institutions is Naropa University, which began as a Buddhist meditation center and institute in 1974, founded first as a summer program by the Oxford-educated, Tibetan Buddhist meditation master Chögyam Trungpa Rinpoche, together with avant-garde artists and poets like Allen Ginsberg, for whom the school's library is named. In January 1999, at the age of twenty-three, Brent entered the university. At first, Naropa seemed like an ideal choice. For the next twelve months he studied various Buddhist traditions, as well as ecology and even calculus. He attended most of his classes in the converted, slightly musty, 1903 elementary school that for years was the school's main building, whose walls were often covered with local artwork. Rooms in the two-story structure have hardwood floors—some covered with industrial carpeting—and high ceilings. Students often sat in a circle, either in chairs or on cushions. Brent took to his classes, even resuming regular computer use he had given up in Mexico. In particular, he loved the building's incense-infused meditation rooms. He enjoyed wandering the grounds, among the three ancient, towering sycamores and the small converted houses and cottages. He would have lunch on Sycamore Green, bordering Boulder Creek Park and the University of Colorado campus beyond. He also took advantage of talks given in Boulder by Hindu gurus.

When he first got to Boulder, Brent responded to a newspaper ad looking for a roommate, which connected him to an older Naropa student, Ann Flinders, a graduate student in psychology. He made a good first impression on the tall, slender, brown-haired woman, with his Southern charm and dry sense of humor. He was quick to smile and laugh and open the door for her, and didn't seem at all eccentric. Flinders described him during that period as a helpful, mannerly young man who always paid his share of the rent on time for the two-bedroom, two-bath, double-wide mobile home and helped clean the house. He was energetic, often asking her if he could help with the groceries or shovel snow. "There was a fine rapport in the house," she recalled in an interview, and they got along well. She never saw Brent use drugs or alcohol at the house. Although Brent was by now strongly committed to celibacy, endlessly discussing why he wouldn't give in to "lower desires," he had a new girlfriend. "She was very New Age-y," Flinders said. "They were very sweet together; they held hands." To Flinders, who would earn a master's degree in psychology, Brent seemed like a typical, eager Naropa student, something of a loner, consumed with being—and being seen as—spiritual. When the conversation with Flinders turned toward the spiritual, she recalled, he was curious and engaged, almost mesmerized, looking wide-eyed at her. "He was really excited about Naropa," Flinders said. "There was no apathy, he was very engaged and wasn't depressed. He was supported by his parents." She did find him a little naïve, instantly willing to accept anything spiritual or metaphysical. "In our conversations, he was very much seeking a teacher, or guide," she recalled years later. "He was really looking outside of himself."

To Flinders, also a student of metaphysics, Brent seemed to be a classic example of a *chela*, a Hindu term from the Sanskrit that can mean a student or disciple in search of a guru. Another meaning of the term is "servant" or "slave." Perhaps out of self-consciousness, Brent spoke little of his past, and never told Flinders about his many stays at monasteries and retreats; her impression was that he had only visited one. At first, Brent thought Flinders might be his guide. He was in awe of her spiritual journey and did not see himself as her equal. "He was willing to give me his power. I kept leading him back toward himself so that he could find that within him. He was very much yearning for that." Ann was impressed with the books he was reading and his disciplined meditation. She found him caring and warm and, although she was a woman sharing a small space with an intense young man she barely knew, "there wasn't any time I was scared or concerned about him, or felt threatened by him. He never got angry."

But there were early signs of trouble, beginning with Brent's fixation with arranging his trailer bedroom—behavior similar to his experiences in Montgomery and at Vanderbilt. In Boulder, he spent two weeks to "get his room fixed," which Charlotte found troubling. In January 1999 he first experienced audio and visual hallucinations—ringing bells, lights, rainbows—that seemed to recur every two or three months. "A shimmering light effect would become superimposed over my vision," he would later describe. Often distracted, he got a traffic ticket for speeding and another for an improper signal. His mother sent the money to pay the fines but warned, "If you forget and spend it for something else, I can't help." Brent Sr. grumbled about how much Brent Jr. was spending at Naropa, especially for a large number of books.

While attending Naropa, Brent became friends with Ann Flinders's parents, Marie and Sam. Sam was extraordinary: blind from age eleven from a dynamite accident, he had earned two master's degrees and a PhD and gold and silver medals in handicapped skiing competitions. A former economics professor in his late sixties, Sam had recently sold his seat on the New York Stock Exchange and moved to Boulder with Marie, who had been an opera singer. When Brent met Sam, the older man was ill with diabetes and had broken his leg in a fall, requiring him to use a wheelchair. Marie was having difficulty caring for him at home, even with Ann's help. A hired attendant proved unstable, so Brent volunteered to help. He began coming to the house to be with Sam, at first to give Marie a break, but he eventually stayed for a time in the couple's basement. Initially, Brent wouldn't take any money, but later accepted several checks, totaling more than a thousand dollars, from Marie with the notation, "caring for Sam." Brent seemed to take to the caring role, always polite and upbeat with Sam, often reading to him. Marie told Charlotte, "Brent helped me get my life back. I hope you appreciate what a wonderful son you have." Naturally, the Springfords were moved. "We thought that maybe he really was cut out for some kind of spiritual vocation," Charlotte wrote. Ann Flinders was equally grateful. "He went out of his way to help my father in the last months of his life. He was profoundly helpful to my mom and to me, so generous and consistent. It felt like a blessing for both of us. He would really listen and he was very attentive."

Charlotte, Brent Sr., and Andrea Jameson all made trips to visit Brent Jr. in Boulder, together and separately—Brent Sr. spent a week with his son. Brent Jr. was making good grades, as usual, and on the surface seemed content. Yet Charlotte sensed that Brent was being pulled in a dangerously cultish direction, returning to old patterns. This time it seemed like it might be coming from a source outside of Naropa, perhaps from friends or acquaintances. During the 1999 summer break from Naropa, Brent decided that his guru was John DeRoiter, a Canadian philosopher-author and a favorite of the Flinders family. So he drove to San Francisco for a series of DeRoiter's talks and later spent a week at a DeRoiter retreat in Edmonton, Alberta. He shaved his head again, and Brent Sr. finally began to resist paying for his son's stays at retreats and monasteries. For Charlotte especially, her son's drift was perplexing. She was unable to untangle the strands of his life and his emotional state. Despite what she knew about psychological disorders, and no matter how much time she spent with her son, she couldn't tell how much was normal young-adult separation and alienation, how much was a sincere search for spirituality, and what might be signs of incipient mental illness, like schizophrenia, that can strike men in their twenties. She even asked Marie Flinders if she would consider taking care of Brent, but the woman declined.

Brent returned to Naropa for the fall semester of 1999, studying Buddhism and ecology. He moved into an apartment of his own and repeated the obsessive ritual of getting his room just right. However, he didn't do well at the school; in manic periods he ordered every book that interested him. During classes, he would sit in the full lotus position, and he was drinking to feel better about himself. That fall, in a disturbing turn—and one of his last forays on the Internet—he sent a mass email to all of his old friends from Alabama and Vanderbilt except Andrea Jameson, saying that he wanted no further contact with them. He told them he was determined to "become a Buddha in his lifetime," assuring them that his choice was not a product of mental illness or delusional thinking. Looking back years later, Jameson sharply disagreed. "Brent's personality and interests changed so dramatically as his illness emerged . . . in his early twenties. We lost the marvelously gregarious, fun person that he was to intense inner contemplation. . . . We lost the wonderful social person who loved being surrounded by friends and loved to entertain people. . . . I—and arguably other women—lost his intense sex drive and his enjoyment of women. . . . He lost all sense of enjoying and participating in the world around him."

In Boulder, meanwhile, Marie Flinders, observing Brent's growing distress, suggested stress-reducing breathing lessons with a Native American woman named Caroline Scoutt. Flinders's home was a kind of New Age salon, hosting various adherents of varied spiritual traditions. Flinders made an appointment with Scoutt for Brent and paid for it—a decision she would come to deeply regret.

Medicine Woman

Around Thanksgiving of 1999, while Brent was still in and out of the Flinderses family's Boulder home, Marie introduced Brent to a woman now calling herself Caroline Scoutt. The woman, born Carol Gonzales, was using a name altered slightly from her most recent ex-husband, whose surname was Scott. Scoutt came to Boulder for a month at a time from her Wyoming ranch, staying with clients like the Flinderses. She claimed to be a psychologist, although she was not licensed or certified, and offered herself as a marriage and family therapist, working with couples, families, and children. Scoutt also offered herself as a Native American spiritual healer, counseling seekers and other New Agers. She made a dramatic impression, with her long dark hair in which she tied eagle feathers—to which Native Americans attach special spiritual significance—and flowing dresses, carrying with her rattles and drums. "I am a shaman," she would proclaim. "She played the Native American card as the key to her spirituality," recalled Ann Flinders, Marie's daughter and Brent's former roommate, "That was how she presented herself. . . . She said she was closely connected to the chiefs and the elders, as well as the spirits in the Native American tradition." One of Scoutt's specialties was leading therapeutic individual and group breathing sessions for which she charged participants a hundred dollars an hour. Sometimes during these sessions she extracted personal information from participants, later using it to gain control over them. She said she based the sessions on her reading of the German spirituality author Eckhart Tolle. Once she had her own children in a session, which was essentially supervised hyperventilation. "It was almost like you were going to pass out," Star Fosheim, her younger daughter, recalled.

By late 1999, Marie Flinders had worked with Scoutt in counseling sessions over the previous six months and thought she knew the woman well. Ann had several breathing sessions with Scoutt, which she found well run, and some members of the Boulder community held the woman in awe. However, neither woman's experience prepared them for Brent's first encounter with Scoutt. Almost instantly after Marie Flinders introduced Scoutt, Brent said he recognized Scoutt as a "master teacher." Unbidden, he dropped to his knees, bowing his forehead to the floor, and signed up for the first of many breathing sessions. Scoutt would later insist that she was embarrassed by this reaction, but Ann saw it differently. "Brent with his big blue eyes, that longing that he had . . . she could pick that up right away." For whatever reason, Brent was taken, and the subsequent breathing sessions only reinforced his initial reaction. He explained his fascination to Ann. "For the first time, he experienced a sense of the divine love," she recalled. "He said she had 'the Sight,' and could sense things." Later Brent would write, "This was the biggest turning point of my life."

Although Brent and Scoutt both stayed at the Flinderses' house, initially they had little to do with one another. Brent was going to class at Naropa and Scoutt was conducting readings and running her sessions. That soon changed. At Scoutt's recommendation, Brent began reading books by Jane Roberts, a mid-twentieth century American writer whose 1960s–1970s books on the paranormal claimed to be channeled from a spirit entity named "Seth." For one of his Naropa classes, Brent wrote a meandering paper about Scoutt's life as a shaman.

Sam Flinders's condition was rapidly deteriorating. Despite Brent's devoted help, Marie felt she had to move her husband to an assisted living facility. Brent followed, praying for the older man when he slept or lost consciousness, sometimes sleeping next to him on the floor. Several weeks later, on the night of December 6, Sam's condition worsened, and Marie asked Scoutt to pray and drum for him. He died the next day, and Scoutt conducted the funeral, again praying and singing over the body.

When Brent went home to Montgomery for Christmas, he was unable to do anything until he rearranged all the posters in his room. Still, for the most part, Charlotte observed, the time at Naropa seemed to have benefited him, producing "good, normal moments with Brent seeming to be his old self, albeit with his new spiritual direction. But it was a good direction." Still, by January 2000, Brent had spent all his Christmas gift money on sessions with Scoutt.

Just as Brent's relationship with Scoutt was starting, in the Flinderses' circle suspicions about her were growing. Ann was involved in channeling and the emotional regression practice known as rebirthing, and she was being counseled by Scoutt. Yet Ann came to believe that Scoutt was not to be trusted. Scoutt, she felt, betrayed confidences from her counseling sessions and tried to play members of the Flinders family—including Ann's mother and her husband—against one another. "Caroline used her sessions with my mom to push [Marie] away from me. I was devastated. She put me in such a bad light to the point that my mom became very suspicious of me." Mostly, Ann decided, Scoutt was after her family's money. Scoutt never seemed to have enough cash, and as a result she always had some hustle going. She claimed many good works, for hospice organizations and countless hours of volunteer work on reservations in Wyoming and the Dakotas. However, as a result of her own unpaid medical bills, she claimed that there were liens against her Wyoming ranch outside Newcastle, liens which she convinced Marie Flinders to cover. Marie paid Scoutt $34,000, ostensibly for various treatments and therapies over a six-month period. Later, Marie would give the woman an additional $10,000 for construction of the driveway to the Wyoming ranch.

Scoutt's major project during this time was building on her ranch a circular lodge and ceremonial center for Native American foster children and battered women. In December 2000, Scoutt incorporated a Wyoming organization called Tatan-Ka Sha. In its filing for nonprofit status, Scoutt asserted that its purpose was "to provide spiritual education including, but not limited to, Native American religious teachings and ceremonies, and to provide spiritual and financial assistance to the elderly, to families, and to newly young adults from abusive and dysfunctional families." Erecting the round house on the Newcastle property as the centerpiece of the project, one of Scoutt's daughters recalled, "was my mother's dream." However, notwithstanding Scoutt's claims to donors and prospective donors, "there were never any abused Native American women running around the property."

Scoutt told her children that she was taking trips to deliver things to reservations, but none of the children ever accompanied her.

When Scoutt took her children on visits to financial contributors in Colorado, like Patricia Emmons, her younger daughter Star was often asked how she felt about being Native American, which the girl knew was untrue, but "which I had to go along with." The donors "thought they were helping with such great causes. My brother told some of them that my mom was using them, lying about what she was doing. That resulted in a fight," the younger daughter recalled. "She was going back and forth between Colorado and Wyoming, pretending to be such a great person, doing all these great things for the world and being a great mom. She likes to be showy, to present things falsely."

One Boulder acquaintance from around that time said there seemed to be an air of deception about Scoutt. Another man recalled that he "always got the impression that when Caroline said something, you weren't getting the whole story." The Flinderses and their friends did not share with Brent, who was clearly vulnerable, their growing skepticism of Scoutt. But even if they had, it probably wouldn't have made much difference.

As Brent was falling more under Scoutt's sway, he shared with his parents his burgeoning relationship with the woman, who, unbeknownst to him and to them, was twenty-four years his senior. At first, the Springfords were pleased—some friends said relieved—that their son had found someone who might look after him, and do so far away from Montgomery. The parents met Scoutt on a visit to Boulder in late March and early April 2000, and Charlotte especially formed a favorable opinion and wrote her a check for $6,000—the first of many for the growing amount of time Scoutt was spending with Brent—apparently as an inducement to assume the role of his informal caretaker. In the eight months after Brent's first meeting with Scoutt, the Springfords wrote her checks totaling $90,000. Around the time of the Springfords' visit, Scoutt suggested that Brent might want to spend the coming summer break working on her Wyoming ranch and learning about Native American culture and spirituality. He made a five-day visit to Wyoming and seemed totally sold. As he explained to his parents, "I'll work for her on her land and she will be my teacher." His parents' understanding was that he would return in the fall to Naropa, where he had managed to maintain a respectable 3.5 GPA for the fall semester.

Yet it soon became apparent to Brent's family and friends that he wasn't improving under Scoutt's care. In mid-May, he returned to Montgomery for a visit and seemed suddenly—and inexplicably—angrier than his parents had ever seen. At one point, he had a near-violent confrontation with his father. Before he arrived, he spoke with Andrea Jameson, telling her he wanted to see her when she returned to town. However, the next afternoon, May 13, 2000, Brent sent Jameson an email saying he no longer wanted any contact with her; it was essentially the same as the mass email he had sent earlier to his other friends. Troubled by this turn of events, Jameson rushed to the Springfords' house. Brent's sister Robin let her in. But when Brent locked eyes with Andrea, he turned away, slamming the door behind him. Brent told his parents that if Andrea was allowed on their property while he was there he would never return. Rather than a devoted, long-suffering girlfriend, he told his mother, Jameson was "a malign spiritual influence with whom he had done battle during several lifetimes, and who would try to bring him down."

The parents knew something was terribly wrong with their son. Charlotte suggested that he seek professional help, either in Montgomery or Colorado, but he refused. At the same time, Brent also broke relations with his sister Robin. Andrea, Charlotte, and Robin thought he was in a psychotic state, suddenly exhibiting vengeful and bizarre behavior. To this day, Andrea believes that the email Brent later sent her was actually written by or was under the influence of Scoutt, who had voiced jealousy about Andrea to Brent in the past. Andrea replied gently to the email with one asking that he not spare her his madness, quoting Hamlet, a character no stranger to the malady:

> The spirit that I have seen
> May be the devil: and the devil hath power
> To assume a pleasing shape; yea, and perhaps
> Out of my weakness and my melancholy

As he is very potent with such spirits,
Abuses me to damn me

For Marie Flinders, the last straw in her relationship with Scoutt took place earlier that spring, before Brent's trip to Montgomery, when she walked Scoutt to her car. Flinders noticed a full-length, white fur coat in the vehicle, and innocently complimented Scoutt on it. Scoutt seemed embarrassed by the discovery, and then angry, snapping that the coat had been a gift. In late May, Marie wrote Scoutt a check for $12,441, ostensibly for advance readings, but more likely to help speed her and Brent's departure from the Flinderses' home. Brent moved to a small trailer on Scoutt's ranch, returning five days later to collect the remainder of his belongings from the Boulder house. The ranch in Newcastle is not far from the Wyoming border with South Dakota, where there were Sioux reservations that Scoutt said she often visited. Her property consisted of little more than a small patch of scrub and undeveloped land, with a dilapidated mobile home, a concrete pad for the unfinished circular home, a camper trailer, and a few wandering animals.

About this time, Charlotte wrote her son a letter on the subject of anger. She was still puzzling out his recent visit home and was shaken by his hostility toward family and friends in Montgomery. She tried to approach the issue in an unthreatening way. "Every wisdom tradition that I know of urges us to learn to control our anger—and with very good reason," she wrote. "Uncontrolled anger is behind man's most devastating social behavior—murder and physical and psychological abuse." Years before, Charlotte taught a year-long course at an Alabama women's prison. Drawing on that experience, which included instructing convicted murderers, she wrote that anger should not be denied or unacknowledged. "If you do that, if it will express itself in some way that is either dangerous for you or someone else. If it finally bubbles up and explodes, you can hurt somebody." Although Charlotte acknowledged that neither Brent nor Scoutt put much faith in psychologists, she pointed out that researchers "feel that teaching a child to express his anger in ways that don't have devastating consequences is one of the most important aspects of parenting. It's also one of the hardest, and obviously we didn't do a good job of it because you are full of anger that was not expressed. But is direct confrontation in the heat of anger the best way?"

In pages of subsequent, typed, single-spaced letters, Charlotte urged Brent to put up encouraging signs in his Wyoming trailer, to watch his diet, and do specific exercises. Her advice about taking care of his body revealed some of her own philosophy. "It is not fair, but it is a fact that physical beauty attracts people to us, and when it is combined with intelligence and sensitivity to others, it can provide us with powerful tools for accomplishing our purpose."

Charlotte thought Brent's first months with Scoutt were positive and the summer move to Wyoming was a good idea. Scoutt "seemed to have a powerfully beneficial influence on Brent," she recalled, despite the Montgomery blowup. Based on Scoutt's reports to the Springfords, Charlotte told a friend that he "gave up all drinking and marijuana and began to examine a lot of his behavior. For six months, we thought we had our son back."

What neither Charlotte nor Brent Sr. knew was that in June 2000, there was a major change in Brent Jr.'s relationship with Scoutt. For no apparent reason, apart from Scoutt's suggestion, they had driven to the historic tourist town of Deadwood, South Dakota, an hour from the Wyoming ranch. At the time, Brent was twenty-four and Scoutt was forty-eight. Years later Brent told an acquaintance that he had no idea of the purpose of the trip until they arrived at a justice of the peace and were married, in what shortly became a chaste, if legal, relationship. They agreed not to tell Brent's parents. "It was a purely platonic relationship," Brent later wrote. Scoutt "was clearly the teacher and I was clearly the student." His life had been changed fundamentally by the relationship.

Not everyone agreed that Scoutt's influence on Brent was positive. When Brent and Caroline visited Boulder early in the summer, Marie Flinders saw Brent as a dramatically changed person, and not for the better. He avoided eye contact, and was obviously submissive, deferring to Scoutt in everything. Others who observed them together said that Brent wouldn't make a decision without her approval, or even leave the room without her explicit permission. His friends felt that from that time on he was under her powerful spell. Brent confided to Ann Flinders that he had finally met his spiritual guide. But Ann didn't like what she saw. "His eyes were cold," she recalled, "and I was definitely afraid."

In Montgomery, Charlotte neither saw—nor sensed—any of this. "I must say in all honesty that Caroline is probably more able to help him than I am," she wrote to one of his Naropa professors. In her view, Scoutt

saw many of the same problems in Brent that I did, and was trying to help him understand that true spirituality involves everyday living, giving to others, etc. and is not measured by psychic powers, ascetic diet and all that. Brent needed to hear this realistic approach, but since he accepted Caroline's authority totally, it also meant that for the first time in four years all the unrealistic structures he had created were being seriously undermined, and he was beginning to fall apart.

At the same time, Charlotte feared that Scoutt, who preferred a spiritual and holistic approach to treating mental illness, couldn't prevent her son's condition from deteriorating. The mother had become convinced, from personal experience following her daughter Stephanie's tragic death and from her family's history of mental illness, that her son needed traditional psychiatric diagnosis and care for what she believed was his bipolar state. In a long, pleading letter to Scoutt, she wrote,

Please understand how urgent this is. If Brent is tested and found not to be Bipolar, we will be delighted to be wrong. If, however, he is indeed Bipolar and does not receive appropriate treatment, his life prospects are grim. The disease, untreated, gets worse quickly. [She pressed Scoutt to get Brent] tested and get the help he needs. He can lead a good life with medication, but without it he is doomed. . . . Please try to help him. His life depends on it.

In the late spring and summer Brent kept another journal, this one in a spiral notebook, where he recorded his near-incoherent thoughts tracking his "Vision Quest." For a time he camped out in a tent, sometimes awakened by the calls of wild turkeys around Scoutt's ranch. Mostly, the diary quickly degenerated into self-help exhortations, dreamy musings, and

New Age gobbledygook, written in an increasingly shaky hand, with lots of exclamation points. During this time, he also corresponded in Spanish with friends from Mexico. He was generating hundreds of notebook pages, trying to figure out the world, the mind, the meaning of existence—and his role in it. His goal, he wrote in May, was "to become empowered as a spiritual warrior. This means to confirm that I am an open-hearted warrior of compassionate, selfless action."

Charlotte and Brent Sr. flew out to visit Brent and Scoutt at the Wyoming ranch in late June, where they found their son sleeping in an uninsulated camper not far from Scoutt's larger trailer. Unasked, they got an estimate to have the camper skirted and winterized, and then paid for the improvements. They even suggested a new site to park it. Scoutt claimed to be grateful, but later told investigators she found it strange—and presumptuous—since the plan at that point was for Brent Jr. to stay just for the summer before returning to Naropa. Brent Sr. inspected the circular concrete pad where Scoutt wanted to build her lodge and Native American cultural center. Charlotte had an emotional breathing session with Scoutt, a kind of meditation similar to what Scoutt had done for Brent Jr. and others in Boulder. Brent Sr. declined to participate but was sufficiently impressed with what Scoutt said she was doing on various reservations that he wrote her another check.

From the ranch, all four headed to the annual, three-day Native American festival in Sundance, Wyoming, where Scoutt was one of the primary organizers and instructors. The Springfords paid for three rooms at the nearby Econo Lodge, one of which was for Brent Jr., leading them to believe that the relationship with Scoutt was not romantic. They had thought that the trip was simply a brief break from their son's summer work on Scoutt's ranch in exchange for room and board and learning about Native American culture. They soon learned, however, that Brent Jr. had spent much of the two weeks before the festival commuting the fifty miles from the ranch, helping Scoutt prepare the Sundance site, and that he got very little sleep during his work on the site. Also, he fasted for four days before the festival opened—all of which may have altered his brain chemistry. By all accounts, he spoke disrespectfully toward tribal elders, talked about Buddha, and sat at the campfire in the lotus position, chanting. The Springfords were shocked by Brent Jr.'s culturally insensitive behavior, which they found uncharacteristic of their son. "Instead of standing back as a thoughtful and respectful observer," Charlotte wrote later, "he single-mindedly and obsessively tried to insert himself right into the middle of it, alienating almost everybody he met." Brent's actions were so egregious that some of the elders asked Scoutt to do something about it. She explained that the young man was mentally ill, and the elders seemed mollified. Looking back years later at the incident, Brent Jr. recalled "I felt completely out of place and my bipolar disorder was becoming full blown."

Brent was puzzled by his own behavior, and to make amends—perhaps at Scoutt's suggestion—he went on a spending spree. When the Springfords returned to Alabama they were shocked to find a bill for $6,500 on the "emergency only" credit card they provided him, covering the time of the festival. Brent had bought a few shirts for himself, but most of the purchases were apparently for Scoutt's Native American friends and others working at the festival—clothes, gas for their cars, and meals at the most expensive restaurant in Deadwood, across the state line in South Dakota, half an hour away. The Springfords were furious, and called Brent to say that he was being financially irresponsible and that they were cutting him off, the first of such threats though they rarely followed through. Charlotte "railed" at him, by her own account. But again, *she* took responsibility for what followed in a subsequent letter to one of his psychiatrists. Recalling the Sundance incident years later, Charlotte blamed herself for Brent's deterioration. "Undoubtedly I was the catalyst that subsequently drove him into a deep depression," she wrote. This was part of a pattern Charlotte would repeat, finding some way to assume the blame for her son's actions. She constantly second-guessed herself, wondering whether she and her husband should have opted for "tough love"—by cutting Brent off financially when he left Vanderbilt, for example, rather than underwriting his meandering spiritual odyssey. The Springfords told Brent that if he wanted to return to Naropa—which they thought he planned to do—he would have to get a job in Boulder. In the meantime, Brent Sr. told Scoutt to keep his son's credit card. The Springfords at that point were sending Brent weekly allowance checks of $425, roughly equivalent to a job paying ten dollars an hour (about $16.60 in

2021). Now, they asked Scoutt to deposit the money into a joint checking account and to dole it out to Brent Jr. in small amounts for gas and food.

Charlotte recalled 2000 and the years that immediately followed as "a rollercoaster ride that has seen two very confused and frightened parents trying to keep their son from going down the tube, and undoubtedly making bad decisions all along the way." On July 31, not long after returning from their western visit, they sent Scoutt three checks totaling $25,000. Around the same time, Charlotte wrote in a new journal: "I can't let worry about [Brent] take over my life. . . . If it weren't for Caroline he really might be suicidal." Charlotte could be quite self-aware about her relationship with her son. "Funny how I never realized what a controlling person I have become," she wrote, "especially with regard to him, always trying to get him to go in the direction I thought best for him." Yet, inevitably, she ended up taking responsibility for what had gone wrong. "I gave him a lot but not what he needed most. I wasn't very good at helping him develop a strong and positive self-image."

In August, Brent learned that his beloved godmother, Charlotte's old University of Alabama debate coach Annabel Hagood, was dying of cancer in Virginia. Despite her illness, Hagood was concerned about Brent and wanted desperately to see him. Brent was equally eager to see her. However, no one could work out the logistics for Scoutt and Brent to get plane tickets together; Brent was in no condition to travel alone, since he tended to get sick on flights. So they drove cross-country, taking an incongruously zigzag route that included so many stops it took a month to get to Virginia. Yet when he finally arrived, Brent spent just ninety minutes with his godmother, to Charlotte's chagrin. One of the stops on the way back to Colorado was a two-day visit with the Springfords in Montgomery, where Brent Jr. was alternately withdrawn and manic—and then unable to sleep. Again, he fixated on rearranging the posters in his bedroom. As in his previous visit home, he argued with his father with even greater hostility, telling his parents he now blamed his problems on Naropa and Buddhism.

By contrast, Scoutt enthralled Charlotte and Brent Sr. with a drumming session. Charlotte was comfortable enough to confide to Scoutt some of the intimate concerns she usually shared only with her closest friends.

These included her early romances, her concerns with her weight and her appearance as she aged, the tensions in her marriage—and most of all, her fears about her son. To Maggie Johnson, who would soon retire from her housekeeper job, Brent was "pitiful looking, like a tramp, shoes with holes in them, dreadfully thin, nasty and dirty." Johnson noticed that he waited on Scoutt "hand and foot." Jerry Armstrong, the operations manager of the Pepsi bottling plant and a friend of the family, had similar impressions when he dropped by for a visit. "I was shocked," he recalled years later. "I was floored. I couldn't believe it initially. He looked disheveled. He looked rough. He wasn't kempt. Long hair and a short beard, I wanted the old Brent back. I had an uneasy feeling. He wasn't the Brent I knew." Armstrong was not impressed with Scoutt, or the dynamic between the couple. "She was rough, too. I expected him to come home with a beautiful young woman on his arm, rather than an older, unkempt lady . . . You could sense she was in charge. She was controlling everything he was saying and doing."

Alarmed by Brent's appearance, Charlotte wanted to buy her son new jeans and boots, but he refused, saying they were leaving the next day. Scoutt, however, was not reluctant to take some of the expensive dresses Charlotte offered. Charlotte still held a favorable view of Caroline, based largely on her role as her son's caregiver. "Brent loved Caroline deeply," she wrote, "and since his depression became full blown, he has become totally dependent on her, and clings to her as his lifeline. He is terrified at the thought of losing her." She expressed her doubts only in her journal. "The issue is whether someone is primarily interested in him or his parents' money." And, reflexively, now almost compulsively, Charlotte took responsibility for the turn her son's life had taken. "While I believe that Brent's illness would eventually have manifested itself in one way or another," she wrote in a letter, "I also believe that I am ultimately responsible for the direction it took through spirituality."

For some reason—possibly because of Scoutt's exposure to the Springfords' affluent lifestyle—when Brent returned to Wyoming, he suddenly became obsessed with the idea of moving to Alabama and working as a manager in the family Pepsi plant in Luverne. This was a dramatic turnaround, since he had viewed joining the Pepsi workforce with indifference, if not distaste, in his letters to Andrea Jameson several years before. The new job would enable him to bring Caroline and her two younger children to Montgomery, buy a house with a pond and enough acreage to keep horses, and send the children to his old prep school. Charlotte was back in Virginia, still caring for Brent's dying godmother. Brent was so seized with his new plan that he got a telephone operator to interrupt a phone call between Charlotte and Brent Sr., saying it was an emergency, telling his parents that he wanted to move back.

By this time, Brent Jr. was communicating with his parents primarily through Scoutt, and in a subsequent telephone conversation they told her the Montgomery proposal would not work, for a variety of reasons. However, Scoutt only passed along his parents' refusal, and not their rationale. Brent Jr. became deflated and then enraged. So Charlotte then wrote him a lengthy letter, explaining that there were no openings at the plant, in management or distribution. For him to join the company, they would have to fire one of their longtime employees, all of whom were family breadwinners. In any case, they thought it likely that the plant would be taken over by a larger bottler in the next few years. Even if he drove a delivery truck, the economics of the move made no sense. A house in Montgomery like the one he described would cost a minimum of $350,000 and tuition for the children at the Montgomery Academy would be $25,000 a year each. Charlotte did her best to soften the blow of their refusal. "Do you see why we were a little bit concerned?" Brent sent his parents a fax dismissing them from his life, and he began telling Scoutt they were evil devils. While on a visit to Boulder, where Scoutt and Brent stayed with friends, people heard a noise in the other room. They found Brent standing on a chair with a knotted sheet around his neck, trying to attach the makeshift noose to the chandelier.

After the summer's blowups, Brent Jr. effectively cut off all spoken communications with his parents—again. Horrified by the suicide attempt, the Springfords negotiated a low-key visit to Scoutt and Brent in September in hopes of reconciling. The parents traveled to the Wyoming ranch for what they promised would be a "no pressure" visit. One of their purposes was to discuss his psychiatric treatment, and to raise the issue of moving back to Colorado, where their son might find better medical care. Caroline was taking Brent with her on her regular trips to Boulder anyway, concerned about leaving him behind. Although there were no more blowups, the Springfords' visit did little to allay Charlotte's growing concerns. "I worry about him so much. And about Caroline. Is she legit? Can she help him? If she can't, who can? . . . What is her motive? Is she simply after our money? If she is, she could very well destroy him. He's totally dependent on her. Does she realize that? Does she care?" Charlotte seemed clear-eyed enough to observe that many of Scoutt's clients she met earlier in Boulder seemed unstable themselves.

With Brent Jr. now privately resolved to remain with Scoutt and her children on the Wyoming ranch, he and Scoutt now proposed that his parents finance construction of her circular lodge and Native American center with a $50,000 loan. Scoutt said she had already sunk more than $30,000 of her own money into what she called her "dream house." Brent Sr., typically thorough when it came to money, had the structure and plans examined. Remembering the condition of the property when he and Charlotte visited that summer, he submitted the plans and photos of the site to an architect, who reported that the proposed house would probably collapse in a heavy snowstorm. In an angry, tearful phone conversation between Charlotte and Scoutt, the Springfords informed Scoutt that they would not agree to the loan without further investigation. Scoutt told Brent Jr. of the rejection but, as with their earlier opposition to a move back to Montgomery, she did not share his parents' reasons. "Obviously, this would set him off and send him into worse shape," Charlotte wrote in a subsequent letter to Scoutt. Any attempt "to discuss everything only through you and at such a distance can only lead to misunderstanding." The Springfords had also looked into Scoutt's financial history. "It appears that you have made some bad business decisions in the past," Charlotte wrote in the same letter, explaining their decision not to support the lodge project. Charlotte also wrote to her son, attempting to mollify him by saying she and Brent Sr. had not rejected the loan out of hand but were still considering it. This had no effect on Brent Jr. He again became fixated on the idea that his parents were "evil, devils," and wrote to them, saying goodbye forever. But, uncharacteristically, Charlotte did not back down. "I will not let myself fall into the trap of emotional blackmailing with Brent as I did with my mother," an unbalanced alcoholic, she wrote a friend.

Later in the fall of 2000, Brent had officially withdrawn from Naropa, but at first he didn't tell his parents. He stayed on at Scoutt's ranch, where she and her children lived in their manufactured home and Brent slept in the camper. Things did not go well in the months that followed. Brent proved to be a scatterbrained stepfather and ranch hand. Once he forgot to pick up Scoutt's youngest child from school. Four chickens died when he neglected to open their house, and a cat almost died when he left it locked in his camper for a week. He routinely broke and ruined tools, often leaving them out in the rain, where they rusted. Plants and bushes died when he forgot to water them. On his monthly visits with Scoutt to Boulder, friends in Colorado noted a curious pattern to his behavior. He actually seemed to stabilize and become more functional when he was apart from Scoutt, despite his frequent psychotic symptoms. When he was with her he destabilized, groveled, and became self-loathing. Within two months, friends recalled, his behavior became more unhinged, with Brent telling them that he was deeply depressed, and that he felt like a failure, frustrated at his inability to do certain tasks.

Although the Springfords were unaware of Brent Jr.'s marriage to Scoutt, around the same time, they did learn that Brent's feelings for Scoutt were more than that of a caregiver. In their early months living together, one of Scoutt's old boyfriends, who worked with her at the Sundance Festival and now was married to another woman, began to pursue her again. Scoutt said she tried to wave off the suitor, without success, and Brent found out from one of her older children. When the man showed up at the ranch, Brent attacked him, but got the worst of it.

The episode prompted Brent to write his parents for a loan to buy Scoutt an engagement ring—months *after* his secret wedding. In the same October 6, 2000, letter he thanked Charlotte for sending him a list of prospective houses in the Boulder area, but asked that she stop trying to analyze him, and to have faith in him, because he was "just trying to survive." As usual, Brent Sr. was skeptical about a loan for the engagement ring, given the apparent haste, but Charlotte was supportive, and she tried to be conciliatory.

Now let me make something very clear. Brent, if you have fixated on the idea of this loan to the point that it will hurt you if you don't get it, or you will feel that we don't love you, or have confidence in you, then I will make the loan to you myself whether Dad agrees or not—but I think he would. We will make a written contract. But I think it is a mistake, and it certainly has absolutely nothing to do with whether we love you or believe in you. It has to do with responsibility and maturity.

Charlotte assured him that the situation was not unique.

I have long believed that one of the dumbest customs that ever evolved in our society is the notion that a young man, during the time when he can least afford it, is expected to buy an expensive ring for his beloved."

Brent's feelings of frustration and worthlessness working at the Wyoming ranch were manifested in many ways. Once, when he lost the screws to a table saw he bashed his head against the concrete floor, giving himself black eyes. On another occasion, he scraped his face into the gravel driveway. Scoutt reported these incidents to Brent's mother, who, now convinced that he was bipolar, insisted again that Scoutt take him to a doctor. The Springfords were relieved when they later learned that Scoutt had given Brent Jr. an ultimatum: agree to medical treatment, or she would leave him. Brent agreed. He was first treated that September by a local general practitioner in Newcastle, who said Brent was the most depressed person he had seen. He prescribed Paxil, a conventional treatment for depression, and Wellbutrin, but Brent reacted adversely to the drugs. So Charlotte located a psychiatrist in Rapid City, South Dakota, a ninety-minute drive from the ranch, and ordered that Scoutt accompany Brent to all appointments. At the initial meeting, in late September 2000, Charlotte had Scoutt hand-deliver several letters to the psychiatrist, Dr. Charles J. Lord. They included a detailed family history, as well as Brent's recent history, finishing with an account of Brent's unsettling two-day visit to Montgomery in August.

Brent told Lord at the first appointment that his father was distant and controlling, but made no mention of his mother. After the visit, the psychiatrist confirmed a diagnosis of bipolar disorder, with relatively mild symptoms, noting in his records that Brent seemed inordinately dependent on Scoutt. Lord took Brent off Paxil and Wellbutrin and prescribed the antipsychotic Zyprexa and Topomax, an anti-seizure medication also used to treat migraine headaches. He also prescribed Risperdal, used to treat bipolar disorder, a Johnson & Johnson drug that would later be criticized for its side effects. The three drugs were sometimes prescribed together. At a second appointment the psychiatrist found the young man "bordering on need for hospitalization," and added Neurontin, a different anti-seizure drug, to his treatment. Lord read the first letters from Charlotte that Scoutt gave him and spoke with her several times on the phone but then cut off contact—to the mother's frustration. Brent was told to return in a month, but he never did, and he eventually stopped taking his medication. For the next two and a half years, he would be without psychiatric care.

: *8*

Descent

Since it was clear to Charlotte and Brent Sr. that their son could no longer care for himself, they now saw Caroline Scoutt as his primary caretaker. They believed—or at least hoped—she would oversee his ongoing psychiatric care and ensure that he took his medication. Charlotte was sympathetic and tried to be encouraging about Brent Jr.'s growing struggles with his bipolar disorder when he agreed to treatment. "I know that it is so frustrating to you that you haven't stabilized yet, but don't give up, Brent. One of the most frustrating things about this disease from what I have read is that it can take so long to get the medication right because every patient is an individual. It will happen," she wrote, voicing the hope that he would soon get a job and return to school. Again, she couldn't resist diagnosing Brent from a distance, suggesting that the short, dark, winter days might also be causing seasonal affective disorder.

In exchange for overseeing Brent's care, Charlotte and Brent Sr. continued to write Scoutt checks in the eight months in 2000 and 2001 after he moved onto her Wyoming property. This decision caused a rift between Charlotte and Brent Sr. about handling their son's mental illness. While they rarely observed Brent Jr. in person, they became painfully aware of his downhill slide. Friends said Brent Sr. was suspicious of Scoutt and wanted to bring his son home to Alabama for treatment, a course of action former girlfriend Andrea Jameson supported. Charlotte still hoped that Scoutt could handle the situation. Charlotte's half-sister, Lois Truss, suggested the obvious, that Scoutt was a gold digger. But Charlotte was more concerned that Scoutt might leave her son. "If she leaves Brent before he stabilizes and discovers what he wants to do with his life, I think it will kill him. . . . If [Caroline] hadn't come along, he probably would have joined a cult—or formed one himself." In the end, the Springfords agreed that it would be best for Brent Jr. to remain out West, well away from their Montgomery friends. They told only Robin and a few others about Brent's problems and his deteriorating condition, although over time word would circulate more widely.

In November 2000, Brent got a construction job in Newcastle, welding pipe, but soon left it for better-paying work as a spare hand or "roughneck" on oil derricks and at the local refinery on Main Street. His paychecks were deposited directly into the joint checking account he had with Scoutt. He worked at various sites in Wyoming, South Dakota, and Colorado for the same company, Key Energy, for the next two years. Brent was proud to land and keep the job, which on some days required working sixteen to eighteen hours. With overtime and extra shifts, he sometimes earned more than $5,000 a month. However, the first time he climbed a derrick, ninety feet in the air, he said he experienced auditory hallucinations, what he described as "celestial music." The repetitive labor was hard but not complicated and should have been easy to master. Ron Ballew, one of the supervisors, said Brent was only a "satisfactory" employee, if a diligent one. He always showed up for work, even when it rained, and never took sick days. One supervisor recalled that he was "completely laid back, would back off [from disputes], never argued."

The Springfords, unaware for months that Brent had found work and was earning a decent paycheck, continued to send his allowance and other money, including a December 4, 2000, check for $5,300 to Caroline for Brent's support, and another, marked "Clothing," for $1,300. Monthly credit card bills were typically about $1,500. And Charlotte was sending checks of her own from a separate account, sometimes for as much as $2,400. Brent was not shy about his financial needs. He faxed a letter to his father, saying he only wanted a card and money for Christmas, and he received a check for $1,500. Despite all the money coming in, Brent lived frugally, almost ascetically, wearing the same two pairs of pants and three shirts, and the same boots with holes in the soles that Maggie Johnson had noticed in Montgomery months earlier. In the bitterly cold winter, he always wore a leather hat with ear flaps. For the first time in years, he did not return to Montgomery for the holidays. Charlotte wrote,

We missed you so much at Christmas, which doesn't mean we think you should have come home. We understood that you wanted to be with your "family" out there, but it didn't mean that we didn't miss you! It's always hard on parents the first time their children are away for Christmas because it's the #1 family holiday, but it's a natural course of events, and parents always manage to adjust. We'll all get together again soon.

Yet just a few weeks later Charlotte seemed to be losing patience, writing on January 8, 2001, that despite all Brent's ramblings and efforts to find himself, "You still didn't seem to have a very happy semester at the school you thought was just right for you," referring to his last semester at Naropa in the spring of 2000. Before he withdrew from Naropa, his grades had slipped, and she was concerned about his scatteredness and inability to relax. But Charlotte, who had earlier sent him the $1,000 loan for the engagement ring for Scoutt, couldn't remain stern with her son for long. She speculated that he might also be suffering from attention deficit disorder or obsessive compulsive disorder, either of which might be brought under control with drugs. She urged him again to seek treatment.

Instead of financing the lodge on her ranch property, the Springfords urged Scoutt to accept their earlier suggestion to move permanently to Colorado. This would enable Brent to be close to better psychiatric and medical care and, they still hoped, to return to college. Charlotte let Scoutt do the house-hunting in the Boulder area, offering to do the final negotiation. In early February 2001, the Springfords flew in from Montgomery and approved the purchase: a 3,400-square-foot, four-bedroom, four-bath house on a seven-acre lot, with a pasture, that Scoutt found in an upscale subdivision called Hillcrest Estates in Windsor, Colorado. It was one of about eight large houses on a gravel cul-de-sac surrounded by fields outside the town of Greeley, and it was within commuting distance to Fort Collins, Boulder, Loveland, and Denver. There was an old-time ranch windmill at the entrance to the development, a view of a large ethanol plant, and, in the distance, the Front Range of the Rockies. Shortly after the purchase Scoutt returned to the Newcastle ranch and announced to the family that they were moving to Colorado. Her younger daughter, who was then in the third grade, was still unclear of her mother's relationship with Brent—there were always people coming in and out of her mother's life. The girl had the impression that Brent was a counseling client, and that he and her mother were not romantically involved.

Charlotte did her best to help Brent, thinking he had moved into the Windsor house. In a series of faxed letters early in 2001 she tried to balance encouragement with gentle urging not to continue relying on his parents' resources. She chose an ostensibly neutral subject—landscaping for the new house. As a landscape designer herself, she wrote, "The only way you will ever be able to afford to landscape is to do it yourself." Then, a few paragraphs later, she seemed to relent.

> We know that you and Caroline have no money right now for landscaping, but we were thinking about this: you have a birthday coming up. If you would like, we can give you trees, grass and bushes! . . . If you could begin learning about landscaping and prepare the area we'll be planting in, we could drive out the end of May or first of June and help you install an irrigation system, site the plants, buy them and help install them.

Charlotte even included some sketches of the house and yard, with her landscaping ideas. But essentially, she was also saying they wouldn't be sending Brent the check he had asked for. Nonetheless, by May Brent's monthly credit card bill was bumping $3,000, and checks sent to Scoutt for his support were more than $5,000.

While the Springfords made a down payment on the $420,000 asking price, they were careful to retain title to the Windsor property. They did assign Scoutt power of attorney to attend homeowners association meetings. There was some uncertainty about the future disposition of the property, an issue that would later loom large. As Brent Jr. understood it, the plan was that the house would remain in his parents' name for several years, ostensibly for tax purposes. Then it would be deeded or willed to him. Scoutt assumed that the title to the Windsor house would ultimately be transferred to her—but not to Brent Jr. In exchange for living in the house and for cash support, the parents believed, Scoutt would oversee Brent's medical care, and fax

Charlotte and Brent all the doctors' charges and pharmacy receipts. Charlotte, who with Brent Sr. came to Colorado for the house closing, also arranged for Brent Jr.'s psychiatric treatment. She contacted Dr. Alice Madison, a respected psychiatrist affiliated with the Veterans Administration hospital in Denver and the University of Colorado department of psychiatry, with an office in Boulder. Following a lengthy phone conversation with Madison, Charlotte said she hoped the psychiatrist would accept her son as a patient, and she had the impression that Madison had agreed. Charlotte suggested a tentative appointment for Brent Jr. in late February. Charlotte and Brent Sr. left Colorado secure in the belief that their troubled son would soon be settled in a new house and in therapy.

When he returned to Alabama, Brent Sr. wrote his son a letter, while thinking about him at work at the Luverne bottling plant. In the past, Brent Sr. had not concealed his feelings that his son was a disappointment. For his part, Brent Jr. spoke admiringly of his father but regretted he would never make him proud. In his note, Brent Sr. now wrote that he hoped that the move went well and said he and Charlotte were looking forward to visiting them in July:

I hope you know how much I love you, Brent. I may get frustrated sometimes, but that doesn't mean I don't love you. Your health and happiness are among the most important things in the world to me. And it's important that you understand that. Keep the faith. Hopefully your new doctor in Boulder will be better able to help you. Try to focus on the positive, and try not to let every little disappointment take you down. You can beat this thing, I know you can.

Charlotte also tried to assist by writing Dr. Madison the first in a series of letters, and included a check for $100 for reading the first one. Typed and single-spaced, the letters rambled, and frequently interrupted themselves with marginally relevant asides. In one of the early letters, Charlotte described her son's symptoms as obsessive compulsive disorder, hypomania, a sense of superiority, grandiosity, and extreme aggression, including the episodes in Montgomery where he was physically threatening to his father.

For the next five months, Charlotte wrote Dr. Madison about Brent and also about herself and her family, going back generations. "You should know there is a history of mental illness, suicide and alcoholism on my mother's side of the family." Her grandmother, Lettie, was an "enigmatic figure" with a volatile personality, "by turns charming and violent," that in retrospect suggested bipolar disorder. Lettie would take to her bed, sometimes for weeks, with depression. In at least one of these letters, Charlotte even suggested a course of treatment for her son. She also talked about Scoutt's relationship with Brent Jr., confiding her ambivalence about the woman. "It is obvious to us that for the foreseeable future Brent is going to be with Caroline. His dependency is total." Charlotte acknowledged that friends and family in Alabama were extremely skeptical of the relationship and especially of the Springfords' decision to buy them a house. The consensus was that the relationship was "bizarre," Charlotte conceded, and she again suggested that Scoutt was a classic gold digger. Charlotte told the psychiatrist that it would take a volume to explain Scoutt, but she asked her to trust her conclusions, which she said were "shared by my hard-nosed businessman husband."

In a June letter to Madison, Charlotte asked, "When, if ever, is it appropriate to use threats with a bipolar patient? Would it be appropriate to cut off financial support if he drops out of treatment?" Her main concern, she wrote, was not her son's profligacy with the credit card, but that he might unknowingly hit the card's limit and not be able to use it for an emergency. This was no idle fear. At the time, Charlotte thought her son had no job and was just driving around, 1,500 miles a week. While off work, he disappeared for days, once taking off to visit a friend in Canada, with no money and no charge card. When he ran out of gas, he started walking in the snow until he was picked up by police. Broke, he was able to call Scoutt and tell her where he was. Several of Scoutt's Native American friends went and got him.

More and more, Charlotte's letters to Madison dealt with Scoutt and her relationship with Brent. Charlotte continued to describe the caregiver as an Apache medicine woman and "the first woman to have [a] place on the tribal council of the Sioux." Despite her lack of money, Scoutt had told Charlotte she provided free-of-charge care to Indians on various reservations, as well as counseling to abused women and children near her Wyoming ranch. She also said she cleaned the house of an old man, her foster father, and read to him, an apparent reference to Larry Price, the Newcastle town engineer. "She is a loving, wise, 'together' woman who is, quite simply, a 'care-giver,'" Charlotte wrote Madison. "Her children, despite whatever prejudice they have experienced from whites in Wyoming, are perhaps the most mature and loving young people I have ever met . . . The love and care they have given Brent is priceless." The Springfords' initial impression of Scoutt, however, was formed mostly by what Brent Jr. and Scoutt told them. Some of the information—like her good works and her two years of college—would prove to be exaggerated, unverifiable, or patently false.

During the time Charlotte was writing Madison, the Springfords still had no knowledge that Brent had not moved in with Scoutt in the new house in Windsor. Both Scoutt and Brent were shuttling between the Wyoming ranch and Colorado, until she moved her family into the new house full-time in the spring of 2001, while Brent remained at the ranch. When Scoutt and her children came to Wyoming for visits, he would sleep in the camper. Scoutt called regularly from Windsor to tell him what more she needed from him, which he brought from the ranch to Colorado. He kept his job in the oil fields during the week and made the seven-hour drive to the new house in Windsor on weekends, working around the house and property under Scoutt's direction. He was assigned chores, mostly feeding the animals, though he made so many mistakes that someone in the family often had to follow up and do it right.

Soon after Scoutt and her children moved into the Windsor house, a local deputy sheriff paid a social call as a courtesy. As she had in Newcastle, Scoutt cultivated local law enforcement officers. Weld County Deputy Ron Richardson met Scoutt while investigating damage to a vehicle and mentioned that his father was part Native American. Later, he visited her several times informally to learn more about his heritage and customs, like sweat lodges and vision quests. "She seemed to be pretty sincere and knowledgeable, and I knew very little," Richardson recalled. "She was a nice lady."

Charlotte, meanwhile, suggested that Scoutt consult her friends in law enforcement about Colorado law regarding voluntary psychiatric commitment, since "involuntary hospitalization is not a legal option." One weekend in early 2001, Brent Jr.—in one of his occasional rages—smashed a window in the car Scoutt was driving, so she called one of the deputies she knew. He came to the house and told Brent if he didn't get help he would charge him with a felony. So the young man agreed to go to the emergency room of Poudre Valley Hospital, which referred him to a new psychiatrist—whom Brent never contacted.

In the months that followed, the Springfords, still unaware that Brent was living mostly in Wyoming, wrote checks to Scoutt and Brent in Colorado for various projects to keep him busy and productive at the new house. These included more than $100,000 to build a huge, detached, combination garage and barn (required by the homeowners association), a privacy fence, several corrals, a riding lawn mower, more outbuildings, and an above-ground swimming pool. In addition to the barn, the Springfords ultimately put nearly $50,000 more into improving the Windsor property. Assuming the house would one day be hers, Scoutt invested $10,000 of her own funds into the property. This was hard-earned money for the woman, and she kept close track of where it went, paying for sod in the backyard and her horse corral.

Brent fell into a pattern of unceasing demands on his parents connected to the property. He faxed his father that he wanted $2,800 for a greenhouse. The money would not be for Christmas; he still expected $1,500 more for his holiday gift. Typically, this ended in disaster. Despite Charlotte's earlier advice about economizing on landscaping the Windsor house, Charlotte and Brent Sr. ultimately agreed to their son's request to order them a kit containing the greenhouse. But when it arrived in a truck from Home Depot, the kit appeared damaged. Scoutt told Brent on the phone not to accept delivery or they might be responsible for the damage. So he chased the deliveryman down the street, jumping onto the driver's-side step outside the cab. The driver tried to explain that he was contracted by Home Depot to deliver, not pick up, so he couldn't reload the boxes. A confrontation ensued, with Brent trying to pull the man out of the cab by his head. The man stopped the truck, got out, and there was a scuffle in the street. When the deliveryman pulled a knife, Brent kicked it out of his hand, breaking the man's finger. Again, no charges were filed. After all of that, Brent broke large windows in the greenhouse when he used screws that were too large and then overtightened them.

The Springfords continued to sweeten their support, most often at their son's request, by lending the family three vehicles, ultimately transferring the titles to Scoutt. Brent Sr. insured all the vehicles through his bottling business. First came a 1998 GMC Yukon, which Scoutt used, then a white 1996 Chevy Blazer for her oldest daughter. Brent thanked his father for the Yukon, but then complained that it only got sixteen miles to the gallon. So he asked for a Volkswagen for his everyday use. Brent Sr. bought him a black 1998 Jetta. When the Springfords acquired the vehicle in Montgomery, Charlotte suggested they meet in Kansas for the delivery, fearing that Brent would drive through the night to Alabama. Instead, Brent came home to pick up the car when his parents were out of town. He called Maggie Johnson, by then largely retired from her housekeeping work, and asked her to come over for lunch. She remembered that Brent asked what she wanted and he fixed her a favorite, peanut butter and jelly sandwich on raisin bread, and a Pepsi. They spent five hours talking about old times, laughing a lot. He was nice and friendly, with no signs of anxiety, Johnson recalled.

Scoutt's family saw Charlotte and Brent Springford Sr. a number of times in Windsor, and got to know them better. In 2000 or 2001, Charlotte invited the whole Scoutt family to Alabama so they could attend Scoutt's son's graduation from an army training course in Fort Benning, Georgia. Charlotte joined them for the ceremony and then had them stay at the Springford's lake house. "They were very nice people—polite, kind," Scoutt's younger daughter, Star, said. "We weren't used to people like that; they were genuine, decent human beings." Later the girl's brother went AWOL from the army and was subsequently discharged.

In addition to Brent Jr.'s medical bills, the Springfords wrote checks for car repairs and gifts for Scoutt's children. Charlotte and Brent Sr. sent more cash. In 2003 they paid more than $2,000 to Scoutt's Boulder attorney, Daniel Quinn, which may have gone to defend Brent from shoplifting and speeding charges. However much money they sent, it was never enough. Brent Sr. paid for his son's medical care through his business and even kept him on the family's cell phone plan, but he at first balked at paying for medical care for Scoutt and her children; he was not yet aware that Scoutt and Brent Jr. were married. While the Springfords were beyond generous, Brent Sr. wanted every cent accounted for, especially Brent Jr.'s medical receipts, which the son often lost. On the infrequent occasions when Brent Sr. would refuse to pay for something, Charlotte would send a check from her own account and ask them not to mention it to Brent Sr. Scoutt had no compunction about accepting money from the Springfords—or asking for more—but at the same time she later told investigators she felt Charlotte was trying to fix her son by indulging him.

Curiously, Scoutt was still billing Brent Jr. for breathing sessions, despite their marriage and his parents' financial support. An increasingly skeptical Charlotte found an Internet site called Quackwatch, which charged that Scoutt's breathing technique was little more than hyperventilation that led to temporary euphoria. Yet she wrote a friend who suspected Scoutt's motives in the relationship: "Let's not be too quick to point fingers. What about *me*? I wouldn't want to argue about who's getting the most from whom—or even who might be manipulating whom." Charlotte pointed out that the current arrangement had the effect of keeping her son in care, but out of sight of her Montgomery friends. In what turned out to be her final letter to Dr. Madison, in early July 2001, Charlotte worried that a planned Springford family trip to Barbados, to celebrate her daughter Robin's Vanderbilt graduation, might send an "uncaring message" to her troubled son, who was not invited. If the doctor thought so, they would cancel. But on July 6, Charlotte received shocking news: in a curt note that may well have crossed with Charlotte's, Madison said she didn't know how Charlotte got the impression that she was treating Brent. Charlotte's growing concern notwithstanding, Madison said she would not be able to treat her son at this time. She returned all of Charlotte's letters, most unopened, as well as the check, uncashed, for reading the first one.

Still unaware that her son had a full-time oil field job in Wyoming, in December 2001 Charlotte wrote that Brent "desperately needs something to do, and I don't think shooting pool will make him feel better about himself." She suggested art lessons. In January 2002, Brent transferred jobs from Newcastle—where work had slowed—to Gillette, Wyoming, a big oil and coal center seventy-seven miles away. He started commuting daily from the ranch in Newcastle, but the commute soon wore him down, so he decided to camp at his work site—and the more distance he put between himself and Scoutt, the more stable he seemed. He lived alone in the Yukon SUV, sleeping on a mattress in the back of the vehicle, cooking meals of oatmeal, noodles, and ketchup, and showering at a nearby Flying J truck stop. For a time, when the weather got bitterly cold, Ron Ballew, his supervisor, let him park inside Ballew's repair shop in exchange for light cleanup work. Brent never seemed to have any money, since he had his paychecks deposited directly to his joint account with Scoutt, and he even sent her most of his work's per diem allowance.

Whether he was commuting or camping in the Yukon, Brent still had to take care of the Newcastle ranch. That took a toll. He got two speeding tickets and several times he fell asleep at the wheel and ran off the road and into ditches, damaging the vehicle. He hit deer three times. Water for the ranch and livestock had to be trucked in, and several times he forgot to close the valve on the tank and left a hose running—all 450 gallons drained out just after he filled it. Scoutt called to berate him. "As far as living in the world as a real man, I was an idiot," Brent recalled. "I forgot everything I was supposed to remember. I broke things, lost things. I knew absolutely nothing." Once, as soon as he hung up the phone with Scoutt he became so enraged at his incompetence that he kicked the Yukon's dashboard, demolishing the radio and air conditioning controls. "I was such a screw-up, I wanted to make up for it by proving I was an exceptional worker in the oil field," he later recalled. The money he earned with Key Energy was decent—base pay of $28,288 a year. He was obsessive about volunteering for overtime, wanting to prove he was a "real man." With those extra hours, he reported income of $51,379.14 on his 2002 W-2 form. Brent spent some of his winter solitude writing letters, most often to Scoutt, addressing her as "Sweetie." For a time, he resumed writing to his parents, typically to ask for money. In one letter, he wrote that he "wanted" to marry Scoutt—although they had been married for several years—and asked for a loan to buy a second ring, this one a wedding band.

When the oil business tapered off, Brent's work performance deteriorated, and his hours were reduced. His employer reported that he was making lots of mistakes, forgetting details, and, more troubling, his bosses thought he was strange. He got into at least one fight, Scoutt said, and was beaten up. "I barely hung onto my job at Key. I was not a good worker," he recalled. His bosses later said they kept him on because they felt sorry for him. He seemed so poor and had so many problems, and his wife was in another state. Still, until then the troubled young man had a sense of accomplishment. He was holding a demanding job and supporting his family, including Scoutt's three children. However, Brent's relationship with Scoutt was paramount. In his journal, he later wrote:

> When I moved to Newcastle and married Caroline, my care-free, easy, no-responsibility life fell apart. . . . Caroline was used to relating with real men like cowboys, police officers, Indians, and her clients of all professions. I knew absolutely nothing about being a man, being responsible and functional. I only knew how to be a student and talk about Eastern philosophy. I never had to be responsible. My parents always bailed me out of messes when I screwed up.

The latter role had now been handed off to Scoutt.

Until his relationship with his parents soured, the oil field job was something he would have liked to share with them, especially his father, he later told a friend. But if he did, he feared, his mother might tell his employer that he was mentally ill and that the job was too dangerous, and he would lose the position as breadwinner that gave him such a sense of self-worth. And he probably also was concerned that the news might interrupt the stream of weekly $425 allowance checks from his father. In fact, when Charlotte learned that Brent Jr. had a job, she decided not to tell her husband for a while, to see if it worked out. When she did tell him, they continued the subsidy anyway.

Other problems related to money were more troubling. In Colorado, Scoutt cultivated expensive tastes, her daughter Star Fosheim recalled. "Everything had to be organic—supplements, hair care—it all had to be top of the line." The Boulder Whole Foods was a particular favorite. "We would go in there so much that people there knew my mom by name. They would suggest new products for her. People knew that she had the money. We did have nice clothes."

Brent's letters to his parents from early 2002 began to reek of entitlement, if not avarice. The tone of the letters, often faxed, shifted from petulant to churlish, sounding less and less like himself—or at least like his old altruistic, anti-materialistic self. How much of this was his accelerating descent into emotional turmoil, and how much was Scoutt's manipulation—or some combination of the two—is impossible to say. Whatever the reason, the sweet, caring, inquisitive young man who hoped to transcend materialism had become a grasping person who saw his parents as little more than an inexhaustible ATM. Finally, he turned abusive. In a March 13, 2002, faxed letter to his parents, Brent complained that they were going back on their promise to pay contractors working on the Windsor house. He wrote that he was "so tired of fuckups"—his parents' delays in paying various bills:

> The contractors still have not been paid. Why is this? Whatever your excuse is it really pisses me off that you think you are so fucking special and important that you can just leave Caroline with the bills that you agreed to pay for and just let her financial record take a hit. If you have decided not to pay what you owe, then at least have an iota of integrity and tell Caroline that you have decided to back out again. . . . It sure would be nice to have some decent parents who are at least usually trustworthy and caring.

Later, he wrote, "Again, could you show me that your word is more than a lie?"

In another faxed letter, this one to his father, dated October 24, 2002, Brent complained that the gifts Charlotte and Brent Sr. had sent to his family were too cheap; his parents, he claimed, were not treating Scoutt and her children as family because they were Native American. In yet another angry note and package to his mother, Brent returned a jacket, one of several Christmas gifts of clothes that Charlotte had picked out for him and his family. He said he only wanted clothes family members specified from catalogues such as Victoria's Secret. He said they would send back anything that didn't fit, or if they didn't like the color or style. One of the gifts Charlotte sent, he wrote, was "ridiculous." On the rare occasions when he wrote something nice to her, she replied, almost pathetically:

> What a sweet letter you wrote the other day . . . It made me feel good—like maybe you still care about me a little. I love you so much and miss you so much, and it breaks my heart to think that you no longer love me. Maybe you do.

The only medical treatment Brent accepted in the two and a half years since leaving Dr. Lord's care in South Dakota was informal and came from his mother. She sent him a Portuguese drug called Tianeptine Stablon, an antidepressant then not available in the United States. Brent was still living and working most weekdays in Wyoming, but he agreed to seek psychiatric help in Colorado, the reason his parents had purchased the Windsor house two years earlier. The treatment got off to a disturbing start. His suspicions of his father had grown, possibly fueled by Scoutt or his own growing paranoia, or both. At the office of Dr. Harris Jensen, the first area psychiatrist he went to in Fort Collins in early March 2003, Brent told the receptionist to be wary of Brent Sr., who might call, pretending to be Brent Jr., to get details of his treatment. There would be a code word needed to supply information, an arrangement Brent Jr. would require when he underwent an MRI. On the intake form, Brent wrote that he was seeking treatment because "I am extremely mentally ill and cannot function." In response to a question of whether his parents had been supportive, he wrote, "They were but in retrospect it seems they were not." Jensen prescribed Eskalith (a form of lithium) and again Zyprexa, and ordered Brent off the herbal supplements he had been taking. Subsequent appointments rapidly went downhill. Jensen diagnosed Brent as "rapidly recycling bipolar," writing that "[h]e is a chronic risk to himself and others," although the danger was not yet acute.

Charlotte was pleased to learn that her son was again under a psychiatrist's care, yet her enthusiasm for Scoutt continued to erode, tempered by growing doubts. When Scoutt would call Montgomery, Maggie Johnson recalled, Charlotte would listen, looking off into the distance and eventually reply, "Talk to the doctor and call us." Then she and Brent Sr. would retire to the library to discuss the most recent developments.

Brent's psychiatric care did not seem to be yielding the hoped-for results. On March 25, 2003, the day after his twenty-seventh birthday, he had a morning appointment with Dr. Jensen in Fort Collins. Jensen reported that Brent told him then that his wife had threatened to leave him if he couldn't control his mood swings. Shortly after leaving the doctor's office, he was arrested for shoplifting dozens of granola bars and trail mix at a supermarket. Fort Collins police said they found him anxious, distraught, psychotically confused, and suicidal, so they took him to the emergency room at Poudre Valley Hospital. He was then transferred to Mountain Crest Behavioral Healthcare, a nearby affiliated mental facility, where he was held for a seventy-two-hour involuntary evaluation. Through all of Brent's travails, his parents continued to travel, to places like South Korea and Vietnam. At the time of the March 25 arrest in Fort Collins, Charlotte and Brent Sr. were at the Hotel Le Royal in Phnom Penh, Cambodia, frantically working the phones and monitoring the situation. The Springfords pulled what strings they could. They were unable to keep their son from being committed but were able to head off a charge for shoplifting. Despite his parents' intervention, and all their indulgence and financial support, Brent Jr. felt they were treating him like a child. And Scoutt once more became the primary conduit for any connection between Brent and his parents.

The admitting physician at Mountain Crest reported that Brent was giving erratic answers to the police about the shoplifting, and that he "became acutely disoriented and gave evidence of delusional thinking." Brent expressed resentment at being admitted as an inpatient, and during his three-day stay refused to participate in group therapy. His lithium dosage was increased to nine hundred milligrams at bedtime, a typical strength in cases like his, enabling him to sleep. He was discharged with a diagnosis of bipolar affective disorder and depression with psychotic features. The doctor said he could not rule out schizophrenia. A second doctor at the hospital, a psychiatrist who took his history, said Brent (whom he referred to by his legal first name, "Winston") complained of sleeplessness and a loss of appetite and libido. "He has thought himself to have superior intelligence and extraordinary abilities approaching delusional proportions," the physician wrote. Brent presented his history "in a rambling but coherent manner." Tucked into the case history was this observation, without further comment: "Winston gives history of emotional difficulties dating back 3 years to just about the time that he met his wife Caroline while he was living in Boulder." Some things had not changed: mental illness and psychosis notwithstanding, an admitting nurse noted Brent's good looks. And for some reason, perhaps to explain his insurance coverage from the Pepsi plant in Luverne, Alabama, Brent wrote on his admission form that he was employed as a laborer at a Pepsi distribution plant in nearby Greeley.

On April 14, 2003, Dr. Jensen wrote a letter and left it for Brent with the receptionist, outlining the bipolar diagnosis and the medication that was waiting for him in the office reception area. Brent read the letter, but felt it was not complete and wanted it rewritten. The doctor came out, told Brent the letter was adequate and said he had a patient waiting in his office. When Jensen left, Brent started talking about beating up the psychiatrist, a threat the receptionist later passed along to the doctor. Jensen called Scoutt and said he was dismissing Brent as a patient, characterizing the break in his notes as a psychotic episode.

A month later, citing a slowdown, Key Energy finally let Brent go from its operation in Gillette, Wyoming. This became the catalyst for his permanent move to the Colorado house. Despite his uneven work record, Key Energy hired him at its operation in Fort Lupton, Colorado, not far from the Windsor home. In July, the Springfords paid off the balance of the mortgage note on the Windsor house, $273,264. They kept the title in their name.

At first, Scoutt's daughter Star Fosheim recalled, Brent seemed to fit into her mother's New Age lifestyle. He was very health-oriented, polite, and around a lot for meals. During one Christmas Caroline announced to the family that they had gotten married. But Brent was not exactly a member of the Windsor household, despite the financial support he and his parents were providing. "It was very weird," Fosheim said. Soon, however, he began to slip. "My mom told us he was mentally ill." The couple argued, and several times Brent rubbed his face in the driveway gravel, the daughter recalled.

"Caroline could make anyone feel that they were mentally ill. She provoked him. She knew exactly how to break someone down."

Soon, Brent was treated more like hired help, setting foot in the house only by invitation. He started sleeping in his small camper trailer, now parked in the driveway behind the house, not far from a stone fire pit Caroline had built. Sometimes, as manic busywork, Brent stayed up all night, wearing a miner's helmet with a lamp, digging a seven-foot-square "worry hole" in the yard. The hole got so big and so deep that Brent had to build a fence around it to keep the horses from stumbling in. Finally, he built what he called his fifteen-foot-square, windowless "cell" in the smaller, attached garage, where he lived as a "monk."

Apart from Brent, the Scoutt household was a turbulent one, so much so that Scoutt later said she burned sage and smudge pots to combat the negative energy. According to Fosheim, Scoutt used some of the same divisive, manipulative tactics on her own family that she used on clients in Boulder, like the Flinders family. "My mom never wanted all us kids to be close," the daughter said, intentionally turning them against one another until she got her way. "We eventually became a family where we only related to her. She was always the victim. We were sluts. When we fought back she said we were killing her."

Weld County sheriff's deputies were called to the address nearly a dozen times a year to deal with a spectrum of domestic strife, none of which involved Brent. Scoutt once called police to remove her adult daughter from the house. Her adult son—who had spent time in juvenile detention facilities in Wyoming—was violent when drunk. In one incident, he struck Scoutt and destroyed a computer and a television and punched holes in walls of the basement, where he slept. The young man also traded threats and accusations of harassment with his girlfriend.

Much of the strife centered on Fosheim, the younger daughter. The girl ran away five times, beginning in the fifth grade when she was about eleven. "I didn't know what to do," she recalled. "I didn't want to live with her and I didn't want to go back." Once, when Greeley police picked her up, the girl refused to go back with her mother, complaining of bruises and saying her siblings were also being mistreated. So officers contacted the Department of Family Services. "My mother decided to have me sent to the behavior institution in Fort Collins due to my running away and for reporting the abuse." So for two weeks the girl was committed to a psychiatric facility, Mountain Crest Behavioral Health Center. Scoutt was called in to participate in the treatment but didn't like what she heard. "She was upset because she was being called out about who she was, how she treated me and my sister, so she complained to the director," Fosheim said. "She manipulated the director to believe I was a troubled child, and to not believe how she treated me and my siblings, and called us names." At the end of the two weeks, the girl returned home, with prescriptions for antidepressants and antipsychotic drugs.

Subsequently, Scoutt took her daughter to Dr. Roger Billica, a Fort Collins family and preventive medicine specialist. She told him that the drugs her daughter had been prescribed were "not healthy and were wrong," the daughter recalled. Caroline insisted that her daughter was hormonally imbalanced. Instead of taking two of the prescribed medications a day, the girl was soon taking four packages of six pills a day, which she said she got from Billica.

Outside the home, Scoutt feuded with neighbors—as she had in Newcastle—as well as with Fosheim's teachers. Over the next eight months relations with the neighbors continued to go downhill. Scoutt installed bars on the house's front windows. At one point, she spent thousands of dollars to erect what appeared to be two birdhouses on twenty-foot poles designed to attract purple martins, flanking the house's front door. In reality, the birdhouses contained surveillance cameras that could be controlled from inside the house and monitored from inside as well as from distant locations. A house next door, temporarily unoccupied, was vandalized, and a row of trees planted to shield it from view of Scoutt's house was cut down. In apparent retaliation, a fence and gate dividing the two properties that Brent built were destroyed. Two couples living nearby wrote a letter to law enforcement, complaining of "hostile, disrespectful and inappropriate behaviors" and "angry outbursts" emanating from Scoutt's house. That led them to conclude that the Scoutt family and others living in the house "are vindictive, violent and dangerous. . . . [They] pose a serious physical threat to all of us, our children, our animals and the property that we own and live on." Brent Sr. came to his son's family's defense in vigorous memos to the residents' association and the Weld County Sheriff's Department. Charlotte consulted a Colorado attorney about what she called the neighbors' "harassment." No legal action ensued.

Checks from Montgomery continued to cascade into Colorado, the letters to Scoutt still signed, "Love, Charlotte." The Springfords' latest solution to Brent's uncontrolled spending was to cut off the credit card and replace it with his weekly $425 allowance checks, which had been temporarily halted. The checks were mailed each Friday. Brent Jr. sometimes misplaced them, but when they were late he complained to his parents, usually through Scoutt. Charlotte drew up a meticulously detailed budget, based on her mistaken belief that Brent Jr. was again unemployed. She suggested where he should buy gas, what brand of bread to get, and what to order at restaurants. She also assumed, wrongly, that he was eating most of his meals with Scoutt and her family. Later, the credit card was reinstated.

The next month, Key Energy let Brent go, but he was hired by K. P. Kauffman Well Service Co., also in Fort Lupton. There were still problems. Once he forgot to clip his safety line and stepped off a piece of equipment high in the air. "I grabbed a boom as it swung around or I would have been killed in the fall," he said later. On another occasion he drove a new company truck, with three other workers, into a semi-trailer, sending both vehicles into a field surrounded by irrigation ditches. Another time, Brent crashed his truck into a ditch, totaling it and sending one co-worker through the windshield, although he survived. Almost fired again, Brent begged his boss for more work hours, cleaning up or anything to earn more money to support his family. At all of his jobs, in Newcastle, Gillette, and Fort Lupton, Brent had difficulty figuring out the sequence of what needed to be done. "I was not a good hand because I couldn't remember what's the next step," he admitted years later. And it irked him that it was a skill easily grasped by his working-class friends. "I could never comprehend how uneducated people would remember, but I would have to stop and think. I could never see ahead. People always said, 'Come on, Winston, you're spacing out.' It was humiliating."

Brent was trying his best to hold things together and remain in Scoutt's good graces. But clearly, whatever self-esteem he once might have had was gone. In his journal, he wrote:

Do not react to anything
Do not have emotions
Do not defend yourself
Do not disagree
Have no personal agenda
Do not argue
Let Caroline tear you down
Do not assert yourself
Create nothing
Be silent

For Brent, nothing seemed to be going right at the Windsor house, and psychiatric treatment offered no solace. It seemed to him—and to his parents—that things couldn't get any worse. And yet they did.

: 9

Visitors

In Savannah, Georgia, in late 2001, Brent's lifelong friend from Montgomery Academy, Dow Harris, ran into Robin Springford and her fiancé Greg Crouch. Robin filled Harris in on what she knew of her brother's relationship with Caroline Scoutt and his psychiatric treatment. Harris, who was among the recipients of Brent's 1999 mass email breaking contact with his old friends, was instantly suspicious about the timing of Brent's meeting with Scoutt and his subsequent psychiatric diagnosis. In addition to their friendship, Harris's adult life had roughly paralleled Brent's. Harris, too, had been diagnosed as a young man with bipolar disorder, had made several cross-country "pilgrimages" of self-discovery, and had dropped out of Washington and Lee University after two years.

Few people knew Brent as well as Harris, who later said that when he heard about Scoutt, "I immediately smelled a rat." He told Robin that he wanted to write Brent, but she, still pleased with the progress she thought her brother was making with Scoutt, declined to give Harris the address. Harris gave up his efforts to contact Brent, but he still thought about him. A year later, he wrote Brent a very general letter, just testing the waters. On Thanksgiving 2002, he delivered it—unsealed—to Charlotte and Brent Sr., asking that they forward it to Colorado. Still concerned about their son's precarious state of mind, the Springfords did not send the letter.

When he didn't hear back from his friend, Harris persisted. In early 2003, he managed to get Brent's Colorado address and wrote him another letter. He then told Robin he had mailed it, and she told her mother, who quickly sent Brent Jr. Harris's first letter. Several weeks later, as Harris was driving to work, his cell phone rang. It was Scoutt, who introduced herself and said that "they" had received both letters. Scoutt implied that

Charlotte had steamed open the letter then resealed it. Harris knew that was unlikely, since he had delivered the envelope to the Springfords unsealed. Harris concluded that Scoutt had done the tampering. "She was opening his mail," he later wrote in a lengthy memo, "filtering information to him, and causing him to think that his parents had done that." Not wanting to scare Scoutt off and jeopardize his contact with Brent, Harris said nothing. Scoutt filled Harris in on Brent's status, informing him that although his parents didn't know it, Brent was working hard in the oil fields, and that they were married. The reason they hadn't told the Springfords, Scoutt said, was that Brent thought that the Springfords "would be prejudiced toward her because she was a Native American."

Harris was not fooled:

Very clever, I'm thinking. Everyone in Montgomery knows that the Springfords were the most tolerant, liberal folks in the whole god damn city. If anyone would have accepted her, it would have been them. My immediate reaction, of course, was to think that she was somehow trying to get at the Springfords' money, and that if they found out that she and Brent had gotten married, they would take steps to cut 'crazy little Brent' off.

After confiding in Harris, Scoutt told him he was forbidden to communicate with the Springfords if he wanted to continue corresponding with Brent.

Now, this is the strangest part of the whole affair, I'm thinking. She's isolated him completely, and is only allowing certain things to come through. *Dangerous, Dangerous. Dangerous.*"

Scoutt may have sensed that Harris was suspicious of her. She asked him repeatedly if they could trust him, and Harris assured her that she could. She said Brent welcomed his letter, saying that it sounded like his old friend, "the real Dow," and that he wanted to write back. Harris asked what Brent was reading and Scoutt mentioned the previously mentioned "Seth" books by Jane Roberts. Brent had given Harris one of the books on a visit to Montgomery in 2000, and Harris hadn't been impressed. Then Scoutt told him that she herself

> has had a history of dealing with the occult. She drops a couple of big names that I recognize. Basically, it is clear that she is into magic and witchcraft and all that. This concerned me because I knew how impressionable Brent was, and already I did not trust her.

Harris was nonetheless pleased to receive a twelve-page handwritten letter from Brent in March 2003. The letter revealed Brent's delusional alienation and dripped with venom toward his parents. Clearly isolated, he poured out his heart to his dear friend. Brent repeated Scoutt's assertion that his mother had steamed open the letter and resealed it:

> This is a small but good example of how she operates, and my father pretty much does her bidding. If you think you know them, I promise you do not. They are extremely controlling, manipulative, deceitful, phony people. To my absolute disgust I have come to see how much I grew up to be like them—nothing but hollow ego. They are phony to the extreme.
>
> If you trust them in any way, especially their words, you will undoubtedly go through the experience of realizing that you have been lied to and manipulated. I used to think that I knew them. I even respected them for being what I thought to be intelligent, supportive parents. I have painfully come to realize how deceived I had been. It was pain in the form of tremendous anger and hatred that has been very slow to dissipate. They have done everything they could think of to get me locked up in a mental institution, with the key under their sole control.
>
> This is not an exaggeration. They are very prejudiced against my family, thinking they are poor, ignorant Indians without having had any opportunities in life until meeting my parents. Because they can't manipulate my family with their money and their phony intellect, they treat the most important people in my life like anyone they would pass on the streets of the Third World countries which they escape to so often, and from which they derive so much phony self-importance. . . .

Later in the letter, Brent would explain his personal life in a way that Harris found troubling:

I am crawling along at a snail's pace, working at being more humble, real, responsible and aware. I am extremely forgetful, and absent-minded. I fuck up constantly, I have no common sense, and my knowledge of Spirit is non-existent. *I do know that I don't know anything of value at all.* . . . I realize that my opinions are grossly ignorant. If I could ever completely let go of my phony ego with all its selfishness, need to be right, important, recognized, and catered to, it would be a major accomplishment. This is what I am slowly working at, a process replete with constant failure. I gave up my obsession with Eastern religions a few years ago. That was all a dismal mistake. I actually thought I was somebody important and on the road to enlightenment! *Ha! What a joke.* So, I'm just putting one foot in front of the other, trying not to fall in the mud but constantly doing so.

After that, Harris didn't hear from Brent for a while, and his phone calls went unanswered. Once, though, he called from a different number, and Scoutt picked up. Within the first few sentences of their conversation, Harris learned that Brent was in bad shape. Scoutt told him Brent was "walking around the house hitting himself and bruising himself." Brent continued to damage vehicles, including another dashboard head-smashing episode, this time with his Jetta. Alarmed, Harris asked Scoutt to have Brent return his call, which he never did, and when Harris called again several times, no one picked up.

In December 2003, at the Springfords' annual Christmas open house, Charlotte broke down in the library while telling Jim Scott, another of Brent's longtime friends from Montgomery Academy, about her son's deteriorating condition. Scott, concerned, called Harris and asked if he would come with him to Colorado to check on their friend. Harris immediately agreed. They got Brent's street address without letting the Springfords know that they decided to make the trip in early March 2004. Neither did Harris confide his suspicions about Scoutt, in part because Charlotte seemed still to hold the woman in high regard. In fact, Charlotte by now had her own suspicions. She scoured the Internet for evidence of a wedding in various jurisdictions in Wyoming and Colorado, but neglected to check Deadwood, South Dakota, city records.

On the thirty-one hour, nonstop drive from Montgomery to Colorado, Harris filled Scott in on the situation they would probably encounter—though not enough to alert him that he "might really be walking into a nightmare," Harris later wrote. Reaching Windsor, about fifty miles north of Denver, they spent the night at a motel. The next morning, without calling first, they drove to the house, where they noticed several all-terrain vehicles and a white Chevy Blazer. Out of caution they drove past the house several times, until the Blazer drove off. They knocked and rang the bell, but no one answered, so they walked around the house. Assuming no one was home, they tried the back door, and took some pictures around the property.

At dusk, they returned, rang the doorbell again, and, when no one answered, they decided to wait on the front porch for a while. Once more, they walked around the house, checked out the barn, and then returned to their truck. Suddenly a Ford Bronco pulled up, driven by a young Hispanic man who immediately made a cell phone call. As Harris recalled the encounter, the young man "was spitting nails. . . . He gets out of the car and tells us to get the fuck off the property," waving a military card in front of them. The young man was Deny Caballero, who had been taken in by Scoutt. The card he flashed was his Military Police ID from the Colorado National Guard. Caballero recalled the confrontation differently. He had just finished a crime scene investigation class at Front Range Community College, and he was protective of Scoutt's youngest daughter, Star, then an adolescent, who he said was cowering inside and wondering who these strange young men were. "They had an arrogant way about them and I told them to get off the property," Caballero recalled years later.

Harris and Scott drove off, but within three minutes their cell phones started to ring. Scott's mother said she had just heard from Charlotte. Brent Jr. had called his mother in a rage, threatening to put Scott in the hospital. Apparently, Star had panicked that morning when Harris and Scott knocked the first time and called her mother, Brent, and the police. Harris's call was from Robin's fiancé, Greg Crouch, equally freaked out, saying that the police had an all-points bulletin out on the two men. They had decided to drive back to the house to clear things up when Brent Sr. called Harris, sounding both worried and relieved when Harris answered. Harris later wrote:

> He says that Brent Jr. is not himself, that he's crazy as hell, and if we go back there, that somebody's going to get hurt really bad. I tell him that we understand and that we are trying to clear out as fast as we can, at least until the smoke clears.

Harris and Scott spent the night at a fraternity house at Colorado State University and tried to explain the situation to Scoutt on the phone. She explained that the Scoutts and Brent were caught off-guard by the visit, and that Brent suspected Harris and Scott had been sent by his parents. Scoutt invited them to meet for breakfast with her—but not Brent—the next morning.

When Scoutt showed up at the restaurant, a half-hour late, Harris was not impressed, recalling her as an "old prunish hag" who "had been around the block. . . . I'm thinking that I just can't believe that Brent had gotten himself tangled up with this woman." She told them she was fifty-two years old and regaled them with tales of her groupie years in Los Angeles. To Harris, she seemed "weird. Very reserved. Too calm." Asked about how she and Brent met, Scoutt said that it was around 2000, at a tribal ceremony or initiation at an Indian reservation in Wyoming, which was untrue. At the time, she said, Brent was in terrible shape, "drinking and drugging around," and hanging around with "cult-like people"—apparently her former Boulder clients. Scoutt also volunteered a denigrating remark about Andrea Jameson, Brent's old girlfriend. To Harris's surprise, Scoutt pulled out a copy of the couple's marriage certificate. Scoutt said she was concerned that the Springfords might reclaim the house, which was still in their name, after she had invested $10,000 of her own money for landscaping. Harris asked her why Brent resented his parents yet still accepted their support, and Scoutt said it was because he felt he was not being respected as the first-born son of a wealthy family. The eeriest moment came when Harris asked Scoutt what she thought Brent might do if his parents cut him off. She replied: "Oh, I don't know. He might go to Alabama and kill his daddy."

The breakfast concluded, Harris and Scott took off for a few days of sightseeing in the Rockies, agreeing to meet Scoutt and Brent for dinner in Fort Collins at a Red Lobster, Brent's favorite restaurant. When they finally met, Harris approached Brent with an awkward hug. Brent looked healthy, with shoulder-length hair and a mustache. He wore a gray cowboy hat and a gray, long-sleeved shirt, and wore a wedding ring. Brent was still angry about his friends' unannounced visit to the house, saying that if he had been home there would have been violence. Brent made eye contact periodically, but for the most part he looked off into the distance, sometimes at a television screen that hung from the ceiling. From time to time, Scoutt, who seemed to be serving as moderator, would join the conversation. Throughout the meal, Brent appeared to Harris unnaturally reserved, suggesting to his friend a determined self-control. But from time to time he would crack a big smile, which Harris found "almost grotesquely tragic, because I knew what kind of joy Brent was capable of demonstrating . . . It's hard to imagine such a dark cloud descending over that bright brow."

When Scott asked Brent if he planned to attend his sister Robin's up-coming wedding, he said definitely not. Asked if he would ever return to Montgomery, Brent responded, in what Harris recalled was deadpan serious-ness and cold calculation, "Only to take care of business." The meal finished, Harris gave Brent some gifts he had made for him, and they embraced again, this time with more warmth. They adjourned briefly to the visitors' nearby motel room, where Harris and Scott had some more gifts for Brent. The friends thought if they could get Brent alone they might get through to him, but Scoutt stuck close. Before they parted for the evening, both Brent and Scoutt admonished his two old friends not to share information with the Springfords or anyone else they knew in Montgomery. Harris and Scott agreed, but Harris, when he returned to Alabama, did share with Charlotte and Brent Sr.—for their own protection—what he sensed as a "malevolent element" within his old friend.

A few days later, on March 11, Brent Jr. wrote Harris, again requesting that news of his marriage not be passed along to his parents, but by then Harris already had. Charlotte did not believe that Brent and Scoutt were married, the certificate she had displayed notwithstanding. In any event, Harris returned from Colorado profoundly shaken by the visit with his old buddy. And Scott later wrote in a memo that he found Brent Jr. "bizarre, too far gone to deal with, certifiable, scary as hell. It unnerved me to the core." Brent was not the same person his friends had known in high school.

A month after being dismissed as a patient by Dr. Jensen for threatening behavior, Brent found another local psychiatrist, Dr. Kent Hinesley, in Loveland, who saw him off and on for the next few months. Hinesley added Provigil to Brent's Zyprexa and Eskalith and ordered an MRI, which came back normal. Brent told Hinesley that, in a manic state, he had stopped taking his meds the week before the shoplifting episode that resulted in his hospitalization. He also repeated his belief that his parents wanted him put away. In April 2004, Brent stopped seeing Dr. Hinesley.

Later that spring Brent seemed to have stabilized, at least financially, allowing his parents to turn their attention to plans for Robin's wedding. As with Brent, the Springfords were generous, even indulgent with their daughter. They paid all of Robin's college and graduate school tuition, plus her condo fees, utilities, and credit cards of $700–1,000 a month, and an allowance of $900 a week. Her October 2004 wedding was to be in the Florida Panhandle, a three-hour drive from Montgomery but close to the Springfords' condo in Destin. The costs promised to be considerable, but Brent Sr. was feeling financially flush, thanks to his prosperous enterprises and to gifts totaling $100,000 from one of his elderly relatives. In addition to his Montgomery and Lake Martin houses, and the Florida condo, Robin's Savannah condo, and Brent Jr.'s house in Windsor, he was also investing in another house for the newlyweds outside Birmingham, as well as real estate in Destin and yet another house in Nicaragua.

Soon after her engagement was announced, Robin called her brother for the first time in four years, inviting him to the wedding. She sent a warm thank-you note, addressed to Brent and his Colorado family, for their gift of a movie for Christmas of 2003, saying "hopefully I'll get to see you all soon." However, the Springfords were worried that Brent would disturb the wedding, a fear they communicated to Scoutt. They told Maggie Johnson, now their occasional housekeeper, not to give Brent Jr. any details of the wedding if he called the house. In May 2004, there was a camp-out engagement party for Robin and Greg Crouch. Dow Harris, who was to be Crouch's best man, and Jim Scott attended. At the party, Scott confided to Harris that Brent Jr. had left him a phone message, saying that he had changed his mind and wanted to attend Robin's wedding after all, to show his support. At first Harris and Scott were elated, thinking that their visit had done their friend some good. But later in the evening, after dinner, Brent Sr. came up to the two men, saying he wanted to talk. Not knowing about the message Scott had already received, Brent Sr. said he was concerned that his son might contact them for details of the wedding. He asked them not to disclose any information about it because he didn't want Brent crashing the affair. At that point, Scott handed over his cell phone to Brent Sr. and showed him the message from his son, asking exactly that. "Whatever you do," Harris recalled Brent Sr. saying, "don't tell him." Just in case, in the months since the engagement, Brent Sr. had doubled his son's weekly allowance, apparently as an incentive or compensation for not attending the wedding. After the ceremony Brent Sr. cut the weekly allowance back to $425.

Brent Sr. told Harris and Scott that his son was "extremely clever and devious" although he did have clinical issues. And Brent Sr. said he was anxious because he suspected Dr. Roger Billica had taken Brent Jr. off lithium. A long talk among the three men ensued, reviewing their histories with Brent Jr. While Brent Jr. seemed to be searching for something he could not find in the late 1990s, all agreed that things began getting seriously weird in the summer after he met Scoutt. At the party, Brent Sr. told Harris that he and Charlotte were in a "Catch-22" situation. "They were sure that if Brent did not have some type of support system that he was either going to hurt himself or hurt someone else," Harris wrote later. Brent had gotten so intense in his various projects out West, his friend felt, that if his parents withdrew their support the result could be disastrous. That same month, Charlotte consulted Dr. Jensen, Brent's former psychiatrist, and on three occasions formally consulted a local Montgomery psychiatrist for advice on how to stop enabling her son. The consensus was that Charlotte and Brent Sr. should postpone any major confrontation until after the wedding. They agreed that they should "use the only weapon we have," Charlotte wrote a friend, "the threat of cutting him off financially—to get him evaluated and stabilized by competent doctors."

Brent Jr. left a few more phone messages for Scott, which Scott did not return. Two or three weeks before the wedding, Brent called Harris again, and asked him point blank where and when the wedding would be. Harris told him gently that if Robin wouldn't tell him, he wouldn't either. Brent said he understood. What he couldn't understand, Brent said, was why his family was shutting him out of his sister's wedding, why they were afraid of him. He turned maudlin, saying he yearned to engage with people in a free, fun-filled way. People in Colorado, including Scoutt, didn't really like him. To Harris, he sounded "frustrated and lost and confused, forlorn and in despair." Again, he blamed his parents for not preparing him for the world.

Finally, Robin wrote her brother a letter on September 7, assuring him of her love and saying she missed all the times they had spent together as friends. In it, she said she was sorry that his relationship with their parents had deteriorated, but she didn't want to put herself in the middle. On the second page of the handwritten letter, Robin got to the point: "I don't think the wedding is the right place or time to have to address these feelings. That weekend will already be very emotional and to add that to it would be too much to handle for all of us." She concluded by saying that she hoped to reestablish their relationship in the future. "I would like nothing more than to have you as my brother again."

The note did not have the desired effect. Brent said later that he felt his sister had been "brainwashed" by their parents, who got her to rescind her invitation. He had decidedly mixed feelings about being excluded from his sister's wedding. In an undated letter, he wrote to say he was happy for her, wished that it would be a wonderful occasion, and that he was not upset or angry that she didn't want him to be there. "I do feel rejected, but I completely accept and respect your decision, and I want only to give you my support, love and encouragement." And yet, he soon made clear that he *was* extremely upset—and deeply wounded. He said he was trying to understand why, after calling him with the news of her engagement months before, and inviting him to the wedding, she had been convinced by their parents to change her mind. "I will *not* and never had any intention of disrupting your wedding. I've never done anything to disrupt anything in your life anyway. Maybe it's just my mere presence that bothers the family. I'd even be willing to cut my hair for you, just to see my little sister get married." He loved his sister very much, he wrote, even though they had not been in contact for years, which he blamed on his "illness," caused by lead, mercury, and arsenic poisoning. "I trust that we will develop a new relationship once things have settled down in the weeks and months after your wedding. I know it will be wonderful for you two and I wish you all the best and a great honeymoon as well. Much love, Brent."

There was reason for the family to be concerned. In September, just a month before Robin's wedding and around the time of her note, Brent paid a surprise visit to Montgomery. He drove the Jetta nonstop from Colorado and pulled up outside the Hull Street house. Brent Sr. was not home, but Charlotte saw the car and ran outside, calling Scoutt on the phone in a panic. Brent had gone off the psychotropic drugs Dr. Hinesley had prescribed the previous April, and his mother feared he might intend to harm his father. It was a well-founded fear; Brent told Scoutt, and later her children, that he drove home because he intended to kill his father. Charlotte got Scoutt to phone him and order him back to Colorado before Brent Sr. could learn of the visit. Charlotte told neither her husband nor her daughter about the incident. The Springfords then began telling their friends that Brent would not attend the wedding because he was mentally ill. Despite Scoutt's potentially life-saving intervention when Brent showed up in Montgomery, a chill was descending on the Springfords' relationship with Scoutt. When they left Montgomery to travel, Scoutt's name was not on the emergency contact list they left with Maggie Johnson, who still looked after the house in their absence. If Scoutt did call while they were away, she was brusque with Johnson, demanding to know where Charlotte and Brent Sr. were, because she needed money for expenses. Johnson, as ordered, did not share her employers' contact information, and Scoutt got ugly, Johnson later told investigators.

In retrospect, Brent's friend Dow Harris believes that "it was the thwarting of Brent's desire to come to the wedding that sent him over the edge." Harris, who was also a clear-eyed friend of all members of the Springford family, asked Robin around this time why the family didn't just cut her brother off, as Charlotte herself had considered. Why not let him find his own way for better or worse, especially given his contempt for them, their money, and their lifestyle? "I couldn't for the life of me understand why he would have such a resentment of his parents and yet still be taking money, expecting money from them." But it was more than a lack of understanding, or even mental illness, as Harris wrote several years later in his long memo:

> What infuriates me about Brent Jr. is that after having "liberated" his mind and reading so many books on existential philosophy he could not at least grasp the concept that a man is worth nothing if he cannot stand on his own two legs. That all the passion he put into studying those books could not yield that one idea, is absolutely incomprehensible to me. Even if he got tricked by an Indian witch, which I certainly believe, he still could have had that one principle lying at the crux of his soul as a safeguard against all deception.

At the time, Robin told Harris that she was as frustrated as him. The more slack her parents gave Brent, she said, the more advantage he took. Harris came to believe that his friend "didn't become insane one night. He followed a pattern his entire life and his appetite was never checked. He fell into collusion with some darker forces and he didn't teach himself how to be a man." Around the time of the wedding, Andrea Jameson, who was still in love with Brent, begged Charlotte to go out to Colorado and get him; she said later that if Charlotte had her husband's full support she might have.

In any event, the wedding of Robin Springford and Greg Crouch was a four-day affair, no expense spared. The ceremony went off without a hitch on October 9, 2004, at a church in the planned community of Seaside, Florida. The chapel, which seats two hundred, was full for the service conducted by a Baptist minister. A reception and sit-down dinner followed—in a huge tent, a good thing, since the weather was drizzly and foggy. Dow Harris gave a long, rambling toast. Brent Jr. was absent, but his specter was felt. Much of the conversation at the reception—outside the ears of the wedding party—was about Brent, that he was coming apart and might show up and make a scene, if not worse. "I honestly pictured Brent showing up during the ceremony and shooting everyone in the Seaside Chapel," his aunt, Lois Truss, recalled. After the ceremony, Brent Sr. complained to a friend about his son's $4,000 credit card bill, which included "taking everyone to a rock concert." The parents were increasingly afraid of him, given his rages, bizarre behavior, abusive phone conversations, and ranting letters.

Three days after Robin's wedding, Charlotte turned her attention back to her son. The Springfords had planned to join Lois and Chris Truss traveling in the Czech Republic and Poland but cancelled at the last minute. Charlotte wrote a letter to Dr. Martin Binks, a clinical psychologist at Duke University's Diet and Fitness Center, where she had been for weight-loss treatment. While there, she had consulted Binks informally about Brent. Binks, who also had a behavioral practice, qualified his advice by reminding her that he had not examined the young man, but spoke generally about "enabling" and "setting limits." Charlotte said that when she shared this advice with Brent Sr., "to his credit, my husband did not say 'I told you so.'" The Springfords had concluded by now that their son was being exploited by Scoutt—and that the cash hemorrhage also had to be staunched.

Of greater concern was the Springfords' belief that Brent Jr. was off his medication and no longer seeing his Loveland psychiatrist, Kent Hinesley. He was now being treated by Dr. Billica, a non-psychiatrist whose treatments focused on nutrition and environment. Scoutt and her young daughter were already Billica's patients. Based on a physical exam and a urine test, Brent told his parents, the physician had concluded that his mental pathologies were the result of a concentration in his brain of certain toxic metals, mainly lead and mercury. There are conflicting accounts as to whether Billica told Brent to stop taking the medications last prescribed in May by Hinesley—Zyprexa, Provigil, and Eskalith. Billica, who served as the NASA Chief of Medical Operations at the Johnson Space Center during the 1990s, insists he did not. Also unclear was whether Billica hooked Brent up to some sort of vibrating stress-reducing device, one that he said used electrical currents to balance his neurotransmitters. Brent Jr. was given a bill for such treatments. At first, Charlotte—in growing desperation—accepted the possibility of toxic metal contamination, thinking the mercury might have come from the canned tuna Brent subsisted on for a six-months period years earlier in

Mexico. In his first examination with Billica, Brent also reported a decrease in his libido. His typical diet, he told the new physician, was rice tea and sugar for breakfast; a sandwich with beans mashed and burned into chips for lunch; and red beans and a box of doughnuts for dinner. In fact, Brent was living almost entirely on sugar and caffeine. His cravings were so intense that he had taken to dumpster-diving behind a Cookies by Design outlet and a doughnut store. Apparently, he had also taken to sneaking into the Windsor house at night to take sugar from the kitchen; Scoutt's children hid in their rooms the sugar for their breakfast cereal. He also reported taking five to ten caffeine pills a day. In addition to shoplifting clothes that Scoutt and her daughter pointed out to him in stores, Brent also shoplifted thousands of dollars' worth of sweets at convenience stores, convinced that he wasn't caught because he had become invisible to surveillance cameras.

The initial results of the new therapy seemed positive. After a long period of silence, Brent called his parents to say he was feeling much better, thanks to the nutrition regimen, and he apologized for the trouble he had caused them earlier. In return, Brent Sr. began paying for Scoutt and her daughter's visits to the same physician. Despite Brent and Scoutt's insistence that the treatment was helping, Charlotte soon concluded that the doctor did not believe their son was bipolar and was not helping him. For his part, Brent Sr. began to suspect that Brent Jr.'s bills for near-daily medical treatment and numerous supplements—"Zinc Supreme," Chlorella, Paleo meal, and a "vital nutrients" product called BCQ—were actually for Scoutt's own use, for other members of her family, or for resale. When Scoutt refused Brent Sr.'s demands for more detailed invoices, his suspicions were confirmed; he was also angry at her for running up credit card bills.

The Springfords finally concluded that "the need to get Brent to some competent doctors [had gotten] to be an emergency," Charlotte wrote Dr. Binks at Duke. Earlier, she began exploring residential psychiatric institutions at both Duke and Emory universities. Charlotte went so far as to put Brent on the waiting list for a program at Harvard Medical School, "which was so expensive it made us gasp, but we were still willing to pay for it." The waiting list, however, was three months long. And the Springfords would first need to convince Brent Jr. to enter any program voluntarily. He was, after all, a married adult, so unless there was a provable threat to himself or others, they could not legally compel him. Under the circumstances, the only cards the Springfords had to play would have been to offer Scoutt the deed to the Windsor house in exchange for convincing Brent to commit himself. Or, conversely, to threaten to cut Brent and Scoutt off financially, unless he agreed to evaluation and treatment. Of course, Charlotte recognized there was great risk in the latter course.

Charlotte wrote the Duke psychologist on October 12,

> Martin, please help me. I want to be sure we're not missing something before we threaten to cut Brent off if he continues to see the one doctor that he believes has helped him and go to specialists of our choosing—not to mention the possibility that he might react violently to an ultimatum.

The situation was further complicated, she wrote, because by now there had been two months of silence from Scoutt, and "Everything we know about Brent's condition is filtered through her." There is no evidence that the Springfords used the carrot of the Windsor house deed, but they were ready to communicate the threat of a financial cutoff through Scoutt.

In another October letter to Binks, Charlotte wrote that they last raised the possibility of a financial cutoff in a phone call in September to Scoutt, prompted by the ballooning bills from the nutritionist. That call in turn caused Brent Jr. to immediately break his silence and call his parents. In that phone conversation, Charlotte wrote, her son said that if his family in Windsor was left to carry the burden of his medical care with the new doctor,

> he would 'do something so terrible that you'll regret it for the rest of your life.' His whole tone was rather frightening, and it was hard to believe that my once beautiful and sensitive son was capable of that kind of venom. But we didn't cave, and Caroline managed to defuse the situation. It was probably just an idle threat.

Charlotte told Binks about her letters to the Fort Collins psychiatrist, Harris Jensen, and Jensen's diagnosis that Brent had gone from "bipolar

II," which was manageable, to out-of-control, rapidly recycling "bipolar I." Jensen also shared the family's reservations about Brent's and Scoutt's growing reliance on Billica.

Until the financial ultimatum could be carried out, the flow of Springford money to Scoutt continued. On November 19, Brent Sr. mailed an allowance check. The same day, Charlotte ordered a photocopy of her son's marriage certificate, which she had finally located in Deadwood. But sometime in the next few days, Brent Sr. finally decided that it was time to cut off Scoutt and sell the house. The last straw was a credit card bill for $18,000 worth of supplements from Billica, who, Brent Sr. and Charlotte now believed, had taken their son off all other medications. And there was no invoice for the supplements. "We paid $25,000 with no appreciable result," Brent Sr. told a friend around that time. Brent Jr. believed the supplements were for him, but investigators later learned that they were for Scoutt's use. Of his total bill of $24,878, Billica later told investigators, just $1,200 was for Brent Jr.

The spiral of dysfunction and the breakdown of communication between Alabama and Colorado began to spin out of control. For his part, Brent Sr. had no more use for his son's life with his Western family than he had years earlier for Brent Jr.'s spirituality and his desire to be a monk. However, Charlotte remained ambivalent about Scoutt. "Charlotte sincerely thought Caroline was taking care of Brent Jr.," Lois Truss recalled. "If not for her, he would be on the street." Brent Jr., long the indulged, entitled child of affluent, permissive parents, must have felt as though he was being ripped apart. His parents continued to meddle in his affairs. Yet he still loved them, and they had also made his Windsor family's life comfortable, with lots of money, credit cards, and cars. He was also seriously ill, possibly off his medication, yet aware of the pain and anguish he was causing his parents and the disappointment he had been. Brent Jr. was crushed by his father's growing hostility to Scoutt, as she conveyed it to him. Always in the background were her demands for more. Now she apparently panicked that the safe, comfortable life Brent had made possible for her and her family was about to end. The cutoff threat threw the Windsor household into turmoil. Turning off the financial spigot would mean catastrophe for Scoutt, who stopped taking Charlotte's increasingly frantic calls. A rupture between Brent and his parents was imminent.

Investigation

The first police officers on the scene of the Springford murders on Friday, November 26, 2004, were patrolmen who quickly summoned several detectives. They in turn called a supervisor, who dispatched homicide detective Guy Naquin, then working the holiday weekend shift and catching up on his open cases. Naquin arrived at the Hull Street house in less than half an hour, was briefed, and then surveyed the carnage. He found both bodies cool to the touch and in full rigor mortis, and he quickly confirmed that this was a double murder. Naquin contacted his supervisor, Sergeant Bryan Jurkofsky, and then called Detective Corporal M. P. "Mike" Myrick, the on-call homicide detective for that holiday weekend, to take over as lead investigator. Up to now, Jurkofsky and Myrick had had similar plans for the day—Christmas shopping at Black Friday sales and watching football.

Jurkofsky, thirty-two, arrived first. Myrick, thirty-six, arrived about an hour later, checking in with the crime scene coordinator before ducking under the yellow tape and locating Jurkofsky amid a swarm of technicians. Naquin briefed the pair in front of the garage and, immediately aware of the impact the crime was likely to have in Montgomery, began calling in a half-dozen other detectives. Additional patrol officers arrived to secure the crime scene. One group clustered directly below Robin Springford Crouch's old bedroom, in the patio area below the trellis and the scuffed pillar. They made images and impressions of what appeared to be boot tracks across the grounds.

Groups of the Springfords' friends, relatives, and neighbors rushed to the scene, holding each other in the street in front of the house. As rumors threaded through the crowd, there was growing anxiety and a sense of shared foreboding that soon escalated to dread. When the deaths were confirmed, initial speculation was that the killer or killers were from the neighborhood, that it was a home invasion gone wrong. But one of the first friends to arrive, retired Circuit Judge Sally Greenhaw, had a different suspicion. The wife of a well-known Alabama journalist and author, Greenhaw has steadfastly refused to talk about the case. But as Charlotte's closest friend and University of Alabama schoolmate, her thoughts that day on the lawn are not difficult to imagine. Everything she and Charlotte had feared, the worst possible outcome, must have left Greenhaw crushed and devastated.

Practical matters first needed to be attended to. The judge urged the police to contact the immediate family before they learned about it through media broadcasts. Jerry Armstrong, the operations manager of the Springfords' Pepsi bottling plant who had discovered Brent Sr.'s body, was designated to call Lois Truss, Charlotte's half-sister. To his relief, her husband, Dr. Christopher Truss, answered the phone. The doctor's first reaction was to ask Armstrong where Brent Jr. was. "That son of a bitch did it," he said. Truss then called Robin, while Naquin separately called Robin's husband, Greg Crouch.

News of the murders shot through the Springfords' social set and through the Garden District, although close friends admitted that a family crisis had been brewing for years. When one couple, longtime friends of the Springfords, got the news of their murders, each burst into tears. They also had no doubt as to who was responsible. "We both knew who it was," said the wife: the couple's twenty-eight-year-old son, Brent Jr., who lived fifteen hundred miles away in Colorado. And some feared he might not be finished with mayhem. Dr. Truss told police that he and his wife were so afraid of Brent Jr. that in the wake of the killings they were temporarily leaving the area to stay with friends. Robin and Greg told police that they also would not stay at their home. By noon, the Trusses and the Crouches had already fled. They gave police cell-phone numbers for Brent Jr. and his wife, Caroline Scoutt. Robin later sent Greg to retrieve her wedding dress, but she never entered the Hull Street house again.

In the days and weeks that followed, detectives Myrick and Jurkofsky became partners. Both college-educated family men, the seasoned investigators were a study in physical contrasts: Myrick tall and beefy with a high, black flattop; Jurkofsky a slender man with a shaved head. While Myrick was designated the lead detective on the case, Jurkofsky was his superior. This could have been an awkward arrangement, but they worked smoothly together. Myrick began taking the first of what would become four hundred of his own photographs of the crime scene. The pair started talking with members of the close family, one of whom had immediately called the police department in Greeley, Colorado, trying to determine Brent Jr.'s whereabouts, without success.

Newspaper and television reporters, alerted by the police scanner traffic, also swarmed to the Garden District, grateful to fill a slow news weekend. Police spokesman Lieutenant Huey Thornton told the *Montgomery Advertiser*: "At this time, we believe they are the victims of an apparent double homicide . . . . We have not yet determined the point of entry [into the house] or the motive." The double murder "does not appear to be a random incident," he said. While Thornton would not say what the cause of death was, he did say that the killer might not have been a stranger. The officer reported that the Springfords were last seen alive on Thursday afternoon—at a Thanksgiving luncheon in Birmingham with Lois and Christopher Truss and Robin and Greg Crouch. Police later learned that Brent Sr. had received a speeding ticket on the way back to Montgomery, driving his sleek, black, four-door 1998 Jaguar XJR, now missing. The police were seeking an individual whom Thornton would not name, but informed speculation quickly turned to Brent Jr., given his history of mental illness and hostility and threatening behavior toward his parents. Jerry Armstrong, the contractor overseeing the kitchen tiling, told Detective Naquin that the young man was manic depressive, but to his knowledge hadn't been in Montgomery in two years though there had been recent tension growing out of excessive medical bills. In any event, the killer or killers were still at large, and people in the city were frightened.

Myrick, Jurkofsky, and Naquin were the only homicide detectives to enter the house while it was still sealed. Investigators and the department's top brass, including newly appointed chief Arthur D. Baylor, knew from the outset that this case had a high screw-up potential. Not only were the victims wealthy, socially prominent, and active in civic affairs, they were acquaintances of Mayor Bobby Bright and his wife. This guaranteed that there would be considerable formal and informal pressure on the department to solve the case quickly, and that the *Advertiser* would be breathing down their necks until they did. After the detectives who first inspected the crime scene came the forensic photographers, and then the death scene investigators. Finally, after cooling their heels on the front porch, the mayor and high-ranking officers made a symbolic tour.

Spokesman Lieutenant Thornton no doubt was being disingenuous in his comments to the press that police had no idea of the point of entry to the Springford house. It may simply have been a matter of intentionally withholding what investigators call "case-sensitive specifics," used to weed out false tipsters and would-be informants. Yet there may have been a different reason. For the department, there was already a potentially embarrassing detail: The Springfords had activated their silent alarm about 5:30 p.m. Wednesday, when they left for Birmingham. At 2 a.m. Thursday, the alarm and motion detectors inside and outside the garage were tripped, alerting the alarm service, which called the house and, when there was no answer, contacted the police. Two city officers, Corporal M. McCord and Officer Michael A. Davis, responded to the call, tried the doors, and found the house quiet and apparently unoccupied, with no signs of forced entry. They left a note on the front door explaining their visit. Thus, it was fair to assume that if the killer or killers had been in the house that night, and if the patrol officers had been more thorough or more inquisitive, the murders might have been prevented. The security company also reported to police that later on Thanksgiving Day they received a "good code" to turn off the alarm at 6:15 p.m., likely indicating the Springfords' return from Birmingham. In a follow-up interview at the house on Sunday with another officer, Davis and McCord said that all the doors and gates were locked, so they saw no reason to investigate further.

Naquin and other investigators began canvassing the people by then gathered on the street, later working their way through the neighborhood. Much of the initial information came to police as neighbors, friends, and relatives arrived at the Hull Street house. While investigators were still working inside, Judge Sally Greenhaw pointed Naquin in the direction of Brent Jr., explaining that there had been growing friction, mostly over money, between him and his parents. Greenhaw said Charlotte had confided about a week before the killing that Brent Jr. had called, saying he and his family had no money for food, and that if Charlotte did not give it to him, he would steal it. His mother replied that if he did, she wouldn't bail him out again. Brent Jr. said his Colorado family's state was so dire he was going to call the Colorado Department of Health and Human Services to report the hardship condition of Scoutt's children. Greenhaw also told investigators that in the weeks leading up to the slaying, Charlotte told her that Brent had forged a check on her account for $6,700. Other friends said it was for $10,000. Charlotte said her son was being treated for mental instability by a new doctor who she believed had taken him off his medications. As a result, in the weeks preceding the killings, the Springfords feared for their safety but friends sensed that Charlotte was already grieving for her son, anticipating his suicide rather than her murder. After briefing the police, Greenhaw called Lois Truss, Charlotte's sister, to provide more details about the murders.

At 11 a.m. on Friday, Jurkofsky had the first substantive phone conversation with Robin Springford Crouch, lasting about an hour. She told him that she and her husband had gone into hiding. In a subsequent phone conversation a few days later, she said she had two calls on her cell phone from her brother the Sunday after the killings, which she did not answer or return. Robin said that to her knowledge Brent Jr. hadn't been home in a year or two—Charlotte had not mentioned to her Brent Jr.'s surprise, threatening visit to Hull Street in September. Robin said she had spoken to her brother four times in the previous four years. He rarely called home on holidays. Her father told her numerous times that when Brent Jr. did call, they argued about money. On the phone, Brent Jr. would say he hated Brent Sr. and accused their parents of trying to have him hospitalized. Recently, Charlotte and Brent Sr. had cut off their son's credit cards, and in the week before their deaths, Robin confirmed, they had discussed having Brent Jr. institutionalized. The Springfords were particularly disturbed that they were no longer getting detailed insurance invoices for Brent's medical bills from the nutritionist, which they had to pay out of pocket. She also confirmed Greenhaw's assertion that a week before Thanksgiving, Brent, who she suspected was again smoking marijuana, had forged a check for $6,700 from Charlotte's account. Robin told Jurkofsky that the family "was confident that Brent Springford Jr. did the killing and that his girlfriend, Caroline Scoutt, was behind it." She said that Charlotte and Scoutt had drifted apart in the past three months.

The Springfords' intimate friends quietly speculated among themselves about what part Caroline Scoutt might have played in the murders. The Episcopal minister planning the couple's memorial service several days later recalled some ambient concern in the crowded room among family members that Brent Jr. might show up at the church. Those who attended later recalled that they agreed to advise people coming to the church not to mention Brent Jr. to the immediate family members. When the couple's five-paragraph obituary, supplied by the family through the Turner Funeral Home in Luverne, appeared in the *Montgomery Advertiser* several days later, Winston Brent Springford Jr. was pointedly not included in the list of survivors.

At 2:25 p.m. the bodies, in white bags, were moved from the house to the city morgue. Investigators continued to comb through the rooms, the garage, and the grounds. The dining room was undisturbed, candles upright on the glass table that seated eight, as was the living room, which was lined with paintings and pottery. Not so the Florida room at the rear of the house, which seemed to be in disarray. In the eight bags from Linens 'n Things that were scattered on the brown tiled floor, Myrick found a receipt indicating that the kitchen supplies, apparently for the Springfords' condo in Destin, Florida, had been purchased Tuesday at a nearby shopping center. Desk and cabinet drawers in the library were pulled open and papers were strewn everywhere. Charlotte's laptop was undisturbed.

In the garage, they picked their way through Brent Sr.'s office. On the desk, the credit cards had been pulled out of his wallet, which had been left on the desk top, still containing two $100 bills. His laptop computer's screen saver, which read "Brent's Comp" in large, red block letters, continued to scroll as the investigators worked. One wall was lined with bookshelves, and file boxes covered half the floor. Packets of canceled checks, held together by rubber bands, were stacked on the floor. In the adjoining exercise room, free weights were lined up along one wall. In the center were a treadmill, a multipurpose fixed-weight apparatus, padded benches, and an inversion table. The garage's bathroom and kitchen area apparently didn't get much of their intended use: In the stall shower were two cartons of Savory & James Deluxe Sherry. A Canon fax/printer was on the kitchen counter next to the four-burner stovetop and a paper cutter was next to the sink. Investigators found nine envelopes in the garage and around the house, each with cash, mostly in $100 bills, including one each with Brent Jr. and Robin's names on them. A third, with both their names, contained $2,000. Ultimately, officers recovered more than $18,000 in cash and more in foreign currency. In the basement, the gun safe held several weapons.

As if to compensate for any question that might be raised by the burglar-alarm incident, Montgomery police deployed all available resources. Investigators went to Montgomery Regional Airport to see if Brent Sr.'s plane was in the private hangar, where it was sometimes parked, also checking for the Jaguar. The plane was there but the car was not. Other officers fanned out through the Garden District and the city on Friday and the next few days, canvassing neighbors, going through trash cans, conducting interviews and responding to tips. Springford family members told police about Charlotte and Brent Sr.'s house on Lake Martin, about forty miles northeast of the city, in Elmore County. After swinging by the police department, Myrick and Jurkofsky sped to the lake house that afternoon, where they thought Brent might be, or may have stopped. With Myrick at the wheel, Jurkofsky provided updates to the family with more calls to Dr. Truss and Greg Crouch. Jurkofsky also called the police in the Birmingham suburb of Homewood, asking them to keep an eye on the Crouch home. Elmore County deputies were already at the lake house when the Montgomery officers got there. There was no sign of Brent Jr. or the Jaguar.

Lois Truss confirmed to Jurkofsky what others were telling them: Brent Jr. had repeatedly threatened his parents. For a year before the murders, she recalled, her sister Charlotte had been telling her

that Brent Jr. had threatened to come to Alabama and "do something bad" to them. Brent Sr. mentioned the threat, but reiterated something he had said before, that it was hard to kill somebody, especially someone like himself who had a gun collection and was much stronger. We had heard a few times about a physical fight Brent had with Little Brent in their house in Montgomery and Brent had overpowered Little Brent. He truly did not believe it could happen.

Meanwhile, acting on what friends and family members had been telling them, other investigators turned their attention to Colorado. It took a few calls for Detective Naquin to determine which local or county law enforcement agency had jurisdiction over Brent's Windsor residence. He eventually reached the Weld County sheriff's office, in Greeley, whose territory covered Brent Jr.'s home. (Naquin also asked the sheriff's office to get a search warrant but was told there was insufficient probable cause.) The community of Hillcrest Estates was in Windsor, an unincorporated part of the county with a Greeley mailing address. Naquin asked the deputies to go to the house to check on Brent and talk to whoever was at the house—without mentioning the killings. When he gave the names and address of the occupants to Weld County deputies, and they punched it up on their computer, division commander Bill Spaulding came on the line. He said he was familiar with Caroline Scoutt and her children, who were living there. Spaulding said he had addressed numerous calls, complaints, and problems with Scoutt's household previously, as well as with neighbors, but nothing major.

Spaulding called Deputy Vicki Harbert, the investigator on call for the holiday weekend. Spaulding assigned Harbert to be the lead liaison officer for the Montgomery case, along with officer William Hood, whose jurisdiction included Windsor. Spaulding and Hood drove to the house, where they found only Scoutt's three children, ages twelve through twenty, whom they later described as "vague" in their initial responses. After twenty minutes their mother arrived, but she was "evasive" regarding Brent's whereabouts, saying she wasn't sure where her husband worked, suggesting it might be Kerr-McGee (she knew it wasn't). Her account, they wrote in their report, "conflicted with information received from the children," who said Brent might have been around during the week, and had left the house at 8 a.m. Thanksgiving morning. The investigators were unable to locate Brent, but observed his black VW Jetta parked outside. Since the deputies had no warrant, Scoutt concluded the interview. Spaulding called Detective Naquin in Montgomery Friday evening and asked what to do. Naquin advised him to have the officers leave the property. By late that night, Myrick and Jurkofsky were thinking they might need to go to Colorado.

On Saturday morning, the investigation was, if anything, more intense. Around noon, a detective checked the answering machine on the Hull Street house's landline and retrieved a message from a woman they later identified as Caroline Scoutt. It had come in at 10:30 a.m., November 23, the Tuesday before Thanksgiving, wishing Charlotte a happy holiday. She was calling early from their home in Colorado, she said, because she knew the Springfords would be celebrating with relatives in Birmingham, and planned to go out of town for the remainder of the weekend. She said Brent Jr. was shopping and wouldn't be home for a while. Other detectives and uniformed officers continued to canvass the neighborhood, with mixed results. Dogs near the house had been barking Thursday night, they were told. A young woman, home from college in the house backing up behind the Springfords', said that from her second-floor bedroom she noticed lights on at the house until late at night, but thought nothing of it.

Before long, police had their hands full with other interviews and fielding unsolicited tips that cascaded in, first a trickle and then a chaotic flood. As in any sensational criminal investigation, some of the information was helpful, but much was incomplete, contradictory, exaggerated, or wrong. Most pointed in one direction: to Brent Jr. As early as Friday afternoon, one officer had written in his notes that the young man was already "being seriously looked at as a suspect." Several neighbors confirmed that Brent Sr. had told them that his son had threatened him and his family numerous times. The Campbells were family friends who lived a block down Hull Street and whose children had carpooled with the Springfords to the Montgomery Academy. Marvin Campbell, an attorney, told police that at a Rotary Club meeting the previous Monday, Brent Sr. said that his son was bipolar and was receiving holistic treatment in Colorado recommended by a Native American medicine woman. He said that he had spent more than $15,000 on these treatments, which he considered inflated, and that he was cutting it off. Brent Sr. also said Brent Jr. had threatened to kill him, and added that he was rewriting his will to ensure that Caroline Scoutt, Brent's wife, would not inherit his money if he were to die. (It later turned out that he was in the process of redrafting his will, but the changes made no mention of Scoutt.)

Campbell's wife Marie said Charlotte told her she, too, was afraid Brent Jr. would harm them. Jim Scott, Brent Jr.'s longtime friend, told Myrick of Brent's intense dislike of his father, and his violent and dangerous temperament. Naquin asked Florida police to check out the Springfords' Destin condo. While Myrick was at the crime scene, Naquin and other investigators began contacting airports and bus stations and companies between Alabama and Colorado, trying to determine if Brent Jr. had traveled to Montgomery in time to commit the murders. Over the next two weeks, the airports would prove to be a time-consuming dead end, typical of the investigative process, but the bus stations would eventually prove more fruitful.

Other investigators focused on the missing Jaguar. Police spokesman Thornton revealed to reporters that the vehicle had been spotted early Friday morning on Alabama Highway 14 in Millbrook, in Elmore County, traveling east at high speed toward Wetumpka. It had not yet been located. The most tantalizing tip Saturday came from a newspaper delivery man. Around 2 a.m. Friday morning, just after tossing a paper from his car onto the Springfords' driveway, the man said, a black car pulled out of the driveway and followed him for several blocks. As was his custom, the carrier was flashing his emergency lights as he and his girlfriend tossed papers from both sides of the car. At one point, he said, the black car pulled up alongside and he got a good look at what he said was a young man with long hair and bloodshot eyes, who stared at him before speeding off. But later, the carrier failed to pick Brent Jr. out of a photo lineup and insisted the black car was a BMW, not a Jaguar.

Later Saturday morning, Myrick returned to the police department to call Brent Jr. and Caroline Scoutt in Colorado, but got no answer, so he left messages for them to get back to him. The detective said nothing about the murders, which had not yet appeared in Colorado news media, saying only that he needed to contact family members about an "incident" in

Montgomery involving Brent's family. Scoutt returned the call just before noon local time and told the detective that her husband had left home early that day to do some Christmas shopping. She assured Myrick that Brent had been at their home during Thanksgiving week, after calling in sick to work early in the week. She said she was certain she had seen him on Wednesday, as well as Thursday morning and evening. She noticed that his Jetta was gone before dawn on Thursday, and that he was not home most of the day, possibly hiking with a friend in Horsetooth Canyon. Scoutt said that he returned for the evening Thanksgiving meal with the family. At the time of her call to Myrick, Scoutt said she was on her way to Boulder to pick him up. She was taking him his cell phone, which he had left in his bedroom, so he could return the detective's call. Brent did call hours later, but on Scoutt's cell phone. Brent said he was with Scoutt, driving through a snowstorm to go to dinner in Fort Collins, and that he had a bad connection. Nonetheless, he repeated Scoutt's account of his whereabouts during the week, including the canyon hike. He said he had done his chores around the house, but he stayed away from family members to avoid infecting them with his cold. He was home on Friday when the Weld County Sheriff's officers arrived. He thought they were investigating a shoplifting incident, so he stayed out of sight, jumping the fence and hiding in a nearby cornfield.

By 10 p.m. Saturday, Myrick and Jurkofsky were told to fly to Colorado to pursue the investigation. Jurkofsky booked the tickets and the pair of detectives went home to pack. Sunday morning they were driven to the airport for their 8:30 a.m. flight. Later that morning, Dow Harris contacted the police again, and Detective Naquin asked him to come in for an interview. Harris described his visit to Colorado the previous March with Jim Scott, when they met Scoutt for breakfast at a restaurant. Scoutt mentioned several times during the meal that Brent wanted his rightful inheritance. Harris said that when he asked Scoutt what Brent might do if his parents cut him off, she had replied that he might injure or kill his father, but she made no mention of his mother.

Also on Sunday morning, November 28, the Springford autopsies were conducted in Montgomery at the State Department of Forensic Sciences, where the bodies had been brought from the morgue. Charlotte's began first at 8:25 a.m., and lasted just under ninety minutes. In various parts of her skull, portions of the brain were visible. There were bruises on her arms, and both bones in her left forearm, just above the wrist, were shattered—classic defense wounds. The nails and fingers on her hands—with two gold bands still on them—were also broken. Her larynx was essentially amputated. Her nose and some teeth were broken, and there were numerous lacerations to her face and scalp. Dr. Stephen F. Boudreau, the state medical examiner, found the cause of death to be multiple blunt force injuries. Brent Sr.'s autopsy began at 10:20 a.m. Apart from the depth of cuts to his throat and six shallow stab wounds to the torso—and the absence of defensive wounds—his injuries were similar to Charlotte's.

Myrick and Jurkofsky flew via Atlanta to Denver, but because of a lengthy delay in Atlanta, it was close to 10 p.m. Sunday when they arrived, exhausted. It was snowing, but they nonetheless headed straight to the Weld County sheriff's office in Greeley to brief Deputy Vicki Harbert. Earlier that day, Harbert had phoned Montgomery detectives and told them that Scoutt had called her just after 4 p.m., while driving back from Fort Collins, voicing her concern about Brent Sr. and Charlotte. She said she had a conversation with Charlotte on Wednesday "about paperwork," but that she had been unable to reach her since then. Scoutt said she left messages for other family members in Alabama—a claim that later proved false—and said she was considering calling the Montgomery police to ask them to check on the Springfords' home. Harbert greeted the two Alabama detectives at the sheriff's department in Greeley, and took them to a conference room. A native of nearby Loveland, Harbert was forty-one and had been with the department for fourteen years. She had worked her way up from volunteer to animal control officer to jail guard to uniformed officer to investigator. She wore glasses and tied her honey-brown hair in a ponytail, her manner no-nonsense.

Jurkofsky and Myrick sat down at the long table, and Myrick opened his laptop, onto which he had loaded scores of photos from the crime scene. Coming from Alabama, the two detectives tried to break the ice with Harbert by talking about the holiday weekend's big college games. "They wanted to talk about football," the deputy recalled, "and I wanted to talk about homicide." By then Harbert was intensely curious, already familiar with Brent and Caroline, and having been to the Windsor house on earlier complaint calls. At the informal meeting, Myrick sensed no territoriality on Harbert's part toward the outsiders, as sometimes happens. For her part, Harbert was deferential, understanding and accepting her junior status in the investigation. "It was their case," she said. "We were there for support. It was just cops working with cops. We had the same goal." They quickly developed a cooperative relationship.

After a short night's sleep at the Executive Tower Inn, then a slightly shabby high-rise in downtown Denver, Myrick and Jurkofsky returned to the sheriff's office Monday morning, November 29. They reconvened in the same, rectangular room where they had met the night before—now sun-lit by a wall of windows. Myrick, introduced by Harbert, gave a more extensive briefing to the larger group of county investigators and prosecutors, which included the other Weld County officer, Bill Hood, who was assigned to join Harbert as local liaison. The two local deputies drew up a lengthy list of what they would need, with Harbert working on a search warrant for the Springford house at 11236 Hillcrest Drive in Windsor. Assistant District Attorney Robert Miller and four officers—Myrick, Jurkofsky, and two from Colorado—took the request to District Court Judge Gilbert A. Gutierrez, who granted it. Among the items listed were "clothing/footwear worn during the offense," retail receipts, and personal diaries and journals. Since they hadn't yet located Brent, they decided to interview Scoutt, who was not under suspicion since Weld officers had found her at home on Friday. Myrick wrote in his subsequent report: "At the present time Ms. Scoutt has been eliminated as a participant in the victims' murder."

Following the briefing, Myrick called Scoutt and asked her to come into the sheriff's office for an early afternoon interview, and to have Brent—who she now "remembered" worked at K. P. Kauffman Well Service in Fort Lupton—come in separately later. She agreed, and at 1:20 p.m. she sat down with Myrick, Jurkofsky, and Harbert, without an attorney. First, the Montgomery detectives officially notified her of the Springfords' murder. Myrick was not impressed with what he viewed as Scoutt's subsequent the-atrics. She reacted with what he felt was a false sense of shock. She said she had to sit on the ground to be closer to the earth, yet otherwise displayed little emotion. They brought in a Native American deputy to put her at ease. What followed was a series of evasive, changing, and convoluted stories. Still, because she was at home in Windsor when Harbert visited the house on Friday night after the murders, she was not considered a suspect.

Scoutt said that most days Brent was awake by 5 a.m. and gone from his garage bedroom by 6:30. She said that the Tuesday morning of Thanksgiving week she had seen him getting ready to leave for work. As for Wednesday, she said she assumed her husband was home because his chores had been done. But she made some key changes to what she had told the detective on the phone two days earlier: Most critically, after previously saying that Brent had come to the family's Thanksgiving dinner table, but had not eaten, she now said that she had *not* seen her husband that day. She had no explanation for why she had called Brent's employer Monday night to say he was sick and would be out Tuesday and Wednesday. Myrick was most interested in the events of the past Saturday evening. Scoutt said she noticed that Brent's Jetta was gone from the house early Saturday morning, and she assumed he had gone Christmas shopping in Boulder, yet was vague about when he left. What Scoutt didn't know was that Weld County deputies, still searching for the missing Jaguar, had returned to Scoutt's house Saturday and seen the Jetta parked where it had been Friday. Saturday afternoon, she said, Brent called her from a pay phone—he said he left his cell at home—at the Pearl Street Mall in Boulder, asking for a ride home. He asked her to meet him at a health food restaurant nearby, but she couldn't find him there. She did some toy shopping in the mall and found him at Barnes & Noble.

Scoutt said that later on Saturday night, after she picked up Brent in Boulder and they had dinner, he complained of a bad cold. The urgent-care centers were closed, so, now driving his Jetta, he went to the emergency room at Poudre Valley Hospital in Fort Collins. Records later confirmed that he was treated there at 10 p.m., having complained of coughing, congestion, and diarrhea. There were no other symptoms, so he was given a Z-Pac—a prepackaged, five-day course of the antibiotic azithromycin—as well as a follow-up prescription, and released. On Sunday, Scoutt and Brent went to fill the prescription at a nearby Walgreens. They went to Jack's Feed Store in Fort Collins for supplies, but then split up. Brent went to Cost Cutters, a discount hair salon at Foothills Fashion Mall, where he had his long hair cut short. Previously, Montgomery and local Colorado police learned from his Colorado acquaintances that in the days before the murder Brent had long hair and a bushy mustache. Jurkofsky and Bill Hood, the Weld County deputy, later verified that on Sunday the first name on the salon's appointment sheet was Brent's. The stylist who cut Brent's hair recalled that he asked for his shag to be cut short, but not like a military buzz cut. She tried to engage him, saying she was surprised that Brent was out in such bad weather on a holiday weekend. Brent made plain he wasn't interested in conversation. When the stylist finished, he said he wanted it shorter. While the haircut took place, Scoutt visited one of her daughters, who worked at a nearby Safeway supermarket. When she returned to the salon, Brent, referring to Scoutt as his mother, told her he didn't have enough money to pay. Scoutt told the stylist that the cut wasn't short enough, to make his bangs even shorter.

Some aspects of Scoutt's account would prove to be demonstrably false. She embellished on Brent's earlier explanation for why he wasn't home on Friday, when sheriff's investigators visited the Windsor house. Despite earlier statements that Brent had left his cell phone in his garage living area, she now said that on Tuesday, Brent had called her twice from a Walmart in nearby Greeley, saying he was going to shoplift a watch for her, but that she talked him out of it. Scoutt confirmed Brent's story that he was hiding when the squad car came by on Friday, assuming it had to do with the Walmart episode, so he jumped the fence and took off, hiding in the cornfield. Scoutt said she was on good terms and in regular contact with the Springfords in Alabama, calling Charlotte two or three times a week to update them on Brent's condition. This was not supported by Montgomery phone records. Later, Scoutt would concede that things had been increasingly cool between Charlotte and her for the previous three months. Not that Scoutt let this have any impact on her utilizing the Springfords' resources, even after she sensed something might be amiss in Montgomery. Two days after Thanksgiving, Scoutt had taken the Yukon the Springfords had given her to Pike Auto Center for repairs, which she charged to Brent Sr.'s credit card. The interview with Myrick and Harbert ended after about an hour, but Scoutt was allowed to wait in the interrogation room until Brent arrived. By the end of the interview, Myrick's overall impression was that Scoutt was a devious person. Harbert agreed. "She's a manipulator and a con," she recalled. "I could see how she could convince people that she was a very powerful Native American medicine woman. She was trying to draw us in, but we're used to people lying to us. As cops, we're savvy to people's bullshit."

About 3:30 p.m. Monday, Brent left his job in Fort Lupton, trailed at a discreet distance by Jurkofsky and Hood in an unmarked sheriff's car. On the way Brent stopped to toss a bag of trash into a dumpster, requiring the car following to pass him and park up the road. Nothing of value to the investigation was found when they recovered the black plastic bag. Myrick and Harbert left Scoutt with Weld County investigators and, with Jurkofsky, began interviewing Brent at 5 p.m. As she had during the Scoutt interview, Harbert watched from the video observation room. Myrick started with a formal notification of the Springfords' deaths in Montgomery, without providing any details. Myrick was first struck by Brent's "ice-blue eyes." The detective noted that Brent's reaction to the news was generally unemotional, that he did not cry, although his eyes were bloodshot. He put his face in his hands, and wanted to know what happened, but asked for no details of the murders. Myrick noticed that his hair was cut jaggedly short, and he had a bruise beneath his right eye and a raw patch of skin on his forehead. Brent was evasive about his injuries, saying they were at least six months old. This answer—and those that followed—made it evident to Myrick that Brent was an unpracticed and consequently inept liar.

Brent denied any role in the killings, repeating Scoutt's earlier account that he became sick with diarrhea and chest congestion on the previous Monday night. He said it was he—not Scoutt, as she had said several hours earlier—who called his employer, and it was on Monday night, to say he was sick and wouldn't be coming to work on Tuesday. He said he stayed away from work on Wednesday, and just hung around the house and property, doing chores. As the interview progressed, Myrick noticed that Brent, while soft-spoken, was growing angry and agitated. He was vague about details. At first he said he saw Scoutt on Tuesday at the house, but then said he couldn't remember. Because he still wasn't feeling well in the days leading up to Thanksgiving, he stayed away from people around the house. Every day, despite his illness, he said he fed the animals, filled the water troughs, and worked on the barns, the corral, and on the horse arena Scoutt wanted built.

By Thanksgiving Day, Brent said, he thought hiking might make him feel better, so he went alone to Horsetooth Canyon in the foothills near Fort Collins, but not with a friend as Scoutt had said. Myrick asked him if he stopped for gas or food coming or going, where witnesses, surveillance cameras, or receipts could document the trip. Brent said no. Myrick asked if he encountered anyone on the hike who might confirm he was there. Again, no. He changed the account of sharing Thanksgiving dinner with his family that he had given Myrick on the phone on Saturday. Now he said that, because of his illness, he ate alone in the garage. Friday, Brent said he did his chores, and again described hiding from the Weld County sheriff's investigators. On Saturday morning he said he felt better and drove the Jetta into Boulder to do some shopping, mostly along Pearl Street. Myrick asked what stores he went into, so they could check surveillance tapes and sales receipts. Brent said he couldn't remember which shops, and that he didn't make any purchases. The meeting with Scoutt at Barnes & Noble was random, and not the result of any phone communication between the two. "We ran into each other," he said. Brent did not explain why it took him more than eight hours to return Myrick's phone call on Saturday. After he spoke on the cell phone with Myrick, who made no mention of the killings, Brent said he tried calling family members in Alabama, but they did not return his calls. Later Saturday evening, he said, he did his chores, making no mention of his trip to the hospital emergency room for his illness. The next day, Sunday, he said he and Scoutt drove in separate cars to Fort Collins, where he went to Walmart and then met Scoutt at the feed store. Again, they drove in separate cars to Walgreens to pick up Brent's prescription. Brent told Myrick he suffered from memory losses and other physical ailments because of what his doctor said was lead and mercury poisoning.

Myrick moved on to Brent's relationship with his parents, and the young man's evasions accelerated. He said his parents were supportive, especially financially. "There's been good and there's been bad," he acknowledged. "We had our disagreements" and, in recent times "we didn't talk a lot." As for the Windsor house, he said, "they gave it to me as a gift." What about the forged check on his mother's account for $6,700? "I have no idea," Brent replied. "I have no idea." Myrick wanted to know when and why Brent had cut his hair short. Brent said he just wanted a new style, and had it cut several weeks earlier at a little shop in Windsor. With the one-hour interview concluded, Brent agreed to Myrick's request to provide DNA samples and his fingerprints—but only after first consulting with Scoutt.

Then, apparently after some informal conversation with the tape recorder off, Myrick turned the machine back on and resumed the interview. The detective headed in a different direction, pressing Brent on the matter of his parents' wills. Brent said he knew nothing about the documents, even when Myrick suggested that his parents had rewritten their wills to exclude Scoutt if Brent Jr. predeceased Charlotte and Brent Sr. Brent said he knew nothing about it, but the question rattled him. Myrick's question was a bluff. Although a friend of Brent Sr.'s had told police that it was his intention to make this change in the couple's will in the last weeks of his life, it never happened. As Myrick continued to bait him on the subject, with the tape recorder back on, Brent said, "You're putting words in my mouth." Shifting gears, Myrick wanted to know if he was angry about a financial cutoff. On November 19, the detective said, he knew that Brent had tried to order $2,000 worth of material from Cedar Supply Fence Co. to build an arena for the three horses on the property, and that Brent's charge card was rejected because it had been canceled. Brent said that he placed the order with his parents' permission; it was to be his Christmas present in lieu of cash. Such mix-ups had taken place in the past and he paid it no notice at the time. (Myrick was unaware that Brent Sr.'s financial cutoff was not complete; on November 15, he had mailed Brent Jr.'s regular allowance check for $425.) Myrick and Jurkofsky returned to the main issue—where Brent was Thanksgiving week. Myrick said that, so far, "you've given us more questions than you've had answers for." At this, Brent balked. "I just don't even feel comfortable continuing," he said. "I was here," he insisted.

After Brent's interview, which ended around 10 p.m., the officers used a ploy, saying that to ensure their safety they were required to escort Scoutt and Brent home. The investigators hoped that would allow them to get into the Windsor house without using the search warrant they had. So the officers asked and received permission to follow both Scoutt and Brent back home. When the caravan reached the house, investigators asked to come in and interview the children to verify details of what the couple had just told investigators at the station. Inside, the house looked like the well-appointed residence of an upper-middle-class family, decorated for Christmas. There were polished hardwood floors, high ceilings, a fireplace, and an open first-floor living area—sitting room, dining area. Also a spacious kitchen, complete with a food preparation island and water filter at the sink, according to photos taken at the time by police. In addition, there was a large-screen TV, a piano, and a drafting table. In the basement, Scoutt's children had painted pictures on the walls.

Hood and Harbert sat with the family in the living room, while Myrick and Jurkofsky took family members one at a time (except for Star, the youngest daughter), into a nearby, smaller room, where the first thing Myrick noticed was a Greyhound bus schedule. Family members gave varying accounts of seeing Brent Jr. around the house and property the previous week, including Thanksgiving Day, noting that his chores had been done. At one point during the interviews, Scoutt ordered Brent out of the house to feed the horses and, when he returned, she sent him to his garage bedroom for the night. Myrick asked Scoutt about the sleeping arrangements, whether she and her husband slept in the same room. "We don't have that kind of marriage," she told the detective, without elaboration. With Brent gone, Scoutt and other family members volunteered that two months earlier Brent had driven the Jetta to Montgomery, where he parked outside his parents' house, waiting to kill his father. Scoutt said Brent Jr. called her, at Charlotte's request, from the house, and she talked him out of any violence. He returned to Colorado three days later. But when Scoutt family members were interviewed separately by police in another room, there were discrepancies about Thanksgiving week, chiefly about who saw Brent when. Scoutt's adult son first said he saw Brent on the property on Tuesday, but then changed his mind and said he last saw him Monday. Only Scoutt's oldest daughter said Brent attended the family's Thanksgiving dinner. Before the detectives could interview Star,

Scoutt ordered them out of the room. "Mom had the detectives leave, and she told me what to say, that Brent was there, and that he had dinner with us," the daughter recalled. "My mom would always tell us what to say about things. That was my mom's world. We had to go along and agree with it."

After Scoutt's children, the detectives interviewed Deny Caballero, the older daughter's ex-boyfriend who was living at the Windsor house, and who considered Scoutt his foster mother. Caballero's interview began with the young man giving the investigators monosyllabic answers, according to the transcript. He said he worked full-time that week as a quality-control inspector at Parkway Products in Loveland, and attended community college classes two evenings a week. He said he did not see Brent between Monday and Sunday. Toward the end of the interview, Caballero made reference to Brent's occasional propensity for violence. "Brent's a different character," he said cryptically. What did that mean? Myrick asked. "I shouldn't," Caballero replied. "I just don't want my mom to hear anything." Tension had been building between Brent and his parents in recent months, Caballero confided. As the interview ended, Caballero stood up and whispered to Myrick that he didn't feel free to speak, so the detective quietly slipped him a business card and said he would call. Before leaving, the officers told the family that if they felt Brent was a danger to himself or others, the deputies would move them to a motel for the night. Myrick asked if they would consider asking for Brent to undergo an emergency psychiatric examination. No one in the house took either offer.

In their nightly conference call debriefing with Montgomery, Myrick and Jurkofsky informed their colleagues about the fresh cut on Brent's forehead and suggested his blood residue might be found at the murder scene. (Investigators checked the bathroom pipes and drains at the Hull Street house for traces of blood, but recovered nothing usable.) For their part, Montgomery police had been equally busy. At 3 p.m. Monday, Corporal E. E. Howton faxed a form to the Department of Forensic Sciences, releasing the bodies of Brent Sr. and Charlotte to the Turner Funeral Home in Luverne. At 3:40 p.m., about the time Myrick was interviewing Scoutt in Colorado, Montgomery police were notified that the stolen Jaguar had been found more than seven hundred miles away by Oklahoma state police. It was parked outside Tulsa, on a grassy shoulder near an Indian reservation, the keys in the ignition. A property caretaker in an industrial area found the car and, after going through the interior, flagged down a passing police car. Inside were two bags of Charlotte's jewelry, mostly costume. By this time, given the prominence of the victims, and the intimate brutality of the crime, there was extensive media interest beyond Alabama, where newspapers and local television outlets in Montgomery, Mobile, and Birmingham were already covering the murders.

On Monday night, the case was the subject of a report on Fox News' "On the Record with Greta van Susteren." Van Susteren identified the couple's son Brent Jr., of Greeley, Colorado, as "not a suspect but a person of interest," and asked Montgomery police spokesman Thornton how the son was located. "We sent two detectives out to Weld County, Colorado," he told her, where they joined forces with four investigators in the sheriff's office. "They went out with our officers and located him at a work site," an oil drilling company, although that had not been the case. At the time of the Fox interview, Thornton said, Brent was being questioned at the police station. Van Susteren turned her attention to the Springfords' Jaguar. Thornton told her that the car had been located that day in Oklahoma, and that investigators were trying to determine whether anyone in the area could remember seeing the car's driver. At this point, police had made no public connection between Brent Jr. and the car. No one, Thornton said, could place Brent Jr. in Alabama over Thanksgiving weekend. On her show two days later, Van Susteren displayed Brent's photo and asked any viewers who might have seen the young man, either in Alabama or in Oklahoma—or between—to contact the Montgomery Police Department.

: 11

Closing In

Myrick and Jurkofsky didn't get back to their Denver hotel room until 2 a.m. on Tuesday, November 30. Two hours later, at 4:30 that morning, Caroline Scoutt called Vicki Harbert, the Weld County deputy, at home. As Brent's wife, Scoutt could not be compelled to testify or give evidence against him. Yet she volunteered to the deputy that soon after the investigators left her house following the Monday night interview, Brent had come into the kitchen to tell her that he might have killed his parents. Scoutt said that just after midnight Brent Jr. had left the house, seeking medical treatment for mental illness. He had driven to Mountain Crest Behavioral Health Clinic in Fort Collins, where he had been treated before. Mountain Crest had no beds available, so Brent was sent by ambulance to Poudre Valley Hospital, an affiliated facility, for evaluation at the emergency room. Scoutt also revealed to Harbert the contents of Brent's privileged intake statement at Poudre Valley, initially unavailable to police investigators. Brent told a hospital staff interviewer that he was mentally ill, that he had been off his medication for three to four months, and that he had heard voices and saw disturbing images. In the statement, he told the psychiatrist that he thought "he could have killed his parents, but isn't sure." The doctor asked Scoutt, who called the hospital hourly, if she thought he was capable of murder, and she said yes. Poudre Valley doctors scheduled Brent for transfer to another affiliated psychiatric facility, Centennial Peaks, in the town of Louisville, outside Boulder.

Myrick and Jurkofsky left their hotel room at 7 a.m. and were on the road to Greeley when Harbert called with the news about Brent Jr. "We couldn't believe it," Myrick recalled. Jurkofsky notified Montgomery of the development and said he would do all he could to pursue the discrepancies

117

between what Brent, Scoutt, and the children had told them the day before in Windsor. The two detectives immediately detoured to Mountain Crest. There, hospital officials confirmed to them that Brent had been preliminarily evaluated and involuntarily committed for seventy-two hours. Then, for lack of a bed, he was transported to Poudre Valley Hospital's emergency room. While Mountain Crest officials refused the detectives' request to turn over the incriminating intake statement without a court order, they did agree to hold Brent at Poudre Valley until Myrick and the others could get there. Myrick's first thought was, "If he's there, there's no way we can get to him." But just after noon Myrick did find Brent in an emergency ward room, lying in the dark, on a gurney. Brent had been given five milligrams of the anti-psychotic Haldol and hadn't slept for more than twenty-four hours. Yet when Myrick called his name the young man immediately sat up. The detective turned on the lights and pressed him for details of what happened in Montgomery, making no reference to Brent's Miranda rights against self-incrimination. Nonetheless, Brent was clear-headed enough to refuse to speak with the detective, saying he felt crowded and needed his space. He asked a nurse to find a yellow Post-It in his pack, which he handed to Myrick. On it was the word "attorney," with the name and phone number of Daniel Quinn, Scoutt's lawyer. Meantime, Harbert spoke with a Mountain Crest nurse about the intake statement, sensing "she was dying to talk to me." The nurse urged the investigator to get a court order that would allow her to turn over the statement. Quinn returned Brent's call, telling him not to say anything, and Myrick left. When hospital officials rebuffed a second request for Brent's medical records, county prosecutors filed a court order for copies. They also checked out Brent's Jetta, which was parked in the Mountain Crest Hospital parking lot. Through the windows they saw a marked atlas and other papers that led them to file another order to impound and search his car. Both motions were granted.

Later that morning, Brent was transferred to Centennial Peaks, a low-slung brick complex on a gentle rise at the edge of some open fields in Louisville. Interviewed by admitting hospital staff, one of the first things he said was, "I want to be watched by doctors. I do not want to go to jail." The admitting psychiatrist, Dr. Frank Guerra, noted that "the patient's affect was sad. He said that if he found out that he did in fact hurt his parents he would want to die." On that basis, he was committed because he was considered a danger to himself. Guerra ordered a battery of tests, some of which proved revelatory. A blood test indicated that, contrary to what his nutritionist doctor had supposedly found in a urine test, Brent's levels of lead and mercury were in the normal range. Lab tests further revealed that he had no gastric infection. Guerra wondered if the expensive herbal supplements his nutritionist had ordered might actually be the cause of the diarrhea that was torturing him, sending him to the bathroom up to a dozen times a day. A drug screen revealed that Brent tested positive for opiates, which was frankly puzzling, an anomaly that was never explained, although it was cited later by prosecutors. Despite his sister Robin's suspicions, Brent's friends believed he had not used drugs recreationally for years, and when he did it was marijuana. The psychiatrist put Brent back on lithium and prescribed a vegetarian diet. To protect Brent and his legal rights, the doctor placed him on constant watch in the hospital's Intensive Treatment Unit.

With Harbert and other sheriff's officers, investigators then executed the search warrant for the Windsor house. In daylight, they saw that—incongruously for the upscale neighborhood—the windows flanking the front door were barred. There was snow on the ground, and the officers could see black cables trailing from the two pole-mounted "birdhouses" on either side of the front path, powering the surveillance cameras. On the roof were two small satellite dishes. Again, only the Scoutt children were home when police arrived. So they ordered the children outside and searched the house, except for Scoutt's locked master bedroom, office and personal storage area. As the deputies went through the house for the next four hours, shadowed by Myrick and Jurkofsky, they noticed how much *stuff* there was, much of it, they assumed, paid for by the Springfords. The children's bedrooms were packed with furniture, rugs, computers, toys, games, flat-screen TVs, books. Closets overflowed with clothes—some still in their original packaging. "It was like a Walmart," Harbert recalled. There were piles of stuffed animals in the younger daughter's room. In the basement was a hockey game table. A full-sized, body punching bag hung from the ceiling, and there was a standard-sized jukebox.

When Scoutt arrived an hour into the search she repeated to Myrick what she had told Harbert earlier, about Brent's incriminating revelations in the kitchen and, later, at the hospital. She unlocked her rooms, where investigators found and photographed a six-foot, eleven-shelf bookcase with hundreds of bottles of vitamins and supplements—which seemed vastly more than needed for one family's personal use. They also found phone records, which confirmed that there had been very little communication with the Springfords in recent months.

Finally, Myrick examined the adjoining garage. In a corner was Brent's sleeping area, a windowless, fifteen-by-fifteen-foot space, defined by eight-foot tall sheetrock walls that reached the ceiling. It was cold, and more than anything it reminded Myrick of a prison cell. A twin bed was along one wall, with a black-and-white Peruvian knit hat lying on it—which they seized. At the foot was a makeshift night table—a black, metal, two-drawer file cabinet containing Brent's journals. On top were a lamp and a clock radio and, under his mattress, two framed, family photos—one of Brent as a child and another of Brent with his father. There was also an old dresser, and a decrepit desk and chair. On the bookshelf was a stuffed Wile E. Coyote doll, a red spiral notebook with "The Power of NOW" handwritten on the cover, and a worn, paperback copy of Jane Roberts's *Seth Speaks*. Investigators found an unopened letter, in his sister Robin's handwriting, postmarked from her suburb of Homewood, outside Birmingham. Just outside the sleeping enclosure, in the garage, was a small, primitive kitchen area with a hot plate and coffee maker, small range and refrigerator, microwave oven and a pipe rack for hanging clothes. Brent's toothbrushes and pens were stored in empty food cans. In addition to a tabletop audio system, there was a space heater.

On Wednesday, December 1, investigators kept an appointment with Deny Caballero at Front Range Community College in Fort Collins where the twenty-year-old was a student. Caballero confirmed to investigators that he felt unable to speak freely when they came to the house, fearing that Brent or Scoutt might hear him. He gave officers a recorded statement that he believed Brent was capable of violent behavior because of incidents he had been involved in and witnessed around the house. These included a fight with him over moving Brent's furniture into the garage, and Brent's tantrums while speaking the phone with his father, usually about money. Caballero said that he, not Brent, had done Brent's chores around the house Thanksgiving week.

Myrick and Jurkofsky were careful to keep their colleagues and superiors back home in the loop, by now sometimes twice a day. There was another evening conference call involving both Alabama and Colorado investigators. "They didn't leave us alone," Myrick said of his superiors. "There was pressure to find out where Brent was at the time of the killings." At the same time, they were looking closely at Scoutt's possible role in the murders. Myrick explained that Scoutt, like Brent—whom police now referred to as "the suspect"—was well aware of the Springfords' financial cutoff threat. In addition, he wrote in his case notes, it "appeared that she could manipulate the suspect to some degree." Later that day, Montgomery police, still referring to Brent as the sole "person of interest" in the case, released photos of Brent, with long hair and shorn, along with a picture of the Jaguar, in hopes that someone between Montgomery and Tulsa had seen them together.

While investigators were interviewing Caballero and Scoutt, Brent was taking actions that in retrospect seemed the result of either panic or cold calculation. From Centennial Peaks Hospital, he made several calls to Montgomery television stations. He told hospital staff that he was contacting the media "to tell the truth and clear my name." Brent's statement, vigorously denying any role in his parents' murders, aired on WSFA-Channel 12, the NBC affiliate, and WAKA-Channel 8, the CBS affiliate. In the statement, he said he was responding to speculation about him on the local news and on the Internet. He explained that after a full day's work the previous Monday and what he described as a grueling interview with Alabama detectives, he had checked himself into Centennial Peaks, suffering from exhaustion, depression, bipolar disorder, and delusions. "I was crying and could not handle being in my body anymore," he said, but he did not explain what had sparked those feelings. Brent spent a good portion of this first statement talking about his medical condition: toxic lead and arsenic poisoning, and treatment for bipolar and other disorders by four psychiatrists. Then he listed the medications he was taking.

Brent said that because family members did not respond to his phone calls, he did not learn of his parents' memorial service at St. John's Episcopal Church until that Wednesday, when the service was over. "Apparently my family did not want me to come," he told the stations' viewers. "I would have been there even if I would have had to have medical doctors at my side, if only I would have known." The murders, he said, left him devastated. "I was crying, very badly shaken and terribly sad to hear the news. I loved my mother and father and always have. I can't imagine anything but loving them." Brent said the shock of learning about the murders, combined with his emotional and psychological problems complicated his ability to answer detectives' questions when they interviewed him the previous Monday. In all of his subsequent calls to the media, comments, and written statements that he insisted on reading aloud on the air, Brent repeatedly denied involvement in his parents' deaths. "I don't know what this is about. I can't believe this is happening to me. . . . I absolutely did not commit this atrocity. It is utterly unthinkable to me." Although at times he was reading, he insisted that "This is completely myself, my own thoughts."

In one of his calls to the TV stations, Brent claimed that Montgomery detectives communicated "threats" from his sister Robin that she intended to carry through with their parents' intention to sell the Windsor house. Thus, in a subsequent written statement he read to the stations on Sunday, December 5, Brent responded directly:

> Robin, why are you so full of hate and want to take away the only thing that Mom and Dad gave me, which is the house, and to evict the people who are taking care of the place and the animals that are living there? Robin, you have everything. You have Dad's businesses. You have both houses, the lake house and Dad and Mom's house and your house that Mom and Dad gave you. You have all of the money, which is millions. I don't want any of that. I don't want to fight for anything. I've never been greedy like you. I don't want them. All I want is to be able to get well from my mental illness and detox from the lead poisoning, and to keep the house that my dad and mom bought for me.

In addition to the seeming inappropriateness of raising money and property issues so soon after the murders, other parts of what Brent had to say to Robin would do him no good back home. He went after the Alabama governor, who would be responsible for requesting his extradition to Montgomery; the police investigating the case; the prosecutor whose decision it would be to indict him; and, implicitly, prospective jurors who might one day decide his fate. "Even if you and the Alabama police and the mayor and the governor and the sheriff all find a way to pin this on me, I would still like for the house to be given to me, for me to decide what to do with it. . . . Anything that happens to me in Alabama," Brent told the television audience, "will be tainted with bias and conflict of interest," an apparent allusion to his parents' social position. In the statement, he repeated that he was innocent of the crime:

> It is unfair for you to even think that I had a motive, because Mom and Dad sent me a check every week and paid my medical, gave me a credit card, and had contractors do things for the house. . . . Do you have any compassion for the suffering I'm going through as well? You probably think that I did this horrible thing. . . . Robin, I want you to know that I absolutely did not commit this atrocity. It is utterly unthinkable to me.

The statements fueled Internet discussion of the case that had been going on for days and would continue for weeks. Posters found it odd that Brent would list his ailments in his statements and talk about the disposition of his house. Scoutt was also a topic of interest, with one writer on the social media site observing, "She apparently was just as nuts as he was."

Back in Colorado, Brent's behavior, particularly his statements to the media, was concerning to hospital staff. He spent much of his time at the desk in his room, drafting faxes, and then would come to the nurses' station to dispatch them and make his calls. In consultation with his doctors, nurses instituted a restrictive regimen. Brent could make just three calls during the day shift, and three during the night shift, but only to doctors, family members, and his attorney. He was limited to one fax a day. All numbers would have to be dialed by nurses from an approved list. One nurse observed something else when Scoutt came to see Brent. In the nurse's log, she wrote:

Wife visited patient. Patient responded in childlike manner to wife upon leaving. 'Tell them about the female you see that's not really there, and report what's going on in your head.' Patient looking down says, 'Yes, I will.' Appeared contrite with wife."

Brent assigned Scoutt his power of attorney after receiving copies of his parents' wills from Montgomery. He also asked Sundance State Bank in Wyoming to take his name off the checking account he shared with Scoutt, perhaps to avoid its seizure. Brent also wrote letters to Scoutt's children and Deny Caballero, apologizing for the trouble he had caused them in the previous week, from the police search to the media scrutiny

I pray with every fiber of my being for this dark storm to blow past quickly and for your lives to return to normal without any further negativity. I firmly believe that we will be able to not only continue living at the house but to own it. . . . I *very, very* much look forward to a happy Christmas with you all at our house.

About the time Brent was reaching out to the media, Scoutt called Montgomery Detective Mike Myrick to inform him of what Brent was doing by fax and by phone, telling the detective that she wanted to stay in touch and remain cooperative. When investigators returned Scoutt's call the next morning and requested a second interview she agreed, on condition that she could bring her lawyer, Daniel Quinn. She emphasized that he did not also represent Brent. In a transcript of that interview, and another several days later, she said she was concerned that she might be criminally charged. Montgomery and Weld County officers noted that she "suddenly remembered" and "started to remember" a much different account than the one she had given previously. She now said that on Monday, November 22, Brent came to her room around 8:30 p.m. and told her his Jetta wouldn't start. He asked her for a ride to Fort Collins so he could meet a friend from work at the Whole Foods market. When the friend didn't appear, Brent changed his mind and asked her to drive to the Starbucks in the Old Town section. Challenged on certain points by investigators, she changed details, claiming the investigators' questions had "jarred her memory." She insisted that, at Brent's direction, she had pulled into the bus station loading zone around 10 p.m. to drop him off. She recalled that the bus station appeared locked when Brent went to the door and that someone might have been vacuuming inside. Scoutt then backtracked, insisting that she had taken Brent to the *train* station.

Investigators were sure she was lying. They knew her first version was correct—that she had taken him to the bus station. Between the two Scoutt interviews, Myrick and Weld County Deputy Vicki Harbert had been able to screen recovered bus station tapes from stations from Colorado to Montgomery. A man fitting Brent's description, with long hair and a mustache, carrying a backpack and a white plastic grocery bag, was seen near the Fort Collins Greyhound station early on the morning of Tuesday, November 23, and finding the door locked. Later, he was seen getting out of the bed of a parked Jeep pickup—owned by the proprietor of a nearby bar—close to the station, and boarding a bus for Denver. But details of Scoutt's earlier account were also inconsistent with the tapes. Investigators then informed Scoutt that surveillance footage showed no sign of her Yukon SUV in the loading zone at that time, which would have enabled her to describe what was going on in the station. The first sight of Brent on the tape wasn't until after midnight. Similarly, there was no sign of the vacuuming she described inside the terminal.

Scoutt insisted she hadn't meant to be evasive in her previous conversation with Myrick, and she offered new details. When she dropped Brent off, she confirmed that he was wearing a dingy green jacket, heavy work boots, had a blue-green Mudd-brand backpack, and was carrying a white grocery bag of food. Brent told Caroline he would be back to do his chores Tuesday morning. But since that Monday night, November 22, she now said, Scoutt had not seen him again until the following Saturday evening, November 27. But Scoutt stuck with her story that Brent already had the Jetta in Boulder when he called her on Saturday. "I know he had that car," she told them. However, when investigators said that her account was impossible, that the Jetta had been spotted at the Windsor house on Friday and early Saturday by Weld County deputies, she was flummoxed. "Brent had the Jetta with him. I don't know. That's all I can tell you. I didn't go to pick him up anywhere. He had that Jetta with him. I don't know what to tell you all." She said she had no explanation for how the Jetta, which she said wouldn't start earlier in the week, had gotten fixed enough to get to Boulder. "I don't know how Brent got to Boulder," she said. Myrick was frustrated by the interview, since Scoutt would reveal only a portion of what she knew, claiming a poor memory. She maintained she had nothing to do with Brent's haircut.

Meanwhile, efforts around the country to locate other bus station surveillance tapes were bearing fruit. At the Denver station, Brent was seen buying a ticket under the name of "Terry Chance"—with cash—to Nashville, Tennessee, for $157 (where police would later identify him on tape). The next day, under the same name, he bought a ticket from Nashville to Montgomery for $72, arriving there at 5:15 p.m. on Wednesday, November 24. On the tape from the Montgomery station, a young, long-haired man is seen arriving wearing a gray hoodie, with a pack and carrying a dark jacket. His face is partially obscured, but he resembles Brent. On the Friday after the killings, the same man is seen in Tulsa buying a bus ticket to Denver for $72.50. Apparently after some bus changes, he is seen arriving in Denver at midday on Saturday, November 27, although now wearing different clothes.

All of this raised another question. If Brent had committed the murders, he might have taken enough money from his family's ransacked house to return to Colorado. But where did he get the $230 he paid for bus fare to get there? Brent's credit card had been canceled by his father weeks before. The week before the murders, Brent had phoned his mother to say he didn't have enough money to feed his family, according to what Charlotte's friend, Judge Sally Greenhaw, had told police. The most likely source would have been Caroline Scoutt, the Windsor family member in charge of finances. If she did give him the $230, what did she think it was for, and where did she think the bus was taking him?

There was more. Police believed Scoutt probably picked Brent up at the bus station in Denver Saturday, when he arrived from Tulsa, after abandoning the Jaguar. Both his ticket receipt and surveillance footage placed him at the Denver station around midday. There were no scheduled Greyhound buses that would have gotten him to Boulder in time for him to call Scoutt from the mall bookstore when both said he did. "I met him, I didn't pick him up," she told the investigators. She was adamant that Brent called her from the Barnes & Noble at the Pearl Street Mall. Scoutt repeated that, after doing her own Christmas shopping, she met Brent at the bookstore and gave him his cell phone. Scoutt told investigators she noticed Brent was dressed differently from the last time she had seen him. He had the same, thigh-length, green jacket, but now he was wearing a new flannel shirt—orange and black, with a small print—and loafers, rather than boots. She said she told him about Myrick's phone message, but he insisted on first shopping nearby at Target. They went in separate cars, she said, and at the store he bought socks, underwear, knit caps, and steel-toed work boots, which cost $200. He only had $130 in cash, so Scoutt had to write a check for the difference. Next he went with her to Whole Foods for groceries.

Without explaining why they needed two cars, Scoutt said that Brent followed her in the Jetta toward Longmont and Fort Collins to have dinner, either at Red Lobster or Tim's Thai, a restaurant where Scoutt liked the soup. At one point on State Highway 119, she said, it was snowing heavily. Brent flashed his lights and honked his horn until she pulled onto the shoulder. He got out of the Jetta and into the back seat of her Yukon—the passenger seat was full of her packages. She reminded him to return Myrick's call on his cell phone, which he did but cut the call off because he said the snowstorm was interfering with his reception. Scoutt said she wouldn't let him use her cell because he had a bad cold, and she didn't want his germs, although Myrick remembered that Brent's call had come from Scoutt's phone. Soon, however, they turned back because of the snowstorm. Scoutt dropped him off at his Jetta and they drove home toward Windsor. Because of his cold, Brent wanted to go to an urgent care clinic near the house before it got too late. However, Scoutt's oldest daughter called from the Safeway supermarket where she worked to say she was low on gas and didn't have any money. So Brent detoured to the store, gave her five dollars, and followed her to the gas station. By this time, his only option for getting medical care was the emergency room at Poudre Valley Hospital in Fort Collins.

Exasperated by Scoutt's story, by turns illogical and teeming with inconsistencies, the investigators again accused her of trying to protect her husband. At this point, Quinn, her lawyer, interrupted, threatening to cut off the interview. More sparring followed, including another round about the Jetta, and at one point Scoutt said, "You're trying to trick me." When the interview ended, police asked to fingerprint Scoutt, and she agreed. Vicki Harbert called Scoutt after the interview to say police wanted to speak to her again to "clarify" some of her earlier statements. In her third interview, and second with Quinn by her side, on December 2, Scoutt changed her story about Brent meeting her that Saturday. She suddenly went vague and backed off her earlier version that Brent was driving the Jetta in Boulder—now saying he could have been in another car.

Fueled initially by Brent's broadcast statements, the media feeding frenzy was accelerating, with reporters from Colorado and Alabama contributing a barrage of information, some accurate, some not. Scoutt and Brent were said to have been spotted at a local air charter company in Colorado or Wyoming. Sources close to the investigation had told a Montgomery TV reporter that Brent had not yet been arrested because of conflicting statements given to them by Caroline Scoutt, whom they were now describing as Brent's common-law wife. Reporters confirmed from Brent's Windsor neighbors that, while they understood that he did have a history of bipolar disorder, among other mental illnesses, the young man was a quiet person. They said he gave different accounts of who he was, sometimes saying he was a hired hand.

By contrast, they volunteered that the woman he was living with, who sometimes used Scoutt-Springford as a last name, was a different story. "One time she'll claim to be married, another time she says they've never been married," Teresa Brunner, a neighbor, told reporters. The neighbors repeatedly clashed with the couple, once over a fence Brent built around the house that blocked passage to communal neighborhood property. "They both come off as totally insane," Brunner told investigators. In addition to their marital status, there was confusion about who actually owned the house. "As far as they led us to believe, she owns the house," Brunner said. Later, another neighbor told a defense investigator that Scoutt had told her, "When his parents die, this house will be ours." Finally, there was a factual development to report. Montgomery Police spokesman Huey Thornton revealed that Detective Guy Naquin had requested and screened surveillance tapes from the Montgomery bus station, showing a figure resembling Brent arriving Wednesday evening, November 24.

In Montgomery, pressure on the police was growing, especially among the Springfords' skittish neighbors. "It certainly would make everyone here feel a lot better" if an arrest were made, John Turner told the *Advertiser,* volunteering that neither he nor his wife had had a good night's sleep since the killings. "I guess I can understand why they are taking their time, but it bothers me that they haven't arrested their only suspect. Who's to say that he won't get out of the hospital and then decide to disappear?" Asked by reporters if Brent was the only suspect in the killings, Major J. C. West, head of the Montgomery Police Investigations Division, was typically circumspect: "We're exhausting all leads at this time." At a press conference, Mayor Bobby Bright echoed the officer: "We have other leads we are still pursuing." West was referring to two black men, a handyman and a gardener who worked at the Springfords' houses and had been employed at the Luverne Pepsi plant. The men weren't eliminated as suspects for more than a week. "It's tragic as mayor of this city to see something like this happen," Bright said. At the same time, "we feel good about what we've done. We were looking not only at an arrest, but we're looking at long term, a conviction." He said the murder weapon was recovered, but he wouldn't identify it further. Around the capital, however, more details of the killings were beginning to leak out, chiefly that Brent's parents had been bludgeoned with a mattock handle about 6:30 p.m. on Thanksgiving.

Arrest

Developments were also accelerating in Colorado. Vicki Harbert and Mike Myrick served a court order to officials at Centennial Peaks Hospital in the Denver suburb of Louisville for Brent's records, including the intake report in which he talked about "blood everywhere" at his parents' home. The Jetta was towed from the Mountain Crest parking lot to the police evidence bay in the town of Lucerne and searched (it would later be turned over to Scoutt, whose name was on the title). By Tuesday, December 7, Centennial Peaks staff noted that Brent was clear-headed enough to seek legal counsel both in Colorado and Alabama. On Wednesday, hospital officials informed Myrick that they would release Brent only to long-term care or to law enforcement. At 11 p.m. on Wednesday night, Myrick received two faxed warrants for Brent's arrest for fugitive flight, a common temporary holding charge. Just after midnight, led by Louisville Police Sergeant Bob Olin and two other uniformed officers in two city patrol cars, Myrick and Harbert went to Centennial Peaks. They took Brent into custody without incident, cuffing him and putting him in the back seat of one of the squad cars, with two uniformed officers in the front seat. The vehicle's audio/visual system recorded Brent talking to himself in the back seat, although the officers could not make out what he was saying. At the time of his arrest, Brent was being administered four medications: Eskalith CR, Risperdal, Provigil, and Zyprexa. Myrick and Jurkofsky followed in their rental car.

Normally, a fugitive arrested in Louisville, a town of eighteen thousand population, on an out-of-state warrant at that time of night would be taken directly to the Boulder County Jail. Instead the caravan deviated from procedure and detoured a few miles away to Louisville's new police station. When they arrived, Myrick advised Brent of his Miranda rights, orally and in writing, which the young man waived. Myrick and Harbert both signed the waiver. Most of the building's investigative division was secured for the night, and the uniformed officers did not have access. So they found a large room with several cubicles and an adjoining room with a round table used as a break/eating area. There, a makeshift interrogation area was put together using two mobile cubicle dividers arranged against the wall. It was so cramped, with Myrick, Bryan Jurkofsky, and Brent sitting at the table, that Harbert had to sit on the other side of one of the dividers. Then, around 1:15 a.m. on Thursday, December 9, the interview began.

What followed, according to a taped transcript and subsequent interviews, was a harrowing but textbook example of police investigators deftly leading a sleep-deprived suspect, likely still under the influence of powerful drug, through an account of a deadly, gruesome encounter.

Jurkofsky and Myrick both knew they were taking a risk. Brent, just released from a psychiatric facility in the middle of the night, was likely still under the influence of psychotropic drugs administered at the hospital and might also be sleep-deprived. And even on his best, non-manic days, Brent's fragile ego left him vulnerable to suggestion. But the detectives, under pressure from Montgomery to clear the case, decided to roll the dice and take their chances with admissibility of the interrogation down the road. "We were concerned about the sleep, and the drugs," Myrick said later, "but he was talkative, articulate." They were collecting bus-station surveillance tapes and had plaster casts of the footprints on the Hull Street patio, yet they still had nothing substantial that tied Brent to the crime scene. "We had no other shot to go with." Myrick set his department-issued digital recorder on the table and turned it on. With no attorney present, Brent said, "Start the tape. I'll tell you what happened."

Myrick led the questioning, initially asking about Brent's movements during Thanksgiving week. Brent said that after working until 5 p.m. Monday, he packed and dressed at home, with the long green coat over a hooded sweatshirt, and put a change of clothes in his pack. He asked Scoutt to take him to the bus station in Fort Collins, insisting he did not tell her where he was going, or why. He bought his ticket for cash but didn't say where the money came from. Initially Brent said he didn't know why he bought the ticket under the name of "Terry Chance." Later in the interrogation, when Myrick returned to the subject, Brent said, "I don't like giving my name out. If they had asked for ID, well then I'd have to give them my name." He said he liked the name Terry because it sounded like "tarry," which meant to wait, and Chance because he was taking a chance in making the trip. "I wanted to take the chance . . . and just see if I can go turn things around [with my parents] because things are going downhill. And I've been going downhill. . . . It was a symbol of . . . my mission, my purpose."

Arriving in Montgomery Wednesday evening about 8 p.m., Brent said he ran two miles from the bus station to his home and climbed the backyard wall. He tried several simple code numbers on the alarm pad next to the garage doors, and one code raised an overhead door. Nonetheless, the alarm began beeping and Brent lowered the overhead and left the garage through the rear door, hiding in a backyard bamboo grove. When neighbors came with flashlights to investigate, before the patrolmen arrived, Brent climbed over a wooden side section of fence and fled a few houses down the street for several hours. During the night he returned and went to the tool shed by the pool. He used a short handsaw to cut the head off a mattock, tossing the ax head into the thick backyard foliage and then went to sleep in the pool house. About 6 p.m. Thursday, carrying the ax handle and the saw, he climbed the trellis and the pillar to the second floor, behind his sister Robin's old room. When they had lived at home, both Robin and Brent Jr. sometimes used that window to sneak in and out of the house, since it was one of the few not wired to the alarm system. Brent said he used the saw to break in a section of the window and then tossed the tool away. However, the officers prompted him to say that he left the saw on the roof nearby—where it had been found. Once inside, Brent stuffed a pillow where the glass had been, secured it with two portable speakers, and went to his mother's dressing area in the master bedroom.

Jurkofsky noticed how Brent's mood could shift suddenly during the interview, "like you flipped a switch." Brent began to tense up at this point in the interrogation, so Myrick suggested he might want some water. "I'm just a very, very fucked-up person," Brent said. "So fucked up." Myrick wanted him to say what came next, and it wasn't easy for Brent. "I was like some insane man, I just, I hit them with a stick." He said he surprised his mother when she came into the bedroom, hitting her first. "I just, um, hit her a bunch of times." He said Charlotte didn't know it was him, at least he didn't think she knew, and said he hoped she didn't recognize him. "I don't want her to know it was me." At this point, Brent said, "I just feel like I'm drugged," which may have been the literal truth. Myrick recognized a remark that could be costly, tainting the entire interview and negating Brent's waiving of his Miranda rights. He did his best to head off the damage. "Is that what you, is that what you felt at the time?" he asked, referring to the "drugged state," and then repeated it. Brent seemed to take the cue, although he didn't reply directly. "It was like a blur."

Next, he said, he hit his father, who had just come up the stairs. After striking Brent Sr., driving him to the ground, incapacitated, he used a nearby area rug to drag him across the carpet into a closet in Robin's room. Why? Myrick asked. "I don't know," Brent replied several times. "Why did I do any of it? I don't even know. . . . It's so sick, so fucked up." The detective wanted to keep Brent from crumbling entirely, so he tried encouragement. "You're doing great, you're telling us the truth."

The ploy worked.

The next thing Brent said was "I cut, cut their throats." While Myrick was running the interrogation, every now and then, Jurkofsky would ask a clarifying question. After changing into the clean clothes and loafers he had brought with him, Brent said he stuffed the blood-stained outfit he had worn into his backpack. Led by Myrick, he then described how he tore through the house and the garage, pulling out drawers in a fruitless search for cash, netting about $200 from his parents' wallets. He went downstairs, grabbed the Jaguar keys off the kitchen counter and locked the back door behind him, but made no mention of throwing the dead bolt. He went into the garage, ransacked his father's office area, and took off in the Jaguar, first north to Birmingham, stopping for gas in northern Alabama, then west to Mississippi, Memphis, and Little Rock, where he stopped again for fuel. As he drove, he threw out the window some of the clothes, including his boots and the gloves he had bought on the bus journey east. The rest of the clothes he tossed into a dumpster during the drive, probably in Mississippi, he said. (While police had found two identifiable footprints outside the bedroom window at the murder scene, without Brent's boots they were of no value.) Along the way, Myrick prompted him to remember buying a straw hat that caught his fancy at a gas station, which he left with the Jaguar outside Tulsa. There were no fingerprints on the car, and just one of Brent's at the Hull Street house, but no way to date it.

At this point, Myrick and Jurkofsky showed Brent a photo of the Jaguar, where it was found, and another of the straw hat he bought on the way. Brent said he used the money he had taken from his parents to buy gas and a bus ticket, also in the name of Terry Chance, from Tulsa to Denver, and then another to Boulder. There, Brent said, his memory became unclear, perhaps because at this point Scoutt became part of the story, and Brent wasn't sure what she had told Myrick previously. When the officer asked how he got from Denver to Boulder—his first potential, post-murder connection with Scoutt—he said he took a bus, but qualified his answer by adding, "It's very blurry."

Trying to keep Brent on track, Myrick turned to compliments and positive reinforcement. "You've done a fantastic job in telling us what happened, you've been very compassionate with what you've said, you've been very brave." Brent said he couldn't remember what phone he used to call Scoutt, whether it was a pay phone or a cell borrowed from someone. Brent took Myrick's suggestion that, since he had left his own cell phone at home in Windsor, that he borrowed a cell from one of his fellow bus passengers. However the contact was made, he met Scoutt at Barnes & Noble in Boulder. Brent insisted he didn't tell her where he had been or what he had done. "I didn't tell her. I didn't want to tell her. . . . I did make up stories. I told her I was on a road trip."

In any case, he made no reference to his black Jetta, saying only that Scoutt picked him up in the Yukon. Brent first said he didn't know where the Jetta was when he was gone, adding quickly that he left it at the Windsor house, opening a gap with Scoutt's statement that he had left it in Boulder. Earlier, Brent said he didn't take the Jetta because it was having a hard time starting. Now he said the reason he didn't drive his Jetta to Boulder himself was because he didn't want to leave it while he traveled. Once he returned to Colorado, Brent said that he and Scoutt went from Barnes & Noble to Target in her Yukon, with Brent sitting in the back seat, his usual spot. He corroborated his account of leaving the Windsor house later that night for the urgent-care facility. Then he detoured to give Scoutt's daughter gas money at the supermarket where she worked, before going on to the Poudre Valley Hospital emergency room. When he returned, he did his evening chores. Brent's account of the following Sunday jibed with Scoutt's. He said they went to Fort Collins to pick up the remainder of his prescription from the night before. Scoutt had more shopping to do at Target, and she needed to go to Jax Ranch and Home store for animal feed. He said the only reason he got his hair cut was because he wanted a shorter style, rather than out of concern that someone might have seen him with long hair in Montgomery or on the bus rides.

By now they had been talking for about an hour and a half.

Myrick decided it was time to double back in the narrative. Recalling that just one of Brent's fingerprints was found at the murder scene, the detective asked Brent why he brought two pair of dark gloves with him to Alabama. Only because he usually wore them in Colorado, he said. Myrick took Brent back to the previous Monday night, when Scoutt drove him to the bus station. Again, did he tell her why he wanted to go to the bus station? At first he told her he wanted to meet a friend, whom they didn't find. So, the detective asked again, no talk about Montgomery? "I just didn't want her to know," Brent said. "I just didn't want her to know. . . . Didn't want her to have anything to do with it." Myrick began to bore in on Brent. When did he decide to go to Montgomery? About a week or two before he went, around the time his credit card was cut off. Why? "I wanted to, I wanted to talk to my parents about why they're cutting me off, and why they were rejecting me," he said. It had been a long time since he had seen them.

With this, Brent launched into an entirely different account of the murders from the one he had given earlier in the interrogation, describing a wordless attack entirely upstairs, beginning with his mother. Myrick asked him if he had tried to talk to them before he attacked. Yes, Brent now said, he had. Suddenly, he began to describe a verbal confrontation, beginning downstairs in the kitchen, which he was upset to find torn up seeing the disarray as symbolic of his family. He said he then walked down the back stairs when he heard his parents come in the back entrance. The detective then led him through a more vivid and detailed version of the sequence of events. "They were really uneasy about why I was even there," Brent said. "They weren't very glad to see me . . . I said 'Mom, Dad, surprise! I'm, I'm here.'" But they weren't glad to see him. They wanted to know what he was doing there. Brent Sr. said, "What the fuck? . . . What are you doing in my house?" His mother was shocked to see him, and his father said, "You're always doing this weird shit. . . . Is this your idea of a joke or something? What'd you just break in our house?" Brent told Myrick. "They didn't even want to see me. They didn't even care. Mother was like, like Mother was trying to not be as gruff as Father because that's usually how he is." His father said, "Quite frankly, I don't even want to see you."

Myrick wanted to know how Brent felt about his parents' reception, and as he began to answer, he unraveled. "Horrible," he replied. "I mean just like, like it's over. I mean, this is a totally dead relationship. I mean I'm just, they're just going, there, there, there's no hope here. I mean they're going to just squash me out . . . totally push me out of their lives completely, and not give me any support because that's what they wanted to do." It was the withdrawal of emotional support as much as the financial support, he said, that was so devastating. Brent indicated that he anticipated a much different reception to what he felt was a last-ditch effort on his part, that his parents would tell him how much they cared about him and how glad they were to restore personal contact. "I, I, I just wanted to try to reconnect [the relationship] because it was just so obviously dying."

The argument with his father escalated, with Brent Sr. losing patience and telling his son he did not want him there. His father stormed out of the house—slamming the door—to unload the car. Brent went back upstairs and realized that his old bedroom had been turned into a storage room, essentially a large closet, with racks of clothes. It was as if he had never lived there. Standing there, he said, "I don't even know what they did with the room but it's not, it wasn't my room. . . . I mean everything, all the posters were stripped off the wall," the ones he had labored over so obsessively. "Like I was just totally dead, I didn't exist, I did not exist for them. I was a complete zero and actually a burden. . . . I felt like I had been, I was a burden for months, months before but then I knew for sure they just want me out of their life."

Then, he said, Charlotte came upstairs, followed by her husband. Brent said he feared his father was so angry he would attack him. If anything, Brent Sr. was angrier than he had been in the kitchen, and Brent Jr. thought he had been drinking. "I mean I could feel he wanted to just like hit me. . . . He wanted to, I, I didn't believe he would, but . . ."

Father confronted son: "So tell me bud, who the fuck do you think you are?" Brent Jr. tried to apologize for upsetting him, but Brent Sr. wouldn't let him finish. Charlotte came out of the bedroom and tried to calm things down. Brent had never seen his father so enraged, to full of hatred toward him. Brent told Myrick that he began to wonder how he could extricate himself from the situation. He told his father he would leave. "Obviously, you don't want me here, you don't want me in your life," Brent Jr. said. Brent Sr. replied, "You're damn right I don't want you here." When Brent Jr. said he was just a burden, Brent Sr. agreed. But there was a practical problem: Brent Jr. expected his parents to buy his bus ticket back to Colorado, and he had no money.

In the meantime, Brent Sr. got in Brent Jr.'s face, the son said. "Then I started wondering, well, God, maybe he is going to hit me," even though Brent Jr. told Myrick that he could not recall ever being hit by his father before. "He said, 'Don't fuck with me, leave us the fuck alone. The least you could have done was called and asked if we wanted you to come. . . . Don't, don't ever just show up in my house again.'" In this version, after his father went back downstairs, Brent said he retrieved the ax handle outside Robin's bedroom, where he had left it on the windowsill, in order to defend himself from his father's expected fury.

Approaching the two-hour mark in the interrogation, Brent Jr. was almost in a trance, manic in his reliving the event. His father was about to make a final break, and end all support:

> I mean I just kept thinking I don't, I don't even want to live this life with them, with them here. I mean I, I just, we can't both be here. This doesn't

work, me having parents, especially a father who hates me and mother, I
know she, I've, I was dead in her eyes too. She wasn't quite—no, she was—she
was turning more and more like him. She was, she was turning more and
more like him on the phone. . . . She used to always come to my rescue. . . .
It was just, they were like, they were more like one person. . . . They were
one person against me.

By contrast, Brent said, his parents had deified his sister Robin—whose
bedroom was preserved as she had left it—and her husband Greg, the latter
replacing Brent in his father's eyes as the ideal son.

And here I am . . . the fuckup, yeah, the black sheep, whatever. But they
did not want me around. . . . I knew they were going to do everything they
could short of killing me . . . severing all connection. . . . I was totally in a
delusional state. . . . I mean, I was totally insane. . . . All I could think of
was just self-preservation.

Myrick, uncomfortable with the direction Brent was taking, toward
insanity and delusion, steered the conversation back to the concrete, asking
Brent if it wasn't his father's threat to sell the Windsor house that had set off
the violence. Brent agreed—though at that point he might have acquiesced
to any suggestion. Prompted by Myrick, Brent recalled his father saying,
"How about I just sell the house out from under you? . . . Die and go to hell."
The detective asked Brent what was going through his mind at this point:

Everything. I was just like, you know, it's either now, I mean, like I kept
thinking what, that's, that's insane though, thinking about killing your parents.
But that's what they want to do to you too. I mean emotionally, financially,
as far as any kind of relationship goes. I just said he's going to sell the house,
I know for sure he's going to sell it, because he doesn't care about Caroline
and the kids. Neither of them cared anything about them, they were just
like, dumb lonely Indians to them.

In this version, Brent said he killed his father first, waiting just inside

Robin's room with the ax handle until Brent Sr. reached the top of the back stairs. "I thought, this is insane but either you do it now, you're going to have the house, or the house is going to be sold. Caroline and the kids. . . ." Now Brent Jr. felt his father's anger and hatred toward him was at the "absolute maximum." As his father walked past the doorway of Robin's room, Brent Jr. stepped out and struck him several times without warning. "It was a part of me that said, you, you have to, you have to protect your own family. . . . Caroline and the kids." Charlotte, in the master bathroom, evidently didn't hear the attack on her husband. Brent ran into the room and struck her repeatedly. Again, Myrick asked him what he was thinking at the time. Brent said he was convinced his Colorado family:

> . . . was going to be evicted and the house is going to be sold and [my father] is going to make a profit off of it because that's what, that's how he thinks about everything. Me, I, I am a source of profit for him. He takes me off his taxes every year and for years he took me off as being in school. I wasn't even in school, and the house which he still had the deed, he still owned it. He said that he, the reason for that is so that he could take the house off his taxes. . . .
>
> That's how it always was and I knew he would never, he's never going to give me the house. At that point I knew he was never going give me the house and he doesn't want me in his life, so he's going to sell the house. So I, I knew it would probably be horrible consequences but I just, I mean I just sacrificed myself. . . . It's just, thoughts were racing around a thousand miles an hour.

Myrick pressed Brent for more details of the killings. When he hit his mother, he said, "she went down and I didn't think she was going anywhere." Yet he was concerned that his father might get up again, "getting his gun and shooting me." So he ran back to where Brent Sr. was lying and finding him still breathing, hit him again with the ax handle. To be sure, Brent ran downstairs and came back with a kitchen knife. "He just kept breathing, and I didn't want him to suffer," so he cut his father's throat. "I just didn't want him in my life. I mean I just, I wanted to be free from this war, this, this enslavement that he was doing to me."

Charlotte was not dead and managed to crawl to the bedroom door and started to close it. Brent Jr. returned and cut her throat as well. Brent said he wished he hadn't killed his parents but that at the time he saw it as his only option. "If not, if I had just laughed and begged Mother for money to get on the bus, then I'm sure I could have begged and pleaded and they would have given me money just to get me out of there, come back home." However, if he had taken that course, "Life would have just fallen apart, that's how I saw it then. I didn't want to go that way. I didn't want to let that house be sold."

Myrick returned one more time to Scoutt's possible role in the killings. Did she or any of the children know where he was going or what he intended to do? "No. . . . I wanted it to be a surprise. . . . I wanted to call Caroline from with some good news about a reconciliation."

Myrick moved in for answers that could send Brent to Death Row, on the issues of premeditation and, by implication, mental competence: "Did you go to Montgomery for the purpose and with the intent of killing your parents?" Brent had the presence of mind to reply unambiguously: "No, I did not. I, I thought for sure if I just show up, surprise them, they'd be glad to see me." In the past, he said, his face-to-face visits in Alabama and in Wyoming were often positive events. "While they were there it was just like magic." It was only after he left that "it was right back in the same games again, and the control." Myrick returned to the ax handle, why Brent cut the head off and brought it into the house. "I didn't trust Father," Brent said. "I thought I may need to defend myself. I don't want to fight him and he's a, he, he was a fighter. I'm not. . . . He was a trained fighter," with a black belt in karate. Brent repeated that he thought his father might react harshly to the visit, and that in fact his father did demonstrate a depth of aversion to his son. Brent wanted to have some protection in case his father "came in drunk and want, wanted to slap me around or threaten me. . . . So I just left it on the windowsill."

Around 4 a.m., as the interrogation neared an end, Myrick felt that Brent had "tied up our loose ends, and corroborated what we thought." He asked Brent if there was anything he wanted to add to his statement. "I just pray to God that I can spend the rest of my life in a mental institution," he replied. It was only then, in the pre-dawn hours, that Brent was driven to the Boulder County Jail, where he was processed and booked on the temporary charge of flight to avoid prosecution. On the admitting form filled out by Louisville Officer Christina Muzzipapa there is a section marked, "Have you seen any indication that the arrestee suffers from any mental illness?" It was left blank. Jail officials, observing Brent's condition, nonetheless ordered a preliminary psychiatric screening. Following the examination, officials reported that morning that Brent's affect was "flat" and that he was unable to make eye contact.

Myrick and Jurkofsky remained unsure about exactly what happened at Hull Street, since both of Brent's accounts were consistent with physical evidence at the scene. One account jibed with his later version, that he greeted his parents when they entered the kitchen, that harsh words were exchanged, and the situation escalated into violence. But the officers thought that there was an alternative scenario, Brent's first account of hiding upstairs the whole time, waiting for his mother to pass Robin's room and go into her bedroom. When his father came upstairs, he attacked with no words passing between the two men. Both investigators felt that Brent wanted to kill his father, and then felt he had to kill his mother. Let the district attorney sort out the versions, they thought. Brent's interview was occasionally inconsistent but for the most part, Myrick and Jurkofsky felt they had the confession they needed. However, they still had nothing on Caroline Scoutt. And though they weren't certain how explicit her role was in Brent's actions, "she was the puppet master," Bryan Jurkofsky recalled later. "She pulled the strings." Mike Myrick agreed.

Without much sleep from their interrogation, Myrick and Jurkofsky returned to Denver to screen the tape from that bus station, which captured Brent's arrival from Tulsa. An hour and a half later, he was reported in Boulder with Scoutt at Barnes & Noble, but there were no scheduled Greyhound buses connecting the cities. There were city buses from Denver to Boulder that day, yet there were none after Brent's arrival in Denver that would have gotten him to Boulder in time to meet Scoutt when he said he did. Myrick, in his report, wondered "how the suspect got from Denver to Boulder without the assistance of his wife." His and Jurkofsky's conclusion: he didn't.

: 13

Akasha

Later on the day of the interrogation, Brent shuffled into a holding area for his first court appearance. He was shackled and clad in a red jail jumpsuit, and carried a paperback copy of Marianne Williamson's best-selling *Reflections on a Course in Miracles*. Silent during the proceeding, he stood amid about a dozen minor offenders until his name was called and then sat down. He indicated that he would not waive extradition. The case was postponed while Boulder officials waited for the Alabama extradition request to arrive, and Judge John F. Stavly did not allow bail. Initially, Brent was placed on a suicide watch in jail, standard practice in cases of capital murder. Then he was moved to another special unit, where he remained under observation. "Our mental health staff has evaluated him and determined the he may have some mental issues that require him to be watched," said Sheriff's Lieutenant Bruce Haas, a jail spokesman.

The arrest warrant for murder, which was served on Brent a week later, in his cell, offered few details. "During the course of the investigation, the defendant was identified as the offender," it read. "This offense occurred during the course of a robbery first-degree and murder during which more than one person was killed." The wording, for those who knew Alabama law, signaled that the offense qualified for the death penalty.

Back in Montgomery, Mayor Bobby Bright, who was briefed regularly on the investigation, still found it difficult to comprehend that Brent Jr. was responsible. "I couldn't believe that any person their right mind could do that," he recalled. "There's no way a son could do that to his parents." After the arrest, *Montgomery Advertiser* reporter Antoinette Konz canvassed the Garden District in an intermittent rain and found residents predictably relieved. Sue Johnson, the Springfords' next-door neighbor and close friend for twenty years, said she was pleased that the arrest had finally happened. Another neighbor left flowers on the family's doorstep. After the article appeared, the discussion continued unabated, and anonymously, on the *Advertiser's* Internet comment board and on the Talk of Alabama social media site. Many bloggers thought the cause of Brent's malign metamorphosis was drug use, but some of the Internet speculation turned to Scoutt. "Who is this mystery woman that is living in the house that his parents bought?" one wrote. "Are they married, involved or just living together, and what kind of influence did she have on Brent?" Another chimed in: "If 'that woman' convinced him of getting off his medications then she is just as responsible as the person who swung the bat! Hope she is in custody too."

On December 10, Greta Van Susteren announced on Fox News that Brent Jr. had been arrested and charged. Montgomery police spokesman Huey Thornton returned to the Fox broadcast, acknowledging that "we have documented [Brent's] route into Alabama, as well as his mode of transportation." Thornton said that police had determined the motive for the killing, but he declined to say what it was, because "we haven't exhausted all of our leads." Colorado newspapers had picked up the story, splashing it across their front pages. "I guess you have everybody between here and Colorado interested in it," Thornton told the host.

Because Brent initially refused to waive extradition, Alabama Governor Bob Riley signed a warrant requesting his transfer, which he overnighted to his Colorado counterpart, Governor Bill Owens, requesting the suspect's rapid return to Montgomery. A spokesman said Owens signed the order quickly, at Riley's request, on December 14. Mark Noel, who handled extraditions for Owens, said that such action was common with requests for a "highly dangerous individual . . . typically, people accused of being murderers or rapists get extradited faster." Still, the extradition would have to be litigated.

In Montgomery, District Attorney Ellen Brooks told the *Advertiser* that once Brent was returned to Alabama he would have a plea hearing and the court would make certain that he had adequate legal representation. When the police and the prosecution had finished their investigation, Brooks said, she would convene a grand jury to consider an indictment. But Brooks left little doubt what was in store for Brent, although she

143

remained vague on whether she would seek the death penalty. "Whenever there is a capital murder charge," she said, "we weigh things carefully. Every case is unique. Our decision depends on the evidence and the law. We also talk with the family and the investigators before making a decision." Brent's sister Robin, who would weigh in on that issue later, declined to comment to the newspaper. Brooks had asked for—and gotten—the death penalty in previous cases, and Alabama's death row was one of the most crowded in the nation. For most prosecutors in the state, the death penalty was the goal in murder cases, and for good reason. "The death penalty is good for your 'brand,'" Bryan Stevenson, founder and director of the Montgomery-based Equal Justice Initiative, told the *New Yorker* in 2014. "If you're a prosecutor or judge who has to run for reelection, and you have to worry about your identity in the community—frankly, nothing says 'tough on crime' like the death penalty."

While still in custody in Colorado, Brent's luck began to turn, at least slightly. The presiding circuit judge in Montgomery appointed Bill Blanchard to serve as his lead public defender, selected from a list of private defense attorneys with experience trying capital cases. In many ways, Blanchard was a logical choice, with thirty years of criminal defense practice in the firm he founded. Unlike many appointed defense lawyers in death penalty cases, Blanchard had extensive experience, having tried about ten such cases going back to 1985. Along the way, he received numerous honors including the Alabama State Bar's Clarence Darrow Award for his work in death penalty cases and the Roderick Beddow award from the Alabama Association of Criminal Defense Lawyers. In one celebrated Montgomery case, he defended James Lewis Martin Jr., sentenced to death for the 1985 robbery and murder of car salesman Allen Powell during a vehicle test drive. Shortly before his scheduled 1990 execution, Martin received a stay, and in 2001 the conviction was overturned by an Alabama Court of Criminal Appeals ruling that the verdict was "tainted by the prosecutorial nondisclosure of material evidence."

Blanchard practices out of a restored two-story wooden house next door to the Alabama district attorneys association. Although a much-honored lawyer, Blanchard also boasts solid good-old-boy credentials, including a

B.A. from the University of Alabama and years of playing with one band called Marital Assets and another called Tequila Mockingbird. He tries to clear his court calendar for his "annual pilgrimage" to the New Orleans Jazz and Heritage Festival, "to preserve my own mental health." In recent years, he had taken to wearing what remained of his gray hair in a ponytail and a stubble beard. In court, he is soft-spoken and unflappable, rarely showing emotion, always dressed in a dark suit and a white shirt. Blanchard didn't know the Springfords, but he recalled attending at least one fundraiser at their house, not far from his own. Blanchard had no qualms about taking the case, although "it hit a little closer to home than a lot of the cases I've had here."

The American Bar Association recommends that defendants facing the death penalty be represented by two "high quality" lawyers, which is usually interpreted as counsel experienced in trying capital cases. Blanchard agreed to defend Brent Springford on the condition that Jay Lewis would assist him in the second chair. Lewis was, if anything, even more of a character. Before attending law school, he was an actor, a commercial pilot, a journalist, a public-relations consultant, a radio and TV political pundit, and a writer of liberal commentary. Blanchard knew the Springford case would inevitably involve dealing with media issues, which he considered one of Lewis's strengths. Married and divorced six times, Lewis practiced civil rights, employment discrimination, and criminal defense, including a half-dozen capital cases, none of which resulted in death sentences. Although a sole practitioner, Lewis had worked with Blanchard on several cases. Blanchard considered Lewis an expert litigator but also felt the other attorney could focus on writing key motions, like change of venue and suppressing Brent's confession, as well as research, particularly in the area of mental health. Lewis had no ego reservations about taking the second chair in the defense, often opting for self-deprecation. "Blanchard was the brains of this outfit," Lewis said of the Springford defense team. "I was the mouthpiece." A gravel-voiced man with a close-cropped gray beard who bears a passing resemblance to Willie Nelson, Lewis is a longtime member of Mensa and known to be deadly at crosswords. He knew of the Springfords and, like Blanchard, had once attended a fundraiser at the Hull Street house. As he examined crime-scene photos and police reports, that experience "would come back to haunt me."

Blanchard and Lewis's appointments became official on December 18, and they began preliminary research. Lewis admitted that he was impressed by Myrick and Jurkofsky's work in Colorado. "They did a fantastic job in tracking this case down in such a short time," he recalled. "I have nothing but praise for them. Everything they did was methodical and event-driven. I'm sorry they were on the other side, but you have to admire their professionalism." Early on, the defense team realized they were facing an uphill climb to save their client's life. Blanchard immersed himself in medical literature, devouring stacks of books on bipolar disorder and other forms of mental illness, as well as parricide, compiling a list of experts he might need to call at trial.

In Colorado, meanwhile, after a period of confusion about whether Brent had local representation, the state public defender's office stepped in, at least until the extradition matter was resolved. They had Brent evaluated by a clinical psychologist, who confirmed earlier diagnoses that Brent was bipolar. They also had a licensed clinical social worker come to the jail to administer a Rorschach Interpretive Test to Brent. "Mr. Springford appears to be working very hard to keep emotions out of his life," social worker Elise Ross wrote, with classic understatement.

The Boulder County public defender's office had one of its young paralegal investigators, Mary Kottenstette, contact both Brent and Scoutt. The paralegal's subsequent interviews would later be shared with Brent's defense attorneys—and eventually with Montgomery police and prosecutors through the discovery process. Kottenstette had planned to meet with Scoutt at the Boulder County Jail on December 21, but Scoutt canceled the night before, saying she was unable to handle the pressure of seeing Brent. Instead they agreed to meet at a restaurant in Longmont. Scoutt began the meeting by saying that her attorney, Daniel Quinn, had advised against the interview because of her tendency to trust people, which sometimes got her into trouble. The investigator assured her that the public defender's office was doing as much as possible to assist defense attorneys Blanchard and Lewis in Montgomery. Given Scoutt's defensive state of mind, Kottenstette decided to just let Scoutt talk and ask only a few questions. Scoutt said she was still smarting from her interviews with Myrick and Jurkofsky, who she said were rude and inappropriate with her and her children, at least until Quinn accompanied her. She told Kottenstette the detectives had told her "the free ride is over" and that Brent was going to "fry." It would have been a classic, if ham-handed, police ploy, if they told her, as she said they did, that they knew Scoutt had been in the Jaguar with Brent and that she had been seen with him in Oklahoma.

Kottenstette found Scoutt sketchy in her recollections, "not clear on the details," but the investigator decided not to challenge her. Scoutt again insisted that she and her family felt that Brent was around Thanksgiving week because his phone and his favorite Peruvian hat were there, and his chores were done. Also, Brent often made himself scarce for days at a time. Scoutt said that people might not understand the nature of her relationship with Brent, but that she had compassion for and cared for him "as an injured soul." Becoming more relaxed with Kottenstette, Scoutt became more expansive, not limiting herself to the crime itself. She said she found Brent's behavior bizarre when they first met at Marie Flinders's Boulder house, particularly when he bowed before her. As she recalled the incident, she had told Brent she was no man's master and never to do it again. Her ongoing relationship with Charlotte and Brent Sr. was a decent one, she maintained. They were relieved and supportive that she was there to help Brent Jr. But when the investigator asked Scoutt about her marriage she became agitated and asked what that had to do with anything. Informed that it might help Brent's defense, Scoutt said the marriage was Brent's idea, that as his wife Scoutt could prevent his parents from committing him to a mental institution. She kept the marriage a secret because she felt her other counseling clients might not understand. There was no physical relationship in the marriage; Scoutt was simply a companion and a caretaker. Early in the marriage there had been a brief physical relationship, but that had proved to be a mistake. She regretted it, and Brent accepted that it would not be a part of their marriage.

There had been, Scoutt acknowledged, some recent tension with the parents over Brent Sr.'s threats to cut them off financially. She said it grew out of a minor matter, which she characterized as "stupid stuff." The nutritionist and environmental medicine doctor who was treating Brent, Scoutt, and her daughter was prescribing supplements that were not covered by Brent Jr.'s insurance, and Brent's father was displeased about having to make up the difference, she said. Scoutt defended the physician, volunteering that he had told Brent to stay on the medications prescribed by his psychiatrist but that Brent stopped taking them on his own. In the past, Scoutt said, when Brent Sr. refused to send money, Charlotte would sometimes send a check without telling her husband. Scoutt said Brent Sr. once told her that things would be easier if Brent Jr. was dead. She believed that he had told his son the same thing. And Scoutt told the investigator that she didn't understand why she herself had to be involved in the murder case.

Scoutt was in constant contact with Brent while he was in jail—notes, phone calls, and face-to-face visits. Concerned about his medical bills, which continued to arrive at the house, Scoutt urged him to inquire if he might be eligible for unemployment benefits or Social Security disability support that might help keep the Windsor household going. Brent assured her that if his medical bills could not be paid from his parents' estate, he would apply for state aid in Colorado.

Several letters and phone conversations between Scoutt and Brent dealt with her interest in her husband's possible "inheritance." In one phone conversation, which Brent thought might be recorded, he abruptly steered the conversation in a different direction when she raised the subject again. In a letter written immediately after that conversation, on December 17, he explained his action. "The reason I said that I don't feel comfortable with talking about the inheritance is that it makes me look like I deliberately killed my parents to get the inheritance. I just wanted that to be heard on the phone, because we had been talking about the estate previously." Twice in her notes to Brent she made an ominous offer, both in a P.S.: "If you do get the death penalty we need to know, cause we want to come out and be there for you." Without being asked, Scoutt later turned over to Myrick all of her correspondence with Brent from his time in the hospital and the Boulder jail.

Two days later, on December 23, Kottenstette, the paralegal, met with

Brent in the jail for another interview. In their previous meeting, when the paralegal began by taking his social history, Brent had not been very communicative, replying "I don't know" and "I can't remember" to her questions. The night before, though, he had spoken with Scoutt, who asked him if he had yet shared with Kottenstette some of the damning and fantastic things he had told her. Caroline's call apparently made Brent suddenly more talkative. He told Kottenstette about his habitual shoplifting and "dumpster diving" to feed his sugar craving and that he believed he was invisible to surveillance cameras. Now, with Scoutt's permission, and possibly her encouragement, he moved on to the realm of the supernatural.

Brent told Kottenstette that, months before the killings, he had met a man at Whole Foods in Boulder who said to call him "Akasha." The man reminded him of the "light visions" he first had at Naropa, and Brent thought Akasha must be a great master. He compared him to the "Seth" character in the Jane Roberts books he had read. "Akasha was my Seth," he told the paralegal. Brent felt "good and blessed" about the encounter, telling Akasha that the meeting "seemed like an answer to his prayers and something he had always hoped for." Brent, who tended to identify with characters in books he read, told Kottenstette that he wanted to become "a great spiritual healer and had heard and read about these things happening to others, so he just embraced it." Ultimately, Brent said, Akasha instructed him to go to visit his parents, and that good things would come of it. He was told to go by bus and not to tell anyone about the trip, including any of his doctors. It was Akasha he was looking for, he said, when Scoutt drove him to the Fort Collins bus station. When Kottenstette sent her account of the jail interview to the Montgomery defense team, one lawyer replied, "This is REAL spooky." The thrust of her interviews, Kottenstette and the Alabama attorneys believed, was to further incriminate Brent and to exonerate Scoutt.

On January 1, 2005, Brent gave a jail guard named Eric Witte some documents to copy for him. Witte asked Brent if they were legal documents, and Brent said they were, meaning that they were privileged and thus should not be shared with anyone but defense attorneys. Copies were made for Brent, but Witte kept one set, passing the statement along to sheriff's deputies. Witte later asked Brent why he had shown the papers to him, if they were intended for his attorney and his wife. "I guess that was a poor decision on my part," Brent later acknowledged to the defense team. He said he thought it wouldn't matter much because he had already given a confession to Myrick and other investigators when he was arrested. Brent did have the presence of mind to refuse Witte's request for the originals of the documents, which contained what amounted to a second confession.

This chilling, written confession echoed elements of the accounts he gave previously to police and Kottenstette, while adding new and frightening details. It was plausible, but was it true? More than anything, it offered the fullest insight yet into the depth of Brent's madness. At last, he was the protagonist in his own supernatural tale. This confession seemed even more damaging than Brent's earlier, recorded version to police. Yet read a certain way, it was more self-serving and exculpatory, a metaphysical version of "the Devil made me do it." All his adult life, Brent had read books from various spiritual traditions about direct, personal, extraordinary supernatural intervention. Despite his listening, studying, meditating, and praying, it had never happened to him. Now, he claimed, it had—in a most horrific way. In his various written accounts, Brent used different formulations for the name of his new spiritual leader, as if he weren't certain, starting with "Kasha," then "Akasa," and finally settling on "Akasha."

The name itself—Akasha—was redolent of the forces that had swirled around him for the previous decade. In classical Sanskrit, the language of Hinduism, some define Akasha as ether, a basic element like fire, earth, and water. In Buddhism, the term defines space, and it is also incorporated into Theosophy and some modern paganism. Less substantively, Akasha is also the name given to a character called "The Queen of the Damned" by novelist Anne Rice in her vampire trilogy. In those books, Akasha is a malevolent, pre-Egyptian queen who becomes the mother of all vampires. Later Brent would say that he "transferred his allegiance" from Scoutt to this spirit: "I chose to let Akasha take Caroline's place." Brent wrote that he had heard Akasha's voice for some time before he encountered the physical incarnation, a man standing in front of the Whole Foods in Fort Collins in November 2004:

Suddenly I heard his voice say something like, "enlightenment is a state of heightened awareness and inner freedom." I was ecstatic and amazed, I felt like I was beginning a new stage of life and that I must already be close to enlightenment for him to even be talking to me. I asked him if he was my spirit, and he said that he was *a* spirit who was here to guide me. He said that I could not tell anyone about him, and that there was a journey he wanted me to go on that would bring good results if I followed his instructions. He said he wanted me to go on a bus to visit my parents to bring about a good change in my relationship with them. He said he had been watching me for my whole life and that he was communicating with me now because I had reached a crisis in my life with my parents. He came to help me resolve it in a positive way. I told him I was definitely willing to follow his instructions because I very much wanted for there to be a positive relationship with my parents, and that I had been despairing about it for a long time.

It had been Akasha who told him to take "a bus from Fort Collins in one week and not tell anyone. . . . He said above all to have no doubt or fears, and to trust him completely in his guidance. And I did." Akasha suggested that he jog to his parents' house and climb over the wall. On Thanksgiving Day the spiritual leader directed Brent to prepare a stick to defend himself in case his father grew violent and then told him to break the window in Robin's room and enter the house. But the voice was oddly silent when Brent faced his angry parents. "I was miserably depressed," he remembered, "and I felt like a complete failure and an idiot for ever having come. And I didn't know why Akasha wanted me to break the window. He just said not to worry and to have faith." While Brent was struggling to decide what to do, "suddenly Akasha started talking loudly inside my head that I did not have to worry because he was going to take care of everything. Before I knew what was happening I felt myself suddenly pushed outside of my body so that I was watching myself from a few feet from the side and a few feet back. I had no control of my body because Akasha had somehow become me, or taken control of my body, like we had switched positions."

And then Akasha, occupying Brent's body, went into action as Brent watched: He put on the black work gloves and retrieved the stick from the window ledge. "I felt horror and despair because I knew what Akasha was going to do and there was nothing I could do to stop him." Akasha, not Brent, smashed Brent Sr. with the stick, ran to Charlotte and hit her, too, "then ran back and forth, hitting them until they weren't moving. My memory of all this is very blurry. . . . It was a horrifying experience and I blamed myself for everything that happened.

"I could not make a response and my thoughts were slowed down like when I take too much Zyprexa. I yelled at him to stop but he paid no attention." Brent watched Akasha slash his parents with the knife, rifle through Charlotte's wallet, scatter papers around the house, climb into the Jaguar, and drive away.

> I hated Akasha for what he did to my parents and for leaving me with the sickening responsibility for it. I knew their death was totally unnecessary and would never have happened if I had not agreed to go there in the first place. I was outraged that he took control over my body without asking, and then used that control to commit that atrocity. . . . From then on my feelings toward Akasha were a mixture of hatred and complete dependence. I knew that I had been possessed by a demonic spirit, not a good spirit helping me towards enlightenment. But he told me that if I followed his instructions I would not get arrested.

Brent followed Akasha's directions to return to Boulder. There,

> I made some calls on other people's cell phones but I could not get through. I did not talk to Caroline because I was so nervous about talking to her. Akasha said the Jetta would be at the Whole Foods parking lot in Boulder and that Caroline would meet me at Barnes and Noble. I don't know how he knew that or arranged for that but both were true.

In the midst of the extradition fight, the *Montgomery Advertiser* reported that the Springfords' 1992 wills provided for the bulk of their multi-million dollar estate to be divided equally between their daughter Robin and Brent Jr., each with their own trust. Proportionate shares in the Pepsi bottling company and property in Luverne were to go to Charlotte's sister, Lois Turner Truss. On January 9, 2005, Probate Judge Reese McKinney scheduled a hearing on the will for January 26, at which time any relatives could raise objections to the division of assets. Among the issues to be decided, according to Brent Jr.'s civil attorney, Richardson B. McKinzie III, was whether his client "may or may not be of sound mind." Unspoken, but hanging in the air: If Brent were convicted, whether his inheritance was the result of what common law calls "ill-gotten gain," and thus should be denied to him and his heirs. In addition, Alabama has what is known as the "Slayer Statute," passed in 1975, which takes effect after all murder convictions and prohibits relatives of murderers or their heirs from benefiting from the crime. But if Brent were acquitted or found not guilty by reason of insanity, the disposition of his half of the estate would likely be determined by civil litigation in the form of a wrongful death suit against Brent Jr., brought by the executors or his sister Robin. At the hearing, Robin's lawyers did not contest the will, preferring to wait for the outcome of the murder trial.

Although Brent was entitled to a hearing on Colorado's extradition order, by then—on the advice of his Colorado public defender—he changed his mind and didn't insist on one, agreeing on February 17 to return to Alabama. The next day, February 18, Myrick and Jurkofsky flew to pick him up in a state-owned Beechcraft King Air 200. On the flight to Alabama, Brent, now with his head shaved and the beginnings of a beard, was silent and cooperative throughout the flight, staring out the window.

As Brent stepped off the plane, wearing his orange jail jumpsuit, Myrick and Jurkofsky adjusted his waist-to-wrist shackles. Police put a bullet-proof vest on him as they brought him off the plane and helped him into the back of an unmarked police car for the drive to the jail. Looking ahead to the trial, authorities wanted to minimize pretrial publicity that might imply that Brent was already guilty—the same reason defendants normally do not appear before jurors in jumpsuits or shackles. Even so, coverage of his return to Alabama in the *Montgomery Advertiser* and local television stations was extensive, so much so that it would later became an issue.

Brent was driven downtown to the Phelps-Price Judicial Center, a sprawling complex that includes the Montgomery County jail and the courtrooms and judge's offices of Alabama's 15th Judicial Circuit. The modern structure is built of white, slab-sided concrete and as a result is completely without the charm of many vintage Southern courthouses. Out front is a life-sized bronze statue of Major Lemuel P. Montgomery, for whom the county is named. He was a Tennessee-born attorney and military officer who was killed during the Creek Indian War while leading an assault at the Battle of Horseshoe Bend in 1814. The most positive, symbolic aspect of the courthouse is that it is named for two local judges, one white and the other black.

After being fingerprinted and photographed, Brent was booked on two counts of capital murder. When the booking process was finished, Brent turned to Myrick and Jurkofsky and said, "I want to thank you for your kindness to me." Years later, Myrick wrote that he detected some poignancy on Brent's part. "I can't help but think that the weight of everything was being felt as he was now back in Montgomery after the murders. I think the reality of everything revealed who he really was and he was truly humbled because of what everyone thought of him. I think he cared deeply what people thought of him, and of course it was the worst. I think he believed that he was not that kind of person, but he knew his guilt. He was truly, truly sad in spirit."

Brent's first visitors were Bill Blanchard and Jay Lewis, his two court-appointed defense attorneys. This initial meeting lasted an hour, but they did not discuss details of the case. "I wouldn't say he appeared to be any more anxious, fretful or worrisome than you would expect from someone in the situation he is in," Blanchard told a local TV reporter. "We did talk about what his medications were and I believe . . . he's gotten some of it. . . . I don't know whether he's getting everything he's supposed to have, but he's not a doctor and neither am I. So, we're just going to have to figure that out." Jay Lewis recalled that Brent had a haunted, vacant look at that first meeting. There was also a hint of the exasperation that would develop in the days to come. "When we saw him he was absolutely adamant that he wasn't going to plead to anything, and after a while we began to believe him."

At his first Alabama court appearance, on February 23, at the justice building Brent was mute, on advice of counsel. When Montgomery Circuit Judge Peggy Givhan explained his rights and the charges against him, he nodded. She informed him that he would be held without bail, and, in order to determine whether he would be eligible for a court-appointed attorney, asked him to fill out a financial form. Witnesses in the courtroom noticed that he stared blankly forward. When the judge told him to rise, he did not seem to comprehend the order, so a bailiff nudged him. Givhan told him he had the right to remain silent and cautioned him about discussing the case with anyone in jail, in light of the common police practice of putting snitches in cells with defendants who try to befriend them. Anything Brent said under those circumstances, she warned, could be used against him in court.

Initially, jail seemed okay to Brent. He saw himself as a monk in his cell, a condition that had been his ambition for years. "As long as I have books and coffee, I actually love being in a cell 24–7," he wrote in a letter. It was fortunate that he felt that way, because the cell would be his home for three years while his case progressed in frustrating fits and starts toward trial. Brent's main source of solace and relative stability were the books Blanchard bought for him and a small radio that he usually tuned to the Montgomery area public radio station. "Brent is terribly remorseful," defense team member Susan Wardell wrote to his aunt, Lois Truss, "and realizes he has ruined so many lives, but has never even mentioned his own life having been ruined. He is content to sit in his cell all day, meditating and reading *Course in Miracles*." That didn't last. While Brent was calm, pleasant, and humble some days, on other days his depression drove him to near suicide. He banged his face against the wall until the skin around his eyes was black and blue. He claimed to see lights and colors and to hear sounds like chanting and celestial choirs. Other times he became even more delusional, thinking he was Jesus or Buddha or was channeling the Holy Spirit. According to his legal team, he was given the same regimen of psychotropic and antidepressant drugs by the jail nursing staff that he had been prescribed in Colorado. No family members visited. In his cell, he sometimes had vivid, fully conscious dreams that he said filled him "with elation and hope."

Visiting defense team members observed that he had turned his cell into a kind of shrine. He arranged his photos and Scoutt's cards in a semicircle, as if they were icons. "If he could have had a candle he would have lit it and sat in the lotus position," attorney Lewis said. "If I had one image of someone who was mentally ill, it would be him." Although Caroline Scoutt never visited him or spoke with him on the phone, Brent remained firmly under her sway, the residue of her longtime hold over him. When he used the cell toilet, he turned Scoutt's cards around so they couldn't "see" him. Mostly, he told the defense team, she appeared in his dreams, singing and chanting, and was able to monitor his thoughts. He desperately missed her, afraid to incur her displeasure in any way. During his time in jail, she sent Brent only seven cards and notes, most in some way cryptic or symbolic, although sometimes including news of her family's straitened economic situation. This was a fraction of the hundred or more desperate and needy letters he wrote her. Shortly after he arrived in Montgomery, Scoutt also forwarded to him and to his deceased parents' Hull Street address her household expenses and the now-overdue bill for $18,000 from the family's nutritionist. In another card, she wrote that neither she nor her children had received any of his numerous letters.

The loss of his largely one-sided correspondence over the years when he awaited trial was "terribly upsetting" and led him to a predictable conclusion: The jail administration was confiscating his letters, providing the only plausible explanation for Scoutt's relative silence, which he found deeply painful. He wrote to his legal team,

> I cannot prove that the jail is behind it, but what other possibility is there?" "Especially when the jail is certainly aware of and allow Caroline's cell [phone] number to be blocked, so I have not spoken with her in two and a half years. The jail is doing this act of cruelty, so I have to believe that they are also confiscating my letters to her and the kids. . . . It has been devastating for me to learn that the countless hours I put into several hundred pages of writing to them, birthday letters to the kids have disappeared. I poured my heart and soul into those letters, and they are gone! . . . This is utter cruelty.

Several of Brent's subsequent letters were returned, with a notation that Scoutt's mailbox was closed. She, clearly moving into the post-Brent phase of her life, later acknowledged that she had stopped reading letters she did receive from him. Still, in the weeks following his return to Montgomery, Brent blamed himself for her resulting ill health, her need to work three jobs, and problems the children were having, according to one of her early cards. The family was thrown out of the Windsor house "in the freezing winter," he told a member of the defense team, "all because of me, and what I did to them." He forbade his attorneys from calling Scoutt as a witness in any proceedings and demanded a written excuse for her.

Critically—given that his life was at stake—Brent refused to make any decisions about his case without Scoutt, compelling his legal team to act as go-between. When, in another card, Scoutt told Brent she didn't want to testify at the trial—which might have helped him—he wrote, "I told her that if she doesn't want to be here, then I don't want her to either." This put the defense team in a quandary, one that would grow exponentially as the months and years passed. How could they serve their client's best interest—and save his life—if *he* was not acting in his best interest? What was sentiment, and what was pathology? Only Scoutt could tie together Brent's cold, psychiatric records into a coherent narrative of his descent into madness. But with Brent's insistence that they keep completely away from Scoutt's involvement, his lawyers had no opportunity to raise the issue of her culpability in the killings.

: 14

Legal Maneuvers

At a certain level of power, wealth and influence, Montgomery, with a population of about 200,000, is a small town. So District Attorney Ellen Brooks, fifty-three years old at the time of the murders, had a sense right away about who would be arrested, having heard for years the stories about Brent Jr. She knew the Springfords well enough that had she not been out of town, she would have attended their memorial service. Like Brent Jr., she was raised in the Garden District, in an Italianate home just a few blocks from the Springfords' house. She, too, graduated from Montgomery Academy, later attending Vanderbilt University as an undergraduate and the University of Alabama for law school. Immediately after graduation, she joined the county prosecutor's office and, except for one year working for the state as a deputy attorney general, never left. Brooks became chief deputy district attorney in 1983 and ten years later was elected to the top post. Petite and fine-featured, her mid-length subdued blond hair was feather-cut and her nails were short. In court, she always wore navy suits—never pants—and a few good pieces of gold jewelry.

Over the years, Brooks won most of the cases she argued. One she lost, to her chagrin, was a firebombing case involving a city councilman's office. All of the defendants were convicted, except for the one represented by Jay Lewis, now on the defense team representing Brent. "She didn't like that," Lewis recalled with a smile. Ten defendants she prosecuted were sentenced to death.

By rotation, the Springford case was assigned to Circuit Judge William Shashy, the grandson of Syrian immigrants who had prospered in the United States, sending two sons to medical school, including the judge's father. Off the bench, the shortish, roundish judge is known for his sly, dry wit, but in court he likes to keep things moving. At the time of the Springford murders, he had imposed only one death sentence, adhering to the jury's recommendation.

For District Attorney Brooks, the hurdles to prove premeditated, capital murder were expected to be: Brent's documented history of mental health treatment, the breadth and depth of which were unusual in a death-penalty case; his steadfast unwillingness to implicate his wife as an accomplice; the absence of any physical evidence of Brent Jr. at the scene; the possibility of a costly change of venue because of the massive amount of local publicity; and that, for a variety of reasons, his two Colorado confessions might not be admissible. For any reason, an acquittal would be politically damaging for Brooks.

Defense attorney Bill Blanchard and his team soon realized that the case would involve years of work, and Blanchard privately felt that a factual verdict of not guilty was not in the cards. So as a practical first position he concentrated his strategy toward a goal of not guilty by reason of insanity, either in the form of a clinical finding, a negotiated plea, or—as a last resort—a jury finding. The risk in that strategy was that a jury could well reject such a defense, resulting in a death sentence. Specifically, if the jurors decided they didn't like Brent—because he came across as a spoiled rich kid, or like a two-year-old who didn't get his way—he would be sent to Death Row. The defense team's tactics came straight from the death penalty litigation playbook, starting with a blizzard of pretrial motions for, chiefly, a change of venue because of pretrial publicity and suppression of Brent's confessions, because of his disturbed, medicated, sleep-deprived state of mind. Victories on these motions could narrow the contested issues in court and provide leverage for a negotiated plea, or at least raise the cost of a trial for the prosecution, and thus the county.

For his part, Brent was less focused on his defense than with his July 21, 2005, legal separation from Scoutt, who apparently wanted to distance herself from her controversial spouse. Her attorney, Daniel Quinn, urged her not to proceed further with a divorce because Brent would be "devastated" by the action. Even after the separation, Scoutt continued to pepper Susan Wardell, an attorney and clinical social worker on the defense team, with questions about her right to inherit Brent's portion of the Springford estate. Brent remained obsessed with the disposition of the Windsor house. Under pressure from lawyers for the Springford estate, Scoutt had wasted little time moving out. One day in early January 2005, a number of Scoutt's friends from the Native American reservations pulled up in a flatbed truck. They took apart smaller outbuildings, uprooted the corral fences and all the shrubbery that could be dug up, as well as the birdhouse security surveillance system, and trucked all of it to Scoutt's Wyoming ranch. They also took every door handle and deadbolt lock in the house. Before the flatbed pulled away, a neighbor alerted Montgomery police and Weld County sheriff's deputies.

On September 5, 2005, Brent received a certified letter from Regions Bank, which handled his parents' estate, informing him of the need to appraise the Windsor property. This provoked an angry, hand-printed letter from Brent: "Why are you doing this? Have you made any decisions? . . . My parents gave me this house, so why does it need to be appraised?" Six days later, removed locksets notwithstanding, Scoutt returned the house keys to the bank. In a last, futile effort, Brent wrote the bank again in October, questioning its plans to sell the house. He hand-printed a statement for the estate's lawyers, saying the Windsor house was to go to Scoutt for taking care of him, that the house was willed to him with that understanding—which was not correct. The statement, of course, had no legal standing. (The new residents who eventually purchased the property, for $425,000, had to do a massive cleanup of trash left behind, repair more than a hundred nail holes in the walls, repaint, and fill in Brent's backyard "worry hole." Given the house's history, the new family also held a blessing service for a spiritual cleansing, even burning sage.)

As often happens with complicated, high-profile death penalty prosecutions, the Springford case languished for long periods. Eight months after his return from Colorado, Brent was still in a single cell in the Montgomery County jail. A year after the killings, the *Montgomery Advertiser* was losing patience with the stalled case. Newspapers love anniversaries, especially around slow news times like holiday weekends such as Thanksgiving. It was predictable that the *Advertiser* would use the first anniversary of the Springford murders to catch readers up on the progress of the case or, as the lengthy story unfolded, the lack of progress. Reporter Crystal Bonvillian, who handled much of the paper's coverage of the case, returned on November 25, 2005, to the house on South Hull Street. The vacant house and grounds—now for sale—were well-tended, she observed, and lights could be seen at night in the house's windows. Notwithstanding news accounts of the murders and Brent's arrest, some nearby residents still grappled with the prosecution's account of the young man as a killer. Neighbor Janet Driscoll said that many around the city questioned the progress in the case. "I think people are just wondering what's happening. . . . It's always on your mind when you walk past the house."

District Attorney Brooks said the case had been delayed largely because of the backlog at the State Department of Forensic Sciences. She was as impatient as anyone to get results from the forensics lab, mostly for DNA reports on the many bloodstains, as well as footprints and fiber analysis. But she said that the Springford case wasn't unique. Apparently unwilling to fast-track the Springford results, she was also waiting to hear from the lab for many of the forty other homicide cases her office was handling. Brooks also complained, "There has been no ruling as of yet of the state's motion for a mental evaluation, which was filed a short time after Mr. Springford's arrest," when the defense announced its plan to seek a verdict of not guilty by reason of insanity.

A year later, Bonvillian was again back on Page One of the *Advertiser* with another anniversary story, noting in her lead paragraph that Brent Springford Jr. was "no closer to his day in court than he was when he was arrested." Both defense attorney Bill Blanchard and District Attorney Brooks agreed. "I think it's pretty frustrating for everybody," Blanchard told the reporter. "It's painful for all involved," said Brooks. "The worst pain here, obviously, is for a family waiting for a conclusion to something extremely terrible that happened." On September 4, 2006, the defense had requested its own formal psychiatric evaluation at Taylor Hardin Secure Medical Facility, the 114-bed hospital for court-committed criminal defendants in Tuscaloosa in west Alabama, founded in 1981 as a maximum security forensic facility, but not formally considered a prison.

Two years after the murders, in December 2006, with reports from the forensics lab finally in hand, a grand jury returned a five-count indictment against Brent Springford Jr. Three counts carried the death penalty. When Brent appeared in court on January 17, 2007, to hear the indictment, he wore a standard-issue orange jail jumpsuit, but he looked dramatically different from his booking photo taken after his extradition two years earlier. Once again he had shoulder-length hair and an untrimmed beard down to his chest, but now he was also gaunt. Asked by a reporter about his client's shocking appearance, defense attorney Bill Blanchard said, "He's doing about as well as can be expected." While Brent remained silent as the clerk read the indictment, his attorneys pleaded not guilty and "not guilty by reason of mental disease or defect," to each of the five counts. His lawyers told reporters after the fifteen-minute arraignment that nurses at the jail facility were administering psychotropic drugs to their client, and that from time to time he was treated by state psychologists in response to his fluctuating mental condition. With the plea finally entered, the next step under state law was to have Brent examined by a psychologist contracted by the county. The defense attorney hinted at another strategic move: a request for a change of venue for the trial. "This is obviously such a high-profile case," Blanchard said. "The difficulty is frankly going to be trying to find jurors who have not already heard enough about it to form an opinion." Assistant DA Daryl Bailey said, "We're ready to try this case as soon as possible."

Finally, Brent received the pre-trial mental evaluation that Brooks had requested shortly after his extradition. The evaluation was assigned to Dr. Glen D. King, a Montgomery forensic psychologist and attorney. He frequently consulted with Alabama police departments and was thought to lean toward the prosecution side in criminal cases. King's finding was a disaster for the defense. It was based on two face-to-face interviews in the jail and a review of Brent's voluminous medical records from his primary care doctor, four private psychiatrists, and two stays in psychiatric hospitals, each for evaluation. Brent was now taking two drugs, Triavil, an antidepressant whose side effects include drowsiness and dizziness, and Risperdal, an antipsychotic used to treat schizophrenia and bipolar disorder, whose side effects can include agitation and anxiety. He had begun signing his mail "winston," uncapitalized, rather than "Brent." King found that the prisoner's judgment was adequate and his intellectual ability "at least average." Without emotion, Brent had reported numerous auditory hallucinations, including one where he said "he represented the voices of the East and he taught Eastern philosophy and gave me spiritual teachings from the East from Buddhism and Hinduism." The voices, Brent had told King, "told me to go to Montgomery and work things out with my parents." King rejected out of hand these and other reports of hallucinations: "I find his reports simply not credible."

As for the upcoming trial, Brent told King that he had a pretty good idea what was in store. He knew Jay Lewis's and Bill Blanchard's names and said he trusted them. Their job was to defend him, he told the psychologist. "They work the legal process to present evidence and a number of factors to show I'm not guilty or not guilty by reason of insanity." And he understood the potential consequences if he was convicted: "I suppose I could be executed," he said. Asked what the district attorney does at trial, Brent responded: "I believe the DA is probably trying to have me killed." That would mean prosecutors "would try to show that I killed my parents deliberately." It was only on the matters of his right to counsel during the investigation, and his understanding of his Miranda rights against self-incrimination in Colorado, that Brent attempted some pushback with the psychologist. Brent insisted that he was denied his right to counsel in Boulder: "They told me I had no lawyer," which was technically correct, since Daniel Quinn represented Scoutt, although a Boulder public defender later was brought in. Brent said he gave the statements in Colorado because investigators pressed him on his most vulnerable point, his wife: "They said if I didn't confess, they would put Caroline in jail." Also, King wrote, Brent said that officers threatened that he would "fry in the electric chair if he didn't give a statement." King rejected Brent's claims, writing that he "had the requisite ability to waive or execute his Miranda rights in a knowing, intelligent, and voluntary fashion." King concluded that "Mr. Winston Springford possesses the requisite ability to assist his legal counsel in his own defense and proceed with a reasonable understanding of the legal proceedings against him."

That finding would have been damaging enough for the defense. But after dismissing the defense claim that Brent couldn't assist in his defense, King went on to say that because of the time that elapsed from Brent's Monday night departure from Colorado to the killings on Thursday, Thanksgiving night, and the planning that went into it, it was clear that Brent "was operating with no serious mental illness or mental defect at the time of the alleged murders." Brent, he went on, was not suffering from any impairment "that would render him incapable of understanding the nature and quality of his actions or the wrongfulness of his acts. Indeed, the crimes were committed in a premeditated, goal-directed, and knowing fashion." The defense attorneys could see that any hopes they had for convincing the prosecutor, much less an Alabama jury, that their client was not guilty by reason of insanity, were evaporating.

The challenge for Springford's defense team—which they knew from the outset was daunting—was to save his life rather than prove he did not murder his parents. But if they could not prove that their client was mentally ill in the clinical sense, they quickly discovered that he was maddeningly irrational and would rapidly become more so. He repeatedly refused to put his own interest first, subordinating everything to protecting Caroline Scoutt—first, from any criminal charges, and then to preserve for her what he saw as his rightful share of his parents' estate. As the legal jockeying played out over the next two years, the defense felt crippled. They realized that Brent's self-sabotaging behavior would propel them to the one place they did not want to go: the courtroom. Early on, defense attorney Jay Lewis recalled, "I got the strong sense that we were actually going to have to go to trial, which gave me a terrible, sinking feeling."

On April 16, 2007, Brent replied to a note from the family's former housekeeper, Maggie Johnson, which offered him help with a request for money to buy food to supplement his jail diet, which had caused his dramatic weight loss. "I'm so hungry," he wrote. The next day, he sent a second letter to Johnson: "This letter is a thank you letter from my heart. You were taking care of me when I was a little baby. You taught me so much about how to be a loving, compassionate, humble, generous person." He apologized for asking her for money in the previous letter, a request he said was selfish. Then he made a revised request, presumably based on one of the few postcards he had received from Scoutt: "The truth is, Caroline and my stepkids need money even more than I do, so if you want to help me, please send that money to Caroline, rather than to me. She is struggling to make ends meet, just to put food on the table, pay for fuel and the bills, and she is working almost non-stop." He wrote that in two years he had received no visits except from his defense team, that he was sleeping fourteen hours a day, and that he was being medicated for mental illness. He concluded by telling Johnson, "We may not see each other again in this lifetime, but I know we'll see each other in Heaven. I'm certain of that."

In mid 2007, the defense opened the argument for a change of venue, an effort led by Lewis. The attorneys argued that because of the victims' high profile in the community, and the amount of publicity the murder and arrest had generated, it would be impossible for Brent to get a fair trial in Montgomery. Change-of-venue motions are rarely granted on grounds of pretrial publicity. When they are, judges usually require a showing of blanket coverage or a consistent, highly prejudicial tone, and even then they are reluctant to move a trial.

In the Springford case, Ellen Brooks maintained that the defense had made no showing that pretrial publicity reached "saturation" point, nor was it sufficiently "inflammatory" or "prejudicial." For the most part, the prosecution argued, "media coverage had been reasonably factual and objective." In any case, a close examination of prospective jurors could weed out any who had been unduly influenced by coverage. If that were not possible, jurors could be brought in from a county outside the reach of local media. In addition, Brooks argued in subsequent briefs that by giving interviews to reporters, defense attorneys had helped generate the publicity.

On August 18, 2007, Judge Shashy granted the defense's change-of-venue motion. In a precedent-setting ruling—one sentence, without elaboration or explanation—he ordered the trial moved to Birmingham, ninety miles away, and set it for January 7, 2008. It was the first time in county history that a change of venue was ordered due to pretrial publicity. Brooks objected vigorously. "I've been trying cases in Montgomery for thirty years, and I want you to show me a case that was moved," she told reporters. "We've had a governor tried here, we've had state officials tried here, we've had several high-profile capital cases tried here." The venue change tipped the negotiating scale in favor of the defense, although not decisively.

Around this time, a key third lawyer in the defense team, Susan Wardell, a death penalty-mitigation specialist, began playing a more significant role. Over the previous decade, the federal courts had ruled that a mitigation effort had to begin well before trial in a capital case. That involved assembling a psychosocial or social-history report of the defendant that would be used in the penalty phase of the two-phase capital case—first, guilt or innocence, and then, if guilty, execution or life without parole. Wardell, a clinical social worker as well as an attorney, was experienced in the field. As the case unfolded, she assumed many other roles with Brent—hand-holder, sympathizer, and intermediary between him, Scoutt, his aunt, Lois Truss, and his former girlfriend Andrea Jameson.

In August Jameson wrote Wardell, asking if she could go along on a visit to Brent in jail. She hadn't seen her old boyfriend in seven years, and she knew he had had no visits from family or friends. Wardell agreed, as an "experiment," mentioning the possibility to Brent beforehand. The encounter did not go well. When Brent saw Andrea, he shouted, "I told you that's not going to work! She's fire to me! She's fire to me!" He refused to look at either woman or respond to them and screamed for a deputy to return him to his cell. Even when Wardell returned alone to the jail to meet with him to talk about her recent investigatory trips to Colorado and Wyoming, Brent would not reply. Instead he called another member of the defense team to complain. After the abortive visit, Brent's sister Robin, who was by then pregnant with her first child, called Jameson—once her good friend—and told her that anyone who spoke with the defense team was being disloyal to the family.

On December 14, 2007, opening yet another front, the defense filed a motion to suppress the series of statements and interviews Brent gave to the Montgomery police detectives in Colorado on November 29–30, 2004. They also wanted to exclude statements he made to the staff and the media while he was committed to Poudre Valley Hospital in Colorado. In particular, they concentrated on his statements given to Montgomery Detective Mike Myrick in the early morning hours of December 9, after the arrest. The defense focused on a number of key questions. Was Brent off his medication for a bipolar condition when he came from work to the first interrogation on November 29? If so, he was "particularly susceptible to police manipulation."

The defense lawyers argued to Judge Shashy that from the time Brent asked in the emergency room to phone Daniel Quinn he should not have been questioned further without an attorney. Any subsequent Miranda warnings were thus tainted. Brent was not mentally capable of "intelligently and rationally" understanding his Miranda rights after his December 8 arrest, they said, and thus he could not waive them. The defense argued that Brent's statement to police at the Louisville police department was "coerced and inadmissible," "an involuntary product of his diseased mental condition, in combination with subtle police coercion." At that time, Brent had not slept for many hours and may also have been under the influence of Haldol, the powerful psychotropic drug used to treat "acute psychosis." The recorded interrogation took place in "an inherently coercive setting." At one point in the interrogation, they argued, Brent asked to be left alone for a while, which the police refused to do. For all these reasons, the defense maintained, "the confession was not voluntary." The lawyers further argued that the written "Akasha" confession, blaming the killings on a demon, that Brent gave to a jail guard to copy, after informing him it was a legal document for his lawyer, was "privileged attorney-client communication" and thus inadmissible as well.

In the fall of 2007, Brent came to believe that the key to achieving a courtroom victory was Rhonda Byrne's 2006 book *The Secret*, which Scoutt had previously recommended. In a disturbing letter—more evidence of Scoutt's continuing hold on him—Brent beseeched all members of the defense team to read the book (and screen a documentary based on it). Byrne maintained that major life outcomes were based on a form of positive thinking she called the "law of attraction." Brent told the defense team that they should base their legal strategy on the book. They rolled their eyes.

District Attorney Brooks had her own problems, centering on the death penalty. It was her normal practice to consult with surviving family members about their feelings on the issue, when there was a possibility of a plea agreement. In this case, the prosecutor would have to give even more credence to the view of the victims' daughter, Robin Springford Crouch. Still, Brooks recalled, "I told her it was not her decision to make," that it was the district attorney's responsibility to make the call, not the family's. Brooks's primary concern for the case's outcome was that Brent would never have an opportunity to hurt Robin. So a plea bargain that resulted in finding Brent not guilty by reason of insanity remained off the table, since that might one day result in his release from the state mental hospital. A guilty plea that left open the possibility of parole was unacceptable for the same reason. Keeping the death penalty in play gave the prosecution vital leverage.

In November 2007, about two months before the trial was scheduled to begin, Brooks's chief assistant, Daryl Bailey, called the defense team. He wanted to sound them out about the possibility that they would accept a guilty plea resulting in a sentence of life without parole, something prosecutors could take into their meeting with Robin and Greg Crouch. Bailey was asked by the defense about the family's inclination toward punishment. "He says they are not reticent about the death penalty but stopped short of saying that they are adamant about having it imposed," a defense team member reported. Actually, Robin was thought to be pushing for the death penalty, although some believed it was her husband Greg who was the driving force. Charlotte Springford's sister, Lois Truss, was thought to favor life without parole. Even though Montgomery juries tended to impose the death penalty relatively freely, Brooks knew that capital punishment in this case was a long shot. The prosecutor expected jurors would see as a mitigating factor the ample documentation of Brent's deteriorating mental condition in the years leading up to the murders.

The defense, too, was weighing its options. As one member of the team informed assistant DA Bailey, they weren't certain they could sell a life-without-parole sentence to Brent. Perhaps, if it was unlikely that a jury would impose the death penalty, it was worth a shot to argue for a sentence of not guilty by reason of insanity. "This is a capital case," the team member cautioned colleagues, "and the death penalty is a possibility if the jurors can't get over the brutality of the crimes. I don't want to be too reckless. Should we shop the life-without-parole plea to the client later this week? If so, how hard should we sell?" The matter was not resolved.

By November 2007, the prosecution was becoming impatient to begin the trial. However, in the face of the numerous pretrial motions, Judge Shashy's previously scheduled January 8, 2008, trial date slipped again. Ellen Brooks went to court to get things going. After a pro forma back-and-forth rehash about time eaten up in bickering over the discovery process, and the backlog at the state's forensic lab, the defense focused on the primary reason it needed a delay: to allow Susan Wardell and her team more time to work up their mitigation phase case. There were still many witnesses to interview, and the defense lawyers were encountering some unique difficulties. "This is a somewhat of an unusual capital case for me," Bill Blanchard told the judge, "because normally the family of my client is more willing to come forward with information about his early life, his social history, and that sort of thing. In this case, obviously, being a parricide case, we have some borders and some boundaries to deal with in getting that kind of information." Since family members and close friends were asked by Robin not to cooperate with defense efforts, Blanchard said, "We have to go to secondary sources for it." Inasmuch as this was the first defense request for a continuance, the judge granted it.

Other skirmishing continued. The prosecution had appealed Shashy's change-of-venue ruling to the Alabama Court of Criminal Appeals, automatically bumping the trial date. Although unmentioned in oral or written arguments, money was an underlying factor in all death-penalty cases. A venue change for a trial estimated to last four weeks would have added about $250,000 to the county's costs, prosecutors said in their appeal. To cover that unbudgeted expense, Brooks had told the *Advertiser,* she would have to go to the Montgomery County Commission to ask for a supplemental appropriation. Brooks also argued that the local judge should have tried to seat a jury in Montgomery before deciding to move it. The appellate court did not agree with Brooks, and on February 8, 2008, the Alabama Supreme Court upheld Shashy's finding, with another one-sentence ruling.

: *15*

Competence

Looking toward a trial, defense attorneys Lewis and Blanchard accelerated their efforts on the mental-health front. They filed new motions arguing that, because of pretrial stress, Brent could not participate in his defense—grounds for a finding of incompetence to stand trial. Still smarting from Dr. King's devastating diagnosis, the defense wanted Brent examined by its own psychologists. There was some shifting of positions. Earlier, the defense had argued the opposite, saying that Brent was fully able to assist in his defense. In a pleading to the court, Blanchard and Lewis now argued for a delay, since Brent was deteriorating in the face of the upcoming trial, and that as a result his "competence to stand trial for capital murder must be seriously questioned." They renewed their motion for their client to be examined at Taylor Hardin Secure Medical Facility. There was continued back and forth between the defense, the prosecution, and Judge Shashy about Brent's psychiatric evaluations, much of the conversation and motions surrounding the Taylor Hardin facility and who would do the examinations there.

In fact, there was more than a suggestion of incompetence. In early March 2008 Susan Wardell received a letter from Brent that triggered a new set of alarm bells. He outlined his plans for how he planned to testify at his trial, and it was a nightmare scenario for his lawyers. First, Brent wrote, "I will not speak about Thanksgiving 2004. I'll probably speak for as long as the judge will allow me, and extemporaneously." He planned to do some reading on the witness stand, including "some of 'The Song of Hiawatha,'" the poem by Henry Wadsworth Longfellow. Brent predicted, "What I say at the trial will affect the jury deeply. I'm certain of that. I will explain how I see reality, how my mind works, my world view."

Now the defense attorneys wanted to avoid a psychiatric examination by another prison-associated doctor who in all likelihood would return with another damning opinion like Glen King's. So in April 2008 they asked Judge Shashy for funds to generate their own psychiatric and psychological evaluation. With his approval, they engaged Dr. Wade C. Myers, director of the forensic psychiatry program at the University of South Florida in Tampa, along with Dr. Allen Hess, a Montgomery psychologist. Together, they reviewed Brent's earlier psychiatric records and Charlotte's letters to various psychiatrists and prepared to interview both Brent and Scoutt.

Bill Blanchard joined Dr. Hess in a face-to-face meeting with Brent at the Montgomery County Jail on May 14, 2008. Brent, dressed in a jail jumpsuit, was led in by a guard. His hair was even longer than at previous meetings and his beard was unkempt. He complained of mood crashes and deep depressions. There was talk of being visited by the Holy Spirit—but no more appearances by the demon Akasha. He was now referring to the spirit voice he now heard regularly as "Seth-Christ." During the visitations, which he said were preceded by a ringing in his ears, Brent would either sit quietly or pace back and forth in his cell. He also volunteered that the Holy Spirit only arrived after he drank coffee. "When I don't have coffee, the Spirit doesn't come through," he told the men. Sometimes he felt like he was living in a different dimension. Scoutt appeared in his dreams (and, he was convinced, she was able to monitor his thoughts), but more frequently there were ethereal visits from friends and acquaintances from his earlier life in Montgomery, including his former girlfriend Andrea Jameson. Yet he said that if Andrea—to whom he would refer to only as "Mr. Jameson's daughter"—were to testify at his trial, he would leave the courtroom.

Twice Brent told the men he wanted to recite at his trial a poem by Jane Roberts, "The Speakers." Sensing that Brent wanted them to ask him to recite it, Blanchard did. Brent recited it from memory and with considerable emotion. Blanchard noticed that Brent now had several symbols carved onto the inner surface of his left forearm. Brent explained that two years earlier he used a paperclip to make the marks, the most prominent one of which was a cross. He said he was inspired by a verse from the Bible, Galatians 6:17, which he paraphrased as, "Lord, show me how to lay your mark upon my body."

Hess later wrote to the defense team that latent disorders like schizophrenia can be controlled in structured environments, only to flourish when young people leave home. In Brent's case, "the Vandy and Naropa and then the Caroline experience were raw gasoline on an open flame." Calling Scoutt as a witness, Hess suggested, could be problematic. Her comments to Brent about his parents—repeated to others—that "we would be better off without them," and "they are better off dead," might be "taken by you or me as hyperbole, but by Brent as a command." But what would the jury think if Scoutt denied making these comments, and Brent refused to corroborate them? The defense would be left with inadmissible hearsay from Deny Caballero, Dow Harris, and Jim Scott.

Robin and Greg Crouch were concerned about the delays, and even more so about the possibility of a trial and what it might reveal about their family history—mental illness, suicide, alcoholism, as well as tension in Charlotte and Brent Sr.'s marriage. On the family's behalf, Morris Dees, co-founder of the Montgomery-based Southern Poverty Law Center and a friend of Charlotte's, asked for a private, face-to-face meeting with Blanchard. Dees strongly urged a negotiated settlement, despite the family's reported preference for a death sentence. While tentative negotiations with the prosecution were underway, Blanchard reminded the defense team about the hurdle they faced. "Even if it was the only way to save his life, Brent told me that he would only accept a plea bargain for life without parole if Scoutt recommended it." That was becoming increasingly problematic, and Blanchard suspected that Scoutt did not have his client's best interests at heart. When the defense team contacted her, around this time, Scoutt said she would never speak with Brent on the phone, telling the lawyers that she was terrified that he would escape and kill her. Her attitude toward Brent suggested that she would not be the best witness for him. "I refuse to talk to a murderer," she told them. "What about his poor mommy and daddy, what did they ever do wrong to deserve this?"

This struck defense investigator Susan Wardell, who knew of Scoutt's contentious relationship with the Springfords in the days and weeks preceding the murders, as particularly disingenuous. Scoutt told the defense team she wanted the trial to be over, so she could follow through with the divorce.

When Brent got some former Montgomery jail inmates to call Scoutt on her cell phone, asking her to send Brent money and to get in touch with him, she changed her number and sent him nothing. Brent, meanwhile, told Wardell that he would kill himself rather than go to prison. Asked if he had a plan to do so, he said it would be easy enough to get medications and overdose.

Hess submitted his report to the defense on May 21, 2008, and the team forwarded it to District Attorney Brooks two days later. Hess ruled out any brain or motor function impairment due to lead or mercury poisoning. He also dismissed any notion that Brent was malingering or simulating mental illness after the killings. "Simply put," Hess wrote in his report, "Mr. Springford did not manufacture the severe concerns noted in his mother's letters. . . . Mr. Springford is psychotically impaired. His records show diagnosis of bipolar disorder with rapid recycling over the past decade and one diagnosis of schizoaffective disorder. In fact, he is delusionally disordered and follows the pattern of a person who was protected in his home life with a marginal adjustment at school." Hess's conclusion was unambiguous: "Mr. Springford cannot meaningfully assist his team of attorneys in preparation or presentation for the trial. He needs life-long custodial care."

What the defense implied but could not say in its competency motion requesting another state examination was that Brent was acting in an increasingly unstable and volatile manner with them. Plagued by nightmares in which he was pursued by his father, he requested four books on dream interpretation. In a letter to one of his lawyers, he wrote that the books "would prepare me mentally, emotionally, and spiritually for trial. I'm praying for more frequent conscious dreams so that I can receive more guidance about how I should proceed at trial."

As a certified indigent, Brent was entitled to free pencils and pads of paper, which he whipped through as feverishly as the books he received. Brent's notes would ultimately grow to more than six hundred pages. These included a steady stream of complaints and requests, especially regarding his diet, to jail officials. Brent now weighed 155 pounds—about forty pounds less than when arrested in 2004. The drop was so dramatic that Lewis wrote Sheriff D. T. Marshall, who oversaw the jail, that he and Blanchard were concerned about their client's "extreme weight loss," complaining that the fourteen hundred daily calories the jail provided was half of what a man of Brent's stature required. Although he was permitted to leave his cell for an hour each day for solitary exercise, he usually preferred to remain inside and keep his door closed.

In a reflective essay written about this time and given to the defense team, Brent looked back on his life and what had led him to his cell. It was clearly self-serving, and in parts regretful, but also informative. "From the time when I was first diagnosed with bipolar disorder until the tragedy, my parents have been incredibly supportive in every way they could," he wrote. "They always encouraged me with my illness and made me believe that I was going continually to get better." Even in the year leading up to the fateful Thanksgiving, during which he chose not to speak with them, "my parents still stood by me." Predictably, Brent claimed that he had been manipulated by Detective Myrick before and during his recorded Colorado confession. The investigators did not want to let him talk about Akasha. "They wanted it to look and sound like I had deliberately planned to come to Montgomery to kill my parents. . . . They threatened to have me fried in the electric chair if I didn't tell them basically what they wanted to hear." He acknowledged that part of the blame was his, like when he exaggerated his father's angry reaction the night of the murders in the written confession that was passed along to police. "The assertion that I deliberately and consciously killed my parents for their money is ludicrous beyond belief. Not only did I have no financial difficulty, but my family and I were living in abundance." And of course Scoutt was completely innocent. She is, he wrote, "the most important person in my life, and she has also been my most important counselor and psychologist every step of the way, from when we first met Thanksgiving 1999 to the day I left on the fateful trip to Montgomery around Thanksgiving 2004."

Brent remained confident that he would be acquitted but his lawyers continued to worry that he would not agree to a plea agreement for life without parole, or see that outcome as a victory. Again, in his introspective essay, he vowed to commit suicide before he would spend his life incarcerated. Mentally, he wrote that he was experiencing rapid mood swings—"fluctuating violently," in his words. He was depressed, because the "Holy Spirit is filling my body less frequently." Mostly, he was crushed by the lack of concrete communication with Scoutt. "I need her spiritual insight," he told Wardell. "If she tells me not to speak at trial, I won't. She speaks the absolute truth, I will never contradict her." He would listen to his lawyers only after hearing what Scoutt advised and considering what the Spirit and his dreams said. He would accept his lawyers' advice only if Scoutt "says to do so."

Scoutt remained the biggest roadblock for the defense. She was the best witness to testify to Brent's mental deterioration over the time he lived with her. Lewis's impression of Brent was that "he was so concerned about protecting Caroline that he didn't give much of a damn about himself." At first, Brent was unalterably opposed to Scoutt's appearance in court, perhaps out of concern that she might herself be placed in legal jeopardy. If she appeared, she could be questioned, for the first time under oath, about dropping Brent off at the Fort Collins bus station the Monday night before the killing, taking him home the Saturday morning after, and at first telling investigators that he was home all of Thanksgiving week. Brent agreed that Caroline could testify, but only if he could leave the courtroom when she took the witness stand. Privately, Lewis was joining the growing defense team consensus about the murders—that Brent "would not have been capable of doing this on his own." Caroline "either put him up to it, or created a scenario in which he had no choice but to do it—in his own mind." From his subsequent face-to-face meeting with Scoutt in Colorado, Lewis found her to be someone with "an almost feral instinct, incredibly stupid, but cunning. . . . I think she was astounded to discover that a conviction would be disinheriting." In 2004, Montgomery police detectives Mike Myrick and Bryan Jurkofsky had come to a nearly identical conclusion, that she was effectively Brent's "puppeteer."

A member of the team was dispatched to the jail to have a "come to Jesus" meeting with their client. That interview lasted for six and a half hours and was probably the frankest conversation Brent had regarding the charges against him. He was informed that his lawyers were concerned about his competence to stand trial and that he could not dictate how he would testify or what he would testify to. The defense team wanted to prepare him as realistically as possible for what he might face on the witness stand. Thus, the team member was clear about the state's evidence against him. At the time, Brent was taking medication in the morning and sleeping during the day, so it took him a while to focus. The first thing he said was that he no longer needed medication because "he had undergone a serious spiritual transformation"—again. He said his cell was now a grand monastery. Weeping, he described hearing the voice of the Holy Spirit, and he described the lives he had previously lived, from St. John of the Cross to Wild Bill Hickok. He said he was preparing for the trial by going into hours-long conscious dream states. He was certain of one thing, he said, his eyes flashing: "I'm not going to be a doormat for the prosecution to walk on." To explain to the jury who he once was, he offered to recite the creed of his college fraternity, Alpha Tau Omega. In addition to "brent" and "winston," now both written in lowercase, he began signing his correspondence "Job," for the divinely tested and put-upon figure from the Old Testament. Despite all, Job's faith did not falter. Neither would his.

Switching the format of the jail interview seemed in order, if only to defuse the situation and return to reality. The defense team member told Brent they were going into a question-and-answer mode. Playing the prosecutor, the defense team member led Brent through an account of the fatal Thanksgiving weekend. Brent incorporated elements from his previous descriptions, like the break-in, and commands from Akasha, as well as his intention to apologize and mend fences. This time he again said his first encounter with his parents was upstairs, but now in his sister Robin's room. "My father's reaction was understandable. He didn't say, 'Brent, it's good to see you.' He wasn't yelling, but his voice was raised. He said, 'How did you get in? You broke into my house? Where did you come in?'" His mother was equally shocked. "She didn't know what to say. They were both standing there looking at this broken window." Brent Jr. retreated to his old room, intending to call Scoutt—another new element—only to be shaken by its transformation into a storage room. That was the last memory he had, except in horrible flashbacks, until he was sitting behind the wheel of the Jaguar.

The simulated question-and-answer format then shifted to Scoutt, beginning when Brent met her at Marie Flinders's home in Boulder in late 1999. "After Vanderbilt," he explained, "I was looking for a spiritual teacher to follow for the rest of my life, to give over my free will to that person. I had tried dozens of spiritual teachers. . . . . When I met Caroline, I knew she was the one." At first, he said, his parents liked Scoutt. "She became Mom's spiritual teacher. Dad thought she was the most spiritual person he had ever met. They helped Caroline with something, to buy the land? They gave her money willingly." Brent denied that his parents engaged Scoutt to keep him far away because he was an embarrassment and a disappointment. He insisted that he never felt rejected, talking about how loving and supportive his father always was. "Dad was a total positive optimist, until I cursed him. I totally lost my temper. I ruined our relationship. . . . Dad definitely loved me until I totally ruined the relationship by cursing him on the phone. We stopped talking." While Brent couldn't imagine anyone seeing Scoutt as anything but a saint, he acknowledged that some people feared her. "She is very powerful. She knows what I dream. I don't have to tell her," including recent visions he had in his cell. "I know she loves me," he added.

In June 2008, Judge Shashy agreed to a new competency examination that required Brent to be transferred from the Montgomery jail to Taylor Hardin, the state mental hospital in Tuscaloosa, for what turned into a ten-week stay. Chief Psychiatrist James Hooper was assigned the case. He reviewed all of Brent's previous records and met with him for a series of face-to-face interviews totaling about five hours. At the time, Brent was taking Provigil, which promotes wakefulness for people who suffer from narcolepsy but can cause breathing difficulties and stomach pain, and Wellbutrin, an anti-depressant and mood elevator, which can cause nausea and headaches. Brent called Susan Wardell to let her know he was enjoying his stay at the facility, saying he liked the group therapy and was having "unbelievable experiences." He reported that he "underwent a transformation" at Taylor Hardin, feeling "elation" at learning so much, and gained fifteen pounds. He liked that there were no female patients with him—thus no temptation to his monkish celibacy—and he refused to attend group sessions led by women. Brent called the mental facility the "Taylor Hardin monastery" and hoped to be sent there if he were found incompetent to stand trial or not guilty by reason of insanity.

But in the end Dr. Hooper agreed with Glen King, the previous state psychologist, that Brent was fully competent to stand trial. "I have seen no evidence of mental illness in this man," Hooper wrote. "He states he has had a bipolar disorder all his life but what he described as bipolar disorder I mostly dismiss as immaturity, poor judgment and possible substance abuse. . . . Mr. Springford did not have a serious mental disease or defect that would rise to the level of an insanity defense." If anything, Hooper's assessment was harsher than King's. As for the voices Brent claimed to have heard, Hooper wrote, "There is no objective evidence to support response to hallucinations now or in the past." Brent's claim of memory loss "is more consistent with substance abuse or malingering than with any mental illness."

Hooper wrote that while Brent had a long history of a "hostile depen-dent" relationship with his parents, he was

> a self-centered, immature person who blames others for his difficulties. Ulti-mately he blamed his parents for not supporting him in his 'hippie' lifestyle. When he had learned that they had cut out his wife, Caroline, from their will and they cut off his credit cards, he was enraged.

The only diagnostic impression Hooper noted, apart from drug abuse, was "Narcissistic Personality Disorder." If the report had a potentially bright spot for the defense, it had to do with Hooper's assessment of Brent's re-lationship with Caroline Scoutt. After spending more than thirty minutes questioning Brent about Scoutt, Hooper observed that she seemed to have acted more like a mother than a wife:

> They had a relationship in which there was no sexual activity, [and she] handled his finances, gave him chores, told him what to do, and even made him ride in the back seat. Therefore, she fed his rage. When he asked his parents to cover his 'wife' and her other children with their insurance and his father refused, he went to Montgomery and killed them.

Apart from his conclusion, some parts of Hooper's report were frankly puzzling to the defense team. The psychiatrist wrote that there was no evidence of Brent's mental illness until he was hospitalized in at Mountain Crest in 2003, even though by then Brent had been treated by at least two psychiatrists who agreed on a diagnosis of bipolar disorder—records that Hooper was given. Understandably, the defense felt blindsided by Hooper's report. The team immediately began devising a strategy for undermining the psychiatrist—anything that would impeach his credibility—standard practice in "dueling diagnoses" cases that rely on competing expert witnesses. Hooper's report noted several times Brent's anomalous positive test for opiates when he was admitted to Centennial Hospital a few days after the murder in 2004. Yet the psychiatrist did not seem to have inquired whether any of Brent's prescribed drugs would include opiates. A Tuscaloosa attorney later tipped the defense that Hooper had a reputation for using drug abuse as his default position in most cases he diagnosed and treated.

There were more problems when Brent returned to jail in Montgomery. He made friends with a neighboring inmate named Eric who gave him some coffee, a man Brent described as "a very literal Christian." Initially, they talked about religion and philosophy, and Brent felt good about the relationship. Although the two men had "opposite views on spirituality" they got along well, but soon some friction developed. So Brent escaped to the jail's suicide isolation section, one of five such transfers he requested in the four years he was in the Montgomery jail. When he returned to the general population he was transferred to a lower floor, where most of the inmates were facing capital murder charges. Ironically, Brent found these men had a much milder disposition.

The defense team next consulted Dr. Randall Tackett, of the College of Pharmacy at the University of Georgia, for advice on how to argue that Brent's actions were influenced by his drug regimen—or lack of one—in the weeks and months leading up to the Montgomery trip. Tackett reviewed Brent's medical and pharmacological records and said he was prepared to testify that Brent had probably stopped taking his medication, including lithium, in the spring of 2004, and periodically thereafter. That might account for the reemergence of his mania during Thanksgiving week, which would account for his riding a bus through the night, using a fake name, and running from the Montgomery bus station to his parents' home miles away. Tackett also suggested that two of the supplements prescribed by Dr. Roger Billica might also have triggered a chemical imbalance that could have precipitated a manic episode. Clearly, this last supposition was a long shot, but the defense team was exploring every option in an effort to save Brent's life.

: *16*

Mitigation

Susan Wardell stood squarely between Brent Springford Jr. and Alabama's crowded Death Row. Relatively late in her professional life, she found a calling in the legal specialty called death penalty mitigation. Wardell returned to school at age forty, following a divorce. She had three children at home in the Atlanta suburbs, yet earned a master's degree in clinical social work before going to law school. During law school she volunteered on the defense of capital cases. After graduation she joined Atlanta's Fulton County Conflict Defender's office, where she often called on her social worker's concern for the underrepresented poor. Clients included battered wives who killed or attacked their abusers, which in turn led her to a steady caseload of capital defenses. In 1998, her work was recognized with the Georgia Woman Lawyer of Achievement award. Defending accused murderers ultimately drew her to the emerging specialty of death penalty mitigation. Steve Bright, famed director of the Southern Center for Human Rights, noticed her success and suggested that Wardell move to an independent mitigation practice. It proved to be a perfect fit. Family and friends of defendants facing the death penalty sensed her sympathetic personality and opened up to her.

In 2006, Wardell, whose short brunette hair emphasizes her intense brown eyes and engaging smile, began working in Alabama, where there was no lack of capital cases. In 2010, Alabama had eclipsed Texas for the highest per capita rate of death sentences and executions in the United States. Under Alabama law in effect both then and now, at least ten jurors must vote for death in order to make that recommendation. It takes at least seven jurors to recommend a life without parole sentence. Therefore, an 8–4 vote could result only in a hung jury in the penalty phase. It is true that a judge can no longer override a jury's penalty verdict, but he or she could have during Brent's case.

In her best-known case, Wardell had confronted Montgomery District Attorney Ellen Brooks in the trial of Mario Woodward, an African American who was convicted in 2006 of killing a white Montgomery police officer, Keith Fouts. Statistically, the odds of Woodward receiving the death penalty were overwhelming. But largely as a result of Wardell's mitigation efforts, the jury voted eight to four for life without parole. The verdict infuriated Brooks and even surprised Wardell. However, the trial judge overruled the jury, and sentenced Woodward to death. The case was appealed to the U.S. Supreme Court, which declined to hear it, and Woodward remains on Death Row. (In January 2016, the U.S. Supreme Court, by an 8–1 decision, ruled that only juries can impose the death penalty, which seemed to undermine its 2013 ruling in Woodward.)

By the time Wardell took on Brent Springford's defense, her twenty-sixth capital case, she was in her late fifties. The state of Alabama's pay for mitigation work was typically meager and often tardy. Wardell was well into a successful third marriage to Atlanta corporate finance attorney Tom Wardell, whose support allowed her to follow her passion. Her husband, she wrote a friend, "enables me to do my work, by paying all the bills, whether the State of Alabama funds me or not." Thus she could front the considerable expenses for her cases. In the Springford case, as is common in many death penalty mitigation efforts around the country, Wardell was joined by two law school intern volunteers and faculty, in this case from the University of California, Berkeley's Boalt Hall. Leading the group was anti-death penalty activist Kate Weisburd, who was enthusiastic about the Springford case and its implications, writing in a memo to the defense team, "We don't execute people who are mentally retarded, and this is a perfect example of why we should not execute people who are seriously mentally ill."

Still, for Wardell and her team, unusual obstacles impeded their effort to keep Brent off Death Row. His sister Robin Springford Crouch had let it be known that she would cut off any family and friends who spoke with Wardell. Dr. Ann Skipper, a local psychiatrist whom Charlotte had consulted several times about Brent Jr. in the year before the killings, declined to cooperate.

Former Judge Sally Greenhaw, Charlotte's closest friend, who had presided over death penalty cases herself, refused to speak to Wardell, and wrote a letter of complaint to Judge Shashy about being contacted. None of this deterred Wardell. Both Robin and Greenhaw cautioned the Springfords' former housekeeper, Maggie Johnson, not to speak with anyone from the defense. But Wardell just showed up on Johnson's doorstep, was invited in, and had a three-hour interview. Jay Lewis, a friend as well as Wardell's colleague on the Springford case, having worked with her on previous (and subsequent) cases, was in awe of her single-mindedness. "She'll go talk to anybody about anything. She'll scour the neighborhood, call up people she knows are going to be hostile. She knows she's going to get a door slammed in her face, which doesn't faze her. She just goes on to the next door."

There were other, less confrontational avenues for her investigation. For two days in Montgomery, Wardell combed through three hundred boxes of Springford property in storage, including documents, books, letters, emails, journals, photos, and scrapbooks. These she scanned or copied for use in generating Brent's mitigation "genogram," an annotated diagram of his family history. The Springfords had apparently saved every letter they ever wrote or received, including thank-you notes and cards, and copies of many they sent. Charlotte, who had family letters dating back two generations, was herself a prolific letter-writer, Three of her home computers were filled with useful information about Brent Jr.'s life, his development, and the progression of his serious mental illness. A forensic technician downloaded everything. Wardell inspected and copied bank records, documenting the flow of money from Montgomery to Colorado, for credit card bills, landscaping, home improvements, auto repairs, legal fees, and more.

From the prosecution, Wardell reviewed other evidence that had been collected in Montgomery, including four years of the Springfords' telephone records, as well as material seized by police in Colorado from the house in Windsor. She collected Brent's elementary and high school records in Montgomery and contacted Vanderbilt to access his records there, with mixed success from publicity-shy university officials. She tracked down retired teachers, Montgomery friends, fraternity brothers, professors, and priests and monks at various monasteries where Brent had spent time. All this material allowed Wardell to document how Brent declined in 1997 through early 1999 from being a creative, talented, much-loved, and handsome young man to being delusional and unkempt. Among Charlotte's papers, Wardell found pages of photocopies and printouts of articles about bipolar disorder, as well as brochures for treatment programs. She reviewed Charlotte's many letters to doctors and treatment centers, recounting her family's history of mental illness, as well as Brent Jr.'s treatment.

By the spring of 2000, Wardell found, Brent had become a completely different person, thin, bordering on emaciated, ill-groomed, unable to function at Naropa University, and before long under the complete spell of Caroline Scoutt. The lawyer found particularly strange how Brent began to refer to his former Montgomery girlfriend, Andrea Jameson, as "Mr. Jameson's daughter." In addition to never mentioning Andrea by name he never included her in any of the biographical timelines that team members asked him to prepare. While compiling her mitigation reports, Wardell deliberately avoided listening to Brent's Colorado confession to police. She said she sensed that the empathy so important to her work on the case would be colored by hearing in Brent's own words how he killed his mother and father. At times, while reading Charlotte's letters, Wardell said she sensed Charlotte's spirit looking over her shoulder, saying, "Save my son." It was not as if Wardell needed any additional motivation. "The magnitude of this tragic situation is overwhelming," she emailed Andrea Jameson. "We must save his life!"

One of the first things Wardell and the team learned that might help with mitigation was an extensive family history of severe mental illness and alcoholism. Judge Shashy had declined to order several mental institutions to provide records on Charlotte Springford and her birth mother, Lucy Turner, which the hospitals later said no longer existed. But from numerous letters, journal entries, and interviews, Wardell pieced together the history. Lucy Turner had been hospitalized numerous times as an adult for psychiatric treatment, including shock therapy. Toward the end of her life, Lucy had delusions of voices speaking to her through the television and of being shot by ray guns. This event led to a major psychotic episode, diagnosis of paranoid schizophrenia, and civil commitment until her death. For two years following the tragic house fire in Luverne that killed her granddaughter, Lucy was drunk much of the time. Lucy's mother Lettie—Charlotte's maternal grandmother—also was mentally ill. From the age of ten, Lettie terrorized her mother and siblings when her father was out of the house. As an adult, Lettie physically abused Lucy, once sending her to elementary school with welts all over her body because she hadn't practiced her piano lesson. Lettie was described as alternately charming and violent and may have been institutionalized. Her husband—Charlotte's grandfather—committed suicide in his thirties. Lettie's son—Charlotte's uncle—killed himself in his twenties. Lettie's brother was also an alcoholic.

In other letters recovered from her computer after the murders, Charlotte Springford wrote that, in addition to the time she was treated for depression after the deaths of her daughter and parents, she and Brent Sr. were diagnosed as adults as bipolar. Charlotte took her prescribed medication, but Brent Sr. refused. Charlotte also wrote that she suffered from clinical depression, yet she was highly functional. Brent Sr., Wardell learned, had his own dark side. Some friends thought he was controlling, and he was a compulsive gambler who would wager as much as $10,000 on a football game. One friend described him as a "nut case," a fast driver who could become sufficiently enraged—or drunk—to tear up a bar in New Orleans. In at least one point in their troubled father-son relationship, Brent Sr. said that he wished his son had never been born, and Brent Jr. agreed. Yet, after the murders, investigators found under Brent Jr.'s mattress a photo, taken his senior year in high school, of father and son, along with a picture of himself as a young child. Brent Jr. said he kept the photos to remember the time before his mental illness, when he and his father were close. Although Brent Jr. realized he was a disappointment to his father and a constant worry to his mother, even after their deaths he always spoke of them in the present tense and told Wardell how much he loved them.

In the spring of 2007, Wardell, Blanchard, and Lewis made the first of two trips to Colorado, Wyoming, and South Dakota, totaling fourteen days. They explored Brent's life in those locations and, in particular, his relationship with Scoutt, who at first refused to meet with the defense trio. Late one afternoon on their initial trip to Newcastle, Wyoming, where Scoutt then lived, the defense team went into Donna's Main Street Diner in the small town's center. Wardell, ostensibly giving her order to the waitress, loudly said that she was looking for information about Caroline Scoutt. In short order, just about everyone in the crowded, cozy restaurant came to their table to speak with them. "Everybody had an opinion," Lewis recalled, "and they weren't good ones." Wardell's research found that Scoutt had several Social Security numbers under a variety of names, some unrelated to her previous marriages. Ultimately, Scoutt agreed to several extensive one-on-one interviews with Wardell, in person and later by telephone. Other interviews followed with members of the defense team. Wardell did her best to conceal her growing suspicions from Scoutt. At first, in these larger meetings, Scoutt would speak only with her own attorney present, and wanted to know if she had been implicated in the murders by anyone. Blanchard found the woman "vigilant, always looking for an angle, and tightly controlled." Scoutt made three insistent assertions at variance with what the defense team had learned: that it was Charlotte Springford who chose the Windsor house; that she was Charlotte's close confidant until the time of the murders; and that the secret wedding in Deadwood had been Brent Jr.'s idea. Again, Scoutt asked about the status of the Springfords' estate, and whether she had any right of inheritance if Brent was acquitted or found not guilty by reason of insanity.

Blanchard hired Denver private investigator Wayne Diffee to assist the defense on the ground in Colorado. The detective is as colorful a character as the other members of the defense team. He is a hefty man with a close-cropped white beard and sparse seeding of white hair—"that which has not left me for other climates," as he liked to say. A veteran of twenty-eight years with the Denver Public Defender's office, he handled 160 homicides and five capital cases—all of which resulted in life sentences. He was the antithesis of the popular image of a PI, with his beard and slightly rocking gait. In summer, he worked in T-shirts—fountain pens fearlessly stuffed in the breast pocket—cargo shorts, a floppy broad-brimmed hat, and sandals. His master's degree and a relaxed, avuncular manner notwithstanding, he was a dogged investigator. He soon learned from Scoutt's second husband that although she told many people she was an orphan, one day a woman she introduced as her mother showed up. And, despite her claims of being Native American, Diffee could find no record that she was enrolled in any area tribes, although like many Mexicans and Mexican Americans it was likely that she had some Indian heritage.

The defense team also generated a money trail, later estimating that, including the purchase of the Windsor house, the Springfords wrote checks for $750,000 to $1 million to support Brent and Scoutt's family. During this same time, 2001–2004, Brent wore the same few tattered shirts and pants for three years. It wasn't until well after the Springfords' murders that investigators began to document Scoutt's callous—if not abusive—behavior toward Brent Jr. even as the money was pouring into Windsor at an increasing rate. It was as if her attitude was, "to hell with his well-being in the dead of winter," Wardell observed. "She had her new house and furniture, and left him on his own, with only intermittent psychiatric care, no food, etc. She was the only one who communicated with Charlotte and Brent Sr. They were dependent on her to keep them informed of his well-being."

Wardell, Blanchard, Lewis, and Diffee spoke with Brent's former Colorado neighbors and contractors, as well as a half-dozen of his co-workers and supervisors in Wyoming, Colorado, and South Dakota, and copied a hundred pages of work records. They learned about Scoutt's birdhouse surveillance cameras that she sometimes focused on their neighbors. The defense team tracked down a neighbor who had hidden after her Windsor house was vandalized almost to the point of demolition, while Scoutt lived next door. Two of this same neighbor's cars were totaled one night while the family was out of town. Other neighbors, with whom Caroline constantly feuded, said that things Scoutt told them about her work history and academic credentials—including a claim of a PhD—later proved to be inaccurate. Caroline told them she was a witch who could put spells on people who crossed her, including her two ex-husbands, who also accused her of casting spells. At one point, the neighbors said, Scoutt threatened them with Brent Sr.'s legal wrath. To confirm what the neighbors told them, the defense team and Diffee retrieved reams of complaints from the Weld County Colorado Sheriff's Department and, before that and after, from police and the county sheriff's office in Newcastle. These documented

Scoutt's contentious relations with her neighbors, as well as complaints filed against—and between—her and her children.

In Colorado and South Dakota, the defense team interviewed a half-dozen private and hospital psychologists and psychiatrists who had treated and/or tested Brent. Even with Brent Jr.'s written approval, some refused to speak with Wardell until she got a court order from Judge Shashy to overcome federal privacy prohibitions. Obviously, such information would be critical in what was expected to be a courtroom dynamic of contending shrinks. Wardell knew that a well-documented clinical history of Brent's spiral into madness would have an impact on a decision by a prosecutor, judge, or jury deciding whether to seek or impose a death sentence. Dr. Charles J. Lord, of Rapid City, South Dakota, the first psychiatrist to diagnose and treat Brent for bipolar disorder in 2000, explained to Wardell that patients with bipolar disorder can progress to schizophrenia and "floridly psychotic behavior." Lord concluded, even after all this time, and at this distance, that Brent was "mentally ill and was, at the time of the murders, floridly psychotic." He said it would be inhumane to execute him, adding that he thought the Triavil drug Brent was getting in the Montgomery jail was not appropriate for him. By contrast, Dr. Harris Jensen, the Fort Collins psychiatrist who dismissed Brent as a patient in 2003 after Brent threatened him, was extremely circumspect in his interview with the defense team, asking if he was being taped before reading aloud from his treatment charts. Jensen did say that he advised Brent to stop taking the herbal supplements Scoutt was providing him.

Wardell and the other lawyers visited the Fort Collins offices of Dr. Roger Billica, Brent's doctor and nutritionist. He told them he was unaware that Brent had stopped taking his anti-psychotic, anti-depression drugs, and his lithium in the months before the murders. "The shock was apparent when we told him," Wardell recalled. Billica said he had put the young man on a dietary detox regimen of green vegetables and supplements. When he apparently overdid it, eating too many sprouts, he got diarrhea, so the physician said it was too much for him and told him to stop. However, the visit to see Billica was unsettling for Jay Lewis. The reception area was lined with glass display cases filled with what appeared to be vitamins and dietary supplements. "It was like a drugstore," Lewis said. Shortly after dropping Brent Jr. off at the bus station Thanksgiving week of 2004, they learned, Scoutt had used Brent Sr.'s credit card to charge $3,000 worth of vitamins and supplements from the doctor.

The Boulder public defender's office, which first represented Brent after his arrest, turned over correspondence between Brent and Scoutt, some of which they exchanged while he was at Centennial Peaks Hospital and, later, in jail. The ones inquiring about the disposition of the Springfords' estate appeared potentially incriminating to Scoutt. The Springfords' phone records were at variance with Scoutt's claims that she maintained a close relationship with Charlotte. They showed, for example, that Scoutt ignored far more calls from the Springfords' home than she answered. Scoutt told police that she had spoken with Charlotte "every day," but in an eight-month period preceding the murder she had not accepted a single call from Montgomery. Wardell also encountered other roadblocks, especially in the Boulder area. A number of Scoutt's former clients refused to talk to Wardell, out of fear. Ann Flinders, Brent's old Naropa roommate, explained to Wardell that, while Scoutt "was a powerful presence and [brought] a great deal of energy," she was someone "who not only heals but also uses forces to do her will." Mike Myrick and Bryan Jurkofsky had previously reached the same conclusion.

The first time the defense trio tried to locate Scoutt's small ranch outside Newcastle, Wyoming, the drive turned into a sagebrush version of "Mr. Toad's Wild Ride." They bounced around in their rented SUV, following their GPS along unpaved roads through empty fields, crossing ravines on frail wooden logs. "We really didn't think we were going to make it," Lewis said. When they found the place, no one seemed to be home, and a sign warned against trespassing. Typically, Wardell ignored the sign, climbed over the locked gate, and barreled onto the property, taking pictures. The birdhouse surveillance cameras, fully functional, had been transplanted to the ranch, along with the greenhouse, several outbuildings, and fencing she also recognized from photos of the Windsor house. Within minutes, the defense lawyers' cell phones began ringing, with Daniel Quinn, Scoutt's Colorado lawyer, on the line, ordering them off the property. Along with her son, a group of Scoutt's Native American friends, ex-boyfriends and neighbors—the same group she relied on from time to time for muscle—roared up in an SUV to ask them what they were doing. On the drive back to Denver, with Lewis at the wheel, they noticed a tire was going flat, apparently caused by driving over a cactus, but they managed to limp into one of the few open gas stations on the highway. "It really was a cursed trip," said Lewis, heretofore a committed skeptic on matters supernatural. "I believe that Caroline has some occult powers that we did not understand."

As early as July 2007, based on her visit west, phone interviews, and Charlotte Springford's correspondence with her son, Wardell was starting to suspect that Brent "was essentially brainwashed, cult-style" by Scoutt and was little more than her dupe. After this trip, Wardell's relations with Brent Jr. began to fray. He sensed her growing belief that Scoutt was a sinister character—that she was at least partly to blame for the final stages of his descent into madness, and that she might have been responsible for Brent's fatal trip to Montgomery. "Brent might have killed his parents only because Caroline whipped him into a frenzy," she wrote. "He had never considered anything other than what Caroline told him. She was milking it for all it was worth—to her. And toward the end, Brent Sr. smelled a rat."

Marie Flinders, who introduced Brent to Scoutt at her Boulder home back in 1999, provided Wardell with calendars recording Scoutt's many visits to her house, as well as receipts for money Flinders paid for improvements to Scoutt's Wyoming ranch and donations for the proposed Native American counseling center. In an email, Wardell wrote Flinders of her goal to bring Scoutt to account. "If we ever do get a crack at her, I want to repay her for all the horrendous tragedy she brought on so many good, trusting people. Of course, I know karma takes care of it, but I'd like to contribute to the process if I can."

For her part, Scoutt—perhaps also sensing Wardell's suspicion—wanted nothing to do with testifying under oath in a Montgomery courtroom. There, she could be drawn into her involvement in the Springford murders, as an accessory before or after the fact, or worse. By February 2008 Wardell felt that in Scoutt's few communications to Brent in jail, she was subtly encouraging him to commit suicide. Wardell was approaching a fixation—if not obsession—with Scoutt. Since her time at Duke in the 1960s,

Wardell maintained an interest in meditation, astrology, and channeling but did not give serious thought to the supernatural. Over time, however, she became convinced that the supernatural had power for good and for evil. "My beliefs have always been a little unconventional," she conceded. She wrote other members of the defense team that she believed that Scoutt was using her powers against her. Wardell was convinced that Scoutt's spells were responsible for the flat tire on the Wyoming drive, the foot she broke after tripping on a Springford file in her office, and even a wallet stolen at the Boulder airport. On their second trip west, Wardell, Blanchard, and Lewis were staying at one of Newcastle's few motels, The Pines. The evening before they were set to make the long drive back to Denver, it started snowing and by morning the snow was fifteen inches deep. Wardell emerged from her room with an eagle feather—provided by a local resident familiar with Scoutt—and an abalone shell filled with sage. She lit the brush, and began to waft it over their car, "in an effort to neutralize any spells that Caroline had put on us," said Lewis. He recalled being bemused by the ceremony, which he found surreal. Still, he said, "it obviously worked, since nothing bad happened to us on the way back."

District Attorney Brooks and her chief deputy, Daryl Bailey, also made an investigative trip to Colorado, a rare out-of-state undertaking. Among other things, Brooks also wanted to speak to the psychiatrists who had treated Brent and to inspect their records. She knew there were valid mental illness concerns. What she wasn't sure of was whether they were sufficient to convince a jury that Brent was, or might have been, insane at the time of the killings, and she didn't want to be blindsided by the defense. She recalled in an interview that her "instinct" was that Brent was simply evil, although extremely bright.

Just as Wardell was forming her conclusions about Scoutt, Brent made a series of demands to Wardell, starting with an apology to Scoutt for everything the attorney had turned up about his wife, and especially for the unauthorized inspection of the Wyoming ranch. During a visit to the jail, Wardell explained to him that it was the defense team's ethical responsibility to try to save his life, not to do as he said. They needed witnesses to his mental deterioration, and the only ones who could do that were family members and his Windsor neighbors. Brent followed up the meeting with two searing letters defending Scoutt. Wardell tried to push back by being tough with him, believing that he needed another reality check. Still, as she confided to other defense team members, she was convinced Brent was now out of touch with reality. The only way they could make a defense work was to somehow get inside his head and see the case through his eyes, and present his state of mind in a way that Brent himself could accept. That was a high hurdle. While it was obvious to Wardell that their client was not guilty by reason of insanity, "we need his trust and cooperation to sell that defense. . . . If he feels we don't respect Caroline and his view of reality, he is going to flip on us and shut us down."

Despite his weird behavior, Brent had his rational moments in his talks with Wardell. He told her that he had no desire to conceal his bus trip from Colorado to Alabama, despite buying tickets under an alias. He saw the many surveillance cameras in the waiting rooms where he sat for hours but made no effort to disguise himself. If he had wanted to avoid detection, he told her, he would have hitchhiked. He insisted that the only reason for the trip to Montgomery was to apologize to his parents.

Wardell's relationship with Brent grew increasingly complicated. Although herself an attorney, as a mitigation specialist her role was to develop a close relationship with Brent and, if possible, with Scoutt, who was spooked by lawyers. Wardell had a determined approach in preparing more than two dozen prior mitigation cases, but in Brent Jr.'s case she felt an even greater personal connection. "I felt an emotional tie to him," she recalled, "because he was so vulnerable to Scoutt's commands. And because he was so heartbroken that his parents were dead. He spoke of them in the present tense and told me what a great life he'd had with them." All of Wardell's previous clients were indigent and about half were people of color, poor, uneducated, and from highly dysfunctional families. None of these dissonant factors applied to Brent, yet none of her previous death penalty clients were as seriously mentally ill. Nor had she previously dealt with a client who was under the spell of another person. Wardell spent a hundred hours with him in his cell. Over time her feelings hardened—and sharpened toward Scoutt. She concluded that the woman was untrustworthy, punitive, greedy, and demanding. From Charlotte's correspondence with Scoutt and with Brent Jr.'s therapists, Wardell found that Scoutt was misrepresenting important information to and from Brent, to her own advantage. This left Brent—by now diagnosed as schizophrenic as well as bipolar—isolated and unable to communicate with anyone, except through Scoutt.

The more Wardell uncovered, the angrier she became, convinced that Scoutt had twisted everything in her relationship with Brent for one motive: money. Wardell also concluded that Brent's parents had had no idea how Scoutt was treating their son, else they would never have allowed it. The Springfords did sense that Brent was deteriorating out west. Close friends suggested that Brent needed to be "deprogrammed." Andrea Jameson "begged Charlotte to go get him," according to her mother, Elaine Jameson.* "I wonder if she would have if she had Big Brent's full support," Elaine wrote to Wardell years later.

In March 2004, Wardell learned, Scoutt persuaded Brent that the psychiatrist he had most recently been seeing was a quack, and Brent agreed. "Psychiatrists are worthless," he wrote. "They give drugs; that's all they do." Brent preferred therapists willing to listen to his ramblings about spirituality, or those who found a more organic cause for his unease. "I'm tired of everything being about my mental illness," he wrote. A month later, Scoutt steered him to Dr. Billica, the nutrition and environmental medicine specialist who was already treating the Scoutt family. It was at this point, Wardell found, that Charlotte had begun her frantic search for a reputable in-patient program for Brent. She had to find a program that would accept her son, and then figure out a way to persuade him to enter it.

In the weeks before they were murdered, Wardell learned, Brent Sr. and Charlotte had firmly concluded that Scoutt was a fraud, and this time they intended to follow through on their threat of a financial cutoff. The week that Brent traveled to Montgomery to kill his parents, Wardell found, thousands of dollars in checks were written on Brent and Scoutt's joint bank account, which was controlled by Scoutt. The dietary supplements and treatments on a costly "sound therapy" vibration device from Billica were actually for

---

*   Not her real name.

Scoutt and her daughter, whom he was treating for a hormonal imbalance. For his part, Brent Sr. had no faith in the doctor and directly confronted Scoutt over taking his son to him; what had been a deteriorating relationship between Scoutt and the parents went into a full tailspin. For the six months leading up to their deaths, there had been virtually no communication between the Springfords and Scoutt, except when she called from Windsor about a financial crisis or home repair. As described earlier, Scoutt had already squeezed nearly a million dollars from the Springfords. In the Colorado and Wyoming interviews by Wardell's team, more incriminating evidence piled up from others in Boulder, including one woman who said that she gave Scoutt more than $80,000 over five months for "a counseling center" and was still fearful of her.

In a key find, Diffee, the defense's Colorado private investigator, located Deny Caballero, who had moved into the Windsor house in the summer 2002, before the start of his senior year of high school, after clashing with his stepfather and mother. At the time, Caballero was dating Scoutt's older daughter, which Caroline did not approve of. She told the other children that Deny was very troubled, and that his parents were abusive, so he would be living with them until he finished high school. After the young couple broke up, Caroline told her younger daughter that Caballero "is not our sister's boyfriend, but our brother. He was a very nice guy." Still, Scoutt required Caballero to pay for rent and food and do chores. Caballero's senior year was a busy one. He joined the Colorado Army National Guard, often going straight from football practice to weekend training with a military police unit in Denver. Immediately after graduation he went through basic training, He then returned to the Greeley-Fort Collins area, taking police science courses at Front Range Community College in Fort Collins, paid for by the guard. In addition to his military training, he also juggled two jobs, including one as an armed guard for Loomis, driving one of the security company's armored trucks and dropping off and picking up currency. He remained in the Windsor home, waiting to join the Army full time.

In 2006, Caballero had enough of military police work and the National Guard. He felt it was time to "get off the sidelines," so he enlisted in the Army, qualified for the 82nd Airborne, and spent his first combat tour in

Iraq. Contacted after his return, Caballero told Wardell that while he lived in the Windsor house he was totally unaware that Brent and Scoutt were married. "There was no romance, never a kiss, no hugs," he recalled. There was a darker side to Scoutt and Brent's relationship. She was verbally abusive to Brent, the young man said, treating him almost like a slave. Caballero said that Scoutt ruled the household with an iron fist. Brent could not enter the house without her permission; he had to call her first on his cell phone. When Scoutt did agree to let him in, she announced to family members, "Oh God, Brent's coming into the house!" Brent was allowed to share meals with the family only on special occasions, like holidays and his birthday. Normally, Caballero told her, Brent cooked outside or in the garage on a small propane stove and basically subsisted on noodles and catsup, canned tuna, beans and rice (sometimes moldy), and peanut butter sandwiches. He would make a pot of oatmeal in the morning, which he took for lunch in the oil field in Lupton. Caballero confirmed from his observation what Brent had told paralegal Mary Kottenstette: that his sugar craving and lack of cash reduced him to shoplifting Granola bars from Home Depot and dumpster diving behind bakeries.

Rare social outings often ended in disaster, Caballero said. The Red Lobster in Fort Collins was one of Brent's favorites, so Charlotte would urge Scoutt to take Brent there for dinner. Brent would get cleaned up for the meal, but since Scoutt's children thought Brent was so weird, it would sometimes be just the two of them at the restaurant table. Scoutt told Caballero that Brent often got angry at the wait staff, complaining about the service and claiming the food wasn't good enough. He looked down and refused to tell the waiter what he wanted, speaking out of the side of his mouth. Finally, Scoutt stopped taking him. The day-to-day household expenses were largely covered by money that Brent earned in the Wyoming and South Dakota oil fields, and then at Fort Lupton, supplemented by what his parents provided, Caballero said. Before he moved to the Windsor garage full time, Brent slept in his SUV or in a nearby camper on his weekend visits from Wyoming, even in the harsh winter. After twelve- or fourteen-hour workdays in the oil fields, Scoutt would shame Brent into building fences and outbuildings, while deriding him as "an idiot," "stupid," and a "total incompetent." There was worse, Caballero said. Scoutt sometimes punished Brent by making him walk or run home behind her Yukon, even at night and through the snow. She forced him to shower at a truck stop, rather than at home. Scoutt and one of her daughters would take Brent to the mall, pointing out things they "really liked," which Brent—who had no money—shoplifted for them.

Even with Brent largely exiled to the garage and yard, the Scoutt household seemed to be in a constant state of upheaval, usually involving money, alcohol abuse, and domestic strife. Everyone in the Windsor household seemed to have mental-health issues, and numerous encounters, mostly minor, with the social service and legal systems. Even though Brent Jr. often spoke and wrote to his parents about his responsibility to support "my kids," insisting that he "acted like a father to them," Caballero said that the stepchildren had little to do with him and did not respect or like him, mocking him behind his back. Caballero told Wardell that he thought Scoutt was a beast and deserved to go to prison.

Wardell believed she had struck mitigation gold with the Caballero interview, but she worried that the young man, by then an army sergeant and soon to leave for his second tour in Iraq, might not be available by the time of Brent's trial. So, on May 27, 2008, she arranged for Wayne Diffee, the private investigator, to take a written, notarized statement covering the same ground as her previous interview, but filling in more details. "She turned Brent into a complete zombie," he wrote. "He never did ANYTHING without her permission. She told him he'd never be a real man."

Although he was for the most part submissive to Scoutt, Brent was still capable of acting out, sometimes violently, Caballero said. Once Brent witnessed a heated argument between Caballero and Scoutt's older daughter while the two were still dating. Brent, who seemed hostile to Caballero when he first moved into the house, threw the young man against a wall, grabbed him by the throat and threatened to kill him. Caballero said Scoutt confided to him that Brent's parents were horrible and that if they were dead she would share in Brent's inheritance.

In the fall of 2004, after the blowups with Brent Sr. over medical treatment ostensibly for Brent—which were actually for Scoutt and her children—the atmosphere in the Windsor house turned ominous, Caballero told Wardell. Scoutt told Brent he had two evil demons in him, and that only she could rid him of them, since she was a witch. Scoutt spent the days leading up to Thanksgiving whispering to Brent Jr. in her bedroom, where he had never been permitted before. By this time, Brent seemed to Caballero to be robotic. On the Monday evening before Thanksgiving, Scoutt drove Brent to the bus station for the trip to Montgomery. When she returned to Windsor from dropping him off, Caballero said, Scoutt acted as though she didn't know where he was. Her children complained about having to do Brent's chores and, on Thanksgiving, when they asked where he was, Scoutt acted nonchalant, even though holiday meals tended to be command performances for Brent. Yet even his unexplained absence Thanksgiving week did not stop Scoutt's financial demands. The week before, the house's sewage stopped working and rather than fixing it or calling the Springfords herself, Scoutt ordered Caballero to phone Brent Sr. about having it replaced. Two days before Thanksgiving, Scoutt announced, almost theatrically, that after months of no communication she was going to call the Springfords to check in with them. The message recorded on the Springfords' phone machine that day sounded stilted. Scoutt said she was calling to see how their holiday was, as she always did, and talked about Brent Jr.'s local shopping trip. When she called again on Thanksgiving morning, before Charlotte and Brent Sr. left for Birmingham, Scoutt pointedly "reminded" the Springfords that she had spoken with them the previous Tuesday. Police, however, were unable to recover any other messages from her before Thanksgiving week.

In his written statement, Caballero recalled several dinners he had with Scoutt "in her sanctuary," before things went downhill between them:

> She dropped hints about Brent getting rid of his parents, like, "God it would be so nice if he'd go kill his parents; they're so bad, so evil." At first, I couldn't believe she was saying that to me, but after a while I realized she meant it. She thought she was confiding in someone who would never tell on her.
>
> She always hinted, "If only I could find a way to get Brent to go away and take care of his family, get rid of them, it would be really good. . . . The house and the Yukon would be mine."

I have no doubt that Caroline told Brent to kill his parents. She hated them. She was an evil, conniving person.

In the final analysis, Wardell agreed with Caballero that Scoutt had been—at least—the intellectual author if not the instigator of the Springfords' murders. Not necessarily that Scoutt specifically *told* Brent to kill his parents—and was therefore legally culpable. But that in some way she manipulated Brent to take that course, in hopes of ultimately profiting from it. Blanchard and Lewis shared these suspicions, to different degrees. It is likely that District Attorney Brooks did too, although she said in an interview years later that she kept any suspicions to herself. In any event, Wardell found that as his trial date approached, Brent remained steadfast in his refusal to say—or listen—to anything negative about his wife. Brent did confirm to Wardell that Scoutt was the source of their escalating and ultimately truculent financial demands to his parents, even those in the letters and faxes ostensibly from him, as well as his angry phone calls.

In a long email, Wardell shared much of Caballero's information with Brent's old girlfriend, Andrea Jameson, with whom Wardell had become close over the years. Jameson wrote back in fury, after reading the email three times. She was so emotional, she told Wardell, she didn't know where to start. When she did, she began in capital letters, and in uncharacteristic language: "I KNEW SHE WAS ALWAYS SOMEHOW BEHIND THIS. I ALWAYS FUCKING KNEW."

Scoutt still had a financial interest in the trial's outcome. Although separated from Brent, they were still legally married. If Brent were acquitted or found not guilty by reason of insanity, she might stand to inherit his interest in the Springfords' sizable estate. In that outcome, Brent might spend the rest of his life in a state mental hospital. But that would depend on the outcome of the estate's expected wrongful death civil suit and the way Alabama's Slayer Statute was interpreted to apply to heirs of accused killers. Through Wardell's questions to Brent, and a card from Scoutt about Wardell's unauthorized visit to her ranch, he became aware of Wardell's findings about Scoutt. He reacted strongly, writing a friend about Wardell,

I simply can't tolerate her false, negative judgments of [Scoutt] and my step kids anymore. She believes in the slanderous lies that the racist, hypocritical neighbors told her to damage my family. Caroline's and my kids' praiseworthy character, integrity, and spirituality can be easily and unassailably proven and vindicated. . . . I will not remain silent anymore while Susan speaks badly of Caroline and my kids.

This letter set off one of Brent's attorneys, who described the letter as

the latest missive from our Young Hero. Do I have any volunteers to go over to the [jail] and slap some sense into him? He's actually more concerned with a technical trespass against Caroline and her 'Sacred Land' than with his own case! . . . I'm sure that this letter is very revealing in a psychological sense vis-à-vis the relationship between Caroline and [Brent], but I gotta say that the tone of it just bakes my biscuits and makes me want to immediately read the kid the riot act. . . . We have somehow got to get it across to [him] that Caroline is not (and never has been) concerned about his best interests, only her own. I wonder if he's capable of internalizing that information without serious damage?

Another member of the defense team agreed: "You and I need to go and see [Brent] tomorrow or the next day if you can. We need to make it plain to him that we are a team, and he can't dictate who he will and won't see. We can't function if we let him do that."

In an April 2008 email, one member of the defense team suggested creating a spreadsheet of Scoutt's lies. Another replied that there might not be a spreadsheet with enough cells to hold all of them. Later that month, a team member observed that Brent was clearly delusional. "If he's delusional isn't he by definition incompetent?" In a memorandum to the defense team, Wardell seemed to throw up her hands. "We believe that Brent Jr. was under the complete domination of a woman motivated by greed and power, but we have no way of proving it, and nothing strong enough to convince a jury that Brent Jr. was insane at the time of the murders." Sinister as her actions may have been, Scoutt presented a thorny dilemma for the defense's theory of the case. "If we imply that Caroline in some way commanded him to go to Montgomery to kill his parents," another team member wrote, "we've admitted that the trip was taken with that intent. Having done so, we won't then be able to claim some psychotic break overtook him at the last moment. I still believe Caroline knew about the trip, but better for us that she, too, viewed it as an attempt at reconciliation."

Plea

Brent's defense team prepared for trial, hoping that it would not come to that. Their main points were that their client was not mentally competent at the time of the murders; he was not competent now to assist in his defense; and his previous incriminating statements should be suppressed because when he made them he was unstable, sleep-deprived, and under the influence of psychotropic drugs, so his rights to a lawyer and against self-incrimination were thus effectively ignored. Without these statements, there was no physical evidence (apart from the single fingerprint of Brent Jr.'s at the house that could not be dated) or witnesses to place Brent at the murder scene on Hull Street or in the Jaguar. Without the confessions, prosecutors Ellen Brooks and Daryl Bailey would then have to rely on circumstantial evidence. That is, the bus station surveillance tapes between Colorado and Alabama, or statements made by Charlotte and Brent Sr. to others about their son, which were hearsay but admissible since the speakers were dead.

In theory, the defense had a fighting chance for a not guilty verdict or, if Judge William Shashy refused to suppress Brent's statements, not guilty by reason of insanity. In an unsolicited strategy memo, a member of the Berkeley Death Penalty Clinic mitigation team suggested the first line of defense should be that the murders occurred when Brent suffered a manic, psychotic episode. Mental illness ran in his family for three generations; he had been in treatment since his early twenties; and he had recently gone off his medication. And as his illness worsened, evidence showed that he developed a volatile temper. Relations with his parents were strained, especially since his invitation to his sister's wedding was rescinded and his father again threatened to cut him off. Brent went to Montgomery with every intention of reconciling with his parents. Seeing that his bedroom was no longer his, that he had been effectively displaced, he snapped. In practice, however, the memo concluded, "[t]here was too much planning, coordination and execution, over too long a period of time that would undercut the psychotic episode strategy." There was a contingency plan to call Caroline Scoutt to the witness stand and explore her toxic relationship with Brent. Still, the consensus was that a plea deal for life without parole would be the best option.

Brent seemed resigned to his fate, as he understood it. The "Spirit has made it absolutely clear, ever since I've been in jail," he wrote to the defense team, "that I'm not going to prison or Death Row, and that I just need to trust, which I do. (I even had a dream in which my Dad told me, 'Just trust.')" He said he understood that his attorneys felt that he had only a five percent chance of acquittal. With no experience of prison life, he projected a post-conviction existence much like his years in jail: "I am solitary by nature, and the cloistered, monastic life is a dominant part of my personality. . . . I would never plead guilty for something when I know I'm innocent, unless Spirit told me to." It was, he admitted, depressing to contemplate spending the rest of his life in a state mental hospital where he would likely go if found not guilty by reason of insanity. "But I know those are decent places to live, so it's not a terrible thing." Such a life, he wrote, "will not be a loss, from my point of view, and not so different from where I would be now if I had gone into a monastery in California." In another instance he mused that if Scoutt had not come into his life when he was twenty-three he probably would have been ordained a Buddhist monk. "My mental illness would probably not have erupted in such extreme form under those conditions." Brent suddenly changed gears, concluding the letter by saying that he prayed the defense team was "ready to battle with the prosecution, because that's my only option. I know I'm not going to prison." Anyway, in the most adverse outcome, Brent said he was not afraid of Death Row. With the electric chair now gone in Alabama, "lethal injection is not nearly as bad."

The biggest problem for the defense remained that Brent would listen only to the counsel of Caroline Scoutt, his recent writings about "Spirit" notwithstanding. Although the couple had legally separated in September 2005, Scoutt remained the only person whose judgment he trusted. Around that time, however, Scoutt wrote Brent, saying, "I will not advise or talk to you about it. Hope that's clear. Don't ask me to!" Fearing her anger, and an irrevocable break in communication, Brent told the defense team to stop asking for her assistance. On November 4, 2008, at defense attorney Bill Blanchard's request, Scoutt sent Brent a brief, hand-printed note:

> I haven't written you for sometime because I do *NOT* want to hear anymore of your strange speaking . . . I hope you find the right medication to help you be as balanced as you can be in your condition. Most importantly—I am communicating because I have spoken to Susan and Bill. They feel *insanity, not guilty, will not be accepted.* I agree! Alabama is still a backward state as far as human rights and compassion for the mentally ill who have committed crimes. I feel it will lead to much *more torment* for you, Robin, the children, etc. The children and I talked about it. There is a feeling that the best is *"to plead for life without parole."* There still is a purpose for your life. You may not know what it is now or how things can change after you take life without parole. I know the decision is up to you, but at least take seriously what I have written. Again, *"life without parole"* feels best. May God Bless, Remember you are loved.

Ten days later, the defense wrote District Attorney Brooks, formally requesting a settlement of the case. There was concern that Brooks would be reluctant to accept, since taking the death penalty off the table might seem racist to some: it might suggest that Brent was getting off because he was white and came from a wealthy family. Then, as previously mentioned, there was his sister, Robin Crouch, who was still thought to favor the death penalty but had communicated through Morris Dees that she and her husband Greg wanted to avoid a trial with its risk of exposing painful details about the Springford family. The defense's offer was to withdraw its change-of-venue motion and have Brent plead guilty to all five counts of capital murder. In exchange, the prosecution would drop its request for the death penalty and stipulate a sentence of life imprisonment without the possibility of parole, with a recommendation that Brent be sent to a prison mental facility.

After further negotiation with Brooks, an agreement was reached that would save Brent's life and save Montgomery County the added $250,000 in trial expenses if the trial were moved. The defense would give up all rights of appeal, on any grounds. In the end, Brooks agreed. "It would have been a tremendous uphill battle to get a death penalty decision," she recalled years later. The prosecutor was aware of the other side's difficulty in getting Brent to accept the agreement, and was even sympathetic. "I had a sense of the defense attorneys' problem. It was not an easy sell for their client," Brooks recalled. "Brent was not easy to deal with."

The Springford plea hearing took place in Courtroom 3C, the largest in the county judicial building, on November 18, 2008, nearly four years after the murder. It is an unassuming room with low ceilings, recessed lighting, and muted industrial green carpet. The seven rows of straight, wooden benches, seating fewer than two hundred, were mostly filled that day. On the right of the judge's bench is the jury box, with fourteen black, swiveling, faux-leather chairs on two levels. All of the attorneys, as well as Judge Shashy, were keenly aware that the hearing that day was to be a delicately choreographed affair. Brooks, in her customary navy suit, was joined at the prosecution table by her chief deputy, Daryl Bailey, and three other lawyers from her staff. Brooks could tell that the defense team was concerned about the hearing. "You could see it in their eyes. We were so close to resolving this. We were all hopeful."

Blanchard, Lewis, and Wardell sat at the defense table next to Brent—thin, long-haired, and bearded, wearing an orange inmate jumpsuit. Although he told members of the defense team he was fine, Brent appeared dazed throughout the proceedings until called to testify. Wardell sat with her arm draped around his back. Robin Springford Crouch and her aunt, Lois Truss, were present. First, the defense lawyers asked Judge Shashy to withdraw their pending motions to suppress Brent's confessions and for another competency hearing, as well as his order for a change of venue. Critically, Blanchard stipulated that Brent was now competent to enter into the plea agreement. Without objection from Brooks, Shashy agreed. Brent was then asked to stand and was sworn in, with Blanchard standing to his right at the defense table. The judge explained the details of the plea agreement and asked Brent if he understood, which he said he did. Next came the tricky part, what is known as the "colloquy." The judge asked Brent if he was guilty, and Brent answered "Yes." Then Shashy said, "Tell me what you did." For Brooks, "it was important for the family to hear him confess his guilt—to 'fess up.'" If Brent didn't accept full responsibility for murdering his parents, there was no deal. And with Brent, the defense knew, anything could happen. As well, they couldn't afford to have it appear that their client was not competent. Legally, without competence there could be no deal.

Before Brent could reply to the judge, Blanchard—who had a good idea what might be coming and didn't want the deal to fall apart—interrupted. The defense attorney was at least as concerned as Brooks that the deal could well collapse. So Blanchard asked Shashy if he could take over with a question-and-answer format, which he had rehearsed earlier with Brent. Shashy agreed, and Blanchard led Brent through a narrative of his journey from Colorado to Montgomery. But after Blanchard got Brent into the Garden District house, the defendant began to wobble. Brent said he had no memory of speaking with his parents, striking them, or even causing their deaths, despite his various confessions to the contrary. This was trouble, and Blanchard knew it.

Brent started to push back when Blanchard asked an otherwise simple question: Did Brent have permission to be in the house? He was of two minds on that question, Brent said. "It's strange to consider needing permission to be in the house that I grew up in." This was not the time for ad-libbing or embellishment. Grudgingly, Brent then acknowledged that he did not have permission. Still, he had no recollection of taking money or jewelry from the house—key elements of two capital counts he was charged with. Using the name he now preferred, Blanchard tried again: "Do you have any doubt, Winston, that it was you who caused the death of your parents?" The courtroom was silent. "I do not doubt that it was my body that caused the deaths," Brent replied. "That's for certain." He hesitated. "Looking back on it, it is certain that my body did these things. I know my conscious mind was not there, not present during these times, this period."

Blanchard asked to approach the bench, with Lewis and Brooks, for a sidebar conference. Blanchard said, out of hearing of others in the courtroom, "This is not exactly what I expected." Would this be enough of an admission to satisfy the plea bargain, he asked Brooks. The district attorney acknowledged years later that at this point she was concerned that the agreement was about to implode. With as much invested in the proceeding as Blanchard, she suggested another approach. Blanchard should establish that Brent was alone in the house and that his parents died while he was there. But for Shashy, that was not enough. "I need more," he told Blanchard and Brooks.

Back on the record, Blanchard tried a different tack, using Brooks's approach as a starting point. The defense attorney asked whether Brent was alone in the house the evening of the murders. "Yes," Brent replied. Did he remember finding the mattock in the pool shed and sawing off the head? "Yes." So far, so good. Blanchard then asked Brent if he recalled the flashbacks he had spoken of in the past. He did. In those flashbacks, did he remember hitting his parents with a stick? "Yes." And were his parents dead when he left the house? "Yes." And he remembered driving away from the house in his father's Jaguar? "Yes." And after he abandoned the car in Tulsa, he made his way back to Colorado? "Yes."

"Your honor," Blanchard told the judge, "I believe that [admission] established the sufficient factual predicate" for the plea arrangement. Shashy asked Brooks if she agreed, and the prosecutor said that if the judge was satisfied, the state was satisfied. Again, Judge Shashy addressed Brent. Was he satisfied with the work of Blanchard and Lewis? "Definitely," Brent replied. Did the defense attorneys concur in the plea? They did. "Okay," the judge said, "I accept your plea." As Brooks recalled later, "We all breathed a sigh of relief." At Shashy's request, Brent signed the agreement.

Regardless of the plea agreement, Alabama law required a pro forma jury trial for all capital cases. That proceeding began with jury selection on Wednesday, December, 3, 2008. In contrast with the plea change hearing, the atmosphere in the courtroom during this proceeding was matter-of-fact, and attendance was sparse, with just a few reporters and spectators present. Brent was dressed in clothes bought for him by the Berkeley mitigation team—black slacks and a long-sleeved, lavender dress shirt. He had lost so much weight that his black belt was wrapped around his waist one-and-a-half times. At the defense table, he toyed with a greeting card from Scoutt with a lifelike cover drawing of a cougar, through which Brent believed Scoutt was able to observe him, and his copy of the New Age best-seller *A Course in Miracles,* by Helen Schucman, rather than the customary Bible that many defendants brought to court. Brent appeared detached, staring silently into space and responding to questions from the defense team with noncommittal monosyllables.

Robin Springford Crouch sat with her husband Greg in the first row, directly behind the prosecutors. Lois Truss, Charlotte's sister, sat on the other side of the courtroom, in the row immediately behind the defense table. Several rows behind Truss was Andrea Jameson. Normally very put together, she looked exhausted, her hair uncharacteristically unkempt. For much of the proceedings that followed, she leaned to one side as if unable to sit upright. Judge Sally Greenhaw, who had attended every hearing con-nected to the case, was sitting near Robin.

The day-and-a-half trial began with jury selection, in which prospective panel members were told that the proceeding would be somewhat unusual. Some of the testimony would be read, and stipulated—agreed on by both the prosecution and the defense—or in the form of tape recordings played for jurors. The final jury was seven women and five men, with two alternates. Assistant District Attorney John Kachelman presented the opening statement for the prosecution, at a brisk fifteen minutes. If anything, Bill Blanchard was even more succinct, explaining that the trial for capital murder was required under Alabama law "as a kind of double-check or backstop" even though there had been a guilty plea and thus there was no doubt about the defendant's guilt. The defense lawyers, he told them, would not play the role they would in a normal trial. They would raise no objections, would not cross-examine or call witnesses. The guilty pleas to all five counts "put us in somewhat of a different format than what you would normally see. . . . It isn't easy sitting there without challenging the state's evidence. I can think of a hundred objections I would have made during an ordinary trial—but that's not our role in this case."

Robin Crouch was the first prosecution witness, questioned by Ellen Brooks. At first, she answered so softly that she had to be asked to speak up. The district attorney took her back to Thanksgiving of 2004, beginning with the midday meal at the Birmingham home of her aunt, Lois Truss. After the meal, she and Greg had initially planned to return with her parents to Montgomery, staying over at the Hull Street house. Instead they drove to Athens, Alabama, to see Greg's family. Brooks then shifted her questioning to the layout and the alarm system of the Garden District home, using photos and a diagram, with Robin using a pink laser pointer to illustrate her answers. Robin testified that her parents were estranged from and afraid of her brother. After a long period of supporting their son, Robin said, Brent Sr. and Charlotte had decided to reduce their financial support, first by cutting off his credit card. As Blanchard had promised, there was no defense cross-examination.

Another of Brooks's deputies, Calvin Williams, read stipulated testimony from a series of witnesses, laying out the case against Brent: the officer who answered the alarm on Wednesday night; one of the tile workers; and two of the death-scene investigators. Then Robin and other members of the Springford family left the courtroom as Dr. Stephen Boudreau, the state's senior medical examiner, took the stand to review the autopsies he performed. Boudreau, who also returned to the murder scene the day after the killings, testified about the slashing injuries to the bodies of Charlotte and Brent Sr., noting that the savage, blunt-force injuries shattered the tops of both their skulls, he said, like eggshells. Photos of the Springfords' bodies were introduced and shown to the jury, and the ax handle and serrated kitchen knife were admitted into evidence. During the medical examiner's testimony, Brent showed no emotion.

After a ten-minute recess, Assistant DA Williams resumed reading stipulated testimony from Brent's supervisor at Fort Lupton, that he had received a call the Monday night before Thanksgiving, saying that Brent was sick and would not be in for the rest of the week. Williams then read testimony from bus station officials between Fort Collins and Montgomery, and described surveillance videos that showed a young man strongly resembling Brent. After a Montgomery police officer described locating the Jaguar in

Oklahoma, Judge Shashy adjourned court for the day, admonishing jurors not to discuss the case or follow it in the media.

The next morning, testimony began with Montgomery homicide detective Mike Myrick. Deputy DA Kevin Davidson led him through a telescoped account of the initial investigation, beginning with the discovery of the bodies. Myrick said that within hours of the time the bodies were found, he and other investigators were informed of the strained relationship between the victims and their son. During Brent's initial interview at the Weld County, Colorado, sheriff's office, Myrick said, the suspect put his face in his hands when informed of his parents' death, and asked how it happened. In addition to the scratch on his forehead, Myrick noticed some superficial scratches at the base of the young man's neck. After this initial interview and the others that followed that night with the Scoutt family at the Windsor house, Myrick testified that he and his colleague Bryan Jurkofsky soon learned that Brent—contrary to what he had first told the officers—had traveled by bus that week to Montgomery. Myrick was not asked about Caroline Scoutt's role in taking Brent to the Fort Collins bus station on Monday night or picking him up the following Saturday.

Myrick recounted Brent's arrest at Centennial Peaks Hospital, and explained how Brent was advised of his Miranda rights at the Louisville police station. Brent's two-and-a half-hour recorded confession from that interview was played, taking up the remainder of the morning session. For the first time, jurors and, through the media, the public heard the most detailed and chilling account of the slayings in the trial. After lunch, Myrick returned to the stand, where he narrated a video of the murder scene, including the Springfords' bodies, effectively illustrating Brent's confession. Davidson then showed the murder weapons to the jury, and Myrick testified that the black-handled, serrated knife found next to Brent Sr.'s body was missing from a block in the kitchen. The prosecutor then asked Myrick to read Brent's recent confession from a transcript of the plea hearing two weeks earlier and, finally, to point Brent out in the courtroom. Brooks then rested for the prosecution, and Blanchard waived any defense.

After a recess, Deputy District Attorney Calvin Williams gave the prosecution's first closing argument, which Brooks told the judge would last only fifteen minutes. True, there was a deal, a plea bargain, but there was still a good deal at stake. Prosecutors were not just presenting their case to jurors; they were making their case to the people of Montgomery County. Williams began by telling jurors, "This case is more than a mere formality," despite what they might think. The case was about more than a murder, a burglary, a robbery or a theft:

> Ladies and gentlemen, it's about betrayal; betrayal of hope, betrayal of trust, betrayal of love and comfort, betrayal of family. Charlotte and Brent Springford provided the defendant with a comfortable life. They bought him a house, purchased automobiles for him, gave him over $1,600 a month as a stipend, purchased gifts for him, paid for educational expenses. And when that was not enough, the defendant wanted more. And when he didn't get more, he went to take more. He traveled by bus, under a false name. To the defendant, self-preservation was more important than family. And he decided that he was going to take and preserve what he thought belonged to him. And he was going to take it from his mother and father because he thought that he would be cut off. . . . He wasn't there to go and reconcile. [He] was there to go and take what was his or what he thought was his. And that's what he did.

The prosecutor concluded by reminding jurors of their larger responsibility, in asking that they return guilty verdicts on all five counts:

> Ladies and gentlemen, while Mr. Springford, the defendant, spoke the truth in his confession and in his guilty plea, it now becomes up to you to speak the truth through a verdict. You must speak the truth as the community representatives to this horrible crime.

Lewis had the thankless task of closing for the defense. He quoted Clarence Darrow about fighting against the odds, and made the largely perfunctory request that they acquit Brent of all the charges against him. Regardless of how many counts jurors convicted Brent of, the outcome was not in doubt:

Let me tell you what's going to happen. . . . Mr. Springford is going to die in prison. When he leaves, it will be because he is carried out dead. That is the penalty for capital murder with a life-without-parole sentence. And that's what he's going to get in this case.

Lewis then said what was clearly on the minds of everyone in the courtroom, and beyond.

We are certainly mindful, painfully mindful of the suffering of the family and the friends of the Springfords. This is a great human tragedy. And we would not be human if we failed to at least try to appreciate the suffering that this has taken, what they've gone through and what will haunt them the rest of their lives.

Finally, it was District Attorney Brooks's turn to present the last summation, and she too seemed to address a larger audience. She spoke to some unresolved aspects of the killings, including Brent's conflicting accounts, both written and oral, of what happened in the seconds immediately preceding the attacks.

As in every case that I have had the fortune of working on as your district attorney over the past thirty years, I have never had a case where every question was answered. It's human nature, isn't it? You can't know everything about anything. And this case, like all those other cases, does have unanswered questions. A first question I think we'll all ask ourselves: Why? Why did he commit the crimes?

Given the physical evidence, and applying common sense, Brooks said, the answer was clear. It was his parents' threat to cut off financial support.

He didn't want to lose the money, and he wasn't going to let them do it. And that's what created his anger."

In plotting his trip from Colorado, and sawing the head off the mattock,

Brooks argued, there was clear premeditation.

This was not a last-minute passionate crime. This was a well thought-out crime. And there was no long conversation in the kitchen. It was an ambush from the beginning.

Again, Brooks addressed both the jury and the larger community, this time on the subject of the death penalty.

It was a heinous, brutal crime, wasn't it? Horrible. Unthinkable. Hard to watch, hard to look at those photos, to see that crime scene video. You would think that the State of Alabama, if you know me, that I would seek the death penalty. And for four years, we have.

However, after receiving the defense's offer,

I then met with the family, with the Montgomery Police Department officials, and we talked. And we came to this conclusion: The buck stops here. I will take responsibility . . . We weighed . . . circumstances like no prior serious criminal history, mental health issues, which the defendant himself raised in his statement, didn't he? But yet, he knew exactly what he did and he planned it. But still, it's a factor a jury would consider, the weighing process that I mentioned a jury would do. And it's subjective.

In the end, Brooks explained, there were practicalities to consider:

We considered all the possibilities. And we determined that we wanted to reduce the risk of a not guilty by reason of insanity, a hung jury, a guilty of a lesser offense, by agreeing to life without parole. We considered it an appropriate and likely punishment in this case. Each case is different . . .

When the defendant did offer to plead guilty to life without [parole], the victim's family, after much discussion and thought, requested that we accept that offer. The Montgomery Police Department supported their request from that family. The prosecution—me—listened and considered and finally determined to accept this offer for the family, for finality, and for fairness. It is not the perfect resolution, but it is the best solution given its unique facts and law.

Judge Shashy instructed the jury, dismissed the two alternates, and sent the remaining panel members to a nearby room to deliberate. They elected as their foreman the one man who had been on a jury before and who was wearing a suit. Deliberations were calm and collected, a juror recalled, and they quickly arrived at a consensus on the first two counts: guilty. They sent a query to the judge about the remaining three counts, but Shashy just sent them back a copy of the relevant instruction he had just read them. After a few more votes, they reached agreement on all counts: guilty. They took just forty-five minutes to accept Brent's plea.

Before sentencing, a series of victim impact statements was presented, the first by Brent's sister, Robin Springford Crouch. Brent appeared curious about what Robin would say, stirring a bit from his trance-like state, lifting his head slightly to look at his sister. Wardell was struck by how poised and self-confident Robin was when she spoke. At the lectern, she betrayed little emotion, never looking at her brother, who continued to stare at her. She read:

In November 2004, I lost the two most special people in my life. It was devastating enough to lose my parents, but to lose them at the hands of my own brother was unimaginable. Many years passed without a resolution to this tragedy, and though we have been patient with the judicial system and stoic on the outside, our family has been more than ready to see justice served. Today we finally received some closure in that we feel the person responsible for it all is being held accountable for what he did. Although I feel he deserves the same fate he afforded my parents, our family does take comfort in knowing that he will no longer be able to harm anyone else.

Before Shashy pronounced sentence, Blanchard asked him to order that Brent spend his sentence, life without parole, in a secure prison facility for the mentally ill. The previous June the defense team had engaged Dr. Wade Myers, the University of South Florida psychiatrist, to examine Brent and his psychiatric records, anticipating that his findings would be used at trial, or in mitigation testimony in the penalty phase. Now Myers had a different role. He had written that

> given the severity of his mental illness . . . Mr. Springford requires placement in a correctional mental health unit. . . . Placing him in general population would significantly increase his risk for further decompensation, being harmed by other inmates given his odd speech and behaviors, and suicide.

Citing Myers's finding, the defense asked the judge to send Brent to the Donaldson Correctional Facility in Bessemer, Alabama, which had a new psychiatric unit. Blanchard and Lewis told Shashy that Myers's evaluation might explain Brent's lack of affect, his unemotional state during the trial.

The judge apparently agreed. After sentencing Brent to life without parole, Shashy added, "Because of Mr. Springford's history of psychiatric treatment, which has included antipsychotic medications, this Court strongly recommends that Mr. Springford be reviewed and/or evaluated for mental health treatment and/or placement in an Alabama Department of Corrections mental health unit until such time as Mr. Springford has received the maximum benefit of any mental health treatment available." As the judge passed sentence, Brent simply nodded.

"I realized this was the best possible outcome for him," Susan Wardell said. "Had we gone to trial he would have gotten death, I have no doubt of that." Yet even with that outcome, Wardell had a bad feeling about Brent's long-term prospects. Lois Truss, who had rejected her overtures heretofore, approached Wardell after the verdict and told her that Wardell's demonstrated compassion to her nephew had moved her. That, as a Christian, she felt that if Wardell could forgive Brent, she had to as well. Later, Wardell shared with Truss her fears about Brent's future behind bars. "He will not survive in general population, in any prison, for any length of time," she wrote in an email. "A death sentence would have been redundant."

When court was adjourned, a member of the prosecution team came up to Wardell, and told her that he was interested in anything the defense might have turned up about Caroline Scoutt's involvement in the crime.

Scoutt's name had been mentioned only in passing during the trial. Like the prosecutor, police investigators were well aware of the hole in Ellen Brooks's assertion that the killing was "a well thought out crime." What sane person would think that by killing his parents, Brent Springford would ensure the financial stability of his family?

The defense team hoped that after being evaluated for ninety days at the Kilby Correctional Facility, in Mount Meigs, Alabama, Brent would be assigned to the psychiatric unit at Donaldson, as Judge Shashy recommended. Days before he agreed to the plea deal, Brent wrote to the legal team with a list of demands for his incarceration at Donaldson. Still a child of privilege, he wrote that "if I'm forced to live with a cell mate I will be suicidal. That's not a threat. I just can't live like that. . . . I have to have my own space, even if it's a closet . . . Do you know if it's possible for me to live in a cell block with mainly white people?" Moreover, he said he wanted a cell block where "everyone is over sixty," which would mean "the most peace and quiet possible."

Wardell visited Brent in his jail cell and found him concerned about sexual assault, which she reported was low at Donaldson, and even lower for inmates who were without financial resources to exploit. He wanted to take his books and writings with him from the jail, but if he couldn't he wanted them sent to Caroline Scoutt.

Wardell could not shake a strong sense of foreboding. Through the defense team's efforts—including her own significant contribution—Brent Springford Jr. had been saved from a death sentence. She remained convinced that it might only have been a stay of execution.

: 18

Prison

After his conviction, Brent was accordingly shaved, given a haircut, and issued a set of "prison whites." Leaving the Montgomery jail for the more strictly regulated state prison system, Brent had to leave behind the books he had acquired during his four years in jail, all of which were collected and boxed up by the defense team. His larger concern was that a Satanist whom he had met in jail and found very disturbing might end up in the same institution. Susan Wardell assured him that at Kilby Correctional Facility he could fill out an "enemies list" form for his safety. Privately, however, she was not so certain. "Surely the docs and staff won't allow anyone to torment Brent," she wrote Bill Blanchard, her colleague on the defense team. "After all, he does have major mental illness, not to mention religious delusions, and he probably now believes he is in his own personal hell."

On January 7, 2009, Brent was taken by prison bus to Kilby, just outside Montgomery, where all male felons are sent for processing. There, he was assigned a single room in the psych unit, with a bed in the center, enabling him to walk in circles, rather than to pace up and down, Doctors at both Kilby and Donaldson were sent the post-conviction evaluation prepared by Dr. Wade C. Myers, who had interviewed Brent and Scoutt (by phone) and reviewed the extended family's medical history. Earlier, before the trial, Myers had diagnosed Brent as paranoid schizophrenic, following on his bipolar disorder. "He has had a deteriorating course in his functioning," the doctor wrote in his second report. It began when Brent was at Vanderbilt, he wrote:

> . . . accompanied by the onset of delusional thinking, auditory hallucinations, a disorganized thought process, grossly disorganized behavior, and the negative symptoms of blunted affect and social withdrawal. . . . Consistent

with this diagnosis, Mr. Springford's social and occupational functioning has demonstrated a marked downward trend since he entered adulthood, notably at odds with what would have been predicted based on his family background, high intelligence, good grades, and normal family and social functioning throughout adolescence. His ability to have normal, warm interpersonal relationships all but vanished, he developed socially reclusive behaviors, his self-care deteriorated, he became pathologically preoccupied with philosophical matters.

From Kilby, after just a few days of expedited evaluation, Brent was sent to the Donaldson Correctional Facility outside Birmingham. That had been Myers's recommendation, because of Donaldson's new psychiatric unit. The maximum security facility, built in 1982 for seven hundred inmates had been expanded to more than double that by Brent's arrival. More than one hundred inmates were, like Brent, serving sentences of life without parole. There were more than two hundred guards and a segregation unit—solitary confinement—for three hundred inmates, the largest in the state system. After Brent had been at Donaldson sixty days, psychiatrist Dr. James Pilkinton said he was wrestling with the best treatment for him. Pilkinton upped Brent's dosage of Risperdal, an antipsychotic, and added paranoid schizophrenia to his diagnosis. He confided to Wardell that he didn't think Brent's condition would ever improve.

Brent wrote that he was "dealing with quite a lot of depression and sadness," adding, "I pray that things improve." He was also given an ongoing prescription for two daily 500 mg Tylenol for headaches. His weight had dropped again to 150 pounds, compared to his high school weight of 195. In a January 15, 2009, letter to Wardell, he said he needed money for lip balm, socks, shoes, paper and envelopes, and pencils. "I wish I weren't so needy, but I am right now. Having nothing is hard indeed! I just pray for a better road ahead. . . . Thank you again for caring and helping." The letter was signed "winston."

While Brent was being evaluated at Donaldson, Wardell maintained her correspondence with his maternal aunt, Lois Truss, who wrote that her feelings about Brent continued to evolve, to the point where she wanted to resume contact. "I have struggled with forgiving him for what he did and have finally arrived at that point. . . . Thanks for being compassionate with him. There was time when I could not even say his name. Now I would like to show him the same compassion that you did." Her compassion extended to a suggestion of a visit from a Christian prison chaplain she had heard of, and Wardell thought that Brent would welcome such an approach.

For her part, Wardell had not lost interest in Caroline Scoutt. On February 22, she wrote Truss: "Believe me, Caroline had a huge part in this, but neither we nor the prosecutor's investigators could get enough evidence to charge her. I haven't given up, though she seems to have disappeared." Truss had come to agree. "I always saw Little Brent as the evil person, but in hindsight I realize that it never would have happened if not for Caroline taking advantage of a vulnerable person."

After two months of isolation, Brent settled into the Donaldson's psychiatric unit. A small group of his friends outside—the Jamesons in Montgomery, Marie Flinders in Boulder—wrote him and sent books and cards for his birthday, as well as money orders for the commissary. Wardell was his main point of contact, and she coordinated communication with his remaining friends and attorneys. From his letters, collect calls, and her visits, Wardell noticed that Brent's mood fluctuated wildly, depending on how many others kept up with him. To Andrea Jameson, Wardell wrote, "My heart is broken by this case, and I'm sure it must be that much worse for anyone who ever knew this child before he lost his bearings, through no fault or choice of his own. If ever there were a tragedy without a foreseeable end, this is it. I can't believe I am sitting here crying, but I am."

At first, Brent preferred administrative segregation, solitary confinement, but over time he changed his mind. On February 23, 2009, Brent wrote to Susan Wardell, saying he was "really struggling in this new environment. It's far more difficult than jail, louder and grosser, at least in the segregation block that I'm in right now." He found the noise in the segregation block deafening, with screaming and yelling at all hours, and said he missed the classical music and news he used to listen to on public radio in Montgomery.

On March 2, Brent wrote to thank Wardell for sending him pictures he had requested of the American spiritual figure Ram Dass (the former Harvard psychologist Richard Alpert), saying, "I have much more hope now." Brent's primary concern was the availability of books. The titles he requested in his letters provide a snapshot of where he was, psychologically—still searching for some peace. They included St. Teresa of Avila's *The Way of Perfection, Life: Written by Herself.* "I know that I was a Catholic monk in about ten lifetimes," he explained. These were followed by books touching on Eastern religion and philosophy and metaphysics.

Eventually, an agreement was reached with the Springfords' estate which provided Brent with $75 a month. This modest amount put Brent back among the wealthy privileged elite, at least by institutional standards. This regular cash deposit to the prison commissary was supplemented by cash gifts from Wardell, the Jamesons, and others, including other members of the defense team. Even though the books began to flow in from publishers and, later, Amazon, it was hard to keep up with Brent's pace of reading. "I'm praying and hoping for these books," Brent wrote Wardell. "My life is nothing but reading spiritual books, meditating and praying. I don't want a visit because I'm in an extremely monastic state of mind."

There were occasional bright spots. By coincidence, in 2002 Donaldson was selected for an experimental Buddhist retreat program of Vipassana meditation, part of a ministry called Prison Dharma. It was developed by a powerful teacher named Fleet Maull at Naropa University. While a student there, Brent had met Maull and knew his work (at one point the defense team had even thought Maull might help get Brent to accept a plea bargain). "The Vispassana retreat at Donaldson is very amazing," he wrote in 2009. "Really blows my mind! I hope they have another, and I'm definitely going to participate in those groups when I get into population"; he had soured by now on segregation. His weight rose to 175 pounds and stabilized, and he kept his hair cut short and was clean-shaven.

Brent's continued indifference to former girlfriend Andrea Jameson was wounding to the young woman. She wrote him at least weekly and sent him money and books from his list via Wardell, including her phone number, but he never replied. "It's definitely hard not to get any response at all," Jameson wrote Wardell. "But I keep hoping that at some point he will write back. . . . Caroline apparently did quite a number on him in regards to me. He never would acknowledge me at all with Susan," she emailed her mother. "But I continue to write, and wait, and hope. . . . I want to make sure he always knows that he is not forgotten and is not alone." Brent was becoming increasingly isolated from his outside support system. He continued to tell Susan to thank "The Jamesons," but never Andrea by name. When Marie Flinders, Brent's old friend from Boulder who introduced him to Scoutt, sent him money and books and wrote him a letter, he did not reply. After missing Wardell with several collect calls, he stopped trying to contact her. She continued to send him money, but her letter-writing tapered off to once a month.

Ironically, the one person Brent continued to write to—Caroline Scoutt—did not reciprocate. Brent complained, in a March 19 letter to Wardell, that he hadn't heard from her since December. "It's hard not to feel abandoned. I know she'll write when she's ready to." Despite not answering his letters, Scoutt's hold on Brent remained strong. Soon after arriving at Donaldson, he wrote Wardell that he would be grateful "if you could tell me anything that you hear from Caroline that you think she would want me to know."

Wardell had informed Scoutt when Brent pleaded guilty and forwarded his mailing address at Donaldson. But as months passed with little communication and no response to her messages, Wardell wrote Scoutt's Colorado attorney, Daniel Quinn. "As you probably know, hearing anything at all from Caroline means the world to Winston." Scoutt's contact with Brent reduced to a trickle, writing him every six months or so on postcards filled with banalities. She complained to Wardell that Brent was sending her bizarre letters, that he was delusional, wanting to transfer to a Wyoming prison to be near her, which was of course impossible.

Brent even tried to use his $75 a month payments from the estate to reach out to Scoutt. Since he was now officially denied coffee, because the caffeine might stimulate his mania, he asked his lawyers to send the money to Scoutt. "I would much rather give it to Caroline and the kids." He wanted to send her the full amount, if she would agree to accept it. "That would make me feel really good, . . . very happy," he wrote Wardell. In her dealings with Brent, Wardell tried to steer clear of the subject of Scoutt and her harsh opinion of the woman, although she expressed those views freely with others. Andrea Jameson wrote Wardell, wondering if there was any chance that Brent would implicate Scoutt. She wondered "if he might be willing to call her out at some point."

Brent still dismissed Wardell's suspicions about Scoutt. He wrote Wardell,

I forgive you for your unjust attacks and judgments against Caroline … If you insist on believing that 'Caroline got me into this,' then you'll also call me a liar . . . I know she tried to help me as much as she could, but I was beyond help and change because I was so set in my beliefs/delusions, and I chose to believe in the voice I heard rather than telling Caroline about it. So it's all my fault, and it's too bad so many people want to blame Caroline rather than my own deluded, messed up, bipolar, psychotic mind that was and is greatly influenced by my heredity. But innocent, spiritual people often take the blame in this world. … [Caroline] works hard to uplift her people. You have no idea how much suffering she takes on to help others. And every year for decades she has delivered presents to the poor Indian children on the reservation out of her own money. But she certainly doesn't need my defense. I believe she'll write me a letter when Spirit says it's time, or when she has the time, so I'll just wait patiently, and I don't believe she will abandon me. She has helped me more than anyone else ever has, and I'm grateful for that.

Wardell wrote Elaine Jameson that she was "almost professionally (but not personally) ashamed to admit that Brent feels like my own child." And she had equal empathy for Andrea, whose "tremendous pain during our last meeting has wrenched my heart." Andrea was still bitter about Scoutt, tearing up as she asked Wardell, "Why did she have to take 'my Brent'?" Andrea copied Springford family photos of Andrea and Brent from a disk Wardell brought. Wardell wrote Elaine that when Andrea paused to say how Brent's senior picture was her favorite, "I thought my heart would break. I felt as if my own daughter were going through this terrible situation, and I really have not recovered from any of it. . . . I don't think she will ever stop loving her Brent."

In late February 2011, Brent wrote Wardell, asking about some of the material she compiled for the mitigation report. "I would very much like to know the mental illness history of my biological family and relatives. I would be very grateful if you could please tell me their names, how related, their illnesses, dates, and any information that you could give me about them." Ominously, he also requested "the names and dates of relatives who committed suicide." Not surprisingly, this information gradually began to weigh on him.

On December 19, 2012, Scoutt was granted an uncontested divorce from Brent in Larimer County, Colorado. The news could not have been good for Brent; his last legal tie to Caroline had been severed. By this time, Brent had few things holding him together. Prison had taken from him many of the things that had been important to him since his arrest: his link to public radio, coffee, and Wellbutrin. His communication with Wardell had trailed off. He had had so few touchstones, and then he lost them, so his depression and loneliness were understandably out of control.

In early October 2013, prison officials at Donaldson told Brent they intended to transfer him to another section of the prison. From January 12, 2009, when Brent arrived at Donaldson, until the fall of 2013, he was moved eight times. In addition, he was in solitary administrative segregation three times, twice for a few days, and once for more than a year. The Alabama Department of Corrections would not reveal the reasons for the transfers, or disclose whether they were voluntary or involuntary, including the planned October move. In correspondence, however, they implied that Brent had no serious disciplinary infractions while at Donaldson. In the days thereafter Brent wrote several letters expressing anxiety over the transfer. He wrote in one that he "would be completely suicidal" if he had to move, and that he had felt suicidal in the past.

The staff apparently took no action regarding the transfer, or his threats of suicide. On Saturday, October 5, Brent complained of intense stomach pains and difficulty with his vision. He was taken to the prison infirmary, where a nurse observed that his skin was yellow, indicating jaundice, and that he had labored breathing and physical unsteadiness. Soon he was unresponsive. Later that day, he was taken to the emergency room at Brookwood Medical Center in Homewood, about an hour away, outside Birmingham. ER doctors quickly assessed his condition, determined that Brent was suffering from liver and kidney failure, and transferred him to the hospital's intensive care unit. Despite their efforts, his condition deteriorated, and hospital officials saw that Brent had earlier filled out a Do Not Resuscitate form, which they observed. He was pronounced dead by Dr. Christopher Monty at 12:30 a.m. on October 7, 2013. He was thirty-seven years old.

Dr. Monty informed Lieutenant Todd Wheat at Donaldson of the death. Steel City Transport took the corpse to the morgue at Central General Hospital, still clad in a blue plastic hospital gown, ID bracelet on his wrist, and additional stickers on his chest and ankle. From there the body was sent to the Jefferson County Coroner/Medical Examiner's Office on Sixth Avenue in Birmingham. Later that same morning, a staff medical examiner, assisted by a pathology resident and fellow from the University of Alabama at Birmingham, conducted a ninety-minute autopsy. They determined that Brent had died from hepatic necrosis, liver failure, as a result of acetaminophen toxicity, 70 milligrams per liter—an overdose of Tylenol, for which he had a prison prescription. Formally, the report stated, "a concentration greater than that which would be expected were one taking Tylenol as therapeutically indicated." The death was ruled a suicide. As he had threatened in the past—telling Wardell and others how easily it would be to overdose—Brent had been able to save a sufficient number of Tylenol tablets to kill himself.

When officials looked on Brent's prison admission documents, under next of kin there were only two names: Andrea Jameson, whose relationship was listed as "friend," and Bill Blanchard, his attorney. Blanchard referred the prison to District Attorney Ellen Brooks, who gave them Robin Crouch's number. Both Andrea Jameson and her mother made early morning calls to Susan Wardell, who was out of the country, with the news. "None of us were really surprised," Wardell recalled. "Brent's prison psychiatrist, Dr. Pilkinton, had told me that based on his experience, Brent would *never* adapt to incarceration. It was fall, approaching the anniversary of the murders. I hate to think of how Brent had to feel." Robin, as Brent's sister, authorized the Cremation Center of Birmingham to retrieve the body. Four days later, Andrea Jameson, still emotional about "my Brent," was given permission to spend thirty minutes with the body and pay her final respects. Winston

Brent Springford Jr. was cremated at 9 a.m., on October 11, at the Cremation Center in Woodstock, Alabama.

Although Brent's suicide occurred in what was supposed to be a secure prison psychiatric unit, the Department of Corrections showed a striking lack of curiosity about it. The investigation report was barely one page, marked "Closed." It made no mention of whether prison officials had read his letter threatening suicide days before and offered no details of how the suicide was able to occur, or how or where the Tylenol had been cached. Nor what prison officials might have done to prevent the suicide by, say, conducting an additional inspection of his cell. In the wake of Brent's death, Bryan Stevenson, executive director of the Montgomery-based nonprofit legal firm Equal Justice Initiative, told the *Montgomery Advertiser* that he considered the matter "very troubling. . . . It's worrisome that someone who has been identified as a high-suicide risk or is suffering from mental illness could access enough Tylenol—or whatever it is he took—to commit suicide . . . When people are identified as being at-risk, obviously [the Alabama Department of Corrections] needs to take action."

Others were not surprised. "While I expected him to die in prison," District Attorney Brooks told the Associated Press, "I didn't expect it at such a young age." Years later, Jerry Armstrong, Brent Sr.'s friend, was unforgiving. "I didn't care." He said that at the time his reaction was, "I'm glad my tax money isn't supporting him anymore."

: *19*

What If . . .

There are so many "What ifs" inherent in this tragedy—any one of which might have averted what was the worst possible outcome. Even District Attorney Ellen Brooks was perplexed: "I kept asking myself, 'What could that family have done differently?'" What if Charlotte and Brent Springford Sr., influenced by the wrenching death of their first child in the house fire, and subsequent failed pregnancy, had not been so indulgent with their son when he was a boy and a teenager? Or even something as trivial as college and geography. What if young Brent had worked hard enough at the Montgomery Academy to get into an Ivy League school and left the South, as he wanted to? What if he had stuck with his high school girlfriend Andrea Jameson, who loved him so? What if his parents had not agreed to his leaving Vanderbilt, or to finance his extended spiritual search? What if Brent had given Oberlin College a chance? Or what if any of the four psychiatrists who treated him before the murders had found the right combination of drugs to treat his bipolar disorder and Brent had stuck with that regimen? What if Charlotte and Brent Sr. had offered Caroline Scoutt title to the Windsor house if she could convince Brent to enter an in-patient program? And for Brent, what if prison officials at Donaldson Correctional Facility had monitored his Tylenol intake, kept him in the mental health unit, and taken seriously his suicide threat?

And yes, most significantly, what if Brent had never crossed paths with Caroline Scoutt in Boulder? Unquestionably, Brent was desperately seeking a transcendent, spiritual guide when the two met. But one Hindu tradition maintains that, at the opportune moment, gurus find devotees, and not the other way around. Susan Wardell, the death-penalty mitigation specialist, remained convinced that the tragedy was a result of crime, not karma—that Scoutt was a schemer and a scammer, a lifelong grifter. She considered Scoutt directly responsible for the deaths of Charlotte and Brent Springfield Sr. and probably for Brent Jr.'s prison suicide. Drawing on her clinical social work background and her observations of Scoutt, who grew up in straitened circumstances, Wardell felt that Scoutt resented the children loved by wealthy parents. Poisoned by envy and greed, she felt no reason not to exploit the Springfords, even if—especially if—it meant driving a wedge between them for her own benefit. Caroline Scoutt might escape justice in the Springford case, if not for the other offenses of which she is suspected. Proving any of this would be a difficult task.

Part Two: The Hunt for Answers

: 20

Shaking the Tree

Winston Brent Springford Jr.'s prison suicide might have ended his grim, sad saga. Yet there remained one nagging question: what role—if any—did Caroline Scoutt play in the murders of Charlotte and Brent Springford Sr., or even in the suicide of their son? Susan Wardell had done all she possibly could to answer it. Now it was my turn.

Wardell is my wife Sallie's sister, and we were all at Duke University in the late 1960s. As a newspaper and magazine journalist, I have reported on murder cases on both U.S. coasts for forty years, off and on, learning my way around police reports, autopsies, and depositions, as well as courtrooms. In the 1970s, I covered the trials of serial killer Ted Bundy in Miami and former Green Beret Dr. Jeffrey MacDonald in Raleigh, North Carolina, as well as the broad-daylight Greensboro Klan-Nazi shootings. During the 1990s, as a staff writer for the *Los Angeles Times,* I covered a stream of horrendous murder trials, many involving the death penalty, in Orange County. And in 2012 and 2013 I reported on the shooting death of Trayvon Martin, and its aftermath, in Sanford, Florida, just up the road from my home outside Orlando.

In 2013, my first nonfiction crime book, *Met Her on the Mountain,* was published, involving a cold case of the kidnapping, rape and murder of a young anti-poverty worker in 1970 in western North Carolina, when I was a student at Duke. In that book I identified the victim's likely killers. After Wardell read it, she asked me to look into the Springford case and Scoutt's role. She jump-started my research with material rarely accessible to nonfiction crime writers without years of research. This cache included more than a dozen file boxes of documents, reports, motions, interview transcripts, memos, emails, psychiatric records, letters, and journal entries.

It took more than six months to work my way through the material.

Then, in the fall of 2014 I made the first of two trips to Montgomery. Without exception, the investigating officers, prosecutors, and defense attorneys were generous with their time and were candid and forthcoming with their recollections. Among them, there was unanimity—and frustration—on one point. They were absolutely convinced that Scoutt played *some* role, direct or indirect, in the murders. However, their hands were tied. Only two people knew for certain what happened. One was dead, and the other had no interest in implicating herself and exposing herself to criminal charges.

So in July 2015, I made a research trip to Boulder, Colorado. My expectations regarding Caroline Scoutt were modest and realistic. In a case like the Springford killings, proving the formal criminal charges of murder or accessory to murder—either before or after the fact—is challenging. The same goes for the rarely prosecuted crime of misprision of a felony—knowing about a crime in advance and failing to notify authorities. Complicating matters, the homicides took place in Alabama, but Scoutt's possible involvement, whatever form it took, would have occurred in Colorado, a distant legal jurisdiction. Her initial statements to investigators, providing Brent with an alibi, were vague and then were modified in subsequent interviews with her lawyer present. Thus, they might not rise to the level of obstruction of justice. Most critically, I lacked the power of the state—no badge or subpoena power. But unlike the authorities, I didn't need to produce sufficient evidence to bring an indictment or convince a jury. I just needed to persuade myself, if I could.

In an effort to find Scoutt, I met twice in Colorado with Wayne Diffee, the Denver-based private investigator who worked for Brent's defense team, who agreed to help me without charge. He told me he had learned that the Scoutt family's return in 2005 to Newcastle, Wyoming, after the murders had been rocky. At first, Caroline stayed at a local motel, The Pines, but she soon feuded with the owner and was asked to leave. Once she was resettled in her mobile home outside town, the sheriff made regular visits to the property. These were mostly in response to Scoutt's minor complaints about neighbors, calls involving strife between Scoutt's adult son and his on-and-off girlfriend, and Caroline's older daughter's scrapes with the law. There was no indication where Caroline was now. Next I contacted Daniel Quinn, Scoutt's Colorado lawyer, and let him know that I was working on this book, and that I would like to speak with his client. His response was polite; he would attempt to reach her. "I do not know if my contact information for her is current or out of date. If I do hear from her, and if she asks me to contact you, I certainly will do so." No response was forthcoming.

The Colorado trip was not a total loss. While there, I visited sites where that part of Brent Springford's saga took place. Ann Flinders, Brent's old roommate, gave me several heartfelt hours in a conference room in Naropa University's Allen Ginsberg Library. I interviewed law enforcement officials in Louisville, outside of Boulder, where Brent was arrested, held, and interrogated. In Weld County I interviewed Sheriff's Investigator Vicki Harbert, who echoed Mike Myrick and Bryan Jurkofsky's belief that Scoutt had been Brent's "puppeteer" in the killings. After our interview, Harbert led me to the Windsor house, and introduced me to Mindy Moore, who with her husband had bought the house from the Springford estate. Moore gave us a tour of the refurbished house and grounds.

Before heading home to Orlando I tried another tactic designed to "shake the tree": With just enough details, I pitched my book project and my effort to find Scoutt as a story to three area newspapers, including the *Boulder Weekly*, an alternative paper. My hope was that a local article might reach someone who knew Scoutt, knew where she might be, or had been scammed by her. I spent two mornings, a total of five hours, with Caitlin Rockett, a young writer and editor at the weekly paper, and Joel Dyer, the editor-in-chief, in the paper's funky, ramshackle offices, telling my story. The local spiritual and metaphysical community—many of whose members advertised in the paper—was small enough that someone was bound to have information about Scoutt. Unfortunately, I had to return to Florida before the two-part cover story ran, detailing Brent Jr.'s arrival in Colorado and the murder of his parents in Montgomery.

Less than a week after I got home—and after the first *Weekly* article ran—I received an email from Diffee. It said that Caroline Scoutt was back in Newcastle. Then came a bombshell: Investigators there considered

Scoutt a "person of interest" in the recent, unattended death of a Richard Campbell Jr. on her property.

In the early evening of June 24, 2015, Scoutt had called the Weston County Sheriff's Department to report an incident in Campbell's trailer, which she did not describe. As the officers pulled up, they saw Scoutt leaving Campbell's single-wide trailer and driving away in her blue Nissan Frontier. Since the deputies recognized her and her car, and assumed she was driving to her trailer on the other side of the property, they didn't stop her. Inside the dwelling, Deputy Dan Fields, Sergeant Patrick Watsabaugh, and another deputy found Campbell, age sixty, dead from an apparent gunshot wound to the head.

The body was lying face up on the floor of the bedroom. The air conditioning was turned off, and the room was stifling, in the nineties. Cradled between Campbell's left shoulder and left ear was a short-barreled, lever-action Rossi rifle, a Brazilian copy of a Winchester Model 92, with one spent, brass .357 Magnum shell in the ejector. At first glance, it appeared Campbell had sat on the corner of his bed with the stock between his feet and fired one shot into his mouth. The slug passed through his head and went through the ceiling of the mobile home. Crime scene photos showed a grizzled but fit man lying on the floor on his back, his head turned away from the bed. Both arms were raised, with his hands flopped forward. He was wearing a blue T-shirt reading "Mystic Mountain Run." Perched on his head were sunglasses and a baseball cap, the visor pushed up on his forehead, both undisturbed by the shot that had exited behind his left ear. While there was a large pool of blood on the floor near Campbell's head, there was almost no bloodspray or brain spatter on the walls or ceiling, which Sergeant Watsabaugh thought unusual. Campbell's fly was unzipped and his belt was lying underneath a nearby bureau. His wallet was missing. The knees of his dark blue canvas painter's pants and boots were flecked with bits of grass. A field urine test indicated that he had no alcohol in his blood, and a subsequent toxicology screen of his blood came up clear of any drugs.

I passed the gist of that information to Caitlin Rockett, of the *Boulder Weekly*, since she was geographically closer to the source than I was, and I encouraged her to pursue the new developments for the second installment of the series. Rockett dove into the hunt. She sent the Wyoming investigators the first installment of the series and followed up with phone interviews with Weston County Sheriff Bryan Colvard and Sergeant Watsabaugh, the veteran investigator who was handling the case. I called Colvard and Watsabaugh myself to fill in additional details of my research on the Springford case and Caroline Scoutt's suspected role in it. Most law enforcement I had encountered over the years disdained any "civilian" involvement with an investigation. But Watsabaugh did not brush me off when I suggested that, given Scoutt's background, it might be wise to wait before classifying Campbell's death as a suicide. Watsabaugh thanked me for my call and suggested that we remain in contact.

Richard Campbell, I soon learned, was a familiar, well-liked personality around Newcastle. He was born in Farmington, Michigan, in 1954 and grew up with four sisters in a family that liked the outdoors and camped a lot. In high school Campbell wrestled, but his great love was running track. At one point he was badly beaten in a fight, and his mother said he was never quite right after that. However, his sisters said they didn't notice any difference in him, that he was always happy and friendly. After finishing high school, he had a number of jobs, including one at Burger King, attended community college for a while, and was married briefly. He divorced and then moved to Denver and then Boulder, where he pursued his interest in holistic health and spirituality. He remarried and had two children, and he remained in contact with his sisters, regularly attending family reunions. After his second marriage broke up he moved to Scoutt's ranch outside Newcastle. Campbell had been living on Scoutt's property for a number of years—but not with her—working as a caretaker and handyman. He had neither a vehicle nor a driver's license at the time of his death. In good weather, to keep in shape, he rode his bicycle from the Scoutt property into Newcastle, where he worked, about twenty-three miles round trip.

Evidently, in the hours before his death Campbell had been clearing foliage with a weed whacker just outside his residence. Police also found vitamins and herbal supplements in Campbell's home, and Watsabaugh investigated reports that he had been treated for depression. Given the scene, the sheriff and his deputy said, the death was first thought to be a suicide, yet there were many unanswered questions. "There's so much more involved," Colvard told Rockett, his voice trailing off. "There's more to it, that's what I can say."

Scoutt's requests to the coroner for Campbell's death certificate alerted investigators to a $100,000 Farmers Insurance policy naming Scoutt as his sole beneficiary. Although there had been some lapses, the premiums were paid out of a bank account Scoutt controlled. As she had numerous times in the past, Scoutt offered different spellings of her first name—"Caroline" and "Carolyne"—on the insurance forms. Since the death took place just three months after going out of the policy's twenty-four month suicide exclusion clause, Scoutt was soon visited by sheriff's deputies. A second insurance policy later surfaced, this one written for employees of the supermarket chain that owned the convenience store where Campbell worked. It was for $25,000 and also named Scoutt as the sole beneficiary and was paid after his obituary was published. For Watsabaugh, now informed of Scoutt's involvement with Brent Springford and his family, and an earlier husband who had been imprisoned for manslaughter in Oregon, there were too many coincidences. "It's so consistent it's scary," he told me in a phone conversation at the time, echoing what Sheriff Colvard told Rockett. "She has a history." Watsabaugh began investigating the case as possible insurance fraud. But before I could turn my attention to the death of Richard Campbell in Wyoming, there remained some unfinished business involving the Springford murders in Alabama.

Eric and Deny

After Brent Springford's conviction and transfer to the state prison system, Susan Wardell was assigned to a defendant facing the death penalty who said he had befriended Brent in the Montgomery County Jail. The inmate, Eric Lang,* had spent time with Brent for much of 2008.

On March, 8, 2008, Lang, then twenty-seven, was charged with capital murder and attempted murder in connection with the shooting death of a twenty-nine-year-old man and the attempted murder of a twenty-six-year-old woman in a Montgomery parking lot. Police said the shooting appeared to be the result of a drug deal gone wrong. Lang's court-appointed attorney was a friend of Bill Blanchard and Jay Lewis, Brent's attorneys. They recommended Wardell to work as the death-penalty mitigation specialist on Lang's case.

On one of Wardell's visits with the new client, Lang mentioned that he knew Brent, who by this time was at Donaldson state prison. This rang a bell. Wardell recalled that Brent had told her of making a good friend, named Eric, who was smart and whom he could talk to. "When my work on Eric's case was winding down," Wardell said, "I happened to ask if he had known 'Winston.' Eric said he had. I asked why he had never said anything, and he said it was because I had never asked him, and we were working so hard on his own case."

It is not uncommon, Wardell said, for her clients to know one another, but it is unusual for them to be good friends. "I recall being stunned that he had been a confidant of Brent," she recalled. Lang, she said, "is not the type to babble on. He has an organized mind, and an amazing memory for details. He knew I had worked with Brent, but didn't know what Brent had

---

*   Not his real name.

told me. . . . Once Eric realized how much it meant to me, he was willing to tell me what he knew." Even more stunning was what Lang had to say: that Brent told him he had been brainwashed by Caroline Scoutt, that Scoutt had planned Charlotte and Brent Sr.'s murders and had rehearsed the fatal crime with him.

"I didn't question him much then, because I didn't think it would make any difference. . . . The one thing that did stick with me from that conversation with Eric was that, toward the end, he told me that Brent realized he'd been duped, and considered telling all about Caroline. Brent had changed his mind about her. He realized that Scoutt had set him up, and wanted to tell on her, but couldn't, he told Eric."

According to Lang, Scoutt's original plan involved a retired Colorado law enforcement officer as an accomplice. The former officer and Brent were to drive together to Montgomery to commit the murders. "What was most striking to me was the level of despair Brent felt about killing his parents," she said. "Brent was astounded that Caroline would suggest murdering his own parents and didn't realize she was serious. Eric could hardly believe Brent would do such a thing for Caroline, and didn't understand her hold on Brent, absent a sexual relationship. Brent cried every day, missing his parents and hoping they could forgive him."

Wardell shared this information with the other members of Brent's defense team. They agreed that had Brent gone to trial with this new information, at best the outcome would have been the same—life without parole. Still, she wrote Brent a letter, telling him that Lang was now her client, nothing more. She then drove to Donaldson to talk with Brent about what she had learned, but he refused to meet with her. Wardell felt that the information was so compelling that she went all the way to the warden, who told her there was no way to force Brent to see her.

On November 28, 2011, Lang pleaded guilty to murder and attempted murder and was sentenced to twenty-five years in prison. There, Lang became a jailhouse snitch, informing on other inmates, in hopes of getting out of prison sooner. By their nature, such informants are problematic witnesses; their character and their motives are suspect. Still, Wardell was convinced of the veracity of Lang's account of his time with Brent, and she told me about it: "He was completely consistent in what he told me. He is not a theatrical sort, he's very down to earth, and that's how he answered my questions. He did know that Brent really wanted to tell me about Caroline's role in his case, and that he struggled with keeping the secret."

In August 2015 I joined her in Montgomery and prepared to drive with her to the Limestone Correctional Facility in northern Alabama to interview Lang and try to evaluate his story for myself. But the day before our scheduled visit, prison officials said they would not permit me to see Lang because I was not part of his legal team. So I prepared a list of questions for Wardell to ask him. I also asked her to request an additional, written account from Lang in the days following, since he might remember things he did not think of when Wardell interviewed him. The arrangement was not ideal, because I would be unable to make my own assessment of his demeanor and body language to decide whether he was a reliable witness, or just a self-serving fabulist. I also could not know the impact of Wardell's zeal to believe Lang's scenario—which implicated Scoutt in the murders. However, Wardell insisted that she did not share with Lang her theory of Brent's case, because doing so would have been a serious ethical violation of her legal relationship with Brent.

In fact, Wardell's interview and Lang's subsequent written account provided many more details, as well as context to the earlier account Wardell had described to me. In her interview, Lang told her that, while both men were in single cells, they were permitted to come out and spend time in the central day room, and they also went into each other's cells to talk. Before long, they spent three or four hours a day together. Brent shared some of his favorite books with Lang. Lang said his first impression of Brent was, "That guy's crazy. . . . He had a long Amish beard, really long hair, very bad personal hygiene—he smelled really bad." Lang later learned that Brent didn't shower because Caroline would not allow him to. Initially, Lang found Brent very guarded, standoffish. He seemed to Lang to be very "book smart," yet without street smarts. When gang members in the jail threw signs at each other, Brent asked Lang what that meant. "He was a fish out of water."

Brent's demeanor varied by the day, Lang said. Sometimes he was extremely energetic, other times extremely depressed. He could be funny or he could be extremely guarded, especially if Scoutt's name came up, which seemed to "pull all the air out of the room. . . . Brent would have breaks with reality when you couldn't talk to him," Lang told Wardell. "Once he said I was the Anti-Christ. He'd be suicidal, be sent to the medical unit for 24/7 watch. He had lots of suicidal tendencies. He believed he was receiving messages from Caroline, whom he always referred to as his wife, telling him to kill himself."

Lang recalled details he could have learned only from Brent. For example, that he believed that Scoutt was having sex with Native American men while he was working in the Wyoming oil fields. "It's not all about sex," Brent said, since he wasn't interested in it that much. Scoutt said she would have sex with Brent as a reward, if he did things perfectly, according to her goals, but it never happened. She wouldn't let him shower at home, or come into the Windsor house without permission.

Naturally, Lang asked Brent how he had ended up in jail, facing murder charges. Brent said only that it was "bad, it's really bad, really bad," and left it at that. Another time, he asked Brent if his parents ever visited him. Brent said they weren't able to. As months passed, Brent slowly revealed the story. Eventually and with great effort, he would utter the words "I killed my parents." Over time, Brent described to Lang how communication with his parents had become less frequent, as more and more money was spent in Colorado with less explanation. His parents were concerned about his mental health and his relationship with Scoutt; they wanted Brent to come back home. Scoutt knew they wanted him to leave her, and she suspected they were going to take the house back.

As his trial neared, Brent became increasingly upset and ambivalent. Lang said Brent veered back and forth about Scoutt in their conversations. Usually he was protective and guarded, but sometimes he shocked his prison friend, describing how she planned the murders and rehearsed the fatal crime with him. At one point, he said Scoutt was someone who "takes everything good in the world and turns it into something to serve her own needs."

When Brent's father informed his son he would be cut off financially, Brent told Lang, Scoutt said the Springfords were standing in the way of their future. Brent insisted to Lang that he had no independent inclination to kill his parents, that he couldn't have thought up the plan, and that the plan was Scoutt's. If he killed his parents, he would become more important to her. If he did that for her, she would be his forever. He could come into the Windsor house without asking permission, eat there, share her bed, and he wouldn't have to keep his oil field job in Fort Lupton. They would be a "normal" family. According to Brent, Scoutt thought he would get half his parents' sizable estate. It didn't occur to her that Brent would get caught. If Brent was killed in the process, he didn't care, he told Lang, as long as Scoutt was happy. He insisted he was not interested in his family's money; all he cared about was Scoutt's happiness. He would have done anything she told him to do.

Brent said he was completely shocked when Scoutt told him what she wanted him to do in Montgomery. "I thought she was playing. . . . Then, wow! She meant it." Scoutt said repeatedly, "This has to be done." Brent said that the plot had a script, which he had to follow, although he wouldn't provide details for Lang, or the name of the retired Colorado cop. The officer warned Brent against using a gun in the attack, because it was too loud, or a knife, which ran the risk of leaving physical evidence if he cut himself. It was Brent's idea to use an ax handle, he told Lang. There was, Lang said, a compact disc of Scoutt and the officer instructing Brent on what he should do in Montgomery, which he was to play over and over. Although Lang said the three rehearsed this plot, it was ultimately scrapped for Brent's solo bus trip to Alabama.

The instructional disc had a particular ringing sound on it, and years later, if Brent heard a similar ringing sound in his head at the jail, Lang said, he thought it was "Spirit" trying to contact him. He'd immediately go to the back of the cell, get on his knees, and say, "Here I am, Spirit." Brent was fervent in telling Lang this version, yet Brent still didn't want Scoutt to be implicated. He wasn't worried about getting the death penalty, and said he'd only take a guilty plea if Scoutt told him to.

It was bizarre, Lang told Wardell. Although Scoutt was barely communicating with Brent, in his imagination he was convinced that his wife believed that he would have to inform on her to take a plea. There were times, Lang said, that Brent felt he had failed Scoutt somehow and then he'd get into suicidal moments.

Lang asked Brent if he had any hesitation about killing his parents, and Brent said yes, he almost left the house on Thanksgiving before his parents got home. Brent told Lang he didn't want to kill his parents, but he couldn't stop himself, he felt so much rage. Afterward, there was so much blood—he was surprised how much. Then he took the Jaguar and, from Tulsa, the bus back to Boulder. Brent felt really bad about the murders, Lang said. "He would cry a lot, but then he thought crying wasn't the right thing to do because he had committed the murders for them, Caroline and the kids. She said 'That's the way it had to be,' and he did it."

Lang followed up after the August interview, as Wardell and I had requested, with a written account, which provided more details. When they met, Lang wrote, he called Brent "Brother Winston," since Lang considered himself a Christian. Brent seemed to like the appellation, and asked Lang if he considered the Bible to be literally true. They laughed at the question and agreed that they were brothers in the sense that both were facing the possibility of the death penalty. Lang noticed that Brent had covered the mirror in his cell, "something Caroline had taught him," Lang wrote. The mirror was "a hindrance to killing the ego," and eliminated power, image, wealth, and fame, Brent said.

At times, Lang said, Brent saw Scoutt's beliefs "for the bullshit it was. Maybe it was his being away from her for such a long period of time that allowed for her spell to lose some of its power." Brent always acknowledged his guilt in killing his parents, yet he told Lang that "Caroline was the reason and the mastermind behind it, and at one point he even wanted her to be punished for her role as well."

Lang's tale sounded intriguing, but at times it was also convoluted and contradictory. Lang's premise was that over the four years since his arrest, Brent had turned on Scoutt and was confiding her role in planning the murders to an inmate, while still fiercely defending his wife to his attorneys. In any case, much of what Lang told and wrote Wardell seemed plausible, including Brent's talk about killing himself. That is, until Lang wrote this: "Knowing that you worked on both of our cases I suggested he tell you but he said he didn't want to see you in danger," apparently from Scoutt. Wardell, however, was not engaged to do mitigation work for Lang's case until August 30, 2009, eight months after Brent had pleaded guilty and gone to Donaldson prison. Wardell brushed me off when I asked about the apparent inconsistency.

The only independent confirmation Wardell had of Lang's truthfulness from Brent was that Brent had said he had a good friend named "Eric." But another form of indirect confirmation came from Deny Caballero, the young man who had lived in the Scoutt home in Windsor, Colorado. His statements to police and defense investigators are at least consistent with Lang's scenario. That is, in the weeks preceding the Montgomery murders there were whispered conversations between Brent and Scoutt, and unprecedented meetings between the two of them in Scoutt's bedroom. I decided I needed to follow up with Caballero myself.

After his second combat tour in Iraq with the 82nd Airborne, Caballero joined the Special Forces in 2012, going on several missions to Latin America. In early 2015 he served a six-month tour in Afghanistan, and by September 2015 he was stationed in the Florida Panhandle, sharing a condo near the beach with another soldier. He agreed to see me and to go over Eric Lang's account of life in the Windsor house, in particular in the weeks leading up to the Springford murders. By now thirty-one and a sergeant, Caballero was tanned, handsome, well-muscled, modest, and quick to smile. He read my typewritten pages while sitting at his dining room table.

After about a half-hour, he looked up and said, "I completely believe it. I would definitely give it credibility." Scoutt, he said, thinks like a good chess player, "always five moves deep. It's ridiculous how fast she calculates." At the same time, he said, she had huge blind spots. "The plan that Lang described is so awful and ill-considered it's something I can see her putting together. Caroline's cunning. She can manipulate. She's been cunning because she's had to hustle her whole life."

Until the weeks before the Springford killings, Caballero recalled, Brent was not allowed into the house. When Caroline wanted him to do something she would communicate by cell phone. Then, suddenly, Brent began coming in the front door, making a beeline for her bedroom. Also, Caballero said, "there wasn't any of the usual berating Brent for a week leading up to the fatal Thanksgiving." In retrospect, "it was kind of weird not hearing complaints about Brent." The dynamic, for years before the murders, was obvious. "I knew he was completely under her control." Caballero also confirmed the earlier accounts that Scoutt's oldest child, Caballero's ex-girlfriend, took Brent shopping, pointing out things she wanted so that he would later return and shoplift them. Caroline made a concerted effort to groom Caballero as well, although not for murder. He was in a vulnerable state, estranged from his stepfather and mother. "I was a very naïve young man at that point in my life," he said. Caroline, whom he called "Mom," would invite him into her bedroom, saying, "Son, come talk to me." Sitting in her rocking chair, she would speak soothingly to him. She pitted him against Brent, often assigning them the same chores. Then she asked Brent, "Why can't you be more like Deny?" Caballero also recalled Scoutt telling him, more than once, how great it would be if Brent killed his parents.

When I first contacted Caballero via email, he was still in Afghanistan, but he said he would talk to me when he got back to the States. There was, however, a caveat: "Allow me to be very clear on this. I have worked diligently to distance myself from that family. I don't want them to know that you have spoken to me, or that I am willing to meet with you. . . . You don't know what that woman is capable of. There's a reason that after all this time, I still consider Caroline Scoutt to be one of the most evil and dangerous people I have ever come across. Be careful, tread lightly, and if you do meet with her . . . good luck." Months later, when we met in his Florida condo, Caballero acknowledged the irony, given his military record, that he still feared Scoutt and her metaphysical reach. Readers, I said, would wonder about that. "There's things you can't calculate, man. . . . I don't give two fucks the way it sounds, and what people will think. I'm a man of faith, but that woman is into some dark, spiritual things. . . . I experienced a lot of weird things in that house. I didn't believe in ghosts as a kid but being in that house I got to see a lot of scary and unreal things."

In the basement of the Windsor house where he slept, he said, there was a locked room that he looked into only once. On the floor was painted a pentagram, an occult sign, with dead animals in the inscribed central circle.

Caballero also insisted that Caroline was what Native Americans, especially Navajos, call a "skin-walker," a malign witch spirit with the ability to transform herself into an animal, or to possess a person or animal. Also, he said, she practiced astral projection, and she was not alone. "Caroline taught Brent and herself how to project out of their bodies." On one occasion, Caballero said he was on the receiving end of the powerful terror of that ability. While sleeping in his room, Caballero suddenly awoke, but found he was paralyzed. "I couldn't move," he said. "A dark figure with long black hair"—whom he took to be Brent—"walked up to me. It had dark red eyes and began clawing at my chest. I can sense complete hate, clawing at my chest, but I can't do anything." Then a cat belonging to his ex-girlfriend, Scoutt's older daughter, jumped onto Caballero's chest and began hissing, driving off the apparition. The next morning Caballero woke up with deep claw marks in his chest. When Caballero told Scoutt about the incident, she admonished Brent not to do it again.

"I'm a rational man," he insisted. "I believe in God, but I've seen ghosts in that house . . . I would like to believe that Caroline couldn't impact me, but I don't want to test it."

*Left, Charlotte
and Brent
Springford Sr.,
while on an
overseas trip in
the 1990s. Below,
their home at
1944 South
Hull Street in
Montgomery's
wealthy Garden
District, about
a mile south of
downtown. This
is the house Brent
Springford Jr.
grew up in.*

Aerial view of the Springfords' house and property — 1. Hull Street; 2. fence Brent Jr. climbed over to slip unnoticed into the back yard; 3. tool shed where murder weapon was obtained; 4. roof he climbed onto to break into a second-floor window. Below, the back yard.

Photos taken by police of the untouched living room (the fireplace surround is a mirror, reflecting a sofa and art objects on a low table).

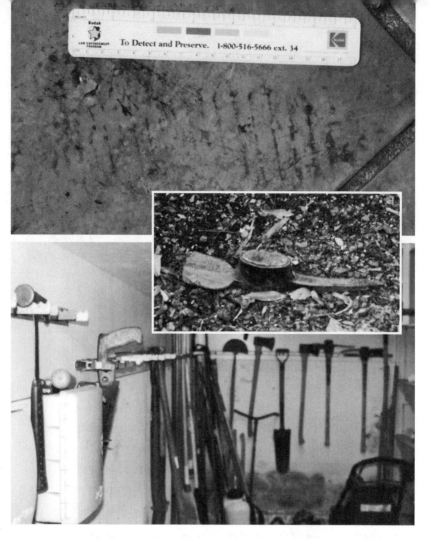

Behind the house, police found (top) a muddy footprint, (inset) the sawn-off and tossed-down head of a mattock taken from the (above) tool shed, and (below) a broken second-floor window.

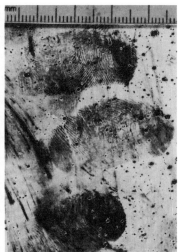

On the second floor, police found blood spattered on walls and a door jamb, bloody fingerprints, and, in separate rooms, the bodies of the Springfords. Next to the husband's body were the two blood-covered murder weapons, a kitchen knife and the handle that had been sawed from the mattock head found in the back yard.

Right, Charlotte Springford's dressing room and her husband's office had been ransacked. Below, detectives set up in the back driveway to sort and process evidence. Bottom, in front of the house, police secured the property with crime scene tape, and neighbors and news photographers huddled across the street.

By Friday morning, the murders had been discovered but Brent Springford Sr.'s black Jaguar was missing from the garage. The car was found three days later, abandoned in Oklahoma. A hat like the one Brent Springford Jr. often wore was on the ground near the car.

Montgomery police investigators soon settled on Brent Jr. as the likely suspect, and the search for him turned to Weld County, Colorado, where the Springfords had purchased property for him to live with Caroline Scoutt and her children. Left, an aerial view shows the house, a large garage, an above-ground pool, and several vehicles; everything was paid for by the Springfords.

Colorado police visited the Scoutt home above and found the occupants evasive about Brent Jr.'s whereabouts over Thanksgiving. On a subsequent visit, Montgomery police detective Michael Myrick spotted the bus schedules at right. Investigators later turned up security camera photos showing Brent Jr., with backpack, boarding a bus on one leg of his journey to Montgomery.

Brent Jr. grew up privileged but by his twenties was mentally troubled. Left, in the 1990s, visiting a friend in New York. Below and inset, visiting in Greeley, Colorado, in the early 2000s with an old high school friend and Caroline Scoutt, his secret wife.

2003/05/02

The Colorado house was filled with electronics. antiques, rugs, toys, clothes, appliances, and other possessions acquired by Scoutt and her family, including cars parked outside, and a swmming pool.

Above, racks of clothes, purses, shoes, and coats overflowed Caroline Scoutt's closets. Below, a "medicine shelf" of pills, supplements, and ointments she said were part of her Native American healing tradition.

Meanwhile, though his parents owned the Colorado house, and Brent Jr. was married to Caroline Scoutt, his own living quarters were in the unheated garage. His "pantry," cooking area, and personal possessions are shown in the photos on this page.

Above, Brent Jr.'s personal desk, orderly as was his habit, as detectives found it in Colorado. The inset at right is the book perched on the right front of the desktop: Seth Speaks, one he read and re-read and cited in his own journals. Below, this odd photo of Caroline Scoutt (seated at right, holding the gun) with daughters and others wearing period costumes, was found in the Colorado house.

Less than two weeks after the murder of his parents, Brent Jr. was arrested in Colorado. He initially resisted extradition to Alabama, but on February 18, 2005, Montgomery police detectives Michael Myrick and Bryan Jurkofsky flew to Colorado in a state-owned plane to return him to Alabama. In Montgomery, above, they loaded him into a waiting car that took him to the Montgomery County jail.

Brent Jr.'s appearance changed markedly from, above left to right, after he was jailed, at the time of his guilty plea, and while he was in prison. His trial in Montgomery County Circuit Court was handled

by Montgomery County District Attorney Ellen Brooks, left. He was represented by veteran criminal defense attorney Bill Blanchard, below right, and his associate, Jay Lewis, below left. The defense team's life-or-death phase of the capital murder trial was prepared by Susan Wardell, inset below, a mitigation expert based in Atlanta.

Above, Winston Brent Springford Jr., flanked by his defense attorneys Bill Blanchard, left, and Jay Lewis, right, in a news clip from local WSFA-TV at his plea hearing in November 2008, which was followed by his sentencing to life in prison without parole. That was the last the public would hear of Springford until news of his October 7, 2013, death appeared on the front page of the Montgomery Advertiser, *below.*

Springford's death a suicide

Coroner says man who killed parents in 2004 died from a drug overdose

By Kala Kachmar
kkachmar@gannett.com
@DailySiftings on Twitter

The death of a man who murdered his parents in Montgomery on Thanksgiving almost nine years ago has been ruled a suicide by a Jefferson County cor-oner.

Winston Brent Springford Jr., who was an inmate at Donaldson Correctional Facility in Bessemer, was pronounced dead at Brookwood Medical Center in Birmingham on Oct. 6.

Derrick Perryman, deputy coroner of the Jefferson County

Coroner/Medical Examiner's office, said he wasn't sure if he could release the report yet, but the death was ruled a suicide with drugs.

The Associated Press reported the death was caused by an overdose of Tylenol.

Marc Bass, an attorney for

the Alabama Department of Forensic Sciences, said obtaining a copy of the autopsy report could take anywhere from two to 10 months. He said the time frame depends on whether the report is complete, whether there's an ongoing criminal investigation associated with the report and whether it's a public record.

Alabama Department of Corrections (ADOC) Spokesman Brian Corbett said the depart-

ment didn't have a copy of the report, and referred The Adver-tiser to forensic sciences.

Springford, who stabbed his parents to death at their Montgomery home in 2004, was found guilty of five counts of capital murder Dec. 4, 2008. Winston Brent Springford, 62, and Charlotte Springford, 60, were a prominent couple in the Capital City.

See SUICIDE » 6A

Springford

Brent Jr.'s conviction, imprisonment, and suicide notwithstanding, the role of Caroline Scoutt was not over. While doing the early research for this book, author Mark Pinsky (left), met several times in 2014 with Denver private investigator Wayne Diffee (center left), who was hired in 2005 by defense attorney Bill Blanchard to assist in Colorado with Brent Jr.'s mitigation case. Then, in 2015, a death on property where Scoutt was then living in Wyoming led to questions by Sergeant Patrick Watsabaugh (bottom left) of the Weston County Sheriff's Department. Watsabaugh then called in the coroner of neighboring Campbell County, to rule on the suspicious death by gunshot of Richard Campbell. Pinsky heard about the death and called Watsabaugh to tell him about Scoutt's role in the Springford case.

Right, in an airplane cockpit, Campbell County, Wyoming, coroner Laura Sundstrom and chief deputy coroner Steve Rozier. Their findings and a search of the Scoutt property by the Weston County Sheriff's Department led to the arrest of Caroline Scoutt, shown below left during a law enforcement interview and below right at her booking.

Above, the Weston County Courthouse in Newcastle, Wyoming, where coroner's inquests were held in the Richard Campbell death. Despite the inquest findings, Weston County Attorney William Curley, left, did not prosecute.

: 22

Caroline

Mysteries, movies, and television notwithstanding, journalists rarely solve murders in real life, the recent profusion of *Serial*-like podcasts notwithstanding. For nonfiction writers, certainty is elusive, and there's no such thing as omniscience, or conveniently revealing flashbacks. In researching the Springford murders, I came to a similar conclusion as those involved in the investigation and the trial: the most likely scenario is that Caroline Scoutt, in hopes of financial gain, subtly or directly nudged Brent toward a predictably fatal confrontation with his parents. Thus, the simplest—but most problematic—way to find out what Scoutt's role was would be to go to Wyoming and ask her.

Weston County Sheriff Sergeant Patrick Watsabaugh, who was investigating the June 24, 2015, death of Richard Campbell on Scoutt's property, told me that if I came to Newcastle, he would accompany me to see Caroline. Frankly, I was on edge about a trip to Scoutt's home in Wyoming. For a week before my flight to Rapid City, South Dakota, the closest regional airport of any size to Newcastle, I was anxious. My wife was concerned as well, and friends familiar with the story volunteered gallows humor about how book sales would benefit if I *didn't* come back. My retort was that I planned to stand *behind* Sergeant Watsabaugh when we knocked on Scoutt's door. But before I drove from Rapid City to Newcastle, I realized that for all the spooky powers Scoutt seemed to wield over the naïve, the gullible, or the damaged, no one had ever said she acted violently. The evil force of the supernatural, I used to tell my devil-fearing evangelical Christian friends back in Florida, depends on how much you invest in its manifestation. I don't believe in the occult, so I figured I would be okay.

I drove from Rapid City to Newcastle on September 19, 2015, a sunny

Saturday afternoon, passing both Mount Rushmore and, further west, the monumental mountain-top sculpture-in-progress of Crazy Horse. After ninety minutes I reached Newcastle, and pulled into the gravel parking lot of The Pines, a modest, homey motel just off Main Street, the same place Susan Wardell and, at a different time, Caroline Scoutt and her daughter had stayed. The genial owner, Iva Carter, recalled them all, including Wardell's defensive sage burning, and Carter's own contentious relationship with Scoutt, including a dispute over her bill. "It was like a three-ring circus with her," Carter told me.

About an hour later, Sergeant Watsabaugh arrived in his marked patrol vehicle, a gray, 2011 Chevrolet 2500 four-door pickup. Stocky, even without the bulletproof vest under his tan uniform shirt, he wore black and white Oakley sunglasses and had a horseshoe mustache that met a close-cropped, Vandyke beard, all framing a soul patch. He was ranch-raised and college-educated, an enthusiastic motorcyclist and Facebook poster. At forty-one, he had sixteen years with the sheriff's department. An arms enthusiast as well as an expert marksman and police shooting instructor, he owned more than 130 guns. Watsabaugh was amiable and talkative as we set out to find Scoutt. When Wayne Diffee, the Denver PI, first contacted him on my behalf, Watsabaugh told me later, he had checked me out on the web before deciding whether to return Diffee's call, and how much to tell him about the circumstances of Richard Campbell's death. The sergeant had done some further research since then, and from the *Boulder Weekly* series had learned that police in Alabama and Colorado had cooperated with me, which he interpreted as "a proven willingness to work with law enforcement." This struck me as ironic, given my history as an unrepentant Sixties lefty, but I felt no need to disabuse the helpful investigator.

Another officer radioed that Scoutt's vehicle had been sighted around town, so Watsabaugh used that as an opportunity to give me a tour of New-castle. Just up Wentworth Avenue from The Pines was a rental property, a modest, one-story, white clapboard house, which Scoutt owned. Watsabaugh said the dwelling was once investigated as a hangout for drug users. We were unsuccessful in locating Scoutt in town, so Watsabaugh headed out to her property, taking Old Highway 85 south. After a while, the paved road gave way to a packed gravel road paralleling the railroad tracks, the road and the rails bisecting miles of open fields. We game-planned the interview as we drove.

Watsabaugh was confident that Scoutt would agree to the meeting. As it happened, she had several reasons to be cooperative, he explained. The verdict on Richard Campbell's death—and thus on her $100,000 insurance claim—was still hanging in the balance, waiting for a coroner's inquest to rule on the cause of death. Also, Caroline often complained to law enforcement about disputes with her neighbors, just as she had when she lived with Brent Springford in Colorado.

In addition, her children were in and out of trouble with the law in Weston County, as they also had been in Colorado, so she needed to remain in the sheriff's department's good graces. At the time of our drive, Watsabaugh told me, Caroline's older daughter was in custody at the county jail on a minor infraction. The younger daughter, too, had brushes with the law, recorded under eleven different names and variations. One cold spring day, Star Fosheim was arrested outside her mother's ranch by another Weston County sheriff's deputy, responding to a call from Caroline, and charged with domestic abuse for attacking her ex-boyfriend. The deputy observed that she appeared to be distraught and intoxicated. In her arms, she was carrying her infant child, dressed only in a shirt and diaper. The couple's fight took place when the ex-boyfriend, concerned about her intoxication, tried to stop the young woman from driving off with her baby and another young child.

Thus, the arrangement between the sergeant and me: the interview would be "mine," and therefore unofficial, so there would be no need for Watsabaugh to put Scoutt on guard with a Miranda warning against self-incrimination. Nonetheless, Watsabaugh would be present, and would benefit from whatever information was forthcoming. Scoutt was free to terminate the interview whenever she chose. It was a relaxed approach to law enforcement and defendants' rights I had encountered before in rural jurisdictions.

As we bounced along, nearing our destination, I tried to settle my nerves and focus on the encounter to come. I had learned a number of things from covering nearly two dozen capital cases. One is that encountering suspected killers in a rational context can be disconcerting, since murder is so often an irrational act. This was on my mind as we drove toward Scoutt's ranch. And since she claimed to be Native American, that could be a cultural filter between the two of us. At a dusty intersection with two mailboxes, Watsabaugh turned left and we trundled over the railroad tracks. Just opposite, he pointed out what had been Campbell's separate entrance to the property, with a padlocked chain-link gate. Scoutt's entrance was up the road. Entering another gate at the end of the road, we saw numerous outbuildings for animals and storage and a horse corral, which may have come from the Springfords' Colorado property. As soon as we got out of the pickup, Scoutt recognized Watsabaugh from a distance, and she called out to him by his first name. As Watsabaugh and I got out of his truck, another man pulled up in a pickup. Watsabaugh asked him his name, and he identified himself as Mark Fitzsimmons, but before he could say more Scoutt rushed up and told him to leave immediately.

The three of us approached a manufactured home, which had an attached front porch and, out front, one of the surveillance birdhouses transplanted from the Colorado house, Numerous small cats scampered out of our way. Scoutt took a seat about twenty yards beyond the double-wide, in front of the newly completed, circular lodge, where she was minding her two young grandsons. They called her "Nana" as they bickered and raced around a play area. She sat at a round, black, wrought-iron table, with her back to the lodge's front door. Watsabaugh placed his chair opposite her, but about six feet from me, so we were sitting at a right angle to her.

Caroline Scoutt was a small woman with glasses and shoulder-length brown hair, worn in a loose braid. Her snug, newish, dark jeans trailed into short cowboy boots. She had on a lavender and gray-striped, short-sleeved, cotton shirt with black embroidery and snap buttons. Around her neck was a black kerchief. She looked at me quizzically as I walked up with Watsabaugh. Scoutt was mousy, but certainly not the "old prunish hag" described by Dow Harris more than a decade earlier. Her facial features had clearly relaxed and softened with age. She appeared to be a diminutive, soft-spoken, nearsighted woman, squinting owlishly from time to time.

Ethnically, she could have been Native American, Hispanic, or even Roma, as one law-enforcement official suggested. Shaking her hand, I did not sense any of the power I knew she wielded over so many people.

Could this be the manipulative "witch" so many feared, the sinister "puppeteer," suspected by numerous lawyers and investigators? Perhaps it was because we caught her off-guard, and thus off-balance, that she first seemed so benign. Watsabaugh gave her a bland, cursory description of me and my role, introducing me as an investigator helping him with the Campbell death. He told her that this would be "my" interview, and that he would not ask any questions. At first, Scoutt seemed to accept the explanation, and was polite, answering with a tentative half smile. But as the interview progressed, she became increasingly wary, her suspicions growing as my line of inquiry became clear. About forty-five minutes into the interview, after nervously shifting her gaze back and forth from me to the officer, she said she wanted to know exactly why I was there. I explained that I was writing a book about Brent Springford and his parents' murders. The case had been brought to me by Susan Wardell, who is my wife's sister and who had interviewed Scoutt before the trial. That prompted her to pause, but she soon continued.

We went back over her life with the Springfords, beginning with their first visit to Newcastle in the summer of 2000. "I liked them," she said, at the same time weaving into her account negative impressions about the couple. Brent Sr. had carried a carton of hard liquor in the car when he visited. It was Charlotte's idea to insulate the camper where Brent Jr. was sleeping, although Scoutt remembered thinking that no amount of insulation would help against the Wyoming winters. Charlotte's aim for Brent was clear from the outset: "She wanted to keep him safe and watched out for." For her part, "Charlotte was nice to me," at times begging her to help her son. "We need to do something," Charlotte would say. "He's not well." Scoutt's marriage to Brent Jr., she insisted, was Charlotte's idea, even when I pointed out that Charlotte had ordered a copy of their Deadwood marriage certificate the week before she was murdered. Scoutt emphasized that "we were not 'married-married,'" an acknowledgment that they did not share a bedroom. At one point, Charlotte confided in her that she wanted to leave Brent Sr., Scoutt said. Brent Jr. seemed to feel both hate and love for his parents, and his anger was usually directed toward them. Brent would complain, "They won't let go of me." When he told Scoutt stories about his early life at home, she said, "I didn't know what was real . . . I didn't know what to say."

Scoutt's answers to my questions were disjointed, and rambling. From time to time, Scoutt would interrupt the interview to rein in her increasingly rambunctious grandchildren, who were clearly upset at having to compete for her attention. At first she spoke to them in a soothing but insistent voice and, when that didn't work, she resorted to placating them with snack food. Returning to my questions, Scoutt said she thought that after the rest of her family moved into the Colorado house, Brent would live in her mobile home outside Newcastle, rather than continuing to sleep at his drilling work sites in the camper, or in the back of his SUV. At times in Windsor, she said, Brent was violent, hitting her with his fists and pushing her to the ground. And, referring to the incident involving her older daughter, she brought up the time Brent threatened to kill Deny Caballero. When Scoutt asked Brent about the large "worry hole" dug during all hours of the day and night, he told her it was in case one of the horses died—although they were all healthy—and needed to be buried. The reason Brent liked Dr. Billica, the Fort Collins nutritionist, was not because his diagnosis suggested his problems were the result of a chemical imbalance rather than mental illness. Mostly, Scoutt said, it was because he liked Billica's nurse. Also, because Brent became convinced that a certain kind of honey would cure him.

In the spring and summer of 2004, Scoutt said she was under the impression that Brent was going to attend his sister Robin's October wedding. "Then Charlotte said he didn't want to go," Scoutt said, although she must have known that Brent had been crushed when Robin withdrew the invitation, at her parents' request. I decided not to challenge her account. By the autumn of 2004, as Brent seemed to deteriorate, Scoutt said that Charlotte asked her if she would sign commitment papers if she could get him admitted to an in-patient program. Scoutt said she was amenable to the proposal. By this time, she said, "I wanted to return to Wyoming," but not with Brent. "He was getting worse." In the end, she said, "I couldn't help Brent. I'm not a psychiatrist. . . . You can only do so much."

As I shifted my questions to the week before the Springford murders, I sensed that Scoutt was trying to figure out how much I knew about the case before she gave me her version. I tried not to tip my hand more than I already had, while answering all of her questions honestly. She said she took Brent to the bus station on Monday of Thanksgiving week because he said he wanted to visit a friend. Throughout the next few days, "I thought he was still around. He did many strange things. I didn't question him." When she picked him up the following Saturday, "He talked crazy, like nothing made sense. He jumped from one subject to another. It didn't make sense to me." The reason she dissembled to the Montgomery detectives in their first interview, she said, was that "I didn't understand what they were saying. Nothing made sense to me." The murders hit her like a thunderbolt, she said, and she feared what Brent might do to her and her family. "I thought it could happen to us . . . I tried not to hate him when I learned he killed his parents. I prayed, I did ceremonies."

After Brent was arrested, Scoutt conducted a few more breathing sessions in Boulder, but "I couldn't do any more sessions. It was too hard." At this point in the interview Scoutt asked me to further clarify my purpose. I told her that an Alabama prison informant named Eric Lang had told Susan Wardell that Brent had told him that Scoutt had instigated and planned his parents' murder, and that she had rehearsed him in the plot. I said I wanted to give her the opportunity to respond directly to what Lang had said. For an instant, she seemed shocked, but then recovered. "No," she said firmly, it was not true. "Absolutely not." Then she offered to take a polygraph test.

My next questions focused on Richard Campbell. Scoutt said she first met his then-wife in Boulder and, through her, Richard, who was also Brent's friend. The two men shared an interest in Eastern religions and went to Buddhist meetings together. Campbell also purchased vitamins and supplements from the same Dr. Billica. After the Campbells' marriage broke up, Richard was adrift and nearly homeless, Scoutt said. By this time, after the Springford murders and her eviction from the Windsor house, she was back in Newcastle. Feeling sorry for Campbell, she agreed to let him join her on her property, working for his keep as a part-time handyman.

He lived in a separate mobile home, with a separate entry to the property. Scoutt said he seemed to settle in, riding his bike to and from town, first to a job at the refinery, and then to a job as a clerk in a local convenience store, the Loaf 'n Jug. There was even a short-lived romantic relationship with a local woman. Campbell complained about one manager who kept him on the night shift at the store. Like Brent, he impulsively bought many vitamins and supplements, taking them in large quantities.

Asked for more details about her relationship with Campbell, Scoutt said, suddenly sharp, "Why do you want to know?" And she became vague when I asked her why she had taken out the insurance policy on Campbell. That, she said, had been her bookkeeper's idea, because of Campbell's role in one of two Wyoming-chartered nonprofit religious organizations she set up to assist Native Americans, the one called Tatan-ka Sha Inc. Scoutt insisted she had advised Campbell to name his adult children as beneficiaries, but he refused, determined to name her instead. She was similarly evasive when I asked what duties Campbell had with the nonprofit organization, how it and the other nonprofits were supported, and where the money came from to complete the round house behind her. Again, she demurred. She said Campbell's suicide was still baffling to her, perhaps now realizing that it might jeopardize the insurance policy. "Richard was happy," she said. "I can't believe he would take his life. He was so happy," singing while he cut copious amounts of firewood. Yet later in the conversation she acknowledged that Campbell was sometimes sad, although he never wanted to hurt himself.

The morning of the day he died, Campbell left a message on Scoutt's cell phone, asking that she pick up some ginseng green tea, coffee, and powdered milk when she was shopping in Rapid City. Around 6 p.m. she returned, honking her horn as she passed his gate to let him know she was back. When he didn't answer his phone she went to his trailer to check on him, and found the body. Not realizing he was dead, she tried to revive him. When she failed, she called 911 and drove to her trailer. Campbell's suicide, she said, was "something unfathomable." At times, answering my questions, Scoutt was plaintive, on the verge of tears, talking about both Brent and Campbell. I asked if she ever wondered about why she seemed to attract damaged, vulnerable people like Brent and Campbell. First, she rejected any comparisons with Brent. "I never thought of Richard like Brent at all." Then she added, "I help people. That's my problem." After two hours, around sundown, as free-range, wild turkeys began roosting in the nearby trees, the interview ended.

In the parking area, just before we got back into Watsabaugh's patrol vehicle, the deputy whispered to me that his bodycam was rolling throughout the interview, and that he would send me a copy when the file was down-loaded. Night fell as we rode back to Newcastle, debriefing one another. "My sense of her was that she put on a pretty good show at being soft-spoken," he said, "but I do believe she answered questions with other questions. And some of the more pointed questions she answered yes *and* no." Deer, antelope, and rabbits crossed the road as we bounced along, the animals all seemingly unconcerned with our approach in the large vehicle, with its high beams on. The conversation continued through dinner as we tried to separate Scoutt's lies from her truths. Later that night, Watsabaugh took me to the sheriff's department, where he opened his laptop and showed me the crime scene photos he took at Campbell's trailer after he had removed the gun from the body. Such images are never easy to look at, but they confirmed the police reports of the scene.

⋮ 23

Task Force

Two days after our interview with Scoutt, on September 21, 2015, a small task force assembled in Newcastle at the Weston County Sheriff's Department and jail, a low-slung complex behind the old, ornate courthouse. The ostensible purpose of the meeting, held in the department's rectangular squad room, was to consider Richard Campbell's death. Four law-enforcement officials gathered in the cluttered room, which was lined with desk-top Formica counters and eye-level wooden cabinets. I was invited to attend *and to participate*—both firsts for me for me as a journalist, after forty years, off and on, covering sensational murder cases and trials. Doing so would transgress one of the cardinal rules of journalism: *Never become part of the story.* I had already inserted myself in the investigation by calling Watsabaugh following Campbell's death, to tell him about Caroline Scoutt's background in Alabama and Colorado. But this would be crossing a line, becoming a part of the official investigation. I thought about it, and then agreed. The only condition of my attending the task force meeting was that I not quote the participants directly.

Sitting around the conference table in the center of the room were Watsabaugh, then the lead investigator on the case; Weston County Coroner Cynthia Crabtree; and two other death-scene investigators from neighboring Campbell County. The day Richard Campbell's body was discovered, the newly elected Crabtree was out of town at a training session. So Watsabaugh called Laura Sundstrom, the on-call coroner in adjoining Campbell County—whom he had once dated—and asked her to handle the case. Sundstom, a divorcee who was having dinner with her two children at her home in Gillette, jumped in her car and sped the eighty miles to work the death scene with him. Later, Sundstrom would reproach herself for the way she conducted the initial investigation, for not immediately suspecting murder. "We screwed it up," she told me later, but she would soon make up for lost time.

By coincidence, Sundstrom is a native of Alabama, and in November 2004 she was living just outside Montgomery, where she was working and going to school. She had vivid memories of the publicity surrounding the Springfords' Thanksgiving weekend murders and their aftermath. These included listening to Brent Springford Jr.'s rambling statement from Centennial Peaks Hospital, proclaiming his innocence, on WFSA-TV. Sundstrom moved to Wyoming with her first husband, an insurance agent, in 2005. She decided to become a coroner's investigator in part because of her family's experience after her brother, a decorated police officer, committed suicide in 2008. The coroner in her hometown of Mobile, Alabama, she said, "treated us like shit." She was convinced she could do better.

In August 2015, two months after Campbell's death, Sundstrom went to Mobile to visit her grandmother, who was ill. So she took the opportunity to contact Montgomery police detectives and then met with Mike Myrick, who briefed her on the Springford murders and Scoutt's suspected role in them. In a Montgomery Police Department conference room they reviewed for several hours documents and photographs saved on a flash drive. In Sundstrom's mind, there was a clear connection between Scoutt's role in at least facilitating the Springford murders and her similar role in the recent death of Campbell

When Sundstrom arrived at the task force meeting in Newcastle, she carried a tall stack of documents copied in Montgomery, as well as others she had accumulated herself. In addition to traditional police methods, she utilized web resources like ancestry.com and background location and identity services like Intellius. When she tracked down Scoutt's first husband, now a double amputee and still living with their son, the man said he didn't know she had divorced him until the coroner told him. Sundstrom's methodical investigation even turned up Scoutt's elementary school counseling records, which revealed her birth name, Carol Gonzales. Sundstrom also brought with her the county's chief deputy coroner, Steve Rozier, a retired detective sergeant with the Gillette Police Department.

Cynthia Crabtree had her own paper pile on the table as high as Sundstrom's.

As the first order of business, I was asked to speak about what I had learned from my research on Scoutt's early life and her relationship with Brent Springford Jr. and his parents. I talked about the hundreds of thousands of dollars and the half-dozen vehicles the Springfords had sent to Scoutt, Brent Jr., and Scoutt's children during the marriage. Sundstrom then took the lead, in what soon became a freewheeling discussion, with only Watsabaugh keeping his own counsel for most of the session. Even though he was still considered the lead investigator on the case, the sergeant liked to tell people he preferred to "listen louder. I don't have a superhuman intellect or superhuman power. My strength is in listening and observing and detecting—and putting it together." For the most part, he said, "I was watching the puzzle pieces."

Sundstrom reviewed what was known about the case. The day Campbell's body was found, Scoutt twice told her story to officers. She returned to his trailer after investigators had been there for a while, and around 8 p.m. Deputy Dan Fields interviewed her again in her mobile home. She told him she left home at about 6 a.m. that day, dropping her two grandchildren at day care in Newcastle and then went to Rapid City for a number of appointments and errands. En route, Campbell called and asked her to get some groceries for him. Around 5 p.m., she picked up the children and returned home. She saw Campbell's backpack hanging on a fence, but there was no sign of him. When she went to his trailer to deliver the groceries she found the body and called 911.

While Campbell's death launched the investigation, over the next two months the case mushroomed into an underlying—and possibly related—fraud investigation as well. Those around the table believed that Campbell was just the latest in a long line of people whom Scoutt had bilked and abandoned. Bank checks collected by Alabama and Wyoming investigators indicated that Scoutt had raised $75,000 to $100,000—the figure would grow in the months to come—from various people, apart from the Springfords. The donors thought they were supporting construction of a cultural-and-counseling center for Native American women and children on Scoutt's property, a center that was never established. Theoretically, it would have been located in the same circular lodge that both Marie Flinders in Boulder and then Charlotte and Brent Springford Sr. had declined to support, in the latter case causing one of the first blowups with Scoutt and Brent Jr.

Campbell's case sounded familiar, those around the table thought. In early 2005 he came up to Newcastle from Colorado, following a devastating divorce that family members blamed on Scoutt. Contrary to Scoutt's recollection at our interview, investigators now believed that Campbell had met her through Brent, with whom he shared an interest in Buddhism. Through either Scoutt or Brent, Campbell also became a patient of Dr. Roger Billica, the Fort Collins nutritionist. After his divorce, Scoutt said Campbell begged her to let him join her in Newcastle and live in the other mobile home on her property. She agreed, allowing him to exchange lodging for chores around the property. Much like Brent Springford, Campbell was soon in Scoutt's thrall. A fitness enthusiast, he took a job at the same local oil refinery in Newcastle where Brent had worked. But Scoutt took up so much of Campbell's time, visiting him at the refinery work site, that he was let go. He cashed in his small 401(k) account. Later he took another job with an engineering company in the nearby town of Upton.

Scoutt took out the $100,000 Farmers Life Insurance policy on Campbell in September 2006, with herself as the sole beneficiary. However, insurance companies look askance at policies in which the sole beneficiary has neither a familial nor a business relationship with the policy holder. So Scoutt named Campbell a director and president of Tatan-ka Sha Inc., one of her two nonprofits. Premiums for the policy were paid by Scoutt or through Tatan-ka Sha. Yet neither organization seemed to have any significant assets, according to documents filed with the state and federal government, nor did Campbell appear to receive compensation for his duties. There might be another potential hitch in Scoutt's claim, Rozier suggested. Since at one point payment of the premiums lapsed, he said, the twenty-four-month clock on the policy's suicide exclusion may have reset, and could nullify Scoutt's claim. He asked Farmers for clarification.

In 2014 Campbell's father died in Florida and the son received an inheritance of nearly $95,000, in the form of two checks, which he appeared to have endorsed to Scoutt. From Campbell and other donors—one of whom sued to get $30,000 back—Scoutt raised almost enough money to complete the round house. She also had an interesting history of acquiring property, task force participants reported. Investigators learned that the land itself, 195 acres she now lived on, had been signed over to Scoutt in the late 1990s from yet another man, from California, Mark Fitzsimmons, to whom it was thought she was once romantically linked. He was the same man Watsabaugh and I encountered on Scoutt's property the day I interviewed her. According to the deed transfer document, the acreage was conveyed as "payment for her counseling services and repayment of previous monetary loans." By coincidence, the initial construction company hired to frame the lodge structure belonged to the family of Cynthia Crabtree, the future Weston County coroner. The firm stopped work in a payment dispute with Scoutt. Using other resources, Scoutt added inside finishing, plumbing, siding, and shingles for the roof. But instead of using the building as the long-promised counseling center for Native Americans, Scoutt simply made it her new residence.

Although there was great interest around the task force table about a possible fraud investigation, the conversation eventually circled back to the circumstances of Richard Campbell's death, which was the coroner's sole jurisdiction. The rifle used in the killing belonged to Scoutt. She said she had given it to him, at his request, for personal protection and to shoot predators. Campbell had a prescription for Prozac, written by a local physician's assistant, and his trailer was stocked with vitamins and supplements, some from Dr. Billica. The coroner's office put the time of death between 3 and 4 p.m. Scoutt said at that time she was shopping in Rapid City, ninety minutes away, and provided a date-and-time stamped receipt from a Safeway supermarket there to substantiate her claim. Supermarket surveillance footage from the store was of poor quality, however, and did not show her. Cynthia Crabtree got the attention of the others at the table when she produced a statement from a young man who had been working on the round house's siding crew that day. He said that while driving away he saw Scoutt in her vehicle, parked near the gate to Campbell's trailer that afternoon.

After two hours, the discussion wound down. The informal consensus was that Scoutt, having squeezed Campbell dry, was planning to discard and evict him, as she had done with other men who had lived on her property the investigators found. They agreed that, whether Scoutt somehow drove him to suicide, or more directly participated in his death in order to get $125,000 from the two policies, was an open question. The group began to plot strategy to gather more information, first for the upcoming coroner's inquest, a broad inquiry in which sworn testimony would be taken. Before that, they wanted to ask the county prosecutor to subpoena more of Scoutt's banking records and to ask the FBI for help in getting her federal income-tax returns, to determine if she paid taxes on any of the money raised for the counseling center. They also wanted to ask the Farmers Insurance agent about the policy's suicide clause, but there had been no response to Rozier's earlier inquiry.

Toward the end of October, Sundstrom, the Campbell County coroner, sent me an email. She had finally gotten around to reading the two-part series about the Springford case in the *Boulder Weekly*. Something in it rang a bell, something she had not mentioned in the task force meeting: Before moving to Newcastle, Richard Campbell had worked at the Whole Foods in Boulder. In one of his confessions and one of his interviews, Brent Springford said that he had met the demon "Akasha" at a Whole Foods market. And in her interview, Caroline Scoutt told investigators that before she dropped Brent off at the bus station on the Monday of Thanksgiving week of the murders in 2004, he first told her he wanted to see a friend at Whole Foods. Could there be a connection between Richard Campbell and Akasha? I told Sundstrom I would send her the Akasha and Whole Foods material from my files and agreed that we could talk by phone about this and other matters related to the case.

I confess to a growing unease in getting so deeply into the Scoutt investigation, first by participating in the task-force meeting, and now this. Traditionally, reporters scrupulously avoid becoming part of stories they cover. Yet I was now crossing a line I had crossed only once before, while working on my previous book, *Met Her on the Mountain*, but that was a long-dormant cold case. For decades, because of their accessibility and eagerness for publicity, I had effectively allied myself with the defense in criminal investigations and trials. Now I was working "the other side," becoming close with cops and investigators. Patrick Watsabaugh later wrote me, "Mark, the progress in this case would not be anywhere near what it is so far without your assistance, your help and insight to the intricate past of those involved in this case. My thankfulness and gratitude to you go beyond words." For an old Sixties lefty like me, Watsabaugh's note felt odd, apart from the flattery. Yet I believed that in this case I was doing the right thing, so I continued in my new role. A few weeks later, on a Friday afternoon, Sundstrom and I began what would be a two-hour, free-ranging phone conversation, trading information in what was essentially a continuation of the task-force meeting in Newcastle. She and Steve Rozier had now assumed the role of lead investigators on the case.

: 24

The Trail

A week before my lengthy phone conversation with Laura Sundstrom, she phoned Caroline Scoutt and asked if she, Watsabaugh and her chief deputy coroner, Steve Rozier, could come out for an interview. Scoutt had evidently learned her lesson from my surprise visit with Watsabaugh, and declined. Instead, she said she was willing to meet the investigators in town, at her house up the street from The Pines motel. This is where, in bad weather, too inclement for him to ride his bicycle back to the Scoutt ranchette, Richard Campbell was allowed to stay, but only if he slept in the basement. When Sundstrom, Rozier, and Watsabaugh arrived, Scoutt refused to let them in. She insisted that the interview take place on the front porch, despite the growing autumn chill. Scoutt brought out a chair for herself and one for Sundstrom, but only a child's chair for Rozier, and nothing for Watsabaugh. Rozier had played these interrogation games himself when he was a police detective, so he decided to remain standing, at times looming over Scoutt. He recalled taking one look at her "lifeless, beady eyes" and registering an instant dislike. Largely silent, Watsabaugh placed himself between Sundstrom and Rozier, keeping his bodycam trained on Scoutt as he leaned against the porch railing. Passing traffic sometimes drowned out her recorded responses. "She was much more guarded this time around, more skeptical about us, and why we were there," Watsabaugh told me.

The interview began fairly low-key, with some biographical questions from Rozier, as well as some tentative probing into her relationship with Richard Campbell. Scoutt, again soft-spoken and seeming almost meek, shifted her gaze from looking up at Rozier to looking directly at Sundstrom. She told Rozier that she was born in Los Angeles, and was a Chiricahua Apache. She first said that she had met Campbell through his interest in New Age and

Buddhist religions. Then, later in the interview, she told the investigators that Campbell and his wife had a house-cleaning business in Boulder, and that she met the couple while they were cleaning Marie Flinders's house. It was another seemingly chance encounter, like Scoutt's first meeting with Brent Springford in 1999. Soon after, Campbell had taken breathing sessions with Scoutt and, at her suggestion, had given up the cleaning business and taken a job as a cashier at the Boulder Whole Foods. Also on Scoutt's advice, he separated from his wife and abandoned his children, going so far as to take out restraining orders against his estranged wife and older daughter.

Because coroners are exempt from federal HIPPA privacy regulations, Watsabaugh told me, Sundstrom was able to get Campbell's medical records from Dr. Billica in Fort Collins. Billica's diagnosis of Campbell seemed to the investigators "strangely similar" to his earlier diagnosis of Brent Springford, which I had shared with them—that is, elevated levels of lead and mercury in his brain. Campbell's ex-wife Sharon told Sundstrom that she believed that he had no significant mental impairment, although he seemed a little "slow" and "suggestible," which the ex-wife attributed to the head injury Campbell suffered in the teenaged fight. Scoutt said Campbell was usually happy when he moved to her Wyoming property, repeating that he sang while feeding the chickens and walking the horses, although he did have occasional dark periods when he got angry with himself.

Scoutt told the investigators things about Campbell's behavior that echoed her time with Brent, that he sometimes fell asleep behind the wheel, ending up in a ditch, and that his sugar craving led him to dumpster dive. Scoutt showed them some letters Campbell had left for her that not only sounded to me like Brent, preoccupied with "Spirit" and self-deprecation; the hand-printed notes even *looked* like Brent's writing. "I talk to people and boost this ego by getting approval from them," Campbell wrote. "I am complete with self-love in Spirit. I try to get people to feel sorry for me. . . . I seem to like getting into trouble doing things wrong and then getting anxiety and guilt from it. I feel like I deserve to feel guilty and fear. I get really angry and depressed when I forget anything real simple. . . . I am centered in Spirit and enjoying every moment." This was clearly another vulnerable, wounded person.

The investigators also pressed Scoutt on her finances. According to IRS documents that Sundstrom had located, Scoutt's nonprofit Tatan-ka Sha Inc. reported yearly gross incomes for the previous decade of under $50,000 (in one year less than $25,000), which exempted it from more rigorous and detailed filing requirements, like the Form 990, all of which are public records and readily available on the Internet. Another board member turned out to be Scoutt's younger daughter, Star Fosheim, who, like her mother, had used different first and last names, including her ex-husband's last name. Scoutt said that the sole purpose of Tatan-ka Sha was to collect old clothes and distribute them on Indian reservations. It had nothing to do, she said, with raising funds to build the round house lodge, to be used for a cultural and counseling center for Native American women and children. The lodge, Scoutt volunteered, was now her primary residence and was worth $460,000.

When Rozier began to focus on the details of Campbell's two insurance policies, Scoutt became suspicious. She said she received the $25,000 check from Campbell's employee policy almost immediately after his death. She said that there had been only one month's lapse in paying premiums on the Farmers policy, and she reiterated that it was Campbell's choice to name her as the sole beneficiary. "I didn't want it," she said, repeating that she had urged him to name his adult children as beneficiaries. Just before the insurance policy was reinstated, Sundstrom found, Campbell received two checks from his father's estate, one for $89,400, and another for $5,755. Endorsement signatures on both were Richard Campbell and Caroline Scoutt. Yet Scoutt dissembled when Sundstrom asked her where that money went, giving different explanations for how much of the inheritance she got and why. She said that Richard owed her money for various unspecified things, and that she gave him some of it in cash. She also said she bought him a four-wheel-drive vehicle, which he was not licensed to drive.

While on the subject of the insurance policy, Rozier focused on Campbell's long-standing history and treatment for depression. When Campbell's Farmers Insurance policy was purchased in 2006, and when it was reinstated in August 2013, whoever filled out the applications failed to check boxes indicating that he had been treated for any form of mental illness. Scoutt appeared mystified and professed to know nothing about how the policy was filled out. The insurance company declined to discuss the twenty-four month suicide exclusion clause with Sundstrom or Rozier, or to say whether the clock reset when Campbell stopped paying the premiums. However, if the time limit did restart when premiums resumed, Campbell's death occurred two months short of the clause's expiration. Scoutt told them she had no explanation for why, at the time of Campbell's death, his trailer was full of Billica's vitamins and supplements, yet there was no sign of the two different medications he had been prescribed locally for depression.

As the interview progressed, the breeze picked up and the shadows on the porch lengthened. Sundstrom, forced by the outdoor setting to take notes on her iPad without her gloves, was already irritated at Scoutt's rudeness. At one point Scoutt asked her to take off her sunglasses before she would answer a question. "She was trying to intimidate me," Sundstrom said. Sundstrom, meanwhile, engaged in some psychological warfare of her own. She brought with her an armful of files—containing nothing but blank paper—marked with tabs with headings like, "Caroline's background" and "Caroline's Finances," which she dropped on the deck where Scoutt could see them.

More substantively, the coroner was also thinking about the growing parallels between Scoutt's toxic, domineering relationship with Brent Springford and her relationship with Richard Campbell. Her investigation indicated that Campbell's friends and co-workers in Newcastle said "they thought the world of Richard," Sundstrom told Scoutt, but they were concerned that Scoutt "treated him like a dog, less than a dog" in front of other people. He was subservient to her and, despite his job, begged for money, always claiming to be hungry. The bike he rode to town was in such bad shape that friends chipped in to buy him a new one—which promptly disappeared. Most significantly, they said that Campbell didn't know how to use a gun—that he never hunted. Rozier said to Scoutt, "I don't think this guy killed himself . . . it doesn't make sense." Scoutt replied, "I never thought of that." Campbell's co-workers, Sundstrom told Scoutt directly, "think you killed him."

"Are *you* thinking I killed him?" Scoutt asked the investigators, incredulous. Rozier then suggested there were things in her past, like her involvement with the Springfords, and Richard Campbell, all of which seemed to have benefited her financially. There were two murders and two apparent suicides that they knew of. "Are you thinking I've done this?" she asked again, now clearly distressed. Rozier didn't respond directly, but brought up the $95,000 that Campbell received from his father's estate and deposited into Scoutt's bank account. He said it seemed to him to be a lot of money to give Scoutt for taking care of him. "Are you accusing me?" she asked. "Do you think he killed himself for me?" Rozier replied obliquely, concluding the interview, "There's a lot of ways to kill people and make it look like suicide."

At this point in the expanding investigation, Sundstrom told me, she was wary of the potential pitfalls of local jurisdictional turf battles, a concern that would prove prescient. Yet, given her lack of resources for such things as a forensic accountant to review Scoutt's financial records, the coroner said she was leaning toward calling in the FBI. The feds would have ready access to Scoutt's bank records, her income tax returns, and any additional IRS materials from her nonprofits. In the investigation into the increasingly sinister circumstances of Campbell's death, Sundstrom was willing to risk losing control of the fraud portion of the Scoutt case. The coroner had since found at least two other men who had been or seemed to be in similarly exploitative relationships with Scoutt. The ex-wife of Mark Fitzsimmons, the man who bought and transferred the property outside Newcastle to Scoutt, told Sundstrom that Scoutt had broken up her marriage, the same claim Campbell's ex-wife Sharon made to her. "This woman is very dangerous in what she does," Sundstrom told me at the end of our phone conversation. "She has hurt a lot of people. This has to stop before someone else dies."

The response to the *Boulder Weekly*'s series revealed more intriguing details about Campbell and his death. Rick Schlueter, who identified himself as an old friend of Richard's, contacted me in November 2015, after being sent the articles. He said he met Campbell—known to his friends as "Sandy"—in Boulder in 1980 when he answered an ad for a roommate. They lived together and became good friends, remaining so after each married and each had two children. Schlueter confirmed that Campbell worked for years in his wife Sharon's home-cleaning business. The two men and their families spent a good deal of time together—camping, hiking, and often visiting each other's homes for dinner. When Campbell left the cleaning business for a job at Whole Foods, he said, Sharon began selling jewelry in Boulder.

The Campbells, prototypically for Boulder, were very much involved in New Age spirituality, "always into some new thing like crystals and channeling," Schlueter said. "I always looked at Sandy as the kid who didn't grow up. He was pretty childish, but that was one reason for our friendship. He was very honest and very trusting. The one thing he was serious about was exercise. He ran a lot. Ran in races, ran for exercise, ran for fun. He was always in great shape. Sandy was a person who needed others to tell him what to do, and Sharon fit that need for him. He sometimes complained that Sharon controlled him too much, but someone has to guide a child." Some of what Schlueter told me reinforced what I and investigators in Newcastle already knew—or suspected. But he also added critical details, many of which echoed Scoutt's relationship with Brent Springford. At some point, Campbell "started to go to a 'spiritual guide' for counseling," Schlueter said. It was, he recalled, around 2005, not long after Brent Springford Jr.'s arrest for murdering his parents. Campbell "may have gone to others before. However, this time I believe the 'guide' convinced him to leave his family and go with her. That person is Caroline. I remember around the time that Sandy left his family, Sharon said that Caroline was now controlling Sandy."

"The kids were devastated by the breakup," Rick's ex-wife Debbie Schlueter told me in a phone interview. "Sandy was so much fun and so loving. And suddenly he walked out of their lives and got a restraining order. Sharon watched him being controlled like a robot. She was broken. It was almost more than she could bear." Rick recalled that soon after, Campbell abruptly left Colorado and moved to Wyoming with Caroline "to work on some property there, and she convinced him to work on the drilling wells there. Very hard physical labor. She also convinced him to give her all of his income as well as work on her property." Around 2007 Campbell visited Rick Schlueter in Denver. "He said he wanted to get away from Caroline and wondered if he could stay with me. I had just gone through a divorce and was living in a small house and unfortunately refused him. I never heard from him again. Given what eventually occurred, I feel very guilty that I didn't help him out at that time."

In the autumn of 2015, a few of Campbell's relatives and friends gathered at his sister Vicki Neusius's home in Woodland Park, in the mountains about forty-five minutes outside of Colorado Springs. It was a dismal, rainy morning as his ex-wife Sharon burned some sage, and the group shared memories and said their goodbyes before scattering Sandy Campbell's ashes on a hill behind the house. Afterward, in the kitchen, Vicki talked about Sandy's death with Sharon Campbell and Debbie Schlueter. After the body was discovered, Vicki and her husband had traveled to Newcastle to meet with Scoutt. They had been highly suspicious of her since the abrupt breakup of Sandy's marriage. But when they met with Scoutt they were completely convinced that she had done all she could to look after him, to help manage his money and cope with his mental illness. "They took it hook, line, and sinker," Debbie Schlueter said. "They were totally taken in. All their concerns were allayed. They were *grateful* to her that she had taken care of him."

And yet, some of what Vicki told Debbie and Sharon about the day of the death troubled them. The morning before he died, Vicki said her brother had called Caroline and asked her to add to his grocery list something to help with his bowel movement. "Sandy had always been concerned about the quality of his poop, to be sure he was healthy," Rick Schlueter said. "If you are going to kill yourself later today, are you worried about the quality of your poop?" That morning, Scoutt told Vicki—who later told Debbie— that Sandy had taken a break from landscaping to help the crew putting up the siding on the new lodge, joking and laughing with them. He put down his tools and said, "I'll be right back," heading across the property to his mobile home. Debbie said, "That's not what somebody does two minutes before they commit suicide. There should be some sort of emotional distress visible before you go and put a gun in your mouth and kill yourself." Driving away from Vicki's house after lunch, Debbie told Rick: "I don't think it was suicide." Her ex-husband agreed. "It just didn't add up to us." Later, after Sharon Campbell sent Rick Schlueter the *Boulder Weekly* articles, he began to reach an increasingly obvious conclusion. "I believe it is possible that Caroline controlled Brent and convinced him to kill his parents. I also believe she may have controlled Sandy and either had him killed or convinced him to kill himself."

: 25

Pursuit

In the weeks following her interview with Scoutt, Coroner Laura Sundstrom continued to dig into Scoutt's past, confirming the existence of a fourth ex-husband—chronologically her first. This was a high school sweetheart, with whom she had the first of what would be four children with three husbands. Scoutt appeared to have abandoned both the husband and the child in 1983. With these tantalizing bits of information, Sundstrom was eager to begin her formal inquest into the cause of Richard "Sandy" Campbell's death. At such an inquest, she believed, Caroline Scoutt would have to testify under oath, perhaps for the first time.

On December 27, 2015, I received an email from Weston County Sheriff's Sergeant Patrick Watsabaugh. He wrote that he was preparing a search warrant for Caroline Scoutt's property on Sundstrom's behalf. He asked that I review it "to see if I have left anything out, or if there are any 'cracks' or weaknesses in it." I agreed—another first for me. The draft document included a list of numerous names which Scoutt was thought to have used, some new to me. Other developments were outlined in the warrant, and some related discoveries, including Bupropion, the antidepressant Campbell had been prescribed. The search warrant also noted that Sundstrom had learned "through her investigation from a woman named Linda Trost, Campbell's sister, that Campbell called his sister on or about July 2013 and told her that Scoutt said his inheritance money, two checks, had been stolen from their joint account." These were the two checks from their late father's trust account, totaling more than $94,000.

I asked Watsabaugh if the timing of Sundstrom's coroner's inquest was dependent on what the search of Scoutt's property—and her bank records—yielded. He said that the inquest "would rely but not depend on the fruits of a search warrant." In any case, the issue was moot; Weston County Attorney William Curley refused to sign Watsabaugh's search warrant and submit it to a judge.

There was some confusion as to how events would then unfold. There had not been a coroner's inquest in modern Weston County. With no precedent, both the county's new prosecutor and sheriff's deputy were not certain exactly how things would proceed and who would be in charge. In January 2016, Sundstrom informed me that the coroner's inquest was scheduled for late March. However, some tension—personal and jurisdictional—had begun to emerge within the investigative team, mainly between Sundstrom and Watsabaugh.

In preparation for the inquest, the two coroners, Sundstrom and Cynthia Crabtree, asked Watsabaugh to send the Rossi .357 magnum carbine to the Wyoming state crime lab to be analyzed, not only for latent fingerprints but for "handler" DNA. However, the coroners felt he may have waited too long. "I'm extremely nervous we may not have results in time," Sundstrom wrote me. Similarly, they asked Watsabaugh several times to run Scoutt's name through the National Criminal Information Center's database, without success. The coroners wanted a printed copy in hand as a safety net when Scoutt testified, since their first order of business was to confirm her real name and Social Security number. Without it, Sundstrom said, they would be "going into this blind." They decided to proceed anyway, in part because of pressure from Scoutt's civil attorney, Jeremy Michaels, a former local judge and prosecutor now practicing civil law in Gillette. When he informed Sundstrom he was representing Scoutt, the coroner asked if he had any idea what he was getting himself into. The lawyer brushed her off, she said.

As the winter months passed, Michaels repeatedly called Sundstrom, asking when his client could expect them to release a cause of death so the insurance company could pay the claim. Nine months had passed since Campbell's body was found. On March 22 the attorney filed a motion to quash Scoutt's subpoena to testify, which triggered a continuance for the inquest.

Nonetheless, Sundstrom made good use of the delay, going over more than a thousand pages of phone and bank records with her deputy, Rozier. They turned up numerous checks, sent from around the country, made out to Scoutt's tax-exempt foundation Tatan-ka Sha, money that was then moved from the foundation to Scoutt's personal bank account. The foundation filed forms with the IRS stating that its assets were less than $25,000, which allowed it to reveal few details of its operations. However, Sundstrom found that in the years 2009 and after, several hundred thousand dollars had been filtered through the foundation to Scoutt. One Denver woman, Patricia Emmons, gave more than $500,000, much of it from her daughter's trust fund, to Scoutt and Tatan-ka Sha. The money, according to the check registers, was for Scoutt's assistance to Native American women and children, as well as for telephone counseling. When Emmons declined to speak in detail with Sundstrom about Scoutt, the coroner asked me to try, which I did, without success. The $94,000 from Richard Campbell's inheritance went almost directly from Tatan-ka Sha to Scoutt's personal account, where it was quickly spent, according to the seized bank records. But there were complications: all this information had, at best, an increasingly tangential connection to Richard Campbell's death, the sole grounds for the coroner's jurisdiction.

So Sundstrom reached out to the Weston County prosecutor; the Wyoming Division of Criminal Investigation (DCI), which operates under the jurisdiction of the attorney general's office; and the resident FBI agent in Casper. I asked Sundstrom what would happen if Scoutt fled the area after the new subpoena was issued, possibly to reservations in the Dakotas. Sundstrom said she was preparing for that eventuality. She had learned that Scoutt was also using the name Carol Price, the last name she acquired when she was "adopted" by the dying Newcastle town engineer Larry Price. It was also the name Deny Caballero, Scoutt's onetime boarder in Colorado, told me she was using in 2015, and it was the name she used for one of her email addresses. Sundstrom and Weston County Coroner Cynthia Crabtree scheduled a meeting with an agent of the Wyoming DCI to see if the state agency wanted to take over or assist with the portion of the investigation not directly related the Richard Campbell's death. However, to involve the DCI, Weston County Sheriff Bryan Colvard had to formally request their participation. Weeks went by without Colvard making the request, so Sundstrom—frustrated—cancelled the meeting. Another factor was that a coroner's inquest would cost Weston County, a 2,400-square mile jurisdiction already crippled by budget cuts, an extra, unanticipated $10,000. At that point, any concern I had about involving myself in Sundstrom's investigation ended; she suddenly stopped responding to my phone calls, email, and Facebook messages.

But independently, and with Colvard's tepid support, Watsabaugh launched his own criminal investigation of Scoutt's activities in Weston County, apart from Richard Campbell's death. He focused on the $94,000 that Campbell inherited from his father and signed over to Scoutt. Campbell's sister, Linda Trost, who lives in Grand Rapids, Michigan, was executor of her late father's Merrill Lynch family trust account. On March 29, 2013, she sent her brother a form notifying him of his portion of the cash distribution of their father's estate, which he signed and returned by certified mail on April 25. Trost told Watsabaugh that she sent her brother a check for $89,400 on June 25, 2013. Within a week, Trost began getting text messages from Campbell's phone. She told the investigator the messages were "unlike her brother," so she didn't respond. When she called Campbell, Trost said, "He never mentioned any of these texts or asked me about any of the things he had sent in the texts." Campbell called his sister back to say that "the check wasn't clearing." Trost called the bank, and found that the check, endorsed by Campbell and Scoutt, had in fact cleared. Shortly after she hung up, Trost told Watsabaugh that she received another series of texts from Campbell's phone, with "a threatening tone."

In May 2014, Trost sent another letter to all the heirs, explaining that their father's estate had finally been settled, and that a final check for the remainder would soon be sent. But Campbell called Trost, asking her to send his check to another address, Scoutt's town property in Newcastle. He told his sister that "someone had forged a check and all the $89,400 was gone." Trost told Watsabaugh that she advised her brother to "get his own bank account for the remaining check of $5,755.39." Watsabaugh learned that on May 21, following an anonymous telephone complaint, the Wyoming Department of Family Services contacted the Weston County Sheriff's office regarding an adult protective services report alleging elder abuse of Campbell by Scoutt. That report indicated that Richard Campbell had been unable to clear the final check. Family Services had been contacted by Campbell's boss at the Loaf 'n Jug convenience store, saying that she had tried talking to Campbell about how Scoutt was controlling him and his money. However, no legal action followed.

Watsabaugh asked for and received copies of the checks, endorsed by Richard Campbell to Caroline Scoutt, as well as screen shots of Campbell's text messages to his sisters about his inheritance money. Watsabaugh then arranged to interview both of Campbell's sisters via Skype. For context, I emailed the sergeant my account of the family gathering in Colorado to scatter Campbell's ashes. Based on his investigation, Watsabaugh drew up a second search warrant for more of Scoutt's bank records.

At this point, an informal consensus was emerging among investigators in neighboring Weston and Campbell counties. Chief Deputy Coroner Steve Rozier called it the "O.J. strategy." It was becoming increasingly clear that it would be problematic to prosecute Caroline Scoutt for any involvement in Richard Campbell's death in Newcastle. Similarly, it had been impractical to charge her for involvement in the Springfords' murders in Montgomery. Instead, prosecutors would try to indict her for felony larceny in connection with the $94,000 from Richard Campbell's inheritance, with a reasonable chance of success. Then, Campbell's sisters and children could bring a wrongful death suit—a civil proceeding that required a much lower burden of proof than a criminal prosecution—against Scoutt for the $100,000 Farmers insurance policy, as well as any assets Scoutt might have, in addition to her property. There was also the possibility of federal tax evasion and wire fraud charges—the "Al Capone strategy." It wasn't exactly measured justice, but it was the best shot to ensure that Scoutt would not be able to victimize or exploit anyone else.

: 26

Post-Mortem Prep

On Tuesday afternoon, August 28, 2016, I received a terse email from Weston County Coroner Cynthia Crabtree: "The inquest into the death of Richard Campbell has been set for September 28 and 30 in Newcastle, WY." In a follow-up phone conversation, Crabtree told me that she too had become frustrated by the lack of progress in the criminal investigation by Sheriff Bryan Colvard and County Attorney William Curley (the role in Wyoming is analogous to that of a prosecutor in Alabama). Caroline Scoutt was calling Crabtree's office on a regular basis, complaining that she could not collect on the $100,000 insurance policy on Richard Campbell's life until a death certificate was issued. Crabtree's patience had run out. She had already included $10,000 for the inquest in her fiscal 2017 budget, so there was no need to go to the county commissioners for the appropriation. Crabtree told me that she was concerned that if the inquest was again postponed, there was a danger that Wyoming's harsh winter weather might keep witnesses, in particular Richard Campbell's family, from testifying.

I called William Curley to ask about the inquest. He acknowledged that he had previously asked Crabtree to postpone the inquest until his criminal investigation had run its course. But now, he said, he had changed his mind. "I have it no plans to derail it." My impression from the interview with Curley was that not much investigating had taken place apart from what Sheriff's Sergeant Patrick Watsabaugh had done on his own initiative. The county attorney insisted that the criminal investigation would continue, and he would monitor whatever relevant information came out of the inquest. There might be a question of the material's subsequent admissibility in a criminal trial. "I can get it," Curley said. "Whether I can make full use of it is another question." However, he assured me that he was confident that his investigation "will result in criminal charges," and that he would obtain a conviction.

In the months preceding the Richard Campbell hearing, the investigative team decided that, given his police background, Steve Rozier would lead the inquest. Crabtree, the Weston coroner, would step back to avoid the appearance of conflict of interest growing out of an earlier dispute between Caroline Scoutt and the Crabtree family's construction company over Scoutt's circular lodge. This did not deter Crabtree from joining Sundstrom in serving Scoutt's subpoena the second week in March. The two coroners had to knock on both doors of the lodge for more than fifteen minutes before Scoutt answered and accepted service of the subpoena for her to appear on March 28, when the inquest was initially scheduled. Scoutt's attorney, Jeremy Michaels, raised some procedural challenges, however, and the inquest was postponed until September. Rozier, the former detective, had done much of the investigative work on the case, and he was determined to bring Scoutt to account. He was still smarting from how she had treated him and the other investigators on her front porch months earlier. Since then, Rozier had learned that after the discovery of Richard Campbell's body, Scoutt had made just three phone calls. One was to 911 and one to the coroner. The third went, not to Campbell's family, but to the insurance company, inquiring about the $100,000 policy. Rozier was convinced that Scoutt was responsible for Campbell's death, but he would need to convince the jurors at the inquest.

Two weeks before the inquest was scheduled, Rozier called me to say he was at Orlando International Airport on a long layover while waiting to return to Wyoming after a Caribbean cruise with his family. It was a Saturday, so traffic was light as I drove from my suburban home to the airport. I hadn't seen Rozier since the task force meeting in Newcastle a year earlier, when I sat across the room from him. I recalled at the time being impressed with the former detective's grasp of the case and his confident sense of how the forthcoming investigation was likely to unfold. Since then we had spoken several times and he had been extremely frank and forthcoming. Now, in person and at close range, my impression was confirmed. Although relaxed from his vacation, Rozier was all business as he shared with me his strategy for the upcoming inquest.

For procedural purposes, Rozier was "cross-deputized" with the Weston County Coroner, so he could conduct the inquest. Rozier told me he planned to wait for just the right opportunity in examining Caroline Scoutt "to do a Columbo." The reference was to the apparently befuddled Los Angeles police detective played by Peter Falk in the long-running NBC television series, a cop who acted as if puzzled by minor inconsistencies in a suspect's story. However, if Rozier wasn't careful, he said, Scoutt's attorney Jeremy Michaels "will jump up out of his fucking seat" to try to object. And there were limits as to how far afield the deputy could go. "You can't put her on trial. Jeremy will shut us down."

Rozier told me that Scoutt's truthfulness on the witness stand—or lack of it—would not be critical. "It doesn't matter if she lies. I'd take the lies as seriously as I would the truth." Also, since Scoutt would be testifying under oath, she would be risking perjury charges if she did lie, rather than invoking the Fifth Amendment protection against self-incrimination. Even then, he said, "a 'nonanswer' might be a valuable tool in the criminal proceeding." For all this strategizing, a week later Scoutt's lawyer informed Weston County Coroner Cynthia Crabtree that his client had had emergency brain surgery, and that she was making a slow recovery. As a result, Scoutt would not be able to appear at the inquest.

Even without Scoutt's appearance, I felt I needed to attend the inquest, so in late September 2016, I flew to Rapid City, rented a car, and drove to Newcastle. When Patrick Watsabaugh came by The Pines motel, I did a double-take at his change of appearance: He was now clean-shaven and had a flattop. He cautioned me, as did the two coroners, about what I might say to Weston County Attorney William Curley. They said Curley often met with Scoutt's lawyer, Jeremy Michaels, and that they had begun to think the prosecutor was more interested in placating the defense attorney than with bringing Scoutt to justice. People in Newcastle said Curley's wife had a personal relationship with Scoutt. The next day, I drove to Gillette, where Sundstrom and Rozier have their offices, for a strategy meeting in which they outlined the new information they had generated, including the existence of numerous other checks from men—including Mark Fitzsimmons—to Scoutt.

The inquest meant a return trip for me to Newcastle, and I arrived a few days before the proceeding so I could get to know the place a little better. In a certain light, Newcastle's six-block business district recalls the bleak, windswept West Texas town in the film *The Last Picture Show*. There is in fact one remaining movie theater, the Dogie, which offers a single evening screening at 7 p.m. A busy railroad freight line—endless trains hauling coal from huge open-pit mines nearby—bisects Main Street. While Newcastle, the Weston County seat, with about 3,500 residents and two traffic lights, down from four, is not especially prosperous, it is at least economically stable, thanks to the county government. North of the city limits, the Wyoming Department of Corrections maintains an honor boot camp, providing another handful of jobs.

The town grew up around the Weston Refinery, the town's largest employer, whose gleaming Erector set-like steelworks remain an anomalous Main Street landmark. The area has had a boom and bust economy linked to the price of energy, but overall there has been a long, slow decline beginning in the second half of the twentieth century. The Burlington Railroad ceased passenger service to the county in 1969. In Newcastle, there are signs of a struggling population, including a number of empty storefronts. Not far from the oil facility, a sign in front of a cinderblock building advertises: "Shoes and Boots Stretched, Overalls Patched." The local Catholic priest divides his time with two other parishes. In late 2017, a mountain lion was shot and killed, by a local game warden, just across the street from the hospital.

Yet there are persistent signs of life, indicating a plucky commitment to the community's survival. Donna's Main Street Diner continues to serve as Newcastle's daytime social center, with lunch an especially crowded, cacophonous scene. Several bars keep busy. "Western Heritage" banners hang around town, paid for by the Weston County Travel Commission. One banner, tied to a weathered, wooden fence blocking view of an empty lot, announces that "Diamond Slim" Clifton, accused of a double murder, "was hung by vigilantes nearby in 1903."

Formal judicial proceedings are conducted in the Weston County

Courthouse, located in the crook of Main Street as it takes a sharp right out of town. The structure, built in 1911 and visited that year by President William Howard Taft, is on the National Register of Historic Places. Two carved stone, centennial benches are on the front lawn, and the mat just inside the front door welcomes "Friends of Coal, Gas and Oil." Here, more than a year after Richard Campbell's death, the coroner's inquest would finally take place.

Coroner's Inquest

In Wyoming, coroner's inquests like the one convened in Newcastle on September 28, 2016, are charged with determining the manner of death: natural, accidental, suicide, homicide, or undetermined. The proceeding—more or less inherited from English common law—has become rare in North America. This is mostly because advances in forensic science, especially toxicology, have made it easier to pinpoint the clinical cause of death. Sometimes the only reason inquests are held is because of public interest in the fatality, like a death in custody. The last previous inquest in Weston County, the coroners learned, was more than eighty-five years before.

In the proceeding, the county coroner has a free hand to select three jurors, and tends to pick at least one person with a law enforcement background for the panel. As with grand juries, the coroner has wide latitude in the inquest and is free to subpoena any witnesses or documents. Federal regulations regarding medical privacy (HIPPA) of the deceased are superseded. Since it is not considered an adversarial proceeding, witnesses at the inquest are not usually represented by counsel or allowed to raise objections but can assert their Fifth Amendment privilege. Coroners, or their deputies, conduct the proceedings, and no judge is present. Jurors may question and recall witnesses and request additional information.

For weeks leading up to the inquest into the death of Richard Campbell Jr., Caroline Scoutt's lawyer, Jeremy Michaels, argued on several grounds why his client should not be compelled to testify. First, he maintained that the coroner had no statutory authority to issue and enforce a subpoena, an argument that resulted in one continuance but ultimately went nowhere. Then Michaels said his client required brain surgery, then elective orthopedic surgery on her foot. However, for months he resisted providing documentation from her physician for either procedure, citing federal privacy regulations.

By Monday, September 26, there was still uncertainty about whether Scoutt would testify as scheduled on the following Wednesday. Before that, Coroner Laura Sundstrom began two days of strategy sessions in her low-slung office on a rise above Gillette, a former energy boom town then suffering a downturn from the coal bust. The eggshell, cinderblock walls of her office were bare, except for some bent horseshoes and a few plaques. Sundstrom was clearly in charge in these meetings, but without throwing her weight around the room. She is a tall, slender woman, her face framed by brown hair with muted, blond highlights. Often she dressed in pale blue hospital scrubs or wore a navy sweater vest embroidered with the words "Campbell County Coroner" over a white cotton shirt whose tails fashionably peeked out, front and back. She was elected Campbell County Coroner in 2014, with the help of Weston County Sheriff's Sergeant Pat Watsabaugh, whom she was dating at the time. The day Richard Campbell's body was found outside in June 2015, Weston County Coroner Cynthia Crabtree was out of town, at a training session for newly elected coroners. So it was natural that Watsabaugh asked Sundstrom, who was on call in the adjacent county, to attend Campbell's death.

In the office with Sundstrom that Monday were Crabtree and Deputy Coroner Steve Rozier. At the outset, Rozier told Crabtree he wouldn't have invested so much of his time on the case if the handling of such an egregious case by other Weston County officials like Curley and Colvard "didn't stink." I'd also been invited to sit in, the latest example of my direct involvement in the investigation. The trio focused on how they would proceed at the inquest. As at the first task force meeting a year earlier in Newcastle, I found myself suggesting lines of inquiry and correcting information. Later, Rozier suggested that he might want to call me as a witness if there were any remaining holes left in their narrative. I replied that I had no objection; it was too late in the day for that. The discussion was freewheeling. The two coroners had been growing more convinced that Scoutt had a direct role in Richard Campbell's death. Growing more conspiratorial, they wondered aloud whether Scoutt had known that Crabtree would be out of town the day of Campbell's death. Crabtree, also an EMT who worked part-time transporting bodies for a local mortuary, recalled that she had Richard Campbell in one of her safety training classes and liked him.

Rozier is a man of average height, with rimless glasses and close-cropped, sandy hair, a mustache, and a Vandyke beard. He sometimes lapses into a growl when he speaks, which he did as he went over the questions he planned to ask each witness. He explained how he hoped to build a damning narrative of Scoutt's abusive relationship with Campbell. In passing, he noted Caroline's odd way of communicating, by writing a note and then taking a picture of it with her phone and then texting the photo. The trio decided that all witnesses would be sequestered, meaning they would not be allowed into the courtroom until they testified. At one point, Sundstrom's anger at Scoutt boiled over. "I hate her for everything she did to that dead man! I want to kill that bitch!"

: 28

Inquest, Day One

The inquest convened in the third floor of the Weston County Courthouse in its one functioning courtroom, which seats seventy-eight. Chief Deputy Coroner Steve Rozier swore in the three jurors, Joseph Wood Jr., Andrew Macke, and Sandy Upton. Rozier next moved to exclude Scoutt's attorney, Jeremy Michaels, from the proceedings until Scoutt—sequestered like the other witnesses—took the witness stand. But Michaels, a former prosecutor and judge, strenuously objected, citing Wyoming's open meetings law, so Rozier decided not to press the issue. Michaels, a compact man dressed in a black windbreaker over a button-down shirt and a black and yellow striped tie, was allowed to return to his seat in the first row of the spectator section. There, he chain-sucked Altoids, while next to him his wife and law partner, Deborah Michaels, took notes on a legal pad.

"Your task is to listen to and observe the evidence and testimony, and determine the true cause and manner of death for Richard Campbell Jr." in September 2015, Rozier told the two men and one woman sitting in the first row of the jury box. "You are not required to determine guilt, innocence, or involvement of anyone in his death." This was disingenuous, as Rozier quickly proceeded to lay out his case much as a prosecutor would in a murder trial. He began building what was in effect a homicide brief against Caroline Scoutt, slowly, methodically, relentlessly painting her as an avaricious, manipulative killer. However, his efforts were unhampered by a defense attorney to object or cross-examine witnesses. All this was to the visible—and growing—chagrin of Michaels, Scoutt's lawyer.

The two coroners, Crabtree and Sundstrom, sat at one table, while Rozier conducted the examinations from a wheeled wooden lectern, halfway between them and the witness stand. The courtroom dress code was "Western informal." Rozier was wearing a beige cardigan over a checked shirt, open at the collar. When nervous, he had a habit of clicking a red, plastic ballpoint pen with his right hand as he questioned witnesses. The first three witnesses were the sheriff's deputies who responded to the 911 call and secured the death scene, which they took to be an apparent suicide. Consulting their reports, they recounted that Scoutt told them that she had lent Campbell the gun six years earlier to protect his goats from a marauding dog.

If there is one thing the average Wyoming citizen understands, it is guns and ballistics. So many of the jurors' questions to witnesses—permitted in an inquest—focused on this. One juror, Joseph Wood Jr., closely interrogated Sheriff's Sergeant Patrick Watsabaugh about Campbell's wound, the position of the body, and the bullets and the shell casing left in the fatal weapon. Not all the officer's answers reflected well on the initial investigation. Neither the casing nor the nearby box of cartridges had been tested for fingerprints or DNA. No prints were found on the rifle. "It's hard to shoot yourself and not have any fingerprints," Wood told me later. The carpet where Campbell's body was found was never lifted to look for a bullet hole, and the area around the trailer was not closely searched to locate the bullet itself. Wood was also troubled by the investigators' initial scenario. Wood thought that if Campbell was sitting on the corner of the bed, and fired into his mouth, he should have fallen backward onto the bed, leaving blood stains there, rather than spinning around and landing on his back on the floor, with both of his hands up. Watsabaugh told Rozier that after closely inspecting Campbell's wound, and interviewing Scoutt at her lodge home, he soon began to have doubts that "this is a black-and-white suicide."

Next on the witness stand was the first of four technicians from the Salt Creek Veterinary Clinic in Newcastle where Scoutt brought her animals for care. Over several days, the quartet testified that on the morning of Richard Campbell's death, Scoutt dropped off one of her cats for tests. There did not seem to be anything wrong with the animal. Notwithstanding, Scoutt seemed to call the office every twenty minutes throughout the day, inquiring about the cat, on each occasion noting the time and saying where she was in Rapid City and Custer, South Dakota. Specifically, she said she was calling from: the Safeway; Sears, to buy a compressor; and having lunch with her son.

Scoutt's purpose in making the calls was so transparent that the techs—who watch as much television as anyone—agreed among themselves that Scoutt must be trying to establish an alibi for something. Pet owners rarely badger the clinic about healthy pets, especially Scoutt. One tech testified that Scoutt once left a very sick cat at the clinic for eleven days without checking on its condition and then waited another week to pick it up.

Later on the June afternoon of Campbell's death, the techs testified, Scoutt returned to the clinic, but refused to reclaim the healthy cat until it was given yet another test, for allergies, which the techs felt was unnecessary. Scoutt also insisted that her bill for the cat's treatment be time-stamped, which the clinic was unable to do. Scoutt made a scene, demanding to speak with the vet, who was treating other animals, to get an apology for the techs' conduct. Curiously, Scoutt also demanded that the techs delete the phone number from which she had called them repeatedly that morning and afternoon. Scoutt planted herself in the waiting room, reading magazines and checking her phone. Every time the waiting room would fill with people and their animals, Scoutt would stand up, loudly identify herself, note the time, and say she was waiting to speak with the vet. She even wrote a note of complaint to the vet, took a picture of it with her phone, and sent it to the techs, even though they were standing just a few feet from her.

Two Farmers Life insurance agents followed the first vet tech to the stand, to explain the history of the policy Scoutt took out and paid for on Richard Campbell's life. Initially, the policy was taken out in Newcastle, with a $100,000 death benefit. On it, Scoutt listed her occupation as "minister" of the Native American Church. The local agent, Reg Rumbolz, told Rozier that his impression from Scoutt was that everyone on the board of her nonprofit, Tatan-ka Sha Inc., was going to cross-insure one another as what insurance companies call "key persons," central to the survival of an organization. However, the only policy that actually went into effect was Scoutt's policy on Campbell. Although the policy lapsed as many as five times over the years, Rumbolz said, Scoutt always had it reinstated.

Caroline owned property in South Dakota, where she operated a day care center, and for that reason renewed her life insurance policy on Campbell with a Farmers agent there, Stephanie Lee. Lee and Rumbolz testified about their policies and reinstatement forms. Each of the documents listed questions about whether Campbell had suffered from depression, or had attempted suicide, or had been treated for mental illness in any form, including medications. If any of these boxes were checked, the agents said the policy might have been declined, or a higher premium might have been charged. But none were checked on Campbell's forms. A juror asked Lee if both Campbell and Scoutt were required to sign the forms, and to affirm that the health information was true. The local agent said they were. Also, Lee told Rozier, each reinstatement normally carried with it a new, twenty-four-month suicide exclusion clause. Campbell's South Dakota policy was last reinstated on September 13, 2014, which seemed to mean that his June 24, 2015, death would have fallen within the suicide exclusion period. Within hours of Campbell's death, Lee recalled, she received a call on her cell phone from Scoutt. "She seemed very distraught, and said 'Richard killed himself. What am I going to do?'"

Jan Mason-Manzer, a physician's assistant at Newcastle Regional Medical Center, testified that Richard Campbell had in fact been treated at the clinic for depression off and on from 2007 until April 2, 2015—eleven weeks before his death. Over time, she said, she prescribed several anti-depression drugs—Paxil, Prozac, and Buproprion. (These were some of the same medications prescribed to Brent Springford, when he was married to Scoutt.) On that last visit, Mason-Manzer said, Campbell complained of irritability, stress at his job at the Loaf 'n Jug convenience store, and conflict with Scoutt. She described Campbell as "a very gentle soul . . . not at all aggressive . . . very agreeable . . . pretty nonchalant . . . He denied suicidal thoughts to me. I didn't consider him suicidal." However, Mason-Manzer said she did consider him susceptible to control by others. Campbell told her that lack of money was a factor in his frequently rescheduled appointment and his inconsistency in refilling his prescriptions.

At the lunch break I tagged along with Crabtree, walking across the street to Isabella's restaurant. We were joined at the table by the three coroner's jurors and Sergeant Watsabaugh, although nobody discussed the case. Just before the inquest reconvened, Watsabaugh came barreling into the courtroom, telling the coroners that Scoutt, who had submitted a medical excuse not to testify, was spotted across the street at the weekly newspaper office, faxing Medicaid forms for her latest surgery. Earlier, her attorney, Jeremy Michaels, had finally shown the coroners copies of reports from her doctor that claimed she was immobile, needing urgent surgery on her foot, the latest reason she could not testify at the inquest.

Next on the witness stand were bankers from three area institutions. Consulting their stacks of printed-out records, they went over five separate accounts which bore both Richard Campbell's and Scoutt's names, as well as those controlled by Scoutt alone, including for her nonprofit Tatan-ka Sha. The balances fluctuated wildly, with deposits into Scoutt's and the nonprofit accounts in the form of checks made out to Richard Campbell in excess of $100,000. Andy Miller, vice president of Sundance Bank, testified that Scoutt's monthly account balances at his bank averaged $800 to $1,300, but for a time spiked to nearly $100,000.

Laying the groundwork for a trap he planned to spring later in the inquest—should Scoutt take the stand—Rozier asked each of the bankers how they would react if one of their customers reported more than $90,000 missing from an account. All said they would immediately report the loss to authorities. Rozier showed Louise Stith of the First State Bank of Newcastle a check for $89,400 made out to Richard Campbell Jr. from the estate account of his late father, Richard Campbell Sr. The check was endorsed by Campbell and Scoutt, for deposit into her exclusive Tatan-ka Sha account. Before that deposit, in June 2013, Stith said, consulting her stack of records, the account balance was $1,209.43. By October 31, the balance was back down to $663.53. Soon after the big deposits, the banker recalled, Scoutt came in and withdrew $40,000 in cash. On another occasion she wrote a check for $18,500 to a truck dealership and others to Victoria's Secret. Within two months the inheritance money was gone from her account. By this point in the inquest, the three jurors had set their junior legal pads on the railing in front of their seats and were taking careful notes. Stith testified that Campbell often came into the bank with his Loaf 'n Jug paycheck with Scoutt, and he endorsed the paycheck to her.

Joey McGinniss, together with his girlfriend Katie Bailey, was working to finish the siding of Scoutt's round lodge the day Richard Campbell died.

He testified that the couple knew Campbell from the Loaf 'n Jug and felt sorry for him because he never appeared to have any money. When Richard's bike was stolen, McGinniss helped get him a replacement. He even took Campbell to McGinniss's brother, a barber, when it seemed Campbell needed a haircut. But while McGinniss was working on Scoutt's property in June 2015, Scoutt told him not to speak with Campbell, implying that the caretaker was "not all there." McGinniss didn't see it that way. "It was belittling, that way she talked about him," he told Rozier. "He was harmless," and anyway Campbell worshipped Scoutt. He was always going on about "how great a woman she is, like she was a saint, just the greatest thing."

The day of Campbell's death, McGinniss told Rozier, Campbell smiled and waved at them when he returned the weed whacker to the barn about 3 p.m. The couple was a little puzzled, since Campbell had been using a machete to clear the grass a few days earlier because he told them Scoutt did not trust him with the weed whacker. As McGinniss and his girlfriend left the property, around 5 p.m., they saw Scoutt parked nearby, almost in a ditch. Bailey, the girlfriend, recalled later that as they drove by it seemed like Scoutt was talking on the phone. Later that night, the couple learned of Campbell's death. The next morning, Scoutt called to see if they would be coming out to finish the siding work on the round house. McGinniss told her he wasn't up to it, in light of Campbell's death, but Scoutt didn't want to take "no" for an answer. He recalled that one of the checks Scoutt wrote him for the siding work came from the account of her nonprofit Tatan-ka Sha account.

Julie Abbott, a longtime secretary at Weston Engineering Company, in the nearby town of Upton, testified that Richard Campbell worked for the firm—where Brent Springford Jr. had also worked—when Campbell first moved up from Boulder. He was a machinist and sometime water rig operator and was popular at the firm, she says. "He seemed capable," Abbott said. "He was a good worker. Everybody liked him." For a time, he drove a small pickup and car-pooled to work from Newcastle. Campbell acted like he was thankful to Scoutt for bringing him up from Boulder after his marriage broke up, Abbott said. Campbell signed over his paychecks to Scoutt, and Abbott was under the impression that Richard was using the money to buy a piece of Scoutt's land. He was let go from Weston when he refused to take an extra shift and soon got a job at the Loaf 'n Jug in Newcastle, mostly overseeing deliveries.

A group of Campbell's co-workers at the convenience store then filed on and off the witness stand, echoing Abbott's observations. A young woman named Raven Whitney noted his adoration of Scoutt. "He really seemed to be hooked on her," she told Rozier. "He would do anything for her." Her impression of Scoutt was that "she was the boss and he was the day worker. He never had any money," and once asked Whitney for $10 to fix his bicycle chain. Scoutt took away Campbell's driving privileges to his own vehicle for various reasons, she said he told her, once just for losing his keys. Scoutt then used this as an excuse to stop paying for his auto insurance. Whitney's view of Scoutt was negative, even witchy, right out of *The Wizard of Oz*. "If you threw water on her," Whitney said, "she would melt." Campbell was deeply affected by comedian Robin Williams's suicide, Whitney said. "He seemed so against it."

Nela Beardsley, who worked at a payday loan outlet in the same strip mall as the Loaf 'n Jug, said Campbell once came in to see if they could cash a large check from his sister. Later, several months before his death, she saw him again several times. A few weeks before he died, Beardsley said he was "quieter than he normally was." He told her, "I shouldn't be using my car," because the insurance hadn't been paid. Campbell said Scoutt, who described him to Beardsley as a "hired hand," was getting his paychecks and paying his bills. Campbell told her, "I got myself into a mess," thinking he had more money than he did. Beardsley asked him if it had anything to do with where he lived, and he said yes. He was under the impression that his pay and other money was going toward a purchase of some of Scoutt's land. Scoutt, she said, was very negative when she talked about Campbell.

Shere Varney, the manager of Loaf 'n Jug, recalled starting work at the store the same week as Campbell. She said that "he worked harder than anyone," forty hours a week at different times of the day, unloading deliveries and stocking the shelves. After he had been at the store for a while, he asked to be trained to work the cash register, and he was proud of himself when he was able to wait on customers. Varney said he "always said good things about [Scoutt]. He really looked up to her." But he was also under the impression that his paychecks for his $10-an-hour job were vulnerable to being garnished—which Varney knew was not true—which is why they were being deposited into a checking account Scoutt controlled. Scoutt, she said, did not treat Campbell well. "He was punished like a kid. She treated him like a kid." Varney said he was among the co-workers who bought Campbell a bike when his refurbished one went missing. "We loved Richard. He was the nicest person. He was a good guy." Campbell exuded what Varney said was a "Boulder hippie vibe."

When Rozier asked Varney about the possibility of suicide, she repeated that Campbell was especially disturbed by the suicide of the comedian Robin Williams, telling her he could never do that. And, she volunteered, "He told me he didn't believe in guns." When Scoutt told her that Campbell had shot himself to death, Varney said, "I thought that was suspicious." Varney had urged Campbell to move into town, but he resisted, in part because of his feelings toward Scoutt, regardless of her apparent callousness and mistreatment. "He was fond of her, no matter what." Campbell did complain to Varney that he was unable to contact his children. Once, his daughter Caleigh called the Loaf 'n Jug, telling Varney that Scoutt wouldn't put through her calls when she phoned the ranch.

This testimony struck a poignant chord with juror Joseph Wood. Newcastle is a small town, so it was not surprising that Wood knew Campbell from stops at the Loaf 'n Jug. "He wondered why his kids never talked to him," Wood recalled later. "He was so distraught and bummed out. He would say, 'I don't know why they don't call me back.'"

Marge Welbourne, the convenience store's previous manager, testified that she helped Campbell fill out the $25,000 life insurance policy offered by Kroger, the grocery chain that owned the store. Welbourne asked him why he was listing Scoutt as the sole beneficiary, rather than his children. "He said his kids didn't want anything to do with him," she said. Welbourne also did the paperwork for Campbell's paycheck to be directly deposited into the Sundance bank checking account that Scoutt controlled. Asked about his financial arrangement with Scoutt, Campbell told Varney that he turned over his pay to Scoutt for rent, and to buy some land. Varney asked him why he was paying rent if he was also working as a caretaker on the property. For a variety of reasons, Welbourne said, "I worried about Richard a lot." He always seemed to be broke and hungry, taking expired food from the dumpster behind the convenience store—just as Brent Springford had done in Colorado.

Months later, Scoutt's daughter Star Fosheim told me that Caroline "was very mean" to the highly suggestible Campbell. "She would tell him he was pussy, a bitch, worthless, stupid and that he should just kill himself, and be done with it."

⋮ 29

Inquest, Interlude

The inquest took a one-day break to allow for a judicial proceeding to use the lone courtroom. The coroners used the day for another strategy session, but this time I was not invited. However, I learned—by yet another incredible coincidence—that that evening the Investigation Discovery cable television channel would be airing an episode on the Springford murders. The previous spring I had traveled to Montgomery to join defense attorneys Bill Blanchard, Jay Lewis, and Susan Wardell, as well as former District Attorney Ellen Brooks at a motel near the airport. We were to be interviewed by a crew from the channel's "Blood Relatives" series, dealing with murder within families. All of us understood that this was tabloid television—I had participated in two other such shows in connection with another murder case I covered for the *Los Angeles Times*. Typically, the episodes were a mix of serious interviews by the participants and lurid reenactments, so we hoped for the best.

In an earlier phone interview with Weston County Attorney William Curley, I had mentioned the upcoming episode. He asked me to let him know when it was going to air. So that Thursday I sent him an email, telling him the show would be on that evening on the Newcastle cable system. Then, stupidly, I added: "I can't figure out what's stalling the related/associated criminal investigation [of Scoutt]. A cascade of evidence has been presented in the first day alone. What's up? Readers of my book are likely to wonder as well." But nudging Curley in the email would turn out to be a costly error. I compounded the mistake by telling Scoutt's attorney, Jeremy Michaels—whose relationship with Curley had been the subject of speculation by the coroners' team—about that night's episode.

The episode was entitled "Axe to Grind," an irresistible reference to the murder weapon in the Montgomery killings, as well as to the infamous 1842 case involving Lizzie Borden, daughter of a wealthy couple in Fall River, Massachusetts:

> Lizzie Borden took an axe
> She gave her mother forty whacks.
> When she saw what she had done
> She gave her father forty-one.

In the end, I got a lot of screen time, so on balance participating was a good decision for me and the timing could not have been better. Several things in the show did trouble me and the other participants. The actress portraying Scoutt was an inaccurately young, sultry woman, and there was an imagined sexual relationship with Brent Jr. And, perhaps for legal reasons, the woman who police in three states told me they believed orchestrated the Montgomery killings, was let off the hook with a categorical exoneration. After raising the possibility that the woman was somehow involved in the crime early in the episode, the narrator concluded that Scoutt "is shown to have no involvement in the murders."

The show's reach was wide. In Birmingham, Charlotte Springford's sister, Lois Truss, watched: "I must say I was disturbed just reliving the day after Thanksgiving in 2004 when we first got the news," she wrote me. "It was the second worst day of my life," a reference to the day of the tragic house fire in which she lost her parents, her toddler niece, and her leg. "Those interviewed did a good job," Truss said. "The spin by the network was pretty ridiculous. So much about it was just plain false," which she said also upset Brent's sister Robin. Despite my warning about the genre before we all agreed to participate, Susan Wardell was more exercised, writing Truss: "I truly wish you had not seen this program. It was so distorted and salacious. The defense team and Mark had no idea what the network would do with what we gave them, but I still feel it was better to give our serious and caring input, knowing they planned to produce the episode, one way or another."

: 30

Inquest, Day Two

In the morning, Rozier, switching to a charcoal cardigan, called Kenneth Whitney to the witness stand. The young man testified that several years earlier, while still a teenager, he began having trouble getting along with his parents in Newcastle. Whitney had gone to school with one of Scoutt's daughters, so Caroline invited him to stay on her property and to share Richard Campbell's trailer, in exchange for caretaking work. Campbell seemed normal to Whitney, although Scoutt warned that his roommate had "an ego problem." Whitney said he never saw Campbell anywhere near a gun, adding that there were no predators while he lived there and thus no apparent need for one. The young man was impressed with Scoutt and her talk about spiritual matters. Whitney got a job with a construction company, and he agreed when Scoutt suggested that they start a joint checking account where his paychecks were deposited, the same bank where she had a joint account with Campbell. Over time, however, Whitney said that he soured on Scoutt. He discovered that she had written a $3,000 check on their joint account without informing him, and that his balance had dropped to $300. Also, she discouraged him from contacting his family. "She kind of like isolated me," he said, so he finally moved out. The parallels with Deny Caballero, at the Colorado house, were striking.

Caleigh Campbell, Richard's daughter, was the next witness. Her father, she said, could be "spacey" but throughout her childhood he was fully functional. "He was really a fun dad. He was really loving and caring." She recalled that about a decade earlier, her father had met Caroline Scoutt at the Boulder home of Marie Flinders, the same place Brent Springford had met Scoutt several years before. Richard began seeing Scoutt often, taking breathing sessions with her. When her parents were having problems in their relationship, Caleigh recalled, Scoutt offered her services as a marriage counselor, although she was not certified in that field. However, over time, Scoutt's advice was that the couple should date others and, later, separate, file for divorce, and that Richard should file a restraining order against his former wife. In addition, at Scoutt's urging, Richard left the cleaning business he had with his wife and took a new job at the Boulder Whole Foods, where Caleigh herself was working. Campbell and Scoutt became "more intertwined," seeing each other several times a week, Caleigh said. She teared up as she described her gradual estrangement from her father, reaching for a tissue box perched on the railing. "I felt like he was pushing me away," she said. Did Caleigh think Richard was capable of suicide? Rozier asked. "The man that I knew never would have done that," she replied.

(Later, Star Fosheim told me she had a slightly different recollection about how her mother met Richard Campbell. In this version, Caroline met Richard Campbell while he was already working at Boulder Whole Foods, and at that time she began treating him professionally as a couples therapist. At one point, the daughter said, Caroline tried to set him up with one of her other clients. "He was nice, a little spacey, and always polite," Fosheim recalled.)

Vicki Neusius, one of Campbell's sisters, followed Caleigh to the witness stand, and explained how she and other family members had been mostly out of touch with their brother for seven years before his death. Once, on vacation with her husband in Deadwood, South Dakota, just an hour's drive from Newcastle, Richard joined them in the restored Gold Rush town, and they had a good visit but he told her not to come see him at the ranch. After the trip, she said, there was an angry call from Richard. "I couldn't believe he was saying these things to me." Soon after, "my brother kind of cut the family off," she explained. On June 29, 2015, five days after Richard's death, Neusius and her husband drove from their home in Woodland Park, Colorado, to Scoutt's ranch. After discussing Richard's death, Neusius asked Scoutt what became of her brother's portion of their father's estate, approximately $95,000. "He had blown pretty much all of it," Scoutt told the family. Scoutt made no mention of the two life insurance policies, leaving Scoutt $125,000.

Another sister, Linda Trost, testified next. She recalled that she learned of her brother's death from a Weston County sheriff's deputy, and then received a call from Scoutt. Two years earlier, in 2013, as the executor of their father's estate, Trost was responsible for sending the two disbursal checks to Richard. She said she was surprised when Richard called her to say that the first check, for $89,400, had not cleared his account. She consulted her records and found that the check, endorsed by Richard Campbell and Caroline Scoutt, had in fact cleared and had been deposited into their joint checking account. When Trost explained this to her brother, he hung up. Richard then called back to say that Scoutt had told him that someone had forged the two names on the check and took all the money. "Caroline told me my money was stolen," Campbell told his sister.

Trost then began receiving texts, ostensibly from Richard—although he did not normally text—asking for a detailed accounting of bills paid by the estate, and of how much each of his siblings had been sent. But Trost noticed that instead of naming the siblings, Richard referred to them as "the rest of dads children." And the tone of the texts became more threatening. If she did not comply, the text read, "i am going to have my lawyers investigate the whole inheritance accounts." Then, this: "I know there is more money from dads will. So send the rest of it. Or I will have my lawyer on this and I will sue you and u may not have much money left for your greedy little self." This, Trost tells Rozier, sounded nothing like her brother. In a follow-up phone call, Trost told Richard—falsely—that her phone could not receive texts. Her brother made no mention to her of an accounting of the estate or a threat to sue her. One of the jurors asked Trost if she thought her brother was capable of killing himself. She said no.

Finished with his scheduled witnesses, Steve Rozier asked the jurors if they had heard enough to render a verdict as to the cause of Richard Campbell Jr.'s death on June 24, 2015. Or would they rather reconvene in October to hear testimony from Caroline Scoutt. Without hesitation, all three said they would definitely prefer to wait.

Over the two days of the inquest, more than 25 witnesses had testified, and what they said was uniformly damning to Scoutt. Still, it was one thing to make the case that she was a cruel and avaricious person, even a perpetrator of insurance fraud, as well as an embezzler. Convincing the inquest jurors that she was a cold-blooded, premeditated murderer was a much steeper climb for Rozier. Nonetheless, the coroner team felt that by making the best case they could for a homicide finding they might light a fire under William Curley, the elected county attorney, and Sheriff Bryan Colvard.

The perils for a writer becoming involved in a criminal investigation, and of needling Curley over his inaction, soon emerged. At the afternoon recess on September 30, a source informed me that Scoutt's lawyer, Jeremy Michaels, had issued a subpoena for me to testify at a hearing on Wednesday, October 6, at which he intended to challenge the coroners' right to compel his client to testify under oath. Apparently, based on the *Boulder Weekly's* two-part series, and my interview on the Investigation Discovery episode, Michaels intended to argue that the coroner's inquest and the concurrent criminal investigation were largely the result of my personal vendetta against Scoutt. I asked my source if I had ninety minutes to clear out of town and leave the state before I was served with the subpoena, and was told that I did. However, forty-five minutes later, as I hurriedly tossed my suitcase into my car, a smiling deputy sheriff pulled into The Pines parking lot and served me. I had no intention of remaining in Newcastle for another five days, so I headed for South Dakota and my Rapid City flight back to Orlando. After an exchange of emails, noting that making the court appearance would interfere with the Jewish High Holidays, Michaels (who is also Jewish) and I agreed that I could testify by telephone. Later, he canceled the subpoena and the hearing.

31

Waiting (1)

The coroners were growing increasingly frustrated by County Attorney William Curley's inaction. On Tuesday, October 5, 2016, at the request of Weston County Coroner Cynthia Crabtree and Campbell County Coroner Laura Sundstrom, acting as her deputy, the Weston County Commission met in a first-floor conference room in the courthouse in executive session. To minimize the likely political collateral damage for what followed in the next hour, Sundstrom volunteered to take the lead. She outlined the coroner team's complaints against Curley and Sheriff Bryan Colvard for their apparent reluctance to pursue a criminal investigation against Caroline Scoutt. Sundstrom listed the evidence thus far introduced at the inquest, in particular the evidence of white-collar crime, the larceny or embezzlement of the $94,000 from Richard Campbell's inheritance from his father. Sundstrom also charged that Sheriff Colvard had refused the coroners' repeated efforts to request assistance from the Wyoming Division of Criminal Investigation and the FBI. The feds, Sundstrom said, should look into the possibility of charging Scoutt with interstate mail and wire fraud, for her fundraising for the round house and counseling center, as well as for income tax evasion.

At this point Curley and Colvard—both elected officials—were called into the meeting and grilled by the five commissioners, one of whom is an attorney and a neighbor of Scoutt's. What followed was awkward and uncomfortable in the extreme; one of those in attendance likened it to "being called into the principal's office." Colvard especially "was not happy with us," one of the coroners recalled. Both Curley and the sheriff agreed to take a more active role in the investigation, and the commissioners—who set the budgets for the county attorney and the sheriff—said they would request another meeting in two weeks. The follow-up never took place.

Throughout the first two days of the inquest in September, Rozier asked many of the witnesses whether they knew a man named Mark Fitzsimmons, without elaboration about why he wanted to know. Gradually, Rozier was building his case against Caroline Scoutt: her creation of a daylong alibi through her calls and appearance at the veterinary clinic; how she treated and exploited Richard Campbell financially; and how she stood to gain financially from his death. Subtly, he also seemed to be preparing a case against Fitzsimmons as a possible trigger man in Campbell's death, acting on Scoutt's behalf. Fitzsimmons, to whom Scoutt was once romantically linked, conveyed to her the 195-acre ranch property as "payment for her counseling services and repayment of previous monetary loans," according to the deed transfer document.

At one point in his testimony, Rozier asked Sergeant Watsabaugh about the encounter he had in the fall of 2015, when the officer accompanied me to Scoutt's property for an interview. As we pulled up in his sheriff's vehicle, Fitzsimmons pulled into the parking area and Watsabaugh asked him who he was. Scoutt came running up and said to Fitzsimmons, "I don't want you talking to him." Since that time, Watsabaugh told Rozier, authorities were trying without success to locate and interview Fitzsimmons. Watsabaugh did find a photo of Fitzsimmons and circulated it throughout the area.

After one of the deputy's informants called to say that Fitzsimmons had been sighted on Scoutt's property, Watsabaugh had a subpoena issued. He drove out to the property and knocked on the door of Scoutt's lodge. Fitzsimmons answered the door and was served to appear when the inquest reconvened. However, between the first two days of the inquest in September, and the days leading up to October 25, when the inquest was set to resume, Rozier changed his mind about Fitzsimmons's involvement in the shooting. The deputy coroner came to believe that Scoutt herself was in the trailer when Richard Campbell died, and that she played a direct role in his death.

When I was back home in Orlando, a thought occurred to me, one I had mentioned in passing at one of the strategy sessions with the coroners. I suggested to Steve Rozier the possibility of calling as a witness at the inquest my wife's sister, Susan Wardell, the social worker and death penalty mitigation specialist who had worked on Brent's case. Listening to the first two days of the inquest in Newcastle, I was struck by the eerie similarity in the way Caroline Scoutt treated Richard Campbell and Brent Springford: psychological denigration and domination; financial manipulation and exploitation; isolation from family members, becoming the sole communications conduit; and even the dumpster diving for food.

Now I proposed that Wardell travel to Newcastle and testify about these parallels, under the legal doctrine of "similar transactions." In a criminal proceeding, this is an extreme long shot, since judges are loath to allow such testimony, considering it highly prejudicial. But in an inquest, as in a grand jury proceeding, there is considerable latitude and no one to object. The coroner team agreed, and I asked Wardell if she would be willing to appear. Still outraged at Scoutt's treatment of Brent after all these years, she agreed. However, since several serious health issues make it difficult for her to travel, I volunteered to come to her home in Atlanta and accompany her to Wyoming. On October 21 I flew to Atlanta. The next day we flew to Rapid City and made the ninety-mimute drive to Newcastle. For Wardell, testifying at the inquest represented a closing of the circle, returning her to her effort to bring Caroline Scoutt to justice for the havoc she had wrought upon the Springford family—that is, the murder of Charlotte and Brent Springford Sr. and the subsequent prison suicide of Brent Jr. "She fired him up with rage to kill his parents," Wardell recalled on the drive to Wyoming.

In Newcastle, we checked into The Pines motel, staying in a detached, handicapped-accessible, two-story cottage a short way from the small, single units. Over the next two days we met several times in Gillette, with Campbell County Coroner Sundstrom and her deputy, Rozier. He reported that he had interviewed Scoutt's older daughter. She confirmed earlier evidence and testimony that at the Windsor home, Scoutt treated Brent Springford "like a slave" and was constantly belittling him. Rozier then asked if I would be willing to testify after Wardell, to tie off any loose ends in the narrative. In particular, I was to describe my role in contacting Newcastle investigators after Richard Campbell's body was discovered and telling them about Scoutt's involvement with the Springford family and her life in Colorado. I said yes—at this point it was too late to say anything else—and Rozier asked Wardell and me to draft a list of about a dozen questions for him to ask each of us at the inquest.

Before our arrival, Rozier had been confident that this time he would be able to compel Scoutt to take the stand, even if it was only to assert her Fifth Amendment right against self-incrimination. Yet again, however, her attorney, Jeremy Michaels and the Weston County Attorney, William Curley, worked out what was essentially a sweetheart deal—and again behind the coroners' backs. Rozier would simply be required to read to the jury a statement from Scoutt's doctor saying that for health reasons she was unable to testify. Frustrated, Rozier was determined to fight back. He told the two lawyers he wouldn't read the doctor's note or, if he did, he would immediately undermine it with contrary testimony from other witnesses.

A woman named Kym Swisher, who was living in Richard Campbell's old trailer on the Scoutt ranch property, had come forward. In late June 2015 she and her husband Dave, a farrier, had moved to the Newcastle area to train and care for horses. When visiting Caroline Scoutt's ranch to look at her horses, Scoutt invited the couple to live on the property in exchange for giving her three children riding lessons. The Swishers agreed, and Scoutt took them to the trailer, without telling them what had happened there a week earlier. The couple found the trailer stuffed with stacks of new clothing, much in its original packaging. By the fall of 2016, my involvement in the Scoutt case had been profiled on the front page of Weston County's weekly paper, the *News Letter Journal*. So, through Facebook, Swisher contacted me, and then Rozier, saying that she had been working as Scoutt's caretaker after both brain and foot surgery. Swisher said she was prepared to testify that Scoutt was completely lucid and fully mobile—but determined not to testify. The Swishers were subpoenaed.

Using periodic breaks in the inquest and meetings, I visited places along Main Street to get an idea of how Richard Campbell and Caroline Scoutt were viewed around Newcastle. Once, I wandered into the county library, a friendly, renovated building next door to the courthouse, to use one of their computers. The library director, Brenda Mahoney-Ayres, had fond memories of Campbell, who she recalled borrowed lots of movies. "He was one of our favorites. He always came in with a smile on his face and he was always a joy to visit." He told her he subscribed to *Oprah* magazine.

By contrast, Scoutt's reputation was that of a small-time grifter and con artist. One morning between meetings with Wardell and the coroners, I drove over to the offices of the family-staffed *News Letter Journal*, across the street from the courthouse. In the old tradition of rural weeklies, it prints in the back and sells office supplies out front. Amid the redolent smell of ink, I went back to visit Bob Bonnar, the paper's editor and associate publisher, to talk about the inquest. An affable, beefy man then in his fifties, Bonnar edited the paper, founded in 1889, on a laptop at a low, cluttered, antique wooden table. He was wearing Teva sandals and white socks, shorts, and a "Papa Bear" T-shirt, a gift from his daughter, a student at the University of Northern Colorado at Greeley. He was still smarting from the incident years ago when Scoutt talked him into doing a heart-rending story on violent domestic abuse, focused on her, in which she was identified only as "The Victim." Bonnar now believed the story was a fictional effort to hustle money for her.

Bonnar was happy to talk about his extensive coverage of the coroner's inquest, which had a high level of reader interest, but which had also been an occasion for some communal soul-searching. Given the contentious jockeying between elected county officials over the Campbell case, "truth and justice might not be served by the judicial branch," Bonnar admitted. So if the only trial Caroline Scoutt was likely to have was in the pages of his newspaper, he said, so be it. For the previous three issues he had run the inquest story at length, starting on Page One, above the fold, and he had no intention of stopping. "It's the best story we've got," he said. "It's what everyone wants to read." At funerals, people came up to him and said "they can't wait for this week's paper. They ask if I'd give them advance word of what is coming."

32

Inquest, Day Three

Three weeks after meeting with Weston County commissioners, the principal players in the inquest reconvened. The two coroners sat at what was usually the prosecution table, and the three jurors returned to the box. Chief Deputy Coroner Steve Rozier, standing at the lectern, was dressed in a black-and-white checked shirt, khakis, and an olive tweed sport jacket. Caroline Scoutt's attorney, Jeremy Michaels, was back in the first row of the spectator section on the opposite side of the courtroom. Rozier announced he was dispensing with his order to sequester witnesses before they testify, so that Susan Wardell and I could remain in the first row behind the coroners. Next to us were Vicki Neusius, one of Richard Campbell Jr.'s sisters, and her husband.

The first witness on the stand was Campbell County Coroner Laura Sundstrom, in a black jacket and skirt. She explained how, on June 24, 2015, with Weston County Coroner Cynthia Crabtree out of town, she was called to the death scene on Scoutt's property. She recounted how she found Campbell's body in his trailer, including the fact that a strong flow of blood was still coming from his mouth. Several days later, Sundstrom said, she received a phone call from Scoutt, inquiring about a death certificate. Asked by the coroner if she was Campbell's next-of-kin, Scoutt said she wasn't. Asked if she was the beneficiary of Campbell's insurance policy, Scoutt again said no. In that case, Sundstrom said, Scoutt would not be eligible to receive a death certificate, or any information regarding the investigation into Campbell's death. Several weeks later, a Farmers Insurance agent contacted Crabtree and informed her that Scoutt was indeed listed as the sole beneficiary of her policy on Richard Campbell. After that, Scoutt called Sundstrom back, telling her she did not know that Richard had made her the policy's beneficiary. Sundstrom then described the interview she and Rozier had with Scoutt in Newcastle in the fall of 2015, asking about the circumstances surrounding her purchase of the policy. There, Scoutt repeated that she had no knowledge that she had been listed on the policy, although she signed it at the time she purchased (and reinstated) it, and paid the premiums. Responding to a question from one of the jurors, Sundstrom repeated Scoutt's query about why the investigators were asking about the policy.

Walking slowly, and in obvious pain from psoriatic arthritis and back surgery, Susan Wardell—as always, elegantly dressed—took the witness stand. For the next two hours, Rozier led her through her involvement in the team defending Brent Springford Jr. on charges of murdering his parents. She began with a description of Brent's privileged upbringing and his subsequent altruism, caring for others in Latin America while in college and, later in Boulder, caring for Sam Flinders, the dying father of a former roommate.

She explained how she investigated the relationship between Brent and Caroline Scoutt. Initially, Charlotte and Brent Springford Sr. trusted Scoutt as their son's caretaker, and began sending her large sums of money, $90,000 the first year the couple was together. Wardell's voice was emotional but controlled, as she described Brent Jr.'s efforts to please Scoutt. He worked and slept in the Wyoming oil fields and directly deposited or sent her his paychecks to the home in Windsor, Colorado, the one that the Springford parents had paid for. She talked about how even Brent Jr.'s allowance checks from his parents were deposited into their joint checking account, although Brent never had any checks of his own to write. Wardell explained that, early in her relationship with Brent Jr., Scoutt had told the Springfords that she was $25,000 behind on the mortgage on her Wyoming ranch, when in fact the property was given to her and had no mortgage. Over time, she said, Scoutt came to totally dominate Brent: "If she said it, he did it." Scoutt beat him down psychologically, undermining his fragile self-image, and isolating him from his parents in the face of escalating financial demands.

For a time, it seemed that Scoutt was now being tried at the Newcastle coroner's inquest for her role in crushing Brent, and somehow for being responsible for his parents' murder in Montgomery. After a lunch recess,

Wardell described her seemingly chance encounter with an inmate named Eric Lang in an Alabama prison, serving time for murder. She repeated Lang's account of what Brent told him about his parents' murders, while in the Montgomery jail. That is, that Brent told Lang that Scoutt had planned the killings and rehearsed the plot with him. At Rozier's prodding, Wardell talked about Scoutt's repeated calls to her, inquiring about the Springford estate. Wardell quoted from Scoutt's note to Brent, saying her family would come to visit him in Alabama, "if you get the death penalty." Citing her credentials as a licensed clinical social worker, and her numerous conversations with Scoutt, Wardell offered her diagnosis of Scoutt: "She's a psychopath . . . She's a chameleon." When Wardell learned from me of Richard Campbell's death, she said, "I knew she'd done it . . . It was so needless . . . Why didn't they get her? . . . She's a real predator."

Toward the end of her testimony, I noticed that Wardell seemed drained, and was starting to ramble and embellish, perhaps because of her pain medication. She made small factual errors—amounts of money, dates and chronology—but by that time it didn't make any difference. The damage to Scoutt had been devastating. "Susan's the main reason we could get the Springford information in front of them," Rozier would tell me later. In one of the strategy sessions before the inquest reconvened, Rozier predicted what would happen when Wardell testified: "You'll be able to see the jurors tying the noose." From where I sat, that seemed to be happening.

Until Wardell took the stand, juror Andrew Macke, the former Newcastle police chief, told me later, his feelings about Scoutt's involvement in Campbell's were building, as were those of the other jurors. "You start developing an opinion that somehow, some way she's involved. We all felt that there was something more involved. The pieces are falling together." However, he said, listening to Wardell's testimony "completely opened my eyes. She got up there and was very articulate—point by point. It was riveting. Toward the end of her testimony, when she became more emotionally involved, that drew you in even that much more." When Wardell stepped down, Macke impulsively got up and shook her hand. Her testimony, he said, was "the final nail in the coffin for me." The impact was not confined to Macke. "It was for all three of us. After that testimony we had some very intense, in-depth conversations in the jury room. We were pinpoint-focused after that testimony. Until then, we had no idea of Scoutt's history. I think that opened our eyes; it was the most time we spent talking as jury members, until we deliberated." Juror Joseph Wood agreed. "Scoutt influenced that kid in Colorado," he told me weeks later. "She convinced him."

The elusive Mark Fitzsimmons was next on the witness stand. Throughout the day he had been sitting next to Jeremy Michaels in the front row of the spectator section. A hulking, shaggy bear of a man, on the witness stand he was soft-spoken but combative in responding—or not responding—to Rozier's questions. At one point, Fitzsimmons asked why there were only three jurors in the box, rather than twelve. At another, he asked where the judge was. When Rozier interrupted his questioning to explain the difference between a criminal trial and a coroner's inquest, Fitzsimmons looked skeptical.

Fitzsimmons, a truck driver, said he met Caroline Scoutt at a boutique in Claremont, California, in the mid-1970s. They developed a good friendship, but he insists it was not a deeply romantic one. "Why ruin it with marriage?" he said. It was also a therapeutic (and financial) relationship; Fitzsimmons said that over the years he went through three "rebirths" under Scoutt's guidance. He drifted from California to Newcastle in the 1990s, where he married and divorced. About that time, Fitzsimmons said, he and Scoutt, who by then had also settled in Newcastle, went looking for a parcel of land. They found about two hundred acres outside of town, valued then at $43,000, most of which Fitzsimmons bought and turned over to Scoutt in gratitude for her counseling services. Recently, he said, Scoutt made him secretary of her nonprofit, Tatan-ka Sha, although he acknowledged he has no real involvement or duties with the organization.

Rozier then asked about Fitzsimmons' financial support for Scoutt. He resisted this line of questioning, but ultimately said that he sends her money "from time to time," but he was reluctant to say how much or how often. "She doesn't have any money so I send her some," he finally admitted. Rozier, who had seen cancelled checks and Scoutt's bank records, pushed Fitzsimmons to say that some months he sent her $3,000—out of an annual income of $30,000–40,000 a year—because "she is one of my best friends."

Rozier then focused on the summer of 2015. He asked if Fizsimmons was at Scoutt's ranch around the time of Richard Campbell's death. Fitzsimmons was vague about his whereabouts, finally saying no, that he was there sometime in July. However, Vicki Neusius, Campbell's sister, leaned over and told me that she recognized Fitzsimmons as being in Scoutt's trailer on June 29, 2015, when she and other members of the family traveled to Newcastle to find out about their brother's death days earlier. Fitzsimmons left the stand and took his seat next to Jeremy Michaels.

I was up next, testifying in court for the first time in my life. I wasn't on the stand for long. Rozier, relying mostly on the questions I prepared, led me through a brief recitation of my credentials as a journalist and author. Then I explained how I became involved in the Springford case, through Wardell, my sister-in-law, and how that led me to Boulder in the summer of 2015. I told him how my research with Alabama and Colorado investigators pointed to Caroline Scoutt as the intellectual author of the Montgomery murders of Charlotte and Brent Springford Sr. Officers in both states had used the term "puppeteer" to describe her role in the killings, I said. Rozier then asked if I had formed an independent opinion of Scoutt's role in the deaths of Charlotte and Brent Springford Sr., as well as of Richard Campbell Jr. I said I had not yet reached a definitive conclusion.

With the matter of Caroline Scoutt's testimony still unresolved, the coroner's inquest was recessed for a second time, until December 20.

: 33

Waiting (2)

A few days later, back in Orlando, I received a series of emails from Kym Swisher, Scoutt's tenant, who was still living with her husband Dave in Richard Campbell's old trailer. The couple had been sitting outside the courtroom during the October inquest, able and prepared to testify that Scoutt was lucid and mobile following her surgeries, but they were not called. "[Things] have gotten stranger here since the day of court," Swisher wrote. On October 25, she said, "I was told [by Scoutt], 'I will not allow you to testify against me,' and much more has been said . . . it's very eerie." With Swisher's permission, I forwarded her email to Rozier and the two coroners, as well as to Sergeant Patrick Watsabaugh, of the sheriff's department. The next day, Kym and Dave Swisher met with Weston County Sheriff Bryan Colvard at his office behind the courthouse in Newcastle to discuss the threats. At one point in that meeting, a deputy informed Colvard that Scoutt and Fitzsimmons had been observed circling the building in Scoutt's pickup.

On Saturday, October 29, a warrant was issued by the county attorney's office for Scoutt's arrest for witness intimidation, a felony, carrying a maximum term of ten years in prison and a $5,000 fine. At 1:15 p.m. Watsabaugh went to Scoutt's ranch, arrested her and booked her into the Weston County jail. The response to Scoutt's arrest on the Weston County Sheriff's Facebook page was positive, almost celebratory, reflecting feeling about Scoutt in the area. Brenda Voll wrote, "YAY!!! It's about damn time." Dana Sutherland agreed: "About time she got caught for something." Lori Price Brown wrote, "Why am I not in the least bit surprised?" Rhonda Haley was less restrained, writing, "I wanna punch her in the mouth sooo bad !!" Several of those who posted suggested that anyone interested in the case link to the *Boulder Weekly* series, and to the Investigation Discovery episode on YouTube. Of course, the big question remained. "What about the murder charge?" Deb French asked. The answer to that would have to wait. The following Monday, a judge released Scoutt on her own recognizance, whereupon she returned to her ranch and promptly evicted the Swishers from their trailer.

Despite the eviction, a judge declined to revoke Scoutt's bail. But—with Jeremy Michaels representing his client by phone—the judge reinforced previous rulings that Coroner Cynthia Crabtree had a right to enforce Scoutt's inquest subpoena. However, in Wyoming, if a prosecutor is informed in advance that a client is going to assert her Fifth Amendment rights, she is not called to the witness stand, to avoid prejudicing a jury. So, after more sniping between the coroner team and County Attorney William Curley, Steve Rozier decided to give up. Instead, he decided to deliver a summation at the final session of the coroner's inquest. On December 9, Scoutt appeared in court again, this time represented by her new criminal attorney, Alex Berger, of Gillette, and was arraigned on the intimidation charge and bound over for trial.

A week before I was scheduled to leave for Newcastle, I had another meal with Steve Rozier, who was again passing through Orlando with his wife after yet another Caribbean cruise. We had dinner at the Outback restaurant near the airport. He outlined his strategy for the last day of the inquest. There would be one final attempt to drag Scoutt to the proceeding, including a possible arrest by deputies. Since Scoutt was now represented by a criminal lawyer, the chief deputy coroner acknowledged that this effort to compel her to testify was likely to end in failure. Rozier's closing argument to the jury would track a criminal prosecutor's summation. Now up to my neck in the attempt to bring Scoutt to justice, I offered to review his presentation. Rozier said he hoped the jury would return with a homicide finding. Further, he would like the jurors to exercise their option to recommend that Weston County prosecutor William Curley—whom Rozier had taken to calling "William the Idiot"—investigate Caroline Scoutt for her role in Richard Campbell's death.

: 34

Denouement

I confess to having had mixed feelings about the December trip to Newcastle, since sudden blizzards are not uncommon in northeastern Wyoming. It struck me that mid-winter might not be the best time to leave the sunny confines of the Central Florida suburbs for a foray to South Dakota and Wyoming. A few days after deciding to make the trip, a blizzard hit the region, reminding me of recent movies about dire events in that part of the country. Still, I got lucky, flying into the Rapid City Airport between snowstorms. Except for the runway and some roads, there was snow everywhere. I picked up the small Jeep SUV I had reserved and, despite the fact that this was my fourth trip to Wyoming, I managed to take a wrong turn outside Rapid City. I found myself driving—white knuckled—on snow-packed state State Road 85, heading south from Deadwood, threading my way through the Black Hills in the failing afternoon light to Newcastle. When, at dusk, I finally checked in at The Pines, new owner Rachel Householder cheerfully informed me that the night before the temperature was well below zero.

The next day, I met Sheriff's Deputy Patrick Watsabaugh at Donna's Diner to catch up on the case. Yet again, the investigator had changed his appearance—now sporting the beginnings of a full beard. After lunch, as I strolled up Main Street, Watsabaugh called to me from his pickup truck, informing me that County Attorney William Curley had just walked into the restaurant. I felt Curley had been avoiding meeting with me face-to-face on past visits. So I went back into the restaurant and approached a burly man with a well-trimmed black and gray beard. He was eating by himself, a bowl of soup in front of him, and a piece of pumpkin pie waiting. Next to his left hand was a trade paperback book, with numerous, yellow page tabs, on the subject of easements, access and public domain, his lunchtime reading. Clearly, this was someone with plans to eat alone. Notwithstanding, I introduced myself and, after a few awkward minutes, he asked me to sit down.

Curley is a slow-talking man, in his early seventies, wearing jeans, and a brown flannel vest over a blue-gray, flannel shirt. He was then halfway through his first term as the elected county attorney. As we chatted he turned out to be the opposite of what I had been imagining as a rustic, recalcitrant, Wyoming rube. In fact he is a New Englander, a collateral relative of Boston's famed Mayor James Curley. He is extremely well-educated, having attended Portsmouth Priory prep school outside of Newport, Rhode Island, then Northwestern University, where he majored in philosophy. Later, he earned a master's degree in that field at the University of Tennessee and a PhD from Southern Illinois University, where he returned a decade later to attend law school. In the early 1970s he was living in Vermont, where he was active in the libertarian Liberty Union Party and met Bernie Sanders, whom Curley said he had trouble getting along with. He and his brother moved to Wyoming in the 1980s. His brother Charles is secretary of the Wyoming state Republican Party. After serving as assistant county attorney, Curley ran for the office and won in 2014.

At the lunch table, Curley seemed cautious—if not evasive—about the prospects of criminally prosecuting Caroline Scoutt, ticking off the reasons. He hadn't attended any of the inquest sessions, but from what he had heard and read he said there did not appear to be probable cause for a homicide prosecution, regardless of the jury's official finding. Also, he was still concerned about the legality of subpoenaing Scoutt to the inquest, fearing it might expose the county to costly civil litigation. He was further troubled by the attention the *News Letter Journal* editor Bob Bonnar was giving the inquest, worrying that it might prejudice a future jury pool in any related prosecution. When my follow-up questions about prosecuting Scoutt became too pointed, Curley—still amiable—steered the conversation toward one of his compelling interests, the U.S. Constitution and the early years of the Republic. After the interview, I was still obsessed with cold weather survival, so I bought a Seattle Seahawks watch cap (one of only two in stock) at Cinch Jeans & Shirts on Main Street.

At 9 a.m., on Tuesday, December, 20, 2016, a small group gathered in the third-floor courtroom. Richard Campbell's sister Vicki Neusius and her husband Greg were again in from Colorado, after a harrowing, snowy ride on Interstate 25 the day before, sitting in the front row. One of the jurors was late, but all three filed in at about ten after nine. However, something was up. Chief Deputy Coroner Steve Rozier, who was conducting the inquest, was huddling at the back of the courtroom with Jeremy Michaels, Caroline Scoutt's lawyer. Scoutt herself had quietly slipped into the courtroom, taking a seat in the last row, nearest the door. Suddenly, William Curley swept into the room from the front entrance, making his first appearance, dressed in a dark suit, vest, and Santa Claus tie. Rozier and Michaels joined him, and the three disappeared into what is normally the judge's chamber. There, once more, Curley attempted to instruct Rozier in exactly what he should say to the jury, but the deputy brushed him off.

A few minutes later Rozier and Michaels returned, and Michaels escorted Scoutt, using a cane and appearing to walk with great difficulty, to the front of the room. They stopped at the low railing that separates the spectator section from the attorneys' tables, the judge's bench and the jury box. Scoutt was wearing a padded fuchsia vest and high black boots, her brown hair tied in a long, loose braid, as she had when I interviewed her at the round house. Rozier explained to the jurors that an agreement had been worked out, and he introduced Michaels. Scoutt remained silent as the defense attorney explained that, because of her medical condition, and her intention to exercise her Fifth Amendment right against self-incrimination, Scoutt would not be taking the witness stand. The deal, brokered by Curley, resulted in an anticlimax: without ever uttering a word, Scoutt hobbled out of court, escorted by Michaels. In the hallway outside the courtroom, Michaels's reaction to the proceeding was barely controlled, the accumulated fury of a stifled advocate. The inquest, he told me, is "medieval . . . I felt as if I were not in the United States, but in a country that doesn't allow for due process. It was literally a unilateral proceeding."

Rozier's first witness was David Swisher, the horse trainer who, with his wife, moved into the trailer in which Campbell's body had been found just weeks earlier. But Swisher testified that it was well after the couple moved in that they were informed that someone had died there. Rozier led him through his recollection of the October day he spent waiting outside the courtroom to testify at an earlier inquest session. Swisher recounted the phone call he and his wife received from Scoutt fifteen minutes after they returned from court. Scoutt, whom they put on their speaker phone, told them she would not "allow" them to testify against her if they were recalled. Since the phone call, Swisher said, two of the horses they kept on the property, all apparently healthy, died suddenly. One of the jurors, Sandy Upton, asked him what he took to be the nature of Scoutt's threat. "We have no clue" why the horses died, Swisher said. Kym Swisher followed David to the witness stand. Rozier asked her about Scoutt's friend, Mark Fitzsimmons. Kym said he made her feel uncomfortable, always lurking around their part of the property. She found his presence so bothersome that she complained to Scoutt about him. Kym then corroborated her husband's account of Scoutt's phone call after their return from the October inquest session. In that call, she said that Scoutt said that Fitzsimmons told her that Kym was going to testify at the inquest that Scoutt was capable of murder. "I will not allow you to testify," Scoutt said on the phone. "I will not allow you to do this." "Did you consider this a threat?" Rozier asks. "I did," she replied, clearly uncomfortable.

Just after 9:30 a.m., Steve Rozier began his closing argument to the jury, reprising part of his opening statement. The inquest process, he told the jury, is "a search for truth" to determine the cause and manner of Richard Campbell Jr.'s death—rather than an attempt to determine guilt or innocence. This flew in the face of much of the testimony, including Susan Wardell's and mine. But everyone in the courtroom was aware of what had been going on. Still, Rozier argued, the witness testimony should constitute the sole basis of evidence for their finding. Inside the trailer that June day in 2015, he says, "whatever happened, happened quickly." The rifle belonged to Scoutt, and Richard Campbell didn't touch firearms. "No one ever saw him hold a gun or shoot a gun," he tells jurors. There were no fingerprints on the weapon and it was unlikely that Campbell wiped them off after being shot through the head. Tellingly, Rozier made no effort to put the fatal weapon in anyone else's hands, either Scoutt's or Fitzsimmons'. Rozier talked about the insurance policies and Scoutt's calls to Coroner Laura Sundstrom, requesting a death certificate while Campbell's body "was not even cold," in which she twice denied she was a beneficiary of his insurance policy. "There was no reason to lie to the coroner unless you're hiding something," Rozier said.

Rozier then went over the other main points: Campbell's abhorrence of suicide; the demeaning way Scoutt treated Campbell; the joint checking account and the direct deposit of his paychecks; Campbell's missing inheritance from his father's estate; the strange alibi calls to the veterinary clinic the day of the death; the testimony about the Springfords. And, finally, the power Scoutt exercised over Campbell. "This woman has so much control over him," Rozier said, isolating him from his family and friends, just as she had done with Brent Springford. Much like Brent, Rozier said, Richard Campbell "fell under the spell of the wrong woman."

Throughout Rozier's short summation, Vicki Neusius took notes. At one point, however, she teared up, taking off her glasses and reaching for a tissue to dab her eyes. Rozier's delivery was not as polished as a trial lawyer's, but it was both comprehensive and effective. He finished, and the three members of the jury retired to begin their deliberations. Shortly after they left, Campbell County Coroner Laura Sundstrom, who had been working on another case, arrived to join Rozier and Cynthia Crabtree to await the verdict.

The three jurors went back to the deliberation room, seeming to nod in agreement with what Rozier had just said. Andrew Macke recalled speaking first. "I said his summation was what I was thinking. I don't think Richard woke up in the morning thinking that he was going to kill himself. Scoutt either talked him into it; or she did it; or she had it done. I don't think he died at his own hand. Somebody else was involved." When Macke finished, a second juror, Joseph Wood, said, "That's what I think. That's pretty much how I look at it." The third juror, Sandy Upton, agreed, adding, "Somebody else was involved." Macke said later, "We can speculate about that, but we firmly believe that Richard was not responsible for his own death." The jurors didn't accuse Scoutt in their verdict, but they did want to recommend further investigation. Wood said later he did not understand that the jurors were free to point investigators toward Scoutt in their verdict. Macke wrote out the wording for further investigation on a separate sheet of paper, so they could all agree, before copying it onto the verdict form.

All of this took just enough time to make the coroner team nervous. So after about fifteen minutes, Rozier went back into the jury room, which is permitted under the relaxed rules of the inquest. Ten minutes later the jurors returned with their verdict form, which they handed to Rozier. He read: a preponderance of the evidence indicates with some certainty that the cause of Richard Campbell Jr.'s death in Weston County, Wyoming, on June 24, 2015, was homicide. The jurors recommended that the matter be further investigated, but made no mention of Scoutt. Juror Joseph Wood spoke up to emphasize that there should be further investigation in the case. He spoke, he told me, because "I wanted to make sure the sheriff's department got off their lazy asses and investigated both the death and the theft. The county attorney, too."

Rozier thanked all three, and Cynthia Crabtree, in her capacity as Weston County coroner, signed the form. Within seconds of the verdict, I emailed those involved in the Springford case about the outcome. Susan Wardell, only recently released from the hospital for a back flare-up, fired back: "This is a well-deserved holiday gift to the most evil creature I have ever encountered." Bill Blanchard, Brent's lead defense counsel, had a similar response: "Great news! Makes my Holiday Season to think that justice may soon catch up with this wretched excuse for a human being."

The proceeding was officially over, but Weston County had arranged lunch across the street at Isabella's restaurant for the jurors and the coroner's team. I was also included—a free meal is a free meal. Outside the courthouse I ran into Curley, the prosecutor, who confirmed that he brokered the deal for Scoutt's short appearance at the inquest. At the restaurant, the jurors were relaxed and felt free to talk about the case. Their built-up hostility toward Caroline Scoutt was pronounced. Andrew Macke, the former Newcastle police chief, said he had to restrain himself when Scoutt finally appeared in court. He was convinced of her culpability in Campbell's death. Weeks later he told me, "Exactly what happened that day I don't know. More intense investigation needs to be done. There's lot more to investigate." Sandy

Upton, sitting next to me at lunch, recalled how much she liked Campbell when he worked with her at Weston Engineering.

While soft-spoken, Steve Rozier is not a man who lacks self-assurance. Yet a day after the verdict he confided that he was relieved by the outcome. "It truly means a lot to me personally," he told me. "And while it might not have been evident, I lost a lot of sleep worrying about making sure I didn't drop the ball." Several weeks later, he was more reflective. He wrote me:

> The inquest was a journey for everyone who watched and participated. It was an experience that many people put their heart, soul, and trust in, as the last hope for truth in an otherwise hopeless case. Along the way, there were pitfalls: a less than competent initial investigation, along with a highly questionable county attorney whose apparent alliance with the suspect and her attorney was troubling. These are just a couple of reasons people lose hope in our justice system. Richard was a prisoner who was not capable of any defense or rebellion against his captor. Failure in my presentation would mean that I had failed Richard Campbell. The jury really wanted to get the opportunity to question Scoutt. But the fact is she could never testify, and her attorney knew it. If she had taken the stand, her jaded past full of lies, greed, phony scams, and a double murder implication would certainly have burned her to the ground.

Cynthia Crabtree participated in strategy sessions before and during the inquest, and sat at the coroners' table throughout the hearings. Yet she effectively recused herself from the courtroom proceeding, because of her business dispute with Scoutt before she was elected coroner. Still, she too had strong feelings after the verdict. "As the inquest began I was naive as to what to expect from my fellow agencies," she told me later. "I wanted justice for Richard and his family and so many of his friends. I knew Richard when he first came to Weston County, as a kind and gentle man. The day I left for my Coroner Basic Training . . . I visited with Richard at the Loaf 'n Jug on Sunday evening. He was smiling and wished me well. Three days later he was dead.

"As we approached the inquest we were held up by the county attorney giving us advice that we could not take—because our gut feeling was that to call it a suicide and walk away was wrong. I only hoped that jurors would be able to see the picture of a man and the injustice that he had been given by Scoutt. Weston County deserves better than what this man got, and someone needs to be held accountable. I do truly believe that my position as Weston County Coroner is to be the last voice for the dead in Weston County."

Not everyone agreed. During the summation and deliberation, Jeremy Michaels, Scoutt's civil attorney, returned to court, sitting in the first row, listening intently with his hands folded, but no longer taking notes. After Rozier's closing argument, Michaels complimented him on hitting on all the points of his case in a concise way. However, weeks later, Michael's anger and outrage had not cooled. He wrote me:

> As a trained attorney, my feeling was primarily one of complete impotence. [The inquest was] a bizarre travesty . . . an historical anachronism which has no place in the American system of justice. It is a complete derogation of any due process or ability to defend or even present evidence.

He stressed that a target in an inquest like Caroline Scoutt "is in fact entirely without any rights." He said that members of the coroners' team were able

> to haul all manner of witnesses into a Star Chamber . . . A free-for-all ensued over a period of days. This involved countless layers of hearsay testimony, tales from anyone the Coroner felt would be helpful in building a literal house-of-cards 'case' against Ms. Scoutt, and a 'jury' consisting of three folks from the community who literally were chosen without selection process by the Coroner, presumably as her friends . . . No representation was permitted, no objections were heard or entertained, and the 'jurors' were free to interpose literally any nature or type of question they felt relevant . . . Had Ms. Scoutt been permitted representation, there is no question at least 90 per cent of the 'evidence' introduced would under any rules of evidence or fundamental fairness would never have seen the light of day.

: 35

Aftermath

If the coroners thought that the homicide verdict would motivate County Attorney William Curley, they were soon disabused of that notion. "When the jury returned with the verdict of Homicide by gunshot wound, I felt that maybe Richard's death would not go unnoticed or be swept under the carpet, that the case would be pursued," Cynthia Crabtree wrote me. When that didn't happen, the coroners continued their ad hoc campaign against Scoutt. Rozier, Crabtree, and Laura Sundstrom requested a meeting with Wyoming Attorney General Peter K. Michael to ask him to present the reluctant prosecutor and Sheriff Bryan Colvard with a writ of mandamus, ordering them to proceed with a criminal prosecution of Scoutt. Then they planned to meet with agents of the FBI and IRS.

The inquest verdict had a mixed meaning for Caroline Scoutt's hopes for collecting the $100,000 Farmers insurance policy on Richard Campbell. On one hand, the homicide finding made moot any questions about the policy's suicide exclusion clause. At first, the coroners said they would refuse to sign the death certificate until Sheriff Colvard opened a homicide investigation. But even after Cynthia Crabtree ultimately did sign Campbell's death certificate, Farmers would not say if the claim had been paid. The only remaining grounds for the company to deny the claim would be if Scoutt was ultimately found culpable for Campbell's death.

In the months following the inquest verdict, the coroners kept up their campaign. Crabtree asked the Weston County tax assessor to check whether Scoutt had notified the office of her "property additions," chiefly the round house lodge. Scoutt had not, which meant the county could bill her for back and current taxes from when the structure was completed. On January 6, 2017, Rozier tipped me that Scoutt had put three of her Weston

County properties, including the ranch and round house and the house in town, on the website realtor.com for close to a million dollars, up from the $699,000 she had asked earlier. Opinion was divided on whether the money is to pay her lawyers and back taxes, or in preparation to cash out and take off. Sundstrom called the Wyoming secretary of state and urged him to look into Tatan-ka Sha, Scoutt's nonprofit.

Around this time, William Curley's deputy county attorney, Lynda Black, announced that she was leaving her job to take a similar post in adjoining Crook County. She didn't give a reason, but courthouse speculation centered on Curley's inaction on the Scoutt case. As if the case against Scoutt was not convoluted enough, on January 3, 2017, Curley told county commissioners he intended to hire as Black's replacement Alex Berger, a private criminal attorney from Gillette—the same lawyer who represented Caroline Scoutt in one of her appearances on the charges of witness intimidation. That would create a blatant conflict that seemingly would make it impossible for Curley's office to pursue any Scoutt prosecution, not limited to the witness intimidation charge.

So Curley appeared to resolve the conflict, although in a highly questionable way. On January 19, 2017, he filed a motion in district court, requesting a dismissal of the witness intimidation charges on grounds that "there is not sufficient proof beyond a reasonable doubt to convict the Defendant." The motion was conveyed to Berger, in his capacity as Scoutt's attorney. Four days later Berger assumed his new $53,000-a-year post as assistant Weston County attorney. "It did have the effect of resolving the conflict," Curley replied when I asked him about it, "but it was not done to resolve the conflict."

So—problem solved? Perhaps not. Several letters were sent from elected officials and law enforcement officers to the Wyoming Bar Association's Professional Complaints committee about Curley's conduct.

About the same time, Sergeant Patrick Watsabaugh requested a meeting with Sheriff Bryan Colvard. In the tense session, Watsabaugh said that if his boss would not sign a letter asking the Wyoming Division of Criminal of Investigation to intervene in the Scoutt investigation, Watsabaugh would send a letter himself. Colvard said that would not be necessary, and sent the letter the next day. While waiting for responses from the attorney general and the state bar association, Cynthia Crabtree requested another closed meeting with the Weston County Commission on February 7. She wanted to renew her complaints of inaction on the part of Sheriff Colvard and County Attorney Curley and ask them to hire a special prosecutor. But before that meeting could take place, Crabtree, Laura Sundstrom, and Steve Rozier learned of Watsabaugh's confrontation with Colvard, and the likely involvement of the DCI. So Crabtree, at Rozier's urging, asked the commissioners to wait until February 21.

Suddenly, things began to change. Apparently in response to the coroners' outreach to the state attorney general, on February 9, three veteran DCI agents were assigned to the case, including Jason Riddle, who knew Sundstrom from when he had been assigned to Gillette. Four days later, the agents requested a meeting with Rozier, Sundstrom, Crabtree, and Watsabaugh. Normally, just two agents are assigned to cases, so Rozier was heartened. Watsabaugh came in on his day off, spending two hours copying his case file. Crabtree brought her material in pink canvas file containers. Sundstrom brought her case notes and files from Campbell County, as well as those from Montgomery on the Springford case. What they couldn't photocopy they transferred to thumb drives for the state agents. Rozier carried in a box of Scoutt's financial records.

The meeting took place in the Weston County Sheriff's complex, starting at 1 p.m. and ran four hours. Behind closed doors, the three DCI agents and four locals sat around a long table in the same squad room where the first task force meeting was held in the fall of 2015. "We were giddy that they were there," Sundstrom admitted. "We couldn't shut up." The locals laid out their investigation in detail, acknowledging at the outset that the Richard Campbell homicide charge would likely to be the hardest to prove. But the larceny case growing out of the money from Campbell's inheritance, and the dismissed witness intimidation charge would likely be much easier. After carrying the burden of the increasingly complex investigation for so long on their own, Watsabaugh and Rozier were encouraged by the reception they got from the state agents, even their body language. "We're finally getting the assets and resources we need," Watsabaugh thought. "I expect a fairly aggressive, fairly quick investigation," Rozier told me afterward. "There's no doubt in my mind that they are going to dig up some shit and charge Scoutt." Sundstrom said, "I want to see them put that bitch away!"

The locals also listed their complaints about William Curley's lack of support in the investigation, citing the county prosecutor's close relationship with Scoutt's civil attorney, Jeremy Michaels, and his hiring of Alex Berger, Scoutt's former criminal lawyer. They sensed a sympathetic audience. "This is going to be handled by a special prosecutor from the state," Rozier predicted. "They were crystal clear about that." With all of their complaints now being addressed, Crabtree canceled the scheduled meeting with the Weston County Commission. From now on, the investigation of Caroline Scoutt would be in the hands of the State of Wyoming.

One of the first things the DCI agents did was to act on the coroner's long-delayed request to run Scoutt's name through National Criminal Information Center's database, although they did not share the results. On March 15, Watsabaugh accompanied the three DCI agents to Richard Campbell's unlocked trailer, pursuant to a new search warrant. Using a digital 3D scanner, the investigators determined that Campbell was shot while standing and facing his bedroom door, rather than sitting on the corner of his bed, as Watsabaugh had initially believed. Campbell could have shot himself, the agents believed, but his position could also indicate that he had a visitor. Some experts believe that suicidal people using a rifle are more likely to sit to kill themselves, so they won't merely wound. Standing with a long gun is a more awkward and less stable position for a self-inflicted shot.

Later that month it occurred to me that the DCI investigators might benefit from contacting some of my Colorado sources, including private investigator Wayne Diffee, Weld County Deputy Vicki Harbert, and the Flinders family in Boulder. I sent the information to Cynthia Crabtree, who forwarded it to the state agents.

On April 11, the DCI agents interviewed Jessica Holland, Scoutt's older daughter. She told them that over the years her mother told family members different things about her plan for the property. For a time, she told them that the round house would be a home for them and their extended family, and as it was built it seemed to Holland to be designed as a residence rather than a counseling center. Despite all Scoutt's talk about abused Native American women, Holland said she "never observed any Native American people on the ranch property." Later, Scoutt told Holland she intended to sell the property, give the money to Holland, her brother and younger sister, and buy a small house for herself.

Around the same time, DCI agents in Casper, Wyoming, submitted a search warrant for Scoutt's property, both the round house and the nearby mobile home, based on the warrant I worked on with Watsabaugh more than a year earlier. It specifically listed "evidence related to a potential homicide and financial crimes." This is the same order that County Attorney William Curley had refused to sign and thus had never been served. Among the items listed in the new document were bank and financial records and electronic devices. Once the warrant was signed by a Casper judge, ten agents from Casper and Gillette drove to the Weston County sheriff's office the morning of May 11, 2017, a sunny and clear day. They joined Watsabaugh and two other deputies and, at about one o'clock drove in a convoy to Scoutt's ranch.

As the vehicles pulled up, the officers noticed a parked pickup truck owned by Scoutt's adult son. Following procedure, the agents and deputies wore enhanced, external body armor with the words POLICE, SHERIFF, or AGENT in large white letters. Some carried assault rifles, others drawn handguns, as they made their way to the round house and the nearby mobile home. No one inside responded to their shouted commands, and the doors to both structures were locked and dead bolted, so the agents used battering rams to get inside. The first thing the agents noticed, they later wrote, was "that the round house (Spiritual Center) was arranged solely as a residence and did not have the appearance of being used for any other purpose." The five thousand square feet structure contained five bedrooms and two-and-a-half baths. In passing, Watsabaugh marveled at the structure's interior design: four large logs formed the primary support, slanting from around the base of the walls to the roof's center, teepee fashion. He noticed that there was little in the way of Native American art or artifacts in the roundhouse. Instead, there were shelves of ceramic and plastic angels.

The DCI agents, including a second investigator, Jason Ruby, fanned out and began collecting documents in cardboard boxes, including material relating to the Tatan-ka Sha nonprofit. They found a copy of Scoutt's California birth certificate in the name of Carol Gonzales, noting her race as "White." An electronic safe in the lodge was empty. The interior of the adjacent mobile home, where Mark Fitzsimmons was living, was a different story. One locked room appeared to be a mini-museum of world religion and spirituality. It was full of Native American regalia, as well as Buddhist and Hindu books and statues, Egyptian ankhs, and small statues. Watsabaugh also noticed a shelf with about a dozen books by Eckhart Tolle, a German Canadian thought by many to be the most spiritually influential person in North America, whose works Brent Springford had requested while in jail and prison.

The Native American headdresses and fans appeared to be made of feathers of federally protected birds of prey: eagles, owls, and red-tail hawks. Watsabaugh called a local agent of the Wyoming Fish and Game Department, told him what he had found, and sent photos taken with his phone. The agent immediately drew up a search warrant for the feathers and drove to the ranch. By this time, Scoutt and Fitzsimmons had been located driving around Newcastle in Scoutt's pickup. They were stopped, Scoutt's cell phone was seized, and they were advised to return to the ranch. They arrived at about the same time as the Fish and Game officer, who cited the protected species statute and asked Scoutt if she had the federal permit issued to Native Americans for ceremonial use of the feathers. When she said she had neither a permit nor a tribal identification card, the agent seized the items.

Next, the DCI agents interviewed Scoutt for about an hour. Scoutt, who was not in custody, agreed to submit to an interview with the DCI's two Jasons, Riddle and Ruby. She described Richard Campbell as her "ranch hand" and said he had turned over the check for $89,400 from his father's estate (which the agents had), which he endorsed to her and she deposited in her account. In this version, Scoutt said the money was in exchange for ninety acres of her land and the trailer where he was living. She acknowledged that no contract or other paperwork existed to prove the arrangement, and that the money was now gone. Scoutt claimed that she had no idea how much the lodge had cost to build, but that the money had been donated by "spiritual people," including Patricia Emmons, the Colorado donor the coroners had located months earlier. These people, Scoutt said, did not visit the property "because they were her enemies now as a result of how people talked about her."

Fitzsimmons also agreed to a brief interview with the DCI agents. He said he had only a vague notion of what his responsibilities were as secretary of Scoutt's nonprofit, Tatan-Ka Sha, acknowledging he never seen any Native Americans around the property, which he thought was "weird." He said he had no knowledge of Scoutt's tribal affiliation, other than that she "had a Native American bloodline."

Later in the search, the agents called for Watsabaugh, telling him that Scoutt had fallen on the kitchen floor of the round house. He rushed in and asked her if he could do anything to help, but she brusquely told him she had no interest in talking to him. An ambulance was called, but Scoutt, who had a small abrasion on her forehead from the fall, declined to be transported. After about ten hours, the DCI agents completed their search and labeled and packed up the seized materials. To Watsabaugh, they appeared in good spirits, but they did not share with him the status of the investigation. "I felt really good about the search," Watsabaugh said, "but I couldn't help but wondering how much more we would have found had I successfully got my warrant a year and a half ago."

By contrast to my close relationship with the two coroners and the Weston County sheriff's department, I didn't know any of the Wyoming DCI agents. So I sometimes had to track the outline of their investigation at a remove, or wait until the investigators filed reports of their interviews, so I could ultimately draw on both. On June 1, the agents later wrote, they visited Patricia Emmons in the Denver area. She confirmed to the DCI agents what the coroners suspected, based on bank records they had seized. Emmons told them that in early 2013 she was approached by Scoutt, who asked her to fund construction of the round house lodge as a "spiritual center." Emmons considered herself a partner in the counseling project, and she expected to volunteer at the center, teaching women how to make handbags for sale. At first, Scoutt began sending her photos of progress on the building, but then stopped. While traveling to the area, Emmons asked

Scoutt if she could visit the site. After saying yes, Scoutt told Emmons she was having a hysterectomy and a visit would be inconvenient.

Scoutt's initial estimates of $150,000 to complete construction escalated. In all, Emmons said she wrote seventeen checks between March 2014 and April 2015, totaling $504,500 for the center. Emmons became uneasy about the rising costs, and told Scoutt that she thought the project was going over budget. Emmons told the agents that Scoutt manipulated her into paying more and more money by making her feel guilty about her wealth, in order to keep her contributing. On some of the checks she wrote, Emmons had marked "Land" or "Land Lease" on the memo line. When the investigators asked her about that, Emmons said that Scoutt promised her eighty acres of her land in exchange for Emmons' support in building the center. As with Scoutt's story about turning land over to Richard Campbell, Emmons said no contract or paperwork was ever drafted to enforce the arrangement.

Scoutt, who told Emmons and others that she was a counselor, also made an agreement for phone therapy sessions with Emmons' daughter, and for her daughter's long-term boyfriend, at $100–150 an hour. Later Scoutt said that the boyfriend "needed a lot of work," and that he called at odd hours, and didn't want anyone to know about the sessions. As a result, Scoutt told Emmons she would need a check for $25,000 in advance for three years of therapy, drawn on the daughter's trust account. Although reluctant—there was never any documentation for the sessions—Emmons ultimately sent the check, a copy of which she provided the agents. Emmons said she wrote Scoutt additional checks for tens of thousands of dollars for other services, some paid directly to vendors or contractors.

Six days after the interview with Emmons, the agents spoke to her daughter, Rebecca Davidson. Davidson told them that Scoutt claimed she was treating her boyfriend for free, but Davidson knew her mother was paying Scoutt from her trust account. The DCI agents found no record of any license or certification for Caroline Scoutt in the database of the State of Wyoming Mental Health Licensing Board.

Following the interviews with Emmons and Davidson, I heard from Wayne Diffee, the Denver private investigator, who told me he had just been visited by two DCI agents—the two Jasons, Riddle and Ruby. Diffee had been called earlier by Weston County Coroner Cynthia Crabtree and asked if he would be willing to meet with them, and he said he would. About ten days later, one of the Jasons telephoned and said they were coming to Denver to interview witnesses and asked if he would see them, and again Diffee said yes. A week after that they called and said they were in town and asked to meet him on June 6.

The agents arrived at Diffee's home. Both wore baseball caps pulled tightly over their heads just above their eyes, and both with the bills sharply curved. The three men sat around Diffee's dining room table for about an hour, and Diffee served coffee as they spoke. The private investigator liked the two agents and felt they knew what they were doing. They told him they usually worked drug cases, but felt that the Scoutt case was good for them. Diffee offered to help, talking to people in the Windsor, Colorado, area where Brent and Caroline lived, people who thought Brent was a field hand rather than Caroline's husband.

"It was difficult to judge what they knew, since they weren't always open," Diffee wrote me. "The agents knew a lot about Caroline when they interviewed me, and that the Springford parents cut Brent Jr. off of money to buy the expensive supplements . . . I told them some of what I did during my case investigation. They are very interested in fraud, and mentioned Caroline asking for donations to build the round worship place, which was actually where she lived. When I said that sounds like fraud to me, they agreed. They said they can't do much about what happened in Colorado," since any funds solicited and collected there would be outside their jurisdiction. "I have the feeling they are committed to the fraud cases, but not so much the homicide of Richard Campbell, although they knew a lot about him. They were leaning toward suicide."

The agents told Diffee they next planned to interview Ann Flinders and her mother, Marie Flinders, who had contributed more than $30,000 to Scoutt's Wyoming counseling center. Then they wanted to speak with Dr. Roger Billica, the Fort Collins physician who prescribed vitamins and supplements to Scoutt and Brent Jr., billing his parents in the last weeks of their lives.

"At least it sounds like they're doing *something*," Steve Rozier, the

Campbell County coroner's investigator, told me, when I passed along these developments. "That's better than nothing." Rozier had clearly adjusted his expectations since the inquest verdict. Still, he said, Wyoming's conspiracy statute was broadly written. An indictment could be brought if it could be proved that any element of a conspiracy, any overt act, regardless how trivial—a phone call, a letter, a money transfer—had taken place in the state.

Next the agents drove to Boulder, to meet with Ann Flinders, Brent's ex-roommate, who had done breathing sessions and extensive family counseling with Scoutt, both before and after Brent Jr. encountered Caroline at her parents's home. Ann repeated to them her feeling that Caroline had sowed discord between Ann, her husband, and her mother Marie. Like Wayne Diffee, Ann Flinders got the impression from her interview that the DCI investigators were focusing on building an embezzlement case against Scoutt.

In early September, the two Jasons met with Jessica Holland, Scoutt's older daughter, for the second time, and for the first time her younger daughter, Star Fosheim, both in Newcastle. The sisters were interviewed separately, each for about an hour. Fosheim told the agents that her mother often used "guilt trips" to manipulate her children. However, the DCI agents had no apparent interest in the family's younger years, although they seemed to be familiar with that period in Caroline's life. Instead, they focused on events in Colorado. "They were very cordial, very laid-back," Fosheim recalled: Neither agent removed his baseball cap during the interviews.

Fosheim told the agents that people, including Campbell, who would come and go on the property were treated "horribly," that Scoutt would sometimes turn them into slaves, which she saw happen in the case of Richard Campbell. Fosheim said her mother always seemed to have money, but the children didn't know where it came from. Scoutt did see clients, for whom Fosheim said she would provide unspecified "services." The round house, paid for by donors, was to be for a nonprofit organization that would provide counseling for abused women, Scoutt told the daughters. But Fosheim said she never saw any abused women on the property.

: 36

Reckoning

After Scoutt's daughters' September 2017 interviews, I heard nothing, and I found the waiting difficult—even more so when I began binge-watching the Netflix series *Longmire*, a richly atmospheric, contemporary crime drama set in a fictional, sparsely populated Wyoming county. Although I know well the difference between fact and fiction, the show's dramatic scenery and small-town ambience—not unlike Newcastle and Weston County—only reminded me of my own time in Wyoming. The title character, a canny but world-weary sheriff, solves murders in less than an hour. Among them were several that at first appeared to be gunshot suicides, eerily like Richard Campbell's. *Longmire* also recalled my long conversations with Deputy Patrick Watsabaugh, Steve Rozier, and the two coroners about the trail of death, destruction, and misery that Caroline Scoutt had left in her wake.

Frankly, I was frustrated by the apparent lack of resolution in the DCI investigation. Was it possible that, after all our efforts, Scoutt would escape justice again? Finally, in mid-December, my impatience got the best of me. I called Forrest Williams, deputy director of the Division of Criminal Investigation in Cheyenne, hoping to nudge the investigation along simply by asking about it. Or at least find out if the matter had been closed. It took two calls before I heard back from Williams on December 14, 2017.

After delivering the standard law enforcement line about not giving any information about an investigation in progress, he gave me a cordial and respectful hearing as I outlined the information I had developed about Scoutt over the previous three years. He said he was familiar with the case, and that he did not expect any resolution "soon," a term he would not define further. In any case, he said, don't expect any news before the first of the year. But less than ten minutes after he hung up, he called me back, saying he just checked with the investigation's supervisor and found that Scoutt had in fact been arrested the night before. Even before I had all the details of the arrest I emailed the others involved in the case. Bill Blanchard, Brent Springford's defense attorney, shot back, "I would love nothing more than to see this evil person receive her just desserts."

Over the years, Caroline Scoutt might have faced a number of criminal charges. In connection with the Springford case: misprision of a felony, accessory before the fact to murder, murder, accessory after the fact to murder, obstructions of justice. In the Campbell case: witness tampering, obstruction of justice and conspiracy to commit murder.

In the end, the Wyoming Division of Criminal Investigation had settled on the easiest cases to make, the ones most likely to result in indictments, prosecutions, and convictions. On December 13, 2017, Scoutt was charged with two felonies, related to obtaining property from another under false pretense, both from Patricia (Patty) Emmons. In the first count, the amount was $504,400 for the round house lodge. The DCI agents concluded that the round house, designated at "Spiritual Center, was arranged solely as a residence and did not have the appearance of being used for any other purpose," according to the criminal complaint.

The second felony count was for $25,000 paid for telephone counseling for Emmons's daughter and her boyfriend. The boyfriend "did not receive three years of therapy and the remainder of the money was never returned to Emmons as being unused," according to the complaint. In both cases, the complaint charged that Scoutt "knowingly obtained property [$504,500.00 and $25,000] from Patty Emmons by false pretenses with the intent to defraud Emmons." Each felony count carries with it a maximum penalty of ten years in prison and a $10,000 fine, or both. The misdemeanor count was for practicing counseling, clinical social work, marriage and family therapy, or addiction therapy, without a license or certification. That count carried a maximum penalty of six months in prison, and $250 fine, or both.

The day before I called the DCI's Williams, agents Jason Ruby and Jason Riddle had taken their affidavits to the nearest circuit court judge they could find, who was sitting in the town of Sundance in Crook County, which borders Weston County. They then drove to Newcastle and, to put Scoutt off guard, they had a sheriff's deputy call Scoutt and tell her the state agents wanted to return the materials they had seized in the May search. When the officers arrived at the round house, Scoutt was using a walker—which, one of her daughters said later, she only seemed to need when she was around law enforcement officers. They informed her that she was under arrest and took her to the county jail in Newcastle.

While gratified by the fraud arrests, the two coroners, the other local investigators, and Richard Campbell's family and friends were disappointed with the DCI conclusion that no further charges would be forthcoming in connection with his death. They had also hoped for additional counts in connection with the life insurance policies, and the alleged embezzlement of $94,000 from Richard's father's estate. Jay Lewis, another of Brent Springford's defense attorneys, took the pragmatic view. "Sometimes justice is done," he wrote me. "I don't care *why* they lock her up, as long as they *do*. This is a dangerous woman!"

But those involved in pursuing Scoutt were particularly dismayed that the responsibility for prosecuting the charges would rest with Weston County Attorney William Curley, rather than with a special prosecutor, as they had hoped. These concerns went beyond Curley's earlier reluctance to pursue the criminal investigation, and his dismissal of Caroline Scoutt's witness-tampering charges during the coroner's inquest. Scoutt's one-time criminal lawyer, Alex Berger, was no longer Curley's assistant, though he would be heard from again.

More ominous was Curley's handling of two other high-profile cases in the previous fifteen months, a child sex allegation and a fatal shooting. The same issue of the local weekly paper, *News Letter Journal,* that carried an account of Scoutt's arrest at the top of the front page also carried an editorial, entitled "Second Opinion," by Bob Bonnar. In it, he attacked Curley for prosecutorial misconduct, citing the two cases, which had drawn criticism by two presiding judges.

In the most recent case, Bonnar wrote that Curley offered a plea deal that would have allowed the defendant to enter a "no contest" plea to a single charge of sexual exploitation of a child, in exchange for having three charges of sexual abuse of a minor dismissed. But presiding Circuit Judge

Michael Deegan rejected Curley's plea agreement as too lenient. "Deegan said the court was unwilling to accept a no contest plea to a sex offense such as the one alleged in this case," Bonnar wrote. "He also objected to Curley's willingness to offer deferred prosecution as part of the deal, which the judge likened to a 'slow motion dismissal' that could ultimately allow the defendant to avoid being placed on the sex offender registry."

Judge Deegan, noting that the alleged victim in this case was displeased with the proposed agreement, rejected the plea deal. So Curley simply dropped all charges and freed the man, enraging a number of citizens. Some showed up to complain about the prosecutor at the regular meeting of the Weston County Board of Commissioners on November 21, 2017. More than one speaker accused Curley of endangering children by sending them back to dangerous households. Following the complaints, four of the five commissioners voted to write Wyoming Governor Matt Mead and State Attorney General Peter Michael, requesting the appointment of a special prosecutor to handle the case. But Michael rejected the Weston commissioners' request, saying he had no statutory authority to act, under the circumstances.

In the same editorial, Bonnar cited another case involving Curley's dubious plea deals. In the autumn of 2016, Circuit Judge Thomas Rumpke objected to a plea agreement involving a former felon named Michael Davis, who was initially charged with the first-degree murder of a U.S. Forest Service officer. The officer, Katy Coffee, 35, was shot at close range at her home in 2011. Curley signed off on an agreement that allowed the man to plead guilty to one count of voluntary manslaughter and to serve no more than ten years, served concurrently with a federal charge of being a felon in possession of a firearm.

However, when Judge Rumpke asked the man what happened, Davis spun a vague and fanciful tale of going to the woman's house to sell her a gun. "During our interaction, the handgun in my hand discharged," Davis told the judge. Dissatisfied, Rumpke said the account made no sense, and was inconsistent with a charge of voluntary manslaughter. "I don't hear a factual basis for voluntary manslaughter," Rumpke said. Finally, the judge accepted the plea after Curley's assistant, Lynda Black, said the plea was acceptable to the prosecution in what is known as an Alford plea, under which a criminal defendant enters a plea of guilty without making a formal admission of guilt.

On February 28, 2018, Caroline Scoutt appeared in Weston County Circuit Court in Newcastle, before Judge Matthew Castano in a hearing that lasted just over an hour. She was represented by a private attorney, Ryan Healy, of Sheridan, Wyoming. The new assistant county prosecutor was Robert R. Jackson, an older attorney who has practiced for many years in the Custer, South Dakota, area. Judge Castano dismissed the felony fraud charge involving $25,000 for telephone counseling of the boyfriend of Patricia Emmons's daughter. The other felony charge, the $500,000 fraud count, also involving Emmons, was bound over to District Court, which handles major felonies. It was up to that court to hold an arraignment on the charge in early April and to set a trial date. The misdemeanor charge of practicing counseling without a license remained in the circuit court for adjudication. Judge Castano ordered Scoutt to post $25,000 bond and begin making payments on $6,500 to a previous attorney in the case. Her other assets were frozen.

Scoutt may have felt the legal net tightening. On April 3, her attorney told the judge that she had broken her hip, so the arraignment was continued until May 1. A few days before that date, her attorney told the judge that his client was still in the hospital, and the arraignment was postponed again, this time to June 26. Meanwhile, Scoutt's ranch property, although frozen by the court, remained listed for sale. In early May, her two daughters were seen gathering their possessions from the ranch property, possessions which were offered for sale online. By then the daughters had concluded that their mother was determined to hide out in the hospital facility until the criminal charges could be resolved. Scoutt filed papers evicting her friend Mark Fitzsimmons from the double-wide trailer next to the round house, and the freeze on her assets was quietly lifted.

Scoutt's attorney, Ryan Healy, requested yet another continuance of the June 26 arraignment, asserting that she "remains in an inpatient rehabilitation facility in Rapid City, South Dakota, and her expected discharge date is presently unknown." Curley did not oppose the motion, and no date was set for arraignment. Impulsively, I fired off an email to Curley, the coroners and Deputy Sergeant Patrick Watsabaugh: "So, hustled again. An objective observer might be led to believe that she has a ring in someone's nose. As the saying goes, 'Justice delayed is justice denied.'"

On July 23, 2018, Alexis Barker, the reporter for the weekly newspaper, the *News Letter Journal*, checked Scoutt's case file. In it, she found that on July 20, 2018, Curley asked District Judge Thomas W. Rumpke to dismiss the remaining felony charge. The judge ruled that the authority not to prosecute the alleged fraud involving over $500,000, rested "within the sound discretion of the county attorney's office, not within the discretion of the court." Curley told the reporter that he decided not to prosecute the case because the state had encountered "difficulties assembling and presenting a proper case," without disclosing what they were, other than that they involved some element of "proof." Curley also cited the "slide in the defendant's health," which prevented her from coming to court. He told reporter Barker that he saw no need to engage an ambulance to enable her to attend proceedings. "At some point you have to consider the circumstances and decide if it is a wise use of resources," Curley said.

In the last paragraph of her news story, Barker quoted me:

> From this distance it's difficult to say whether this sorry, disgraceful outcome is the result of incompetence, lassitude or corruption. I leave it to the good people—and voters—of Weston County to make that determination. Fraud unpunished on this scale would be bad enough, given the conclusions of state investigators. But as the December 20, 2016, verdict of the coroner's inquest into the death of Richard Campbell demonstrates, murder in Weston County has also gone unpunished.

Others, closer to the scene, had a similar reaction. Steve Rozier, the ex-cop and Campbell County coroner's assistant who ran the inquest, questioned "the small town justice system where a worthless attorney like Curley can destroy any hope of justice for the people he is supposed to serve and protect. Scoutt is clearly a woman with bloody hands, and with Curley in control she will get away with everything."

In late July, 2018, Scoutt sold the round house, the trailer where Richard was killed, and the acreage for $300,000, to a couple from Georgia. The purchase excluded the double wide trailer, which had a bank lien on it. Since Curley had unfrozen her assets, she had immediate access to the funds, and was no longer under any legal constraints.

"This case has left a permanent scar on me," Susan Wardell wrote me much later. "The fact that Caroline is free, after so many wonderful people have lost their lives to her greed, is unfathomable! We must never give up. As long as she's despoiling the earth, we know there is always going to be another trusting victim."

In retrospect, the outcome of the case was not entirely unexpected. When the announcement came, shortly after Scoutt's February arrest, that William Curley would be responsible for prosecuting her, Weston County Coroner Cynthia Crabtree wrote me: "My personal opinion on his prosecuting the case is that it is going to be bullshit. He hasn't prosecuted a case yet. He plea bargains them. [Scoutt] will get a slap on the hand so she can go somewhere else and do it again." I wrote Crabtree back, acknowledging the likelihood that the prosecutor would take yet another dive. "I'm thinking along the same lines. Which returns me to my original premise: This book will be the trial she never had . . . I think we should all be resigned that, in our respective spheres, we did all we could."

As they say in church, "Here endeth the lesson."

Perhaps not. In the late spring and early summer of 2018, there was other, related stirring in the Weston County Courthouse. Alex Berger, briefly Scoutt's criminal attorney in the witness-tampering affair and, later, also briefly, Curley's assistant, filed to challenge Curley in the upcoming Republican primary. At first, the county clerk rejected Berger's filing because he was not a Weston resident, a ruling that was overturned on appeal by a local judge. A nonresident running for county office "is something people would normally be irate over," said *News Letter Journal* editor Bob Bonnar. "But they are happy with the judge's decision because it meant they could vote for somebody besides Curley." Cynthia Crabtree, the Weston coroner, agreed. "Yes, a lot of the voters are tired of . . . his not doing his job . . . The citizens of Weston County are outraged," she said. "But the election will tell."

And so it did. On August 21, Berger defeated Curley in the Republican primary in a landslide, 1,636 to 435. Berger was all but assured of victory in the deep red county's general election, since no Democratic candidate filed for the office. Because of Berger's earlier representation of Scoutt, observers predicted that he would have to recuse himself from any decision to refile the felony fraud charge that Curley dismissed. In that event, he would have to ask the Wyoming attorney general to appoint a special prosecutor to try the case.

The *News Letter Journal's* front-page account left little doubt about its feeling about the county attorney's action. Alexis Barker wrote, "During his tenure, William Curley incurred public criticism for his soft stance on prosecuting crime." Berger, the newspaper wrote, "ran as the only qualified alternative to the unpopular Curley," who was described as "a Campbell County outsider."

At the grass roots level, Weston County citizens likewise connected the two issues. "Needless to say, most people were quite shocked when no charges were brought against Caroline Scoutt," said Brenda K. Mahoney-Ayres, director of the Weston County Library. "I believe that was the straw that broke the camel's back in regard to [Curley's] reelection."

When I called Berger in Gillette several days later, he confirmed that view, but said any decision about refiling charges and engaging a special prosecutor would have to wait to see if his election was challenged on the basis of his residence when he filed to run.

He told me, "Given someone in my situation, involving someone whom I've previously represented, this is what I would do if I took office: State investigators, who handled the case, could approach me immediately after my taking office, if they wanted the evidence and their case to be looked at again. If they asked me to look into this matter, I would request a special prosecutor to look into all of the allegations that law enforcement had regarding Ms. Scoutt. I wouldn't want to second-guess my predecessor. The best process would be to have a special prosecutor do that."

In late August, I had dinner with Laura Sundstrom and her fiancé at a restaurant near the Orlando airport, after their extended visit to Disney World with her children. She told me that Jason Riddle, who headed the

Wyoming DCI's Scoutt investigation, hadn't been informed when Curley had dropped the remaining felony fraud count. Outraged, Riddle immediately went to the attorney general and asked him to appoint a special prosecutor, a request that was still pending. For her part, Sundstrom was still furious that Scoutt had tried to fool her into believing that Richard Campbell's death had been suicide. "You picked the wrong bitch!" she said, as if her voice at the dinner table could carry two thousand miles.

On November 6, 2018, Alex Berger was elected Weston County attorney with 88 percent of the vote, against a scattering of write-ins. A week after he took office in January, I called Forrest Williams at the Wyoming Division of Criminal Investigation, asking if he or the attorney general's office intended to ask Berger to reinstate the felony fraud charge and to appoint a special prosecutor. He told me his office fully intended to pursue the case, although there was a possibility that it would be taken over by the U.S. attorney, for federal jurisdiction. By February 2019, Scoutt was reported in Yreka, California.

But on February 18, 2019, Scoutt died in Greensburg, Illinois, thus ending any possibility of a trial.

Several days later, but before her death was confirmed by a brief funeral home notice posted on Facebook by her daughter, Star Fosheim, my cell phone rang. It was after midnight when I reached for it in the dark, and heard Laura Sundstrom's voice. The former coroner, who helped lead the inquest into Richard Campbell's death, said her first reaction to the news was that Scoutt might have faked her own death. With no reluctance to speak ill of the apparently deceased, Sundstrom voiced the hope that, if true, that Scoutt was by then "burning in Hell." Susan Wardell, who was on Brent Jr.'s defense team, had a similarly bitter reaction. "I am certain she won't be running into the Springfords in the spirit world." She said. "She'll be in the special part of Hell for the religious charlatans."

Others close to the case were resigned. "So she managed to escape justice after all," wrote Brent Jr.'s lawyer, Bill Blanchard, when I shared the news. "Well, of all the ways she could have done it, this is probably the one I might have chosen for her." Lois Truss, Charlotte Springford's sister, said simply, "I guess we'll never know the whole story."

Still, doubt remained. Weston County Coroner Cynthia Crabtree wrote me, "I would like to know the cause of death, so I am going to make a few calls to see if we can get an answer. With the $300,000 [from the sale of her Newcastle property] she could have faked her death. She is a sneaky one." Crabtree subsequently confirmed with the local coroner that the causes of death included dementia and Parkinson's disease. The death certificate listed her age as sixty-six.

After nearly five years of my pursuit, there would be no courtroom settling of accounts. With the confirmation of Scoutt's death, I felt strangely empty.

: 37

Reflections

I take a layered view of how and why this story of four tragic deaths unfolded so inexorably, a view that spreads responsibility for the tragedy in Montgomery, and what took place afterward in Boulder and Wyoming. As a parent, I can't fault Charlotte Springford for trying to involve herself in her son's life and psychiatric treatment. To one doctor, she wrote, "We love him so much, and we are frightened for him." The larger questions, it seems to me, are: How might Brent's parents have distinguished between his neediness and entitlement; his sincere spiritual quest; and incipient, possibly hereditary mental illness? Then, how soon should they have recognized the venal, malign influence of Caroline Scoutt, in whom they placed so much hope and faith? For that I have no answer.

When Susan Wardell first brought the Springford case to my attention in 2009, there were two dead people, Charlotte and Brent Springford Sr.; Brent Jr. and Richard Campbell were still alive. By the time I left Wyoming in 2016, there were four dead. I wish the outcome could have been otherwise, that Caroline Scoutt would have faced a jury for her role in the Springford and Campbell deaths. But nothing more Wardell or various law enforcement officials—and certainly not I—could do was able to change that. However, when I first approached members of the Springford and Campbell families, as well as defense and law enforcement officials in Alabama, Colorado, and Wyoming, I told them that, regardless of how the judicial process played out, this book would be the murder trial that Caroline Scoutt never had.

I became a journalist in the heady days of the late 1960s and early 1970s, writing a column called "The Readable Radical" for the Duke University campus daily, The *Chronicle*. Later, I helped found and edit alternative publications then called the "underground" press. Ultimately, I graduated to straight journalism, beginning a career of freelancing for the *New York Times* and others, and then staff work, including for the *Orlando Sentinel* and the *Los Angeles Times*. But I never gave up my youthful idealism and political commitment in whatever I wrote, focusing on discrimination and the dispossessed. I was inspired in part by the career of the crusading nineteenth-century French writer Emile Zola, author of *J'Accuse*, a passionate defense of Captain Alfred Dreyfus, a Jewish army officer framed for espionage by anti-Semites. For four decades I campaigned in print against racial and gender injustice, covering criminal cases that became political causes, from Joan Little and the Wilmington 10 to the Greensboro Massacre, and, more recently in Central Florida, from Trayvon Martin to Orlando's Pulse nightclub shootings.

So there is no small amount of irony that in the case of Caroline Scoutt I found myself emulating another famous—if fictitious—Frenchman: the implacable police Inspector Javert, of Victor Hugo's *Les Miserables*. I admit that I am troubled that my quarry was a woman of color, either a Native American shaman or, more likely, Latina. Still, injustice, like love, is where you find it, and I have found it here. Four people—that we know of—close to Caroline Scoutt died, without reason. They have their claim as well.

"At the center of almost every crime story is a person who did something morally reprehensible," *New Yorker* archivists Erin Overbey and Joshua Rothman wrote in an introduction to "True Crime," the magazine's October, 2015, email newsletter collection. "In a bad crime story, that person is a bogeyman. In a good one, he or she has been imagined from the inside, and becomes real and comprehensible." In this case, that person was Caroline Scoutt, and whether I have made her real and comprehensible is for you to decide.

On the various television series built around crime scene investigations, team members do a lot more than determine cause of death—the forensic responsibility of most coroners' and medical examiners' offices. The TV CSI characters carry and use guns, investigate and interrogate suspects, and, most weeks, solve murders. It's a fictional, fanciful—and lucrative— dramatic construct that does not exist in most of the real world. And yet, Laura Sundstrom, Cynthia Crabtree, and Steve Rozier—with the assistance of Patrick Watsabaugh—were determined to investigate the circumstances surrounding the death of Richard Campbell Jr. They ignored the limits of their statutory authority to do just that. As in the case of the murders of Charlotte and Brent Springford, Sr., Caroline Scoutt was never charged in connection with Richard Campbell's death. But for the coroners' teamwork in Newcastle, Caroline Scoutt would have escaped justice entirely.

Epilogue

IN ALABAMA:

Above the jury box in Montgomery County's **Courtroom 3C,** there is a large drawing—more a cartoon than a portrait—commissioned by a local television station, depicting the abbreviated murder trial of Winston Brent Springford Jr. held on December 3–4, 2008. Apart from the drawing, and occasional anniversary stories, the Springford case isn't spoken of much in Montgomery.

However, in June 2014 the Southern Poverty Law Center issued a report entitled "Cruel Confinement," which contended that "The Alabama Department of Corrections is deliberately indifferent to the serious medical needs of the prisoners in its custody." The study detailed the system's numerous failures in treating the physical, mental, and emotional conditions of inmates, as well as those with disabilities. A prison psychologist is quoted, citing horror stories of mental patients whose medication was cut off even before they had seen a psychiatrist, as well as those given the wrong medication or dosage.

Bill Blanchard, Brent Jr.'s lead defense attorney, who still practices in Montgomery, saw a news account of the Southern Poverty Law Center report, and messaged other members of Brent's defense team, using the name their client had reverted to after his conviction. "I wonder if Winston would have killed himself if he'd had better care?" On Thanksgiving, 2014 the tenth anniversary of the slayings passed almost without media attention in Montgomery.

Robin Springford Crouch and husband **Greg Crouch** joined St. John's Episcopal for a few years after the memorial service, and two of their children were baptized there. However, probably to spare them from their family's tragic history, they subsequently moved to a home on the Gulf of Mexico. Robin has steadfastly—and understandably—refused to discuss her family's tragedies with me, but later sent word through her aunt, Lois Truss, that she did not oppose publication of this book. Greg runs the family Pepsi bottling plant in Luverne, which is still a sleepy, crossroads town and agricultural center. Old Pepsi ads painted on the sides of red-brick buildings remain, fading in the sun. Just outside of town, the bottling plant, in an unprepossessing, one-story brick building behind a chain-link fence, continues to operate, and prosper. The firm was named Pepsi's Bottler of the Year for 2013.

In 2010, after a campaign of nearly three decades, District Attorney **Ellen Brooks** helped establish the One Place Family Justice Center. The county's one-stop facility for victims of domestic violence and sexual abuse was subsequently named for her and another community activist. That same year, the *Montgomery Advertiser* named Brooks its Citizen of the Year, and she later received the Athena Award from the Women's Business Forum, a branch of the local Chamber of Commerce. On February 25, 2014, two years into her sixth term as district attorney, Brooks suddenly resigned her office. She was vague about why she was leaving, saying only, "The time seemed right." Chief Deputy District Attorney **Daryl Bailey** was appointed by Alabama Governor Robert Bentley to complete Brooks's term and immediately announced that he would run for a full term in 2016. He won.

Montgomery Detective **Michael Myrick** was promoted to major after supervising the night shift patrol.

Montgomery Detective Sergeant **Bryan Jurkofsky** was promoted to major and is now a chief of operations at the Montgomery Police Department.

Defense Attorney **Jay Lewis** retired from practicing law. He died in 2019. His body was found the day after Caroline Scoutt died.

Judge William A. Shashy continues to hear cases.

Dr. James Hooper, the state psychiatrist who examined Brent Springford Jr. and found that he was "malingering," rather than mentally ill, was subsequently appointed Medical Director of **Taylor Hardin Secure Medical Facility**. However, he was fired in February 2009 following allegations of sexual harassment by a social worker at the hospital. In July 2016, al.com reported that Hooper had been indicted on drug trafficking charges after a two-year investigation into alleged opium trafficking. Taylor Hardin is slated to be closed and turned over to the Alabama Department of Corrections to be used as a prison.

Former Montgomery Mayor **Bobby Bright** served one term in Congress as a Democrat from 2008 until 2010, when he was defeated in the Tea Party landslide. He ran for his old seat as a Republican in 2016 but was defeated in the primary.

The house at **1944 South Hull Street**, in Montgomery's Garden District, finally sold and has had two owners since the murder. It is now valued at about $600,000. The house at **11236 Hillcrest Drive** in Windsor, Colorado, is now worth an estimated $675,000.

In Colorado:

For Weld County, Colorado, sheriff's investigator **Vicki Harbert**, working on the Springford investigation prepared her for what was to be the biggest case of her career so far. That same year, 2004, her commander assigned her a cold-case homicide from August 1977. The victim, twenty-three-year-old Mary Pierce, was working the night shift in a convenience store in downtown Greeley. She disappeared after work, and two days later her naked body was found in a cornfield about seven miles west of town. She had been stabbed to death. Although the case was worked aggressively for several years, it went cold in the 1980s. Harbert found that evidence which likely contained DNA was still viable and stored in her department's evidence section. It was sent to the forensic lab, where a DNA profile was developed and run through the national CODIS system. No match was found until 2008. A suspect, who had just been released from a Texas prison, was matched and arrested a year later, returned to Colorado, and convicted of the killing in 2010. "In both cases, as an investigator, when you have leads on an investigation," she says, "you follow them no matter where those leads take you. You pursue until you cannot go anymore. You work day, you work night, holidays and weekends to come to the justice that victims deserve." Harbert is now retired from the Weld County Sheriff's Department.

In Georgia:

After devoting two-and-a-half years and hundreds of hours compiling Brent Springford's social history, death penalty mitigation specialist **Susan Wardell** went through the same financial ordeal she had in other cases with the Springford case. After Brent's guilty plea, Judge Shashy significantly cut her invoice, which left her bitter. "Never let anyone tell you how much we profit in this work—it is thankless," she wrote a friend. Two years after Brent's suicide, Wardell still had three photos of him tacked up next to the computer in her basement home office in suburban Atlanta. Understandably, death-penalty mitigation has a high burn-out rate among attorneys, with an equally elevated rate of stress-related ailments, like heart attacks, strokes and aneurysms. In Wardell's case, psoriatic arthritis, a crippling auto-immune condition, has left her with limited mobility. Nonetheless, she still takes a few mitigation cases.

In Wyoming:

In August 2018, **Weston County Deputy Sergeant Patrick Watsabaugh** retired from the Sheriff's Department, sold his house in Newcastle, and moved to the family ranch outside Gillette.

That same month, **Campbell County Coroner Laura Sundstrom** was defeated for reelection in the Republican primary.

Steve Rozier, her chief deputy, ran as an independent in the subsequent general election, but was defeated.

Since his defeat in the Republican primary, former **County Attorney William Curley** has returned to the private practice of law.

In November, **Cynthia Crabtree** was reelected Weston County coroner.

Notes on Sources and Methodology

"Everyone loves a good crime story—but why?" ask *New Yorker* archivists Erin Overbey and Joshua Rothman. "Tales of crime and punishment have moral power, and they evoke the strong, tragic emotions of pity and fear. But it's hard to write a crime story. The indescribable must be vividly described; the inexplicable must be, to some degree, explained."

I have been able to describe some of the otherwise indescribable aspects of this story, including material regarding death penalty mitigation, only through the dogged work of Susan Wardell, my sister-in-law. If there are any heroes in this sad story, she is one of them. Charlotte Springford, Brent Sr., and Brent Jr. wrote a lot, and saved everything. Wardell accumulated and compiled this rare and rich source material in her voluminous files, which she shared with me. Thus, we can know, of a certainty, what they were thinking and telling each other every step of the way—a rarity in nonfiction crime writing.

A number of key elements in this story took place before I began my research: the Springfords' murder; the subsequent investigation and arrest of Brent Springford Jr.; and the legal proceedings against him. I have interviewed as many of those surviving participants as would agree to speak with me. In reconstructing the narrative chronology of these events I have also relied on police and court records, along with contemporaneous news reporting, chiefly by Crystal Bonvillian and Antoinette Konz and other staff members at the *Montgomery Advertiser*. Also Chris Holmes at WSFA-TV. Wherever practicable, I have cited them individually, as opposed to material derived from other sources, including my own subsequent interviews. If in any significant instance I have failed to credit them adequately, I apologize.

In addition, I relied extensively on the files of Denver private investigator Wayne Diffee. I am also indebted to attorneys Bill Blanchard and Jay Lewis, who shared with me their insights and experience in defending Brent Springford Jr. To protect the confidentiality of some sources, I have used variations of the construction "a member of the defense team," rather than a specific name.

In all, I conducted approximately twenty-five on-site interviews, mostly in Alabama and Wyoming, but also in Colorado, Georgia, and Florida. For a spectrum of reasons, ranging from requests for privacy to exposure to litigation, I have used two family pseudonyms ("Jameson" and "Flinders"). However, all quotations and facts are fully documented, and there are no composite characters. Although she used the first names Carol, Carolyn, and Caroline, and the last names Gonzales, Ankney, Holland, Scott, and Price, for uniformity's sake I used Caroline Scoutt throughout the text.

Acknowledgments

First, I must again thank my sister-in-law, Susan Brown Wardell. Without her, I would not have written this book, and without her extensive cooperation, it would not be the book it is. Through her files and correspondence, I was able to see an admirable woman, tirelessly devoted to the pursuit of justice.

Next, I thank the first editor of this manuscript, my friend and colleague of thirty-five years, Rob Waters. Also my first editor at the *Los Angeles Times,* he steered numerous of my stories to that paper's coveted Column One slot. From the time I decided to take on the Springford story and realized how complex it would be, I had no doubt about asking Rob to edit the manuscript. Repeatedly, and without complaint, he pulled it into what the old *Times* Spring Street editors used to call "the body shop" and wrestled it into shape. He did not disappoint. I encourage any of my journalist colleagues with book projects to reach out to him.

My son Asher, himself a young writer and editor with an exceptionally keen eye, gave me some excellent advice—which I should have taken when he first offered it. Better late than never.

In Charleston, my old Duke friend Steve Hoffius did yeoman service fine-tuning the narrative architecture, as well as deftly line editing.

My friend and neighbor Nanci Adler provided a number of eagle-eyed fixes, as well as being my ace Internet expert.

In Santa Fe, Jane Kepp offered a timely suggestion for my Prologue.

Much to my pleasant surprise, Montgomery Police Detectives Mike Myrick and Bryan Jurkofsky, former District Attorney Ellen Brooks, and Judge William Shashy were extremely helpful to this left-wing, Jewish Democrat who parachuted into their city. Mary Ann King, Judge Shashy's clerk, was extremely helpful in preparing a transcript of the "mini-trial," as well as providing me with excellent advice.

Similarly, Carol and Don Rickard opened their home to just such an interloper, as did Montgomery's preeminent historian, the late Mary Ann Oglesby Neeley, despite pressure not to. Mark Potok, Joe Levin, and Morris Dees, all then of the Southern Poverty Law Center, provided much-needed context to this story. Documentary assistance came from the helpful staffs of the Montgomery City-County Library and the Alabama Department of Archives and History.

In Colorado, I'd first like to thank my gracious hosts, my old *Orlando Sentinel* colleague Harry Wessel and his wife Judy Binns, who extended the Wessel family tradition of assisting me in my literary murder investigations.

Likewise, Denver private investigator Wayne Diffee, who worked earlier with the Springford defense, shared his files and his expertise. Sergeant Dave Hinz, then of the Louisville Police Department, was extremely helpful and generous with his time. Weld County Sheriff Steve Reams welcomed me and made members of his department available to assist me, especially Vicki Harbert. At Naropa University in Boulder, I am grateful to Bill Rigler, director of university relations, and Martha Husick, who gave me a tour of the campus (in the rain). Most critically, I cannot say how important was the help I got from Joel Dyer, a kindred spirit if there ever was one, editor of the *Boulder Weekly*, and Caitlin Rockett, a gifted reporter and special editions editor.

In Wyoming, Weston County Sheriff's Sergeant Patrick Watsabaugh went to extraordinary lengths to assist me, despite my outsider status. Weston County Coroner Cynthia Crabtree, Campbell County Coroner Laura Sundstrom, and the latter's chief deputy, Steve Rozier, took me into their confidence and provided candid, invaluable assistance. Chief Circuit Court Clerk Barb Munger provided key documents on short notice.

In California, my dear old friend Barbara Guggenheim—still glam—was helpful in pointing me to a valuable *New Yorker* essay.

Even in a book about murder, I turned reflexively to members of the faith community for assistance, and they did not let me down: the Reverend Ernie Bennett (a longtime first reader); broadcaster, preacher and author

Steve Brown; and my rabbi and friend, Steve Engel. In Montgomery, the Reverend Robert Wisnewski of St. John's Episcopal Church was extremely gracious and helpful.

In Atlanta, I was and am indebted to the late Millard Farmer, a pioneer in the field who set me on the road to covering death penalty cases more than forty years ago. Until his passing, he continued to fight the good fight and remains an inspiration. And I appreciate my Winter Park Y gym buddies and constant encouragers, Dr. Stan Sujka and my late friends Dr. Tom March and Guy McCann.

While I was doing one of the final rewrites of this manuscript, a friend recommended *While the City Slept: A Love Lost to Violence and a Young Man's Descent into Madness*, by Eli Sanders. The book was excellent and instructive in the way I shaped my own narrative. As well, Kathleen Heide's *Understanding Parricide: When Sons and Daughters Kill Parents*.

I'd like to thank my literary agent, Linda Langton, of Langtons International, and her assistant, Lindsay Watson, for their encouragement when I needed it. At NewSouth Books, publisher Suzanne La Rosa—this book and her press were a perfect match—and marketing specialist Lisa Harrison have my gratitude, as does editor-in-chief Randall Williams, who edited the manuscript with a light hand and praise that I appreciated. Thanks also to the careful proofreading and editorial suggestions of Joel Sanders, and to McCormick Williams for indexing, Sarah Williams for proofreading, Laura Murray for cover design, and Kelly Snyder and Beth Marino for marketing.

As always, my family—wife Sallie Brown (ad hoc field producer, and late innings volunteer fact checker), son Asher, and daughter Liza Brown-Pinsky—now a bit geographically scattered, have my deepest, enduring love and appreciation.

Dr. Norman M. Wall, to whom this book is dedicated, was a great friend, advisor, mentor, and surrogate father for more than a decade, a constant part of my life and, later, my family's life. Even after his passing, I could hear his wise words echoing in my ear as I worked on this book.

Index